D0940407

NINETEENTH-CENTURY SHORT STORIES BY WOMEN

This anthology brings together twenty-eight lively and readable short stories by nineteenth-century women writers, many of which are re-published here for the first time since their original appearance. It covers a wide range of genres, from Gothic tales to romances, detective fiction and ghost stories, and includes short fiction by such well-known authors as Maria Edgeworth, Mary Shelley, Elizabeth Gaskell and Margaret Oliphant alongside stories by the less well known.

The volume includes:

- a full scholarly introduction covering such issues as the literary market-place and conditions of production, stylistic considerations, genre, and the relation between short fiction and novel;
- biographies of each of the authors;
- full explanatory notes and suggestions for further reading;
- a full and wide-ranging bibliography.

As well as offering a new source of enjoyment for the general reader, the anthology provides an invaluable resource for students and teachers of nineteenth-century women's writing and for those more generally interested in the history of women in society. The bibliography of resources and further reading will enable those interested in pursuing research on any author or topic to do so with ease.

Harriet Devine Jump is Senior Lecturer in English at Edge Hill University College. Her recent publications include *Mary Wollstonecraft: Writer* (1994) and *Women's Writing of the Romantic Period, 1789–1836* (1997). *Women's Writing of the Victorian Period, 1837–1901* will be published in 1998.

NINETEENTH-CENTURY SHORT STORIES BY WOMEN

A Routledge Anthology

Edited by Harriet Devine Jump

London and New York

First published 1998
by Routledge
11 New Fetter Lane, London EC4P 4EE

Simultaneously published in the USA and Canada
by Routledge
29 West 35th Street, New York, NY 10001

© 1998 Harriet Devine Jump, editorial matter and selection

Typeset in Garamond by RefineCatch Limited, Bungay, Suffolk
Printed and bound in Great Britain by Clays Ltd, St. Ives PLC

All rights reserved. No part of this book may be reprinted or reproduced or
utilized in any form or by any electronic, mechanical, or other means, now
known or hereafter invented, including photocopying and recording, or in any
information storage or retrieval system, without permission in writing from
the publishers.

British Library Cataloguing in Publication Data
A catalogue record for this book is available from the British Library

Library of Congress Cataloging in Publication Data
Routledge anthology of nineteenth-century short stories by women /
[edited by] Harriet Devine Jump
p.   cm.
Includes bibliographical references and index.
ISBN 0–415–16781–7 (hbk.: alk. paper). – ISBN 0–415–16782–5
(pbk.: alk. paper)
1. English fiction – Women authors. 2. Great Britain – Social life
and customs – 19th century – Fiction. 3. Women – Great Britain –
Fiction. 4. English fiction – 19th century. 5. Short stories.
English. I. Jump, Harriet Devine.
PR1309.W7R68   1998
823′.01089287′09034 – dc21   97–23393
CIP

PR
1309
.W7
N56
1998

12233273

ƐR

For my aunt
Margaret Harris
1904–

UWEC McIntyre Library

JUN 1 6 2000

DISCARDED

Eau Claire, WI

Willi... McIntyre Library
...University...sconsin - Eau Claire

CONTENTS

CONTENTS

ACKNOWLEDGEMENTS

My thanks go to Edge Hill University College for research funds and a welcome period of research leave: in particular, I am grateful to Professor John Simons and Dr Gill Davies for their continued encouragement and support, and to colleagues too numerous to mention who have helped to elucidate obscure references. I also thank the staffs of the Bodleian Library, the British Library, the Sidney Jones Library, University of Liverpool and the John Rylands Library, who have all been helpful. Professor Alun Jones, as always, has my gratitude for invaluable practical help and literary advice. Finally I must thank family and friends who have put me up, and put up with me, during this project: they include Sophie Jump, Glyn and George Pritchard, William, Oliver and Benjamin Key, Lucy Bovington, Peter Tong, Liz and Anna Bhushan, and Bill and Nell Frizzell.

INTRODUCTION

Why a collection of nineteenth-century women's short stories? The idea arose from a quite separate research project, an anthology of women's writing of the Romantic period,[1] in which the original intention had been to include some short fiction. However, when the reality of word-limits began to dawn, it became apparent that the fiction was taking up too much space and would have to go. Meanwhile, here were all these enjoyable stories, many of them never re-published since their original appearance. It seemed a pity that readers should be denied access to a hitherto almost untapped source of reading pleasure, especially given the prevailing interest in texts by nineteenth-century women writers. From this the plan for the present anthology was born.

The short story, in its broadest sense, is as old as narrative itself – as long as there have been people to talk and people to listen, stories have been told. Myths, legends, folk and fairy tales, adventure stories, romances – we have all been familiar with the form since we were children. But it was during the course of the nineteenth century that the short story developed from a 'low' or popular genre to one which carried aesthetic and cultural prestige,[2] and women writers made an important contribution to its evolution.[3]

The production and publication of literature by female writers had reached unprecedented levels by the 1790s, and women remained major producers of prose fiction, which was seen as an acceptably 'feminine' genre, throughout the nineteenth century.[4] At the beginning of the century, however, there was a limited market for what was then known as the 'tale' and only later came to be called the short story. A small number of literary periodicals had begun to publish tales by the end of the eighteenth century, but the credit for bringing the genre to the attention of a wide reading public must go to Harriet and Sophia Lee, whose joint collection, *Canterbury Tales* (1798–1805) was extremely successful, and was reprinted several times. In their wake, several well-known authors, including Maria Edgeworth and Amelia Opie, published their own collections between 1800 and 1820. One of Edgeworth's first collections was *Moral Tales* (1801), a title which

1

indicates the strong element of didacticism that was built into the tales of this early part of the century.

There continued to be a limited market for stories in the periodicals of the early part of the nineteenth century: *Blackwood's Edinburgh Magazine*, for example, founded in 1817, began to publish short fiction in the early 1820s. But the demand for short stories was greatly increased by a publishing phenomenon of the 1820s: the birth and proliferation of large numbers of annuals and albums, aimed specifically at female readers. Handsomely produced and lavishly illustrated, with titles such as *The Keepsake, Friendship's Offering, Forget-me-Not* and *Heath's Book of Beauty*, these gift-books were produced once a year, in time to be given as Christmas and New Year presents. Often edited by society women (the Countess of Blessington edited *Heath's Book of Beauty*, and Lady Emmeline Stuart-Wortley *The Keepsake*, for example) the annuals combined poetry, often of a somewhat sentimental kind, with prose fiction. The importance of these apparently ephemeral publications as an outlet for writers may be judged from the fact that in the nine years following the founding of the first annual, Rudolph Ackermann's *Forget-me-Not*, in 1823, the number of annuals in production had risen to sixty-three (Faxon 1973: xi). Publishers were obviously responding to the demands of an avid readership: it has been estimated that in 1828, for example, 100,000 annuals were sold, at a retail value of more than £70,000 (Altick 1957: 362).

By the middle of the century, the annuals were largely replaced by Christmas annuals, which were aimed at the whole family rather than just at female readers. Meanwhile the demand for short stories was further increased by the appearance of weekly papers, most notably Dickens' *Household Words* (1850–9), and its successor, *All the Year Round* (1859–95), as well as countless other fortnightlies and monthlies.[5] The two most celebrated female novelists of the 1860s, Mary Elizabeth Braddon and Ellen ('Mrs Henry') Wood, edited their own periodicals (Braddon was responsible for *Belgravia* and *The Belgravia Annual*, and Wood for *The Argosy*) as well as contributing to numerous others. In the 1890s Ella D'Arcy worked as assistant editor of the notorious *Yellow Book* in which she and many other women writers in the New Woman tradition published short stories. As the century drew to a close, short stories were increasingly collected together and published in volume form: Mary Braddon, Ellen Wood, Margaret Oliphant, Olive Schreiner and George Egerton among many others had considerable success with their short-story collections.

In an age when writing was one of the few respectable means for a woman to make a living, publication in the annuals, magazines and periodicals provided a vital source of income for single or widowed women, or for those for whom a husband added to their financial burdens. The poet, novelist and short-story writer Caroline Norton, for example, married at 19 to an idle and feckless husband, asserted that the first expenses of my son's life were defrayed from the first creation of my brain. . . .The dependence on my literary efforts for all extra resources runs . . . through all the letters I received from [my husband] during our union. The names of my publishers occur as if they were Mr Norton's bankers.

(Norton 1854: 25)

Mary Shelley, widowed at the age of 24, supported herself and her son for many years by her writing, and, though she found writing a slow and painful business, produced at least twenty-four tales for the *Keepsake* and other such publications.[6] Elizabeth Gaskell, whose need for money was less pressing in so far as she had a husband to support her, used her income from writing to finance her extensive travelling and entertaining, and would often dash off a story or two when she needed extra cash: *The Manchester Marriage* was written in Germany, when a holiday proved to be more expensive than she had anticipated (Uglow 1993: 453).

Contributors to the annuals seem to have been surprisingly well paid. It has been suggested that writers of short fiction received as much as twenty or thirty guineas a sheet, although payment presumably varied according to the status of the author: the highest payment on record is that made to Sir Walter Scott, who was paid £500 for two tales and a sketch published in the *Keepsake* for 1828 (Polsgrave 1974). By way of contrast, however, the prolific and hard-working poet and prose writer Laetitia Landon, whose 'editorship' of *Fisher's Drawing-Room Scrapbook* in the 1830s in fact amounted to writing the entire text of the annual (the 1833 volume has one very long poem of thirty-three pages and twelve shorter ones, and two short stories), is said to have been paid only £105 per volume (Jerdan 1852–3, vol. 3: 185). The monthlies and other periodicals appear to have paid less, on average, than the annuals. Mary Shelley sold two of her husband's manuscripts and her own story, *A Tale of the Passions*, to *The Liberal* in 1822 for £36 (Marshall 1960: 148). Elizabeth Gaskell earned £20 for her story *Lizzie Leigh*, which was serialised in the first three issues of *Household Words* in 1850, but ten years later was paid only £40 in total for *The Manchester Marriage*, *Right at Last* and an advance on a third story as yet unwritten (Uglow 1993: 250, 453). Later in the century Margaret Oliphant was paid £3 a sheet for a story in the 1877 edition of the Christmas annual *Good Cheer* (Jay 1995: 283). Although even for the period these are not large sums, clearly a hard-working short-story writer (and most of the women writers of the nineteenth century were astonishingly prolific) could earn what amounted to an extremely useful part of her income from the production of short fiction.

This anthology begins in what is known, in literary terms, as the Romantic period, which is generally taken to have started in 1789 (the year the French Revolution began) and to have ended with the accession of Queen Victoria in 1837. Several of the early stories provide examples of an important and influential Romantic mode, that of the Gothic. This popular sub-genre, which appealed particularly to women writers (the most consistently successful Gothic novelist of the 1790s was Ann Radcliffe) and women readers, allowed for exploration of the darker, non-rational, imaginative side of human experience.[7] The Gothic mode was well adapted to both long and short fiction. Anna Barbauld's early experiment in the genre, *The Story of Sir Bertrand*, has all the hallmarks of an archetypal Gothic tale. Set in a mysterious castle at some unspecified time in the past, the story provides exactly the judicious combination of terror and horror culminating in a happily romantic resolution that readers of the period would have enjoyed. 'David Lynsay', writing in the 1820s, manages to combine traditionally Gothic apparitions with an interrogation of the power of superstition and a keen-eyed assessment of marriage in a tale which recalls, but subverts, Keats' 'Eve of St Agnes'. Mary Shelley's *The Mortal Immortal* has been the most frequently reprinted of all her tales, and it is easy to see why. Set, unusually for a Gothic story, in the present day, it offers a protagonist whose realistically imagined psychological trauma engages the reader even more fully than the supernatural elements of his tragedy.

By the mid-century, Gothicism, which typically was distanced from its contemporary readers by both geographical and temporal location, had developed in two related directions. On one hand it had been transmuted into the ghost story, a popular sub-genre which lent itself more readily to short fiction than to the full length novel. The huge upsurge of public interest at this time in psychical phenomena of all kinds, from seances and table-tapping to well-attested apparitions, can be attributed largely to the spiritual doubts and disquietude which followed in the wake of scientific progress and Darwinian evolutionary theory.[8] In literary terms this interest was reflected in the production of large numbers of stories describing ghostly manifestations. In the present collection the genre is represented by the stories of Mary Braddon, Amelia Edwards and Vernon Lee. These three show how widely approaches to one genre may vary: Braddon's story deals in dark passions, sexuality, jealousy, murder and retribution; Edwards narrates a domestic tragedy in which the supernatural appears only briefly; and Lee's chief interest is in the psychology of the narrator and in the nature of the evil to which he is exposed. It is worth noting, perhaps, that Braddon and Lee have used a male narrator to tell their stories, a practice which is found in many other ghost stories written by female authors of this era. As Jennifer Uglow has perceptively suggested, this helped to give authority and credence to the supernatural tale at a period when men were habitually perceived as reliable and trustworthy while women were seen as emotional and hysterical.[9] The story by Vernon Lee, who never openly acknowledged her own lesbian sexuality, is particularly interesting for the ambivalent sexual feelings of the male narrator, who becomes obsessed with the portrait and voice of a long-dead male singer whose beauty of is of an indubitably female nature.

Another development of the Gothic was the sensation novel, a sub-genre which came into being in the 1860s. Passion, insanity, bigamy and even murder – made more shocking to Victorian readers by being set within a background of detailed domestic realism – are frequently figured in these controversial texts. The best-known examples of this highly popular, subversive mode of fiction are full-length novels: Ellen Wood's *East Lynne* (1861) and Mary Braddon's *Lady Audley's Secret* (1862). However, elements of sensationalism can also be found in the short fiction of the 1860s and 1870s: in the present anthology, they can be seen in Ellen Wood's *The Mystery at Number Seven*, with its rational, middle-class male narrator and its shocking denouement involving unrequited passion and madness. The story also demonstrates the way in which the sensation school of fiction was to contribute to the development of the detective story slightly later in the century.

Short fiction has always lent itself readily to what can most accurately be described as the love story. Many of the stories in this anthology come into this category. Some are happy, like Margaret Majendie's cheerful comedy of innocent deceit, *A Railway Journey*, and Evelyn Sharp's *The Other Anna*, in which mistaken identity allows the female protagonist the freedom to experiment with an alternative persona. Others have a more serious agenda, like Ménie Muriel Dowie's *An Idyll in Millinery*, whose upper-class male protagonist finds his values and beliefs radically called into question, but who acts too late to prevent the loss of the (working-class) woman to whom he finally realises he is willing to commit himself. Other stories in the anthology defy generic classification: Olive Schreiner's *A Dream of Wild Bees* is an allegory of the genesis of a New Woman; Ella Hepworth Dixon's *The Sweet o'the Year* sensitively confronts the tragedy of ageing and loss of female beauty and subjects its male protagonist to a powerful and evolutionary growth in maturity and sensitivity. Two of the women writers of the 1890s deal sensitively with problems associated with the Indian subcontinent: Flora Steel's clever young boy protagonist Govind Sahai, in *Amor Vincit Omnia*, serves as a cautionary demonstration both of the dangers of reading too many romantic novels and of the pitfalls, cultural and psychological, of colonialism; Cornelia Sorabji's *Urmi: The Story of a Queen* draws attention to the ultimately tragic plight of an over-educated Indian woman in an unregenerately patriarchal society.

Above all else, perhaps, it should be remembered that the stories collected here, whatever their generic classification, are women's stories. Not surprisingly, then, they show a recurring interest in women's lives: their relationships with men, their social position and status, their choices, their emotions. The chronological arrangement of the anthology allows readers to see clearly the change in attitudes to gender, marriage, and sexuality that took place during the nineteenth century. In the earlier stories, women are largely denied both an option to choose a partner and a voice to protest if the choice made for them proves unsatisfactory. This issue, touched on lightly in Maria

Edgeworth's comedy *The Limerick Gloves* (1804), takes on tragic dimensions in Catherine Gore's story, *Lady Evelyn Savile's Three Trials* (1832). The irritation which present day readers may understandably feel at Lady Evelyn's sentimentalised decline is more than compensated for by the skilfully ironised treatment of the first-person narrative voice of her husband, whose deranged pathology becomes increasingly evident as the story progresses. His final 'And now she is mine again – mine only and for ever!' insistently recalls the protagonist of Browning's 'Porphyria's Lover' (1842), who voices an almost identical sentiment immediately before he strangles his beloved. Laetitia Landon's witty *Sefton Church* (1834) offers a critique of marriage in a different mode: the cynical persona of its male narrator allows Landon to voice a scepticism that would be otherwise unthinkable in the conventional world of annual fictions.

By the mid-century, women writers were beginning to explore a somewhat riskier side of sexual relations. Elizabeth Gaskell's *The Manchester Marriage* (1860), for example, deals sensitively with the subject of bigamy.[10] Interestingly, in this story, the wife is a somewhat shadowy figure and it is the husband who undergoes a revolution of mind and sensibility as he is forced to protect her from the consequences of an act committed in all innocence but carrying heavy implications, both legal and psychological. Mary Braddon's *Eveline's Visitant* (1867) shocks the reader by its revelation, kept back until the closing paragraphs, of the wife's (implicitly sexual) obsession with the attractive womaniser who persistently haunts her despite the best efforts of her less appealing husband. As is frequently the case in sensation fiction, Eveline is suitably punished for her transgression. Lucy Clifford's classic story of the 1880s, *The End of her Journey*, openly confronts the issue of sexual infidelity. Clifford's protagonist, plain, quiet Mildred, is devastated to discover that her adored husband keeps a mistress and child in a separate establishment. The tragedy that ensues is shown, with great sensitivity and psychological accuracy, to result in part at least from Mildred's inability to express her powerful, repressed emotions.

Not surprisingly, it is in the stories of the 1890s – the era when heated debate on the subject of the New Woman reached its peak – that the discussion of women's lives and expectations opens most fully. There is the protagonist of Mary Angela Dickens' *Another Freak*, whose insistence that the man she loves must marry his discarded working-class mistress, the mother of his child, effectively demolishes what the reader is given to believe is her one chance of personal happiness. There is Janey, in Margaret Oliphant's *A Story of a Wedding Tour*, who escapes the loveless and brutal sexuality of her husband in a radical move which brings both unheard-of freedom and inescapable guilt. There is the heroine of George Egerton's *A Cross Line*, who enters into an extra-marital relationship with a man she meets while out fishing and who indulges in sexual fantasies of passion and seduction, but who finally chooses motherhood rather than escape. Most radical of all, there are the *Yellow Book* stories of Ada Leverson, Netta Syrett and Ada Radford, in which adultery is, if not condoned, at least shown to be a fact of life. Leverson's *Suggestion* offers a particularly interesting confrontation of the mores of *fin-de-siècle* decadence. Elaine Showalter's reading of the story as a straightforward critique of the excesses of Oscar Wilde and his circle is,[10] perhaps, complicated first by the fact that Leverson was one of Wilde's closest friends and supporters, and second by the undeniable charm of its narrator, 'that intolerable effeminate boy', as he is described by another (unsympathetic) character. It is impossible not to warm to someone who can describe his own father as having 'that look of having suffered that comes from enjoying oneself too much'. One of the finest stories in the collection, Ella D'Arcy's *The Pleasure-Pilgrim*, is notable for its refusal either to condemn or to exonerate the central character, Lucy, whose past indiscretions fatally stand in the way of her acceptance by the male narrator. D'Arcy's skill in this story is in her withholding of any final judgement on Lucy, who may be either the irredeemably loose woman her reputation suggests or the reformed, entirely devoted lover that she and her female friend insist she has become.

Clearly, in terms of themes and preoccupations, the development of the nineteenth-century short story runs parallel in many respects to that of the nineteenth-century novel. Are the short stories of this era, then, simply mini-novels, or are there characteristics of short fiction which distinguish it from the full-length novel? If, at the risk of over-simplification, the traditional realist novel of the period is defined as a fiction dealing with everyday life and having a clearly defined structure which tends to end with the marriage or death of the main protagonist(s), then many of the short stories in this anthology do indeed fall into the same category. By the 1890s, however, many writers were using short fiction in a much more consciously subversive way. Even if we leave aside Olive Schreiner's experiments with allegory, which could almost be described as prose-poetry, and George Egerton's pioneering use of a present-tense narrative style, it is observable that many of the stories from the end of the century welcomed the flexibility of the short form, finding that, as one critic has put it, its:

> characteristic inconclusiveness, its open-ended or deliberately evasive resolutions were particularly helpful in overcoming the narrative problems of traditional realism, [avoiding] the tendency of the traditional full length novel to come to definite conclusions.
>
> (Stubbs 1979: 104)

This inconclusiveness can most readily be seen here in Ella D'Arcy's *The Pleasure-Pilgrim*, but it is also found in Netta Syrett's *A Correspondence* and Ada Radford's *Lucy Wren*, among others. These stories, with their deliberate refusal of closure, point forward clearly to the ambivalence and relativism which was to characterise the Modernist texts of the early years of the

twentieth century. I would argue that the fundamentally problematic position of the New Woman in society at the end of the century was such that
women writers were particularly drawn to a style and form which mirrored
the equivocal nature of their role and status.

I had hoped to end this introduction with a discussion of recent critical
approaches to nineteenth-century women's short fiction. Unfortunately,
however, there do not appear to be any critical texts which have concentrated
in any specific way on women's short stories of the period, although the
introductions to anthologies such as Showalter (1993) and Stephenson (1994)
offer some helpful pointers for the direction in which further research might
usefully go. Nineteenth-century women's novels have been a staple of feminist criticism since the 1970s, however, and readers will find lively and
thought-provoking discussions in works such as Auerbach (1978, 1982),
Gilbert and Gubar (1979), Moers (1977), Showalter (1977), Stubbs (1979)
and Pykett (1992, 1996).

I hope this anthology will be enjoyable for the general reader and, above
all, perhaps, useful to students and teachers. At the time of writing,
nineteenth-century women's poetry has become more accessible,[12] but short
fiction has not, despite the fact that the study of women's writing now forms
a part of most 'historical' or 'survey' courses in most institutions of higher
education. Given the fact that nineteenth-century novels are notoriously long
– a source of much complaint from students, and of irritation to tutors who
find the students are not reading them – it is to be hoped that this anthology
will provide an alternative source of accessible texts for a study of women's
prose fiction of the period. My principles of selection have been simple. I
have tried to represent the changing tastes and preoccupations of a hundred
years of literary work, and I have included stories which I myself have
enjoyed. I apologise to readers who may wish I had made a different selection: but I hope that most people will find some pleasant surprises as well as,
perhaps, one or two old favourites.

Notes

1 See Jump (1977).
2 Edgar Allan Poe's assertion, in 1842, that the short story 'affords unques-
tionably the fairest field for the exercise of the loftiest talent, which can be
afforded by the wide domains of mere prose' did much to set the genre on its
evolutionary path towards acceptance as 'high art' (see Poe 1984: 571–2).
3 For a useful discussion of the history and development of the short story, see
Suzanne Ferguson, 'The Rise of the Short Story in the Hierarchy of Genres', in
Lohafer and Clarey (1989: 176–92; see also Harris 1968–9).
4 For the statistics relating to the eighteenth century, see Turner (1992), and for
the nineteenth century, see Tuchman (1989). Gaye Tuchman's argument is
that 'Before 1840 . . . most English novelists were women. By the turn of the
century . . . most critically successful novelists were men' (p. 1). The actual

numbers of women writing both novels and short stories remained high, however.

5 Among the more important fiction-carrying magazines were the market leader, *The Cornhill Magazine* (1860–1875) and its imitators, including *Temple Bar* (1860–1906), *Belgravia* (1866–99), *The St James's Magazine* (1861–82) and *St Paul's Magazine* (1867–74).

6 Owing to the common practice of anonymous publication in the annuals, it is more than likely that other stories by Mary Shelley still remain to be discovered.

7 See Ellen Moers' pioneering discussion of 'the female gothic' in Moers (1977).

8 See Briggs (1977).

9 'Introduction', Dalby (1992).

10 Interestingly enough, Gaskell's story pre-dates the upsurge of interest in bigamy as a fashionable complication in fiction which followed the notorious Yelverton trial of 1861–4 (see Sutherland 1988: 63).

11 See Showalter (1993: xxi).

12 See, for example, Leighton and Reynolds (1995) and Armstrong and Bristow (1996).

THE LIMERICK GLOVES

Maria Edgeworth

Maria Edgeworth (1767–1849), novelist, short-story writer, educational and children's writer, was born in Ireland. She was educated at school in England, but returned to Ireland at the age of 15 to help her Anglo-Irish landowner father to run his estate, and to care for the rest of his twenty-two children by his four marriages. She remained there, unmarried, until the end of her life. One of the most successful novelists of the era, she was admired by Jane Austen. Her fictional works include the Irish novel, *Castle Rackrent* (1800); *Belinda* (1801); *Leonora* (1806); *The Absentee* (1812); *Patronage* (1814); *Ormond* (1817); and *Helen* (1834). She also published educational works, including *Practical Education* (with her father, 1798) and *Essays on Professional Education* (1809). *Early Lessons* (1801), didactic stories aimed at children, was the first of several collections of 'moral tales'; *Moral Tales* (also 1801) was for adolescents and *Popular Tales* (1804) for adults.

Her father Richard Edgeworth's preface to *Popular Tales* states that it has been calculated:

> that there are eighty thousand readers in Great Britain, nearly one hundredth part of its inhabitants. Of these we may calculate that ten thousand are nobility, clergy, or gentlemen of the learned professions. Of the seventy thousand which remain, there are many who might be amused and instructed by books, which were not professedly adapted to the classes that have been enumerated. With this view the following volumes have been composed. The title of *Popular Tales* has been chosen, not as a presumptuous and premature claim to popularity, but from the wish that they may be current beyond circles which are sometimes exclusively considered as polite.

The didactic intent of *The Limerick Gloves* is conveyed by the chapter headings. It is interesting to note that later editions omitted these, however.

Further reading

Blain (1990); Butler (1972); Hare (1894); Jump (1997); Mellor (1993); Myers (1995); Ritchie (1883); Shattock (1993).

The Limerick Gloves

Chapter I

Surmise is often partly True and partly False.

It was Sunday morning, and a fine day in autumn; the bells of Hereford cathedral rang, and all the world smartly dressed were flocking to church.

'Mrs. Hill! Mrs. Hill! – Phœbe! Phœbe! There's the cathedral bell, I say, and neither of you ready for church, and I a church-warden;' cried Mr. Hill, the tanner, as he stood at the bottom of his own staircase. 'I'm ready, Papa,' replied Phœbe; and down she came, looking so clean, so fresh, and so gay, that her stern father's brows unbent, and he could only say to her, as she was drawing on a new pair of gloves, 'Child, you ought to have had those gloves on before this time of day.'

'Before this time of day!' cried Mrs. Hill, who was now coming down stairs, completely equipped. 'Before this time of day! She should know better, I say, than to put on those gloves at all: more especially when going to the cathedral.'

'The gloves are very good gloves, as far as I see,' replied Mr. Hill. 'But no matter now. It is more fitting that we should be in proper time in our pew, to set an example, as becomes us, than to stand here talking of gloves and nonsense.'

He offered his wife and daughter each an arm, and set out for the cathedral; but Phœbe was too busy drawing on her new gloves, and her mother was too angry at the sight of them, to accept of Mr. Hill's courtesy. 'What I say is always nonsense I know, Mr. Hill,' resumed the matron: 'but I can see as far into a millstone as other folks. Was it not I that first gave you a hint of what became of the great dog, that we lost out of our tan-yard last winter? And was it not I who first took notice to you, Mr. Hill, church-warden as you are, of the hole under the foundation of the cathedral? Was it not, I ask you, Mr. Hill?'

'But, my dear Mrs. Hill, what has all this to do with Phœbe's gloves?'

'Are you blind Mr. Hill? Don't you see that they are Limerick gloves?'[1]

'What of that?' said Mr. Hill; still preserving his composure, as it was his custom to do as long as he could, when he saw his wife was ruffled.

'What of that, Mr. Hill! why don't you know that Limerick is in Ireland, Mr. Hill?'

'With all my heart, my dear.'

13

'Yes, and with all your heart, I suppose, Mr. Hill, you would see our cathedral blown up, some fair day or other, and your own daughter married to the person that did it; and you a churchwarden, Mr. Hill.'

'God forbid!' cried Mr. Hill; and he stopped short and settled his wig. Presently recovering himself, he added, 'But, Mrs. Hill, the cathedral is not yet blown up; and our Phœbe is not yet married.'

'No; but what of that, Mr. Hill? Forewarned is forearmed, as I told you before your dog was gone: but you would not believe me, and you see how it turned out in that case; and so it will in this case you'll see, Mr. Hill.'

'But you puzzle and frighten me out of my wits, Mrs. Hill,' said the churchwarden; again settling his wig. *In that case, and in this case!* I can't understand a syllable of what you've been saying to me this half hour. In plain English, what is there the matter about Phœbe's gloves?'

'In plain English then, Mr. Hill, since you can understand nothing else, please to ask your daughter Phœbe who gave her those gloves. Phœbe, who gave you those gloves?'

'I wish they were burnt,' said the husband; whose patience could endure no longer 'Who gave you these cursed gloves, Phœbe?'

'Papa,' answered Phœbe, in a low voice, 'they were a present from Mr. Brian O'Neill.'

'The Irish glover!' cried Mr. Hill, with a look of terror.

'Yes', resumed the mother; 'very true, Mr. Hill, I assure you. Now, you see, I had my reasons.'

'Take off the gloves directly: I order you, Phœbe,' said her father, in his most peremptory tone. 'I took a mortal dislike to that Mr. Brian O'Neill the first time I ever saw him. He's an Irishman, and that's enough, and too much for me. Off with the gloves, Phœbe! When I order a thing, it must be done.'

Phœbe seemed to find some difficulty in getting off the gloves, and gently urged that she could not well go into the cathedral without them. This objection was immediately removed, by her mother's pulling from her pocket a pair of mittens, which had once been brown and once been whole, but which were now rent in sundry places; and which, having been long stretched by one who was twice the size of Phœbe, now hung in huge wrinkles upon her well-turned arms.

'But, papa,' said Phœbe, 'why should we take a dislike to him because he is an Irishman. Cannot an Irishman be a good man?'

The churchwarden made no answer to this question; but, a few seconds after it was put to him, observed that the cathedral bell had just done ringing, and, as they were now got to the church door, Mrs. Hill, with a significant look at Phœbe, remarked that it was no proper time to talk or think of good men, or bad men, or Irishmen, or any men, especially for a churchwarden's daughter.

We pass over in silence the many conjectures that were made, by several of the congregation, concerning the reason why Miss Phœbe Hill should appear in such a shameful shabby pair of gloves on a Sunday. After service was ended the churchwarden went, with great mystery, to examine the hole under the foundation of the cathedral; and Mrs. Hill repaired, with the grocer's and the stationer's ladies, to take a walk in the Close; where she boasted to all her female acquaintance, whom she called her friends, of her maternal discretion in prevailing upon Mr. Hill to forbid her daughter Phœbe to wear the Limerick gloves.

Chapter II

Words ill understood are among our worst Misfortunes.

In the mean time, Phœbe walked pensively homewards; endeavouring to discover why her father should take a mortal dislike to a man, at first sight, merely because he was an Irishman; and why her mother had talked so much of the great dog, which had been lost last year out of the tan-yard; and of the hole under the foundation of the cathedral? What has all this to do with my Limerick gloves? thought she. The more she thought the less connexion she could perceive between these things: for, as she had not taken a dislike to Mr. Brian O'Neill at first sight, because he was an Irishman, she could not think it quite reasonable to suspect him of making away with her father's dog; nor yet of a design to blow up the Hereford cathedral. As she was pondering upon these matters, she came within sight of the ruins of a poor woman's house; which, a few months before this time, had been burnt down. She recollected that her first acquaintance with her lover began at the time of this fire, and she thought that the courage and humanity he shewed, in exerting himself to save this unfortunate woman and her children, justified her notion of the possibility that an Irishman might be a good man.

The name of the poor woman, whose house had been burnt down, was Smith: she was a widow, and she now lived at the extremity of a narrow lane in a wretched habitation. Why Phœbe thought of her with more concern than usual at this instant we need not examine, but she did; and, reproaching herself for having neglected it for some weeks past, she resolved to go directly to see the widow Smith, and to give her a crown which she had long had in her pocket, with which she had intended to have bought play tickets.

It happened that the first person she saw in the poor widow's kitchen was the identical Mr. O'Neill. 'I did not expect to see any body here but you, Mrs. Smith,' said Phœbe, blushing.

'So much the greater the pleasure of the meeting; to me, I mean, Miss Hill,' said O'Neill rising, and putting down a little boy, with whom he had been playing. Phœbe went on talking to the poor woman; and, after slipping the crown into her hand, said she would call again. O'Neill, surprised at the change in her manner, followed her when she left the house, and said, 'it would be a great misfortune to me to have done any thing to offend Miss

Hill; especially if I could not conceive how or what it was, which is my case at this present speaking.' And, as the spruce glover spoke, he fixed his eyes upon Phœbe's ragged gloves. She drew them up in vain; and then said, with her natural simplicity and gentleness, 'You have not done any thing to offend me, Mr. O'Neill, but you are some way or other displeasing to my father and mother, and they have forbid me to wear the Limerick gloves.'

'And sure Miss Hill would not be after changing her opinion of her humble servant for no reason in life, but because her father and mother, who have taken a prejudice against him, are a little contrary.'

'No,' replied Phœbe; 'I should not change my opinion, without any reason; but I have not had time yet to fix my opinion of you, Mr. O'Neill.'

'To let you know a piece of my mind then, my dear Miss Hill,' resumed he, 'the more contrary they are the more pride and joy it would give me to win and wear you, in spite of 'em all; and, if without a farthing in your pocket, so much the more I should rejoice in the opportunity of proving to your dear self, and all else whom it may consarn, that Brian O'Neill is no Irish fortune-hunter, and scorns them that are so narrowminded as to think that no other kind of cattle but them there fortune-hunters can come out of all Ireland. So, my dear Phœbe, now we understand one another, I hope you will not be paining my eyes any longer with the sight of these odious brown bags, which are not fit to be worn by any Christian's arms, to say nothing of Miss Hill's, which are the handsomest, without any compliment, that ever I saw; and, to my mind, would become a pair of Limerick gloves beyond any thing; and I expect she'll show her generosity and proper spirit by putting them on immediately.'

'You expect, Sir!' repeated Miss Hill, with a look of more indignation than her gentle countenance had ever before been seen to assume. Expect! If he had said hope, thought she, it would have been another thing: but expect! what right has he to expect? –

Now Miss Hill, unfortunately, was not sufficiently acquainted with the Irish idiom to know that to expect, in Ireland, is the same thing as to hope in England; and, when her Irish admirer said I expect, he meant only in plain English I hope. But thus it is that a poor Irishman, often, for want of understanding the niceties of the English language, says the rudest when he means to say the civilest things imaginable.

Miss Hill's feelings were so much hurt, by this unlucky "I expect," that the whole of his speech, which had before made some favourable impression upon her, now lost its effect; and she replied with proper spirit, as she thought, 'you expect a great deal too much, Mr. O'Neill; and more than ever I gave you reason to do. It would be neither pleasure nor pride to me to be won and worn, as you were pleased to say, in spite of them all; and to be thrown, without a farthing in my pocket, upon the protection of one who expects so much at first setting out. – So I assure you, Sir, whatever you may expect, I shall not put on the Limerick gloves.'

16

Mr. O'Neill was not without his share of pride, and proper spirit: nay, he had, it must be confessed, in common with some others of his countrymen, an improper share of pride and spirit. Fired by the lady's coldness, he poured forth a volley of reproaches; and ended by wishing, as he said, a good morning for ever and ever, to one who could change her opinion point blank, like the weathercock. 'I am, Miss, your most obedient; and I expect you'll never think no more of poor Brian O'Neill, and the Limerick gloves.'

If he had not been in too great a passion to observe any thing, poor Brian O'Neill would have found out that Phœbe was not a weathercock: but he left her abruptly, and hurried away; imagining all the while that it was Phœbe, and not himself, who was in a rage. Thus, to the horseman who is galloping at full speed, the hedges, trees, and houses, seem rapidly to recede; while, in reality, they never move from their places. It is he that flies from them, and not they from him.

Chapter III

Endeavours to be consistent often lead to Obstinacy in Error.

On Monday morning Miss Jenny Brown, the perfumer's daughter, came to pay Phœbe a morning visit, with a face of busy joy.

'So, my dear!' said she: 'fine doings, in Hereford! But what makes you look so downcast? To be sure you are invited, as well as the rest of us?'

'Invited where?' cried Mrs. Hill, who was present, and who could never endure to hear of an invitation, in which she was not included. 'Invited where pray, Miss Jenny?'

'La! have you not heard? Why, we all took it for granted that you, and Miss Phœbe, would have been the first and foremost to have been asked to Mr. O'Neill's ball.'

'Ball!' cried Mrs. Hill; and luckily saved Phœbe, who was in some agitation, the trouble of speaking. 'Why this is a mighty sudden thing: I never heard a tittle of it before.'

'Well, this is really extraordinary! And, Phœbe, have not you received a pair of Limerick gloves?'

'Yes, I have,' said Phœbe; 'but what then? What has my Limerick gloves to do with the ball?'

'A great deal,' replied Jenny. 'Don't you know that a pair of Limerick gloves is, as one may say, a ticket to this ball? for every lady, that has been asked, has had a pair sent to her along with the card; and I believe as many as twenty, beside myself, have been asked this morning.'

Jenny then produced her new pair of Limerick gloves; and, as she tried them on, and shewed how well they fitted, she counted up the names of the ladies who, to her knowledge, were to be at this ball. When she had finished the catalogue, she expatiated upon the grand preparations which it was said the widow O'Neill, Mr. O'Neill's mother, was making for the supper; and concluded by condoling with Mrs. Hill, for her misfortune in not having been invited. Jenny took her leave, to get her dress in readiness: 'for,' added she, 'Mr. O'Neill has engaged me to open the ball, in case Phœbe does not go: but I suppose she will cheer up and go, as she has a pair of Limerick gloves as well as the rest of us.'

There was a silence for some minutes, after Jenny's departure, which was broken by Phœbe, who told her mother that, early in the morning, a note had been brought to her, which she had returned unopened: because she knew, from the hand-writing of the direction, that it came from Mr. O'Neill.

We must observe that Phœbe had already told her mother of her meeting with this gentleman at the poor widow's; and of all that had passed between them afterwards. This openness, on her part, had softened the heart of Mrs. Hill; who was really inclined to be good-natured provided people would allow that she had more penetration than any one else in Hereford. She was moreover a good deal piqued and alarmed by the idea that the perfumer's daughter might rival and outshine her own. Whilst she had thought herself sure of Mr. O'Neill's attachment to Phœbe, she had looked higher; especially as she was persuaded, by the perfumer's lady, to think that an Irishman could not be a good match: but now she began to suspect that the perfumer's lady had changed her opinion of Irishmen, since she did not object to her own Jenny's leading up the ball at Mr. O'Neill's.

All these thoughts passed rapidly in the mother's mind; and, with her fear of losing an admirer for her Phœbe, the value of that admirer suddenly rose in her estimation. Thus, at an auction, if a lot is going to be knocked down to a lady, who is the only person that has bid for it, even she feels dis-contented, and despises that which nobody covets: but if, as the hammer is falling, many voices answer to the question, Who bids more? then her anx-iety to secure the prize suddenly rises; and, rather than be outbid, she will give far beyond its value.

'Why, child,' said Mrs. Hill, 'since you have a pair of Limerick gloves, and since certainly that note was an invitation to us to this ball, and since it is much more fitting that you should open the ball than Jenny Brown, and since, after all, it was very handsome and genteel of the young man to say he would take you without a farthing in your pocket, which shows that those were misinformed who talked of him as an Irish adventurer, and since we are not certain t'was he made away with the dog, although he said its barking was a great nuisance, and since, if he did not kill or entice away the dog, there is no great reason to suppose he was the person who made the hole under the foundation of the cathedral, or that he could have such a wicked thought as to blow it up, and since he must be in a very good way of business to be able to afford giving away four or five guineas worth of Limerick gloves, and balls and suppers, and since, after all, it is no fault of his to be an Irishman, I give it as my vote and opinion, my dear, that you put on your

Limerick gloves and go to this ball, and I'll go and speak to your father, and bring him round to our opinion; and then I'll pay the morning visit I owe to the widow O'Neill, and make up your quarrel with Brian. Love quarrels are easy to make up, you know; and then we shall have things all upon velvet again; and Jenny Brown need not come, with her hypocritical condoling face, to us any more.'

After running this speech glibly off, Mrs. Hill, without waiting to hear a syllable from poor Phœbe, trotted off in search of her consort. It was not, however, quite so easy a task, as his wife expected it would be, to bring Mr. Hill round to her opinion. He was slow in declaring himself of any opinion; but, when once he had said a thing, there was but little chance of altering his notions. On this occasion, Mr. Hill was doubly bound to his prejudice against our unlucky Irishman; for he had mentioned, with great solemnity, at the club which he frequented, the grand affair of the hole under the foundation of the cathedral; and his suspicions that there was a design to blow it up. Several of the club had laughed at this idea, others, who supposed that Mr. O'Neill was a Roman Catholic, and who had a confused notion that a Roman Catholic *must* be a very wicked dangerous being, thought that there might be a great deal in the churchwarden's suggestions; and observed that a very watchful eye ought to be kept upon this Irish glover, who had come to settle at Hereford nobody knew why, and who seemed to have money at command nobody knew how.

The news of this ball sounded to Mr. Hill's prejudiced imagination like the news of a conspiracy. Aye! aye! thought he; the Irishman is cunning enough! But we shall be too many for him: he wants to throw all the good sober folks of Hereford off their guard, by feasting and dancing, and carousing, I take it; and so to perpetrate his evil designs when it is least suspected: but we shall be prepared for him! Fools as he takes us plain Englishmen to be, I warrant.

In consequence of these most shrewd coagitations, our churchwarden silenced his wife with a peremptory nod, when she came to persuade him to let Phœbe put on the Limerick gloves, and go to the ball. 'To this ball she shall not go; and I charge her not to put on those Limerick gloves, as she values my blessing,' said Mr. Hill. 'Please to tell her so, Mrs. Hill, and trust to my judgment and discretion in all things, Mrs. Hill. Strange work may be in Hereford yet: but I'll say no more, I must go and consult with knowing men, who are of my own opinion.'

He sallied forth, and Mrs. Hill was left in a state which only those who are troubled with the disease of excessive curiosity can rightly comprehend or compassionate. She hied her back to Phœbe, to whom she announced her father's answer; and then went gossiping to all her female acquaintance in Hereford, to tell them all that she knew, and all that she did not know; and to endeavour to find out a secret where there was none to be found.

19

Chapter IV

The Certainties of Suspicion are always doubtful, and often ridiculous.

There are trials of temper in all conditions; and no lady, in high or low life, could endure them with a better grace than Phœbe. Whilst Mr. and Mrs. Hill were busied abroad, there came to see Phœbe one of the widow Smith's children. With artless expressions of gratitude to Phœbe, this little girl mixed the praises of O'Neill, who, she said, had been the constant friend of her mother, and had given her money every week since the fire happened. 'Mammy loves him dearly, for being so good natured,' continued the child; 'and he has been good to other people as well as to us.'

'To whom?' said Phœbe.

'To a poor man, who has lodged for these few days past next door to us,' replied the child; 'I don't know his name rightly, but he is an Irishman; and he goes out a haymaking in the day-time, along with a number of others. He knew Mr. O'Neill in his own country, and he told mammy a great deal about his goodness.'

As the child finished these words, Phœbe took out of a drawer some clothes, which she had made for the poor woman's children, and gave them to the little girl. It happened that the Limerick gloves had been thrown into this drawer; and Phœbe's favourable sentiments of the giver of those gloves were revived by what she had just heard, and by the confession Mrs. Hill had made, that she had no reasons, and but vague suspicions, for thinking ill of him. She laid the gloves perfectly smooth, and strewed over them, whilst the little girl went on talking of Mr. O'Neill, the leaves of a rose which she had worn on Sunday.

Mr. Hill was all this time in deep conference with those prudent men of Hereford, who were of his own opinion, about the perilous hole under the cathedral. The ominous circumstances of this ball was also considered, the great expence at which the Irish glover lived, and his giving away gloves; which was a sure sign he was not under any necessity to sell them, and consequently a proof that, though he pretended to be a glover, he was something wrong in disguise. Upon putting all these things together, it was resolved, by these overwise politicians, that the best thing that could be done for Hereford, and the only possible means of preventing the immediate destruction of its cathedral, would be to take Mr. O'Neill into custody. Upon recollection, however, it was perceived that there were no legal grounds on which he could be attacked. At length, after consulting an attorney, they devised what they thought an admirable mode of proceeding.

Our Irish hero had not that punctuality which English tradesmen usually observe in the payment of bills: he had, the preceding year, run up a long bill with a grocer in Hereford; and, as he had not at Christmas cash in hand to pay it, he had given a note, payable six months after date. The grocer, at Mr.

Hill's request, made over the note to him; and it was determined that the money should be demanded, as it was now due, and that, if it was not paid directly, O'Neill should be that night arrested. How Mr. Hill made the discovery of this debt to the grocer agree with his former notion, that the Irish glover had always money at command, we cannot well conceive; but anger and prejudice will swallow down the grossest contradictions without difficulty.

When Mr. Hill's clerk went to demand payment of the note, O'Neill's head was full of the ball which he was to give that evening. He was much surprised at the unexpected appearance of the note: he had not ready money by him to pay it; and, after swearing a good deal at the clerk, and complaining of this ungenerous and ungentleman-like behaviour in the grocer and the tanner, he told the clerk to be gone, and not to be bothering him at such an unseasonable time; that he could not have the money then, and did not deserve to have it at all.

This language and conduct were rather new to the English clerk's mercantile ears: we cannot wonder that it should seem to him, as he said to his master, more the language of a madman than a man of business. This want of punctuality in money transactions, and this mode of treating contracts as matters of favour and affection, might not have damned the fame of our hero in his own country, where such conduct is, alas! too common; but he was now in a kingdom where the manners and customs are so directly opposite that he could meet with no allowance for his national faults. It would be well for his countrymen if they were made, even by a few mortifications, somewhat sensible of this important difference in the habits of Irish and English traders, before they come to settle in England.

But, to proceed with our story. On the night of Mr. O'Neill's grand ball, as he was seeing his fair partner, the perfumer's daughter, safe home, he felt himself tapped on the shoulder by no friendly hand. When he was told that he was the king's prisoner, he vociferated with sundry strange oaths, which we forbear to repeat, 'No, I am not the king's prisoner! I am the prisoner of that shabby rascally tanner, Jonathan Hill. None but he would arrest a gentleman, in this way, for a trifle not worth mentioning.'

Miss Jenny Brown screamed when she found herself under the protection of a man who was arrested; and, what between her screams and his oaths, there was such a disturbance that a mob gathered.

Among this mob there was a party of Irish haymakers; who, after returning late from a harvest-home, had been drinking in a neighbouring alehouse. With one accord, they took part with their countryman, and would have rescued him from the civil officers with all the pleasure in life, if he had not fortunately possessed just sufficient sense and command of himself to restrain their party-spirit, and to forbid, them, as they valued his life and reputation, to interfere, by word or deed, in his defence.

He then dispatched one of the haymakers home to his mother, to inform her of what had happened; and to request that she would get somebody to be bail for him as soon as possible, as the officers said they could not let him out of their sight till he was bailed by substantial people, or till the debt was discharged.

The widow O'Neill was just putting out the candles in the ball room when this news of her son's arrest was brought to her. We pass over Hibernian exclamations: she consoled her pride by reflecting that it would certainly be the most easy thing imaginable to procure bail for Mr. O'Neill in Hereford, where he had so many friends who had just been dancing at his house; but to dance at his house she found was one thing, and to be bail for him quite another. Each guest sent excuses; and the widow O'Neill was astonished at what never fails to astonish every body, when it happens to themselves. 'Rather than let my son be detained in this manner for a paultry debt,' cried she, 'I'd sell all I have within half an hour to a pawn-broker.' It was well no pawn-broker heard this declaration: she was too warm to consider economy. She sent for a pawn-broker, who lived in the same street, and, after pledging goods to treble the amount of the debt, she obtained ready money for her son's release.

O'Neill after being in custody for about an hour and a half, was set at liberty upon the payment of his debt. As he passed by the cathedral in his way home, he heard the clock strike; and he called to a man, who was walking backwards and forwards in the church-yard, to ask whether it was two or three that the clock struck. 'Three,' answered the man; 'and, as yet, all is safe.'

O'Neill, whose head was full of other things, did not stop to enquire the meaning of these last words. He little suspected that this man was a watchman, whom the over-vigilant churchwarden had stationed there to guard the Hereford cathedral from his attacks. O'Neill little guessed that he had been arrested merely to keep him from blowing up the cathedral this night. The arrest had an excellent effect upon his mind, for he was a young man of good sense: it made him resolve to retrench his expences in time, to live more like a glover, and less like a gentleman; and to aim more at establishing credit, and less at gaining popularity. He found, from experience, that good friends will not pay bad debts.

Chapter V

Conjecture is an Ignis Fatuus,[2] *that by seeming to light may dangerously mislead.*

On Thursday morning, our churchwarden rose in unusually good spirits, congratulating himself upon the eminent service he had done to the city of Hereford, by his sagacity in discovering the foreign plot to blow up the cathedral, and by his dexterity in having the enemy held in custody, at the very hour when the dreadful deed was to have been perpetrated. Mr. Hill's knowing friends further agreed it would be necessary to have a guard that should sit up every night in the church-yard; and that, as soon as they could, by constantly watching the enemy's motions, procure any information which the attorney should deem sufficient grounds for a legal proceeding, they should lay the whole business before the mayor.

After arranging all this most judiciously and mysteriously with the friends who were exactly of his own opinion, Mr. Hill laid aside his dignity of church-warden; and, assuming his other character of a tanner, proceeded to his tan-yard. What was his surprise and consternation when he beheld his great rick of oak-bark levelled to the ground; the pieces of bark were scattered far and wide, some over the close, some over the fields, and some were seen swimming upon the water. No tongue, no pen, no muse can describe the feelings of our tanner at this spectacle! feelings which became the more violent from the absolute silence which he imposed on himself upon this occasion. He instantly decided, in his own mind, that this injury was perpetrated by O'Neill, in revenge for his arrest; and went privately to the attorney to enquire what was to be done, on his part, to secure legal vengeance.

The attorney unluckily, or at least as Mr. Hill thought unluckily, had been sent for, half an hour before, by a gentleman at some distance from Hereford, to draw up a will; so that our tanner was obliged to postpone his legal operations.

We forbear to recount his return, and how many times he walked up and down the close to view his scattered bark, and to estimate the damage that had been done to him. At length that hour came which usually suspends all passions by the more imperious power of appetite – the hour of dinner; an hour of which it was never needful to remind Mr. Hill by watch, clock, or dial; for he was blessed with a punctual appetite, and powerful as punctual: so powerful, indeed, that it often excited the spleen of his more genteel, or less hungry, wife. – 'Bless my stars, Mr. Hill,' she would oftentimes say, 'I am really downright ashamed to see you eat so much; and, when company is to dine with us, I do wish you would take a snack by way of a damper before dinner, that you may not look so prodigious famishing and ungenteel.'

Upon this hint, Mr. Hill commenced a practice, to which he ever afterwards religiously adhered, of going, whether there was to be company or no company, into the kitchen regularly every day, half an hour before dinner, to take a slice from the roast or the boiled before it went up to table. As he was this day, according to his custom, in the kitchen, taking his snack by way of a damper, he heard the house-maid and the cook talking about some wonderful fortune-teller, whom the house-maid had been consulting. This fortune-teller was no less a personage than the successor to Bampfylde Moore Carew, king of the gipsies, whose life and adventures are probably in many, too many of our readers' hands.[3] Bampfylde the second, king of the gipsies, assumed this title, in hopes of becoming as famous, or as infamous, as his predecessor: he was now holding his court in a wood near the town of Hereford, and numbers of servant-maids and 'prentices went to consult him – nay, it was whispered that he was resorted to, secretly, by some whose education might have taught them better sense.

Numberless were the instances which our church-warden heard in his kitchen of the supernatural skill of this cunning man; and, whilst Mr. Hill ate his snack with his wonted gravity, he revolved great designs in his secret soul. Mrs. Hill was surprised, several times, during dinner, to see her consort put down his knife and fork, and meditate. 'Gracious me, Mr. Hill, what can have happened to you this day? What can you be thinking of, Mr. Hill, that can make you forget what you have upon your plate?'

'Mrs Hill,' replied the thoughtful church-warden, 'our grandmother Eve had too much curiosity; and we all know it did not lead to no good. What I am thinking of will be known to you in due time; but not now, Mrs. Hill; therefore, pray no questions, or teizing, or pumping. What I think, I think; what I say, I say; what I know, I know; and that is enough for you to know at present: only this, Phœbe, you did very well not to put on the Limerick gloves, child. What I know, I know. Things will turn out just as I said from the first. What I say, I say; and what I think, I think; and this is enough for you to know at present.'

Having finished dinner with this solemn speech, Mr. Hill settled himself in his armchair, to take his after-dinner's nap; and he dreamed of blowing up cathedrals and of oak-bark floating upon the waters; and the cathedral was, he thought, blown up by a man dressed in a pair of woman's Limerick gloves, and the oak-bark turned into mutton-steaks, after which his great dog Jowler was swimming; when, all on a sudden, as he was going to beat Jowler for eating the bark transformed into mutton steaks, Jowler became Bampfylde the second king of the gipsies; and, putting a horsewhip with a silver handle into Hill's hand, commanded him three times, in a voice as loud as the town-crier's, to have O'Neill whipped through the marketplace of Hereford: but, just as he was going to the window to see this whipping, his wig fell off and he awoke.

It was difficult, even for Mr. Hill's sagacity, to make sense of this dream: but he had the wise art of always finding in his dreams something that confirmed his waking determinations. Before he went to sleep, he had half resolved to consult the king of the gipsies, in the absence of the attorney; and his dream made him now wholly determine upon this prudent step. From Bampfylde the second, thought he, I shall learn for certain who made the hole under the cathedral, who pulled down my rick of bark, and who made away with my dog, Jowler; and then I shall swear examinations against O'Neill without waiting for attornies. I will follow my own way in this business: I have always found my own way best.

So, when the dusk of the evening increased, our wise man set out towards the

wood, to consult the cunning man. Bampfylde the second, king of the gipsies, resided in a sort of hut made of the branches of trees: the church-warden
stooped, but did not stoop low enough, as he entered this temporary palace;
and, whilst his body was almost bent double, his peruke was caught upon a
twig. From this awkward situation he was relieved by the consort of the
king; and he now beheld, by the light of some embers, the person of his
gipsey majesty, to whose sublime appearance this dim light was so favourable that it struck a secret awe into our wise man's soul; and, forgetting
Hereford cathedral, and oak-bark, and Limerick gloves, he stood for some
seconds speechless. During this time, the queen very dexterously dis-
encumbered his pocket of all superfluous articles. When he recovered his
recollection he put, with great solemnity, the following queries to the king
of the gipsies, and received the following answers:

'Do you know a dangerous Irishman, of the name of O'Neill; who has
come, for purposes best known to himself, to settle at Hereford?'

'Yes, we know him well.'

'Indeed! And what do you know of him?'

'That he is a dangerous Irishman.'

'Right! And it was he, was it not, that made away with my dog Jowler,
that used to guard the tan-yard?'

'It was.'

'And who was it that pulled down, or caused to be pulled down, my rick of
oak-bark?'

'It was the person that you suspect.'

'And was it the person whom I suspect that made the hole under the
foundation of our cathedral?'

'The same, and no other.'

'And for what purpose did he make that hole?'

'For a purpose that must not be named,' replied the king of the gipsies;
nodding his head in a mysterious manner.

'But it may be named to me,' cried the church-warden, 'for I have found it
out, and I am one of the church-wardens; and is it not fit that a plot to blow
up the Hereford cathedral should be known *to* me and *through* me?'

> 'Now take my word,
> Wise man of Hereford,
> None in safety may be,
> Till the *bad man* doth flee.'

These oracular verses, pronounced by Bampfylde with all the enthusiasm
of one who was inspired, had the desired effect upon our wise man; and he
left the presence of the king of the gipsies with a prodigiously high opinion
of his majesty's judgment, and of his own, fully resolved to impart, the next
morning, to the mayor of Hereford his important discoveries.

Chapter VI

Falsehood and Folly usually confute themselves.

Now it happened that, during the time Mr. Hill was putting the foregoing queries to Bampfylde the second, there came to the door, or entrance of the audience-chamber, an Irish haymaker, who wanted to consult the cunning man about a little leathern purse which he had lost, whilst he was making hay, in a field near Hereford. This hay-maker was the same person who, as we have related, spoke so advantageously of our hero, O'Neill, to the widow Smith. As this man, whose name was Paddy M'Cormack, stood at the entrance of the gipsies' hut, his attention was caught by the name of O'Neill; and he lost not a word of all that passed. He had reason to be somewhat surprised at hearing Bampfylde assert it was O'Neill who had pulled down the rick of bark. 'By the holy poker,' said he to himself, 'the old fellow now is out there. I know more o' that matter than he does, no offence to his majesty: he knows no more of my purse, I'll engage now, than he does of this man's rick of bark and his dog: so I'll keep my tester in my pocket, and not be giving it to this king o' the gipsies, as they call him; who, as near as I can guess, is no better than a cheat. But there is one secret which I can be telling this conjurer himself; he shall not find it such an easy matter to do all what he thinks; he shall not be after ruining an innocent countryman of my own, whilst Paddy M'Cormack has a tongue and brains.'

Now Paddy M'Cormack had the best reason possible for knowing that Mr. O'Neill did not pull down Mr Hill's rick of bark; it was M'Cormack himself who, in the heat of his resentment for the insulting arrest of his country-man in the streets of Hereford, had instigated his fellow haymakers to this mischief: he headed them, and thought he was doing a clever spirited action.

There is a strange mixture of virtue and vice in the minds of the lower class of Irish; or rather a strange confusion in their ideas of right and wrong, from want of proper education. As soon as poor Paddy found out that his spirited action of pulling down the rick of bark was likely to be the ruin of his countryman, he resolved to make all the amends in his power for his folly: he went to collect his fellow hay-makers, and persuaded them to assist him this night in rebuilding what they had pulled down.

They went to this work when every body except themselves, as they thought, was asleep in Hereford. They had just completed the stack, and were all going away except Paddy, who was seated at the very top finishing the pile, when they heard a loud voice cry out, 'Here they are; Watch! Watch!'

Immediately all the haymakers, who could, ran off as fast as possible. It was the watch who had been sitting up at the cathedral who gave the alarm. Paddy was taken from the top of the rick, and lodged in the watch-house till morning. 'Since I'm to be rewarded this way for doing a good action, sorrow take me,' said he, 'if they catch me doing another the longest day ever I live.'

Happy they who have in their neighbourhood such a magistrate as Mr. Marshal. He was a man who, to an exact knowledge of the duties of his office, joined the power of discovering truth from the midst of contradictory evidence; and the happy art of soothing, or laughing, the angry passions into good humour. It was a common saying in Hereford – that no one ever came out of Justice Marshal's house as angry as he went into it.

Mr. Marshal had scarcely breakfasted when he was informed that Mr. Hill, the church-warden, wanted to speak to him on business of the utmost importance. Mr. Hill, the church-warden, was ushered in; and, with gloomy solemnity, took a seat opposite to Mr. Marshal.

'Sad doings in Hereford, Mr. Mayor! Sad doings, Sir.'

'Sad doings? Why I was told we had merry doings in Hereford. A ball the night before last, as I heard.'

'So much the worse, Mr. Marshal; so much the worse: as those think with reason that see as far into things as I do.'

'So much the better, Mr. Hill,' said Mr. Marshal laughing; 'so much the better: as those think with reason that see no farther into things than I do.'

'But, Sir,' said the church-warden still more solemnly, 'this is no laughing matter, nor time for laughing, begging your pardon, Mr. Mayor. Why, Sir, the night of that there diabolical ball, our Hereford cathedral, Sir, would have been blown up; blown up from the foundation, if it had not been for me, Sir!'

'Indeed, Mr. Churchwarden! And pray how, and by whom, was the cathedral to be blown up; and what was there diabolical in this ball?'

Here Mr. Hill let Mr. Marshall into the whole history of his early dislike to O'Neill, and his shrewd suspicions of him the first moment he saw him in Hereford; related in the most prolix manner all that the reader knows already, and concluded by saying that, as he was now certain of his facts, he was come to swear examinations against this villainous Irishman, who, he hoped, would be speedily brought to justice, as he deserved.

'To justice he shall be brought, as he deserves,' said Mr. Marshal; 'but, before I write, and before you swear, will you have the goodness to inform me how you have made yourself as certain as you evidently are, of what you call your facts?'

'Sir, that is a secret,' replied our wise man, 'which I shall trust to you alone;' and he whispered into Mr. Marshal's ear that his information came from Bampfylde the second, king of the gipsies.

Mr. Marshal instantly burst into laughter; then composing himself said, 'My good Sir, I am really glad that you have proceeded no farther in this business; and that no one in Hereford, besides myself, knows that you were on the point of swearing examinations against a man on the evidence of Bampfylde the second, king of the gipsies. My dear Sir, it would be a standing joke against you to the end of your days. A grave man, like Mr. Hill; and a churchwarden too! Why you would be the laughing stock of Hereford!'

Now Mr. Marshal well knew the character of the man to whom he was talking, who, above all things on earth, dreaded to be laughed at. Mr. Hill coloured all over his face, and, pushing back his wig by way of settling it, shewed that he blushed not only all over his face but all over his head.

'Why, Mr. Marshal, Sir,' said he, 'as to my being laughed at, it is what I did not look for, being as there are some men in Hereford, to whom I have mentioned that hole in the cathedral, who have thought it no laughing matter, and who have been precisely of my own opinion thereupon.'

'But did you tell these gentlemen that you had been consulting the king of the gipsies?'

'No, Sir, no: I can't say that I did.'

'Then, I advise you, keep your own counsel, as I will.'

Mr. Hill, whose imagination wavered between the hole in the cathedral and his rick of bark on one side, and between his rick of bark and his dog Jowler on the other, now began to talk of the dog, and now of the rick of bark; and when he had exhausted all he had to say upon these subjects, Mr. Marshal gently pulled him towards the window, and putting a spy-glass into his hand, bid him look towards his own tan-yard, and tell him what he saw. To his great surprise, Mr. Hill saw his rick of bark rebuilt. 'Why it was not there last night,' exclaimed he, rubbing his eyes. 'Why some conjurer must have done this.'

'No,' replied Mr. Marshal, 'no conjurer did it; but your friend Bampfylde the second, king of gipsies, was the cause of its being rebuilt; and here is the man who actually pulled it down, and who actually rebuilt it.'

As he said these words, Mr. Marshal opened the door of an adjoining room, and beckoned to the Irish haymaker, who had been taken into custody about an hour before this time. The watch who took Paddy had called at Mr. Hill's house to tell him what had happened; but Mr. Hill was not then at home.

Chapter VII

Our Mistakes are our very selves; we therefore combat for them to the last.

It was with much surprise that the church-warden heard the simple truth from this poor fellow; but no sooner was he convinced that O'Neill was innocent, as to this affair, than he recurred to his other ground of suspicion, the loss of his dog.

The Irish haymaker now stepped forward, and, with a peculiar twist of the hips and shoulders, which those only who have seen it can picture to themselves, said, 'Please your honor's honor, I have a little word to say too about the dog.'

'Say it then,' said Mr. Marshal.

'Please your honor, if I might expect to be forgiven, and let off for pulling down the jontleman's stack, I might be able to tell him what I know about the dog.'

'If you can tell me any thing about my dog,' said the tanner, 'I will freely forgive you for pulling down the rick; especially as you have built it up again. Speak the truth now: Did not O'Neill make away with the dog?'

'Not at-all at-all, plase your honor,' replied the haymaker: 'and the truth of the matter is, I know nothing of the dog, good or bad; but I know something of his collar, if your name plase your honor is Hill, as I take it to be?'

'My name is Hill; proceed,' said the tanner, with great eagerness. 'You know something about the collar of my dog Jowler.'

'Plase your honor, this much I know, any way, that it is now, or was the night before last, at the pawnbroker's there, below in town; for, plase your honor, I was sent late at night, (that night that Mr. O'Neill, long life to him! was arrested,) to the pawnbroker's for a Jew, by Mrs. O'Neill, poor cratur! she was in great trouble that same time.'

'Very likely,' interrupted Mr. Hill: 'but go on to the collar; what of the collar?'

'She sent me, – I'll tell you the story, plase your honor, *out of the face*.[4] – She sent me to the pawn-broker's, for the Jew; and, it being so late at night, the shop was shut, and it was with all the trouble in life that I got into the house any way; and, when I got in, there was none but a slip of a boy up; and he set down the light that he had in his hand, and ran up the stairs to waken his master; and, whilst he was gone, I just made bold to look round at what sort of a place I was in, and at the old clothes, and rags, and scraps; and there was a sort of a frieze[5] trusty.'

'A trusty!' said Mr. Hill; 'what is that, pray?'

'A big coat sure, plase your honor: there was a frieze big coat lying in a corner, which I had my eye upon, to trate myself to; I having, as I then thought, money in my little purse enough for it. Well, I won't trouble your honor's honor with telling of you now how I lost my purse in the field, as I found after: but about the big coat, as I was saying, I just lifted it off the ground, to see would it fit me; and, as I swung it round, something plase your honor hit me a great knock on the shins: it was in the pocket of the coat, whatever it was, I knew; so I looks into the pocket, to see what was it, plase your honor, and out I pulls a hammer, and a dog-collar; it was a wonder, both together, they did not break my shins entirely: but its no matter for my shins now: so, before the boy came down, I just, out of idleness, spelt out to myself the name that was upon the collar; there were two names, plase your honor; and out of the first there was so many letters hammered out I could make nothing of it, at-all at-all; but the other name was plain enough to read any way, and it was Hill, plase your honor's honor, as sure as life: Hill, now.'

This story was related in tones, and with gestures, which were so new and strange, to English ears and eyes, that even the solemnity of our church-warden gave way to laughter. Mr. Marshal sent a summons for the pawnbroker, that he might learn from him how he came by the dog-collar. The pawnbroker, when he found from Mr. Marshal that he could by no other means save himself from being committed to prison, for receiving stolen goods, knowing them to be stolen, confessed that the collar had been sold to him by Bampfylde the second, king of the gipsies.

A warrant was immediately dispatched for his majesty; and Mr. Hill was a good deal alarmed, by the fear of its being known, in Hereford, that he was on the point of swearing examination against an innocent man, upon the evidence of a dog-stealer and a gipsy.

Bampfylde the second made no sublime appearance, when he was brought before Mr. Marshal: nor could all his astrology avail him upon this occasion: the evidence of the pawnbroker was so positive, as to the fact of his having sold to him the dog-collar, that there was no resource left for Bampfylde but an appeal to Mr. Hill's mercy. He fell on his knees, and confessed that it was he who stole the dog; which used to bark at him at night so furiously that he could not commit certain petty depredations, by which, as much as by telling fortunes, he made his livelihood.

'And so,' said Mr. Marshal, with a sternness of manner which till now he had never shewn, 'to skreen yourself, you accused an innocent man; and by your vile arts would have driven him from Hereford, and have set two families for ever at variance, to conceal that you had stolen a dog.'

The king of the gipsies was, without further ceremony, committed to the house of correction. We should not omit to mention that, on searching his hut, the Irish haymaker's purse was found; which some of his majesty's train had emptied. The whole set of gipsies decamped, upon the news of the apprehension of their monarch.

Chapter VIII

Good Sense and good Humour are the best Peace-makers.

Mr. Hill stood in profound silence, leaning upon his walking-stick, whilst the committal was making out for Bampfylde the second. The fear of ridicule was struggling with the natural positiveness of his temper: he was dreadfully afraid that the story of his being taken in, by the king of the gipsies, would get abroad; and, at the same time, he was unwilling to give up his prejudice against the Irish glover.

'But Mr. Mayor,' cried he, after a long silence, 'the hole under the foundation of our cathedral has never been accounted for: that is, was, and ever will be, an ugly mystery to me; and I never can have a good opinion of this Irishman, till it is cleared up; nor can I think the cathedral in safety.'

'What,' said Mr. Marshal, with an arch smile, 'I suppose the verses of the oracle still work upon your imagination, Mr. Hill. They are excellent in their kind. I must have them by heart that, when I am asked the reason why

Mr. Hill has taken an aversion to an Irish glover, I may be able to repeat them.

> 'Now, take my word,
> Wise man of Hereford,
> None in safety may be
> Till the bad man doth flee.'

'You'll oblige me, Mr. Mayor,' said the church-warden, 'if you would never repeat those verses, Sir; nor mention, in any company, the affair of the king of the gipsies.'

'I will oblige you,' replied Mr. Marshal, 'if you will oblige me. Will you tell me honestly whether, now that you find this Mr. O'Neill is neither a dog-killer nor a puller down of bark-ricks, you feel that you could forgive him for being an Irishman, if the mystery, as you call it, of the hole under the cathedral was cleared up?'

'But that is not cleared up I say, Sir,' cried Mr. Hill; striking his walking-stick forcibly upon the ground, with both his hands. 'As to the matter of his being an Irishman, I have nothing to say to it: I am not saying any thing about that, for I know we are all born where it pleases God; and an Irishman may be as good as another. I know that much, Mr. Marshal; and I am not one of those illiberal-minded ignorant people that cannot abide a man that was not born in England. Ireland is now in his majesty's dominions,[6] I know very well, Mr. Mayor; and I have no manner of doubt, as I said before, that an Irishman born may be as good, almost, as an Englishman born.'

'I am glad,' said Mr. Marshal, 'to hear you speak, almost, as reasonably as an Englishman born and every man ought to speak; and I am convinced that you have too much English hospitality to persecute an inoffensive stranger, who comes amongst us trusting to our justice and good-nature.'

'I would not persecute a stranger, God forbid, Mr. Mayor,' replied the church-warden, 'if he was, as you say, inoffensive.'

'And if he was not only inoffensive but ready to do every service in his power, to those who are in want of his assistance, we should not return evil for good; should we?'

'That would be uncharitable, to be sure; and moreover a scandal,' said the church-warden.

'Then,' said Mr. Marshal, 'will you walk with me as far as the widow Smith's; the poor woman whose house was burnt last winter? This hay-maker, who lodged near her, can shew us the way to her present abode.'

During his examination of Paddy M'Cormack, who would tell his whole history, as he called it, *out of the face*, Mr. Marshal heard several instances of the humanity and goodness of O'Neill, which Paddy related to excuse himself for that warmth of attachment, to his cause, that had been manifested so injudiciously by pulling down the rick of bark, in revenge for the arrest.

Amongst other things, Paddy mentioned his countryman's goodness to the widow Smith: Mr. Marshal was determined, therefore, to see whether he had, in this instance, spoken the truth; and he took Mr. Hill with him, in hopes of being able to shew him the favourable side of O'Neill's character.

Things turned out just as Mr. Marshal expected. The poor widow and her family, in the most simple and affecting manner, described the distress from which they had been relieved by the good gentleman and lady; the lady was Phœbe Hill; and the praises that were bestowed upon Phœbe were delightful to her father's ear, whose angry passions had now all subsided.

The benevolent Mr. Marshal seized the moment when he saw Mr. Hill's heart was touched, and exclaimed, 'I must be acquainted with this Mr. O'Neill. I am sure we people of Hereford ought to shew some hospitality to a stranger, who has so much humanity. Mr. Hill, will you dine with him to-morrow at my house?'

Mr. Hill was just going to accept of this invitation when the recollection of all he had said to his club, about the hole under the cathedral, came across him; and, drawing Mr. Marshal aside, he whispered, 'But, Sir, Sir, that affair of the hole under the cathedral has not been cleared up yet.'

At this instant, the widow Smith exclaimed, 'Oh! here comes my little Mary: (one of her children who came running in) 'this is the little girl, Sir, to whom the lady has been so good. Make your curtsy, child. Where have you been all this while?'

'Mammy,' said the child, 'I've been shewing the lady my rat.'

'Lord bless her! Gentlemen, the child has been wanting me this many a day to go to see this tame rat of hers; but I could never get time, never: and I wondered too at the child's liking such a creature. Tell the gentleman, dear, about your rat. All I know is that, let her have but never such a tiny bit of bread, for breakfast or supper, she saves a little of that little for this rat of hers: she and her brothers have found it out somewhere by the cathedral.'

'It comes out of a hole under the wall of the cathedral,' said one of the elder boys; 'and we have diverted ourselves watching it, and sometimes we have put victuals for it, so it has grown, in a manner, tame like.'

Mr. Hill and Mr. Marshal looked at one another, during this speech; and the dread of ridicule again seized on Mr. Hill, when he apprehended that, after all he had said, the mountain might, at last, bring forth – a rat. Mr. Marshal, who instantly saw what passed in the church-warden's mind, relieved him from this fear, by refraining even from a smile on this occasion. He only said to the child, in a grave manner, 'I am afraid, my dear, we shall be obliged to spoil your diversion. Mr. Church-warden, here, cannot suffer rat-holes in the cathedral: but, to make you amends for the loss of your favorite, I will give you a very pretty little dog, if you have a mind.'

The child was well pleased with this promise; and, at Mr. Marshal's desire, she then went along with him and Mr. Hill to the cathedral, and they placed themselves at a little distance from that hole which had created so much disturbance. The child soon brought the dreadful enemy to light; and Mr. Hill, with a faint laugh, said, 'I'm glad it's no worse: but there were many in our club who were of my opinion; and, if they had not suspected O'Neill too, I am sure I should never have given you so much trouble, Mr. Mayor, as I have done this morning. But, I hope, as the club know nothing about that vagabond, that king of the gipsies, you will not let any one know any thing about the prophecy, and all that? I am sure, I am very sorry to have given you so much trouble, Mr. Mayor.'

Mr. Marshal assured him that he did not regret the time which he had spent, in endeavouring to clear up all these mysteries and suspicions; and Mr. Hill gladly accepted his invitation to meet O'Neill at his house the next day. No sooner had Mr. Marshal brought one of the parties to reason, and good humour, than he went to prepare the other for a reconciliation. O'Neill and his mother were both people of warm but forgiving tempers: the arrest was fresh in their minds; but, when Mr. Marshal represented to them the whole affair, and the church-warden's prejudices, in a humourous light, they joined in the good-natured laugh, and O'Neill declared that, for his part, he was ready to forgive and to forget every thing, if he could but see Miss Phœbe in the Limerick gloves.

Phœbe appeared the next day, at Mr. Marshal's, in the Limerick gloves; and no perfume ever was so delightful to her lover as the smell of the rose-leaves, in which they had been kept.

Mr. Marshal had the benevolent pleasure of reconciling the two families. The tanner and the glover of Hereford became, from bitter enemies, useful friends to each other; and they were convinced, by experience, that nothing could be more for their mutual advantage than to live in union.

Notes

Text: *Popular Tales,* Johnson, London, 1804.
1 County Limerick in Ireland was noted for the manufacture of very fine leather gloves, reputed to be made from the skin of unborn lambs.
2 Pale phosphorescent flame appearing over marshy land, sometimes called will-o'-the-wisp, believed to lure travellers to their doom.
3 Bamfylde Moore Carew (1693–?1770), the son of a Devonshire rector, ran away from school to join the gypsies. He was elected king of the English gypsies, transported to Maryland, escaped back to England, and became a follower of Bonnie Prince Charlie. The first of many editions of his *Life and Adventures* appeared in 1745.
4 From the beginning.
5 Heavy woollen fabric, used for overcoats.
6 The Act of Union (1800) established the United Kingdom of Great Britain and Ireland.

THE STORY OF SIR BERTRAND

Anna L. Barbauld

Anna Laetitia Barbauld, née Aikin (1743–1825), poet, critic, editor and essayist, was the daughter of the Unitarian minister and teacher Dr John Aikin. She was precociously intelligent, and was educated by her father and his colleagues at the Warrington Dissenting Academy. Her marriage, to Rochemont Barbauld, a dissenting clergyman of French extraction, was increasingly unhappy owing to a mental disorder which eventually led to his being placed in an institution, where he drowned himself in 1808. An important writer of the Romantic period, she published poetry (some of it political) and educational works, and edited the poems of Akenside (1794) and Collins (1797) and the letters of Richardson (1804). Her important fifty-volume edition of *The British Novelists*, with biographical introductions and a prefatory essay, appeared in 1810. Her last published work was *Eighteen Hundred and Eleven: A Poem* (1812) which was heavily criticised for its anti-war sentiments.

The Story of Sir Bertrand, one of her few ventures into fictional prose, first appeared in an early publication which she co-wrote with her brother John Aikin, *Miscellaneous Pieces in Prose* (1773). It was reprinted a number of times.

Further reading

Barbauld (1825, 1994); Blain *et al.* (1990); Jump (1997); MacCarthy in Feldman and Kelley (1995); Ritchie (1883); Rodgers (1958); Shattock (1993).

The Story of Sir Bertrand

Sir Bertrand turned his steed toward the wolds, hoping to cross those dreary moors before the curfew tolled. But ere he had proceeded half his journey, he was bewildered by the different tracts; and not being able, as far as the eye could reach, to espy any object but the brown heath surrounding him, he was at length quite uncertain which way he should direct his course. Night overtook him in this situation. It was one of those nights when the moon gives a faint glimmering of light through the thick black clouds of a louring sky. Now and then she suddenly emerged in full splendor from her veil; and then instantly retired behind it, having given the forlorn Sir Bertrand a wide-extended prospect over the desolate waste. Hope and native courage awhile urged him to push forward; but at length the increasing darkness, and fatigue of body and mind, overcame him; he dreaded moving from the ground he stood on, for fear of unknown pits and bogs; and, alighting from his horse in despair, he threw himself on the ground. He had not long continued in that posture when the sullen toll of a distant bell struck his ears; he started up; and, turning toward the sound, discerned a dim twinkling light. Instantly he seized his horse's bridle, and with cautious steps advanced toward it. After a painful march, he was stopped by a moated ditch surrounding the place from whence the light proceeded; and, by a momentary glimpse of moonlight, he had a full view of a large antique mansion, with turrets at the corners, and an ample porch in the centre. The injuries of time were strongly marked on every thing about it. The roof in various places was fallen in, the battlements were half demolished, and the windows broken and dismantled. A draw-bridge, with a ruinous gateway at each end, led to the court before the building. He entered; and instantly the light, which proceeded from a window in one of the turrets, glided along, and vanished; at the same moment the moon sunk beneath a black cloud, and the night was darker than ever. All was silent. Sir Bertrand fastened his steed under a shed; and approaching the house, traversed its whole front with light and slow foot-steps. All was still as death. He looked at the lower windows, but could not distinguish a single object through the impenetrable gloom. After a short parley with himself, he entered the porch; and, seizing a massy iron knocker at the gate, lifted it up, and, hesitating, at length struck a loud stroke. The noise resounded through the whole mansion with hollow echoes. All was still again. He repeated the strokes more boldly, and louder. Another interval of silence ensued. A third time he knocked; and a third time all was still. He then fell back to some distance, that he might discern whether any light could be seen in the whole front. It again appeared in the same place, and quickly glided away as before; at the same instant, a deep, sullen toll sounded from the turret. Sir Bertrand's heart made a fearful stop. He was a while motionless; then terror impelled him to make some hasty steps toward his steed; but shame stopped his flight; and, urged by honor, and a resistless desire of finishing the adventure, he returned to the porch; and, working up his soul to a full steadiness of resolution, he drew forth his sword with one hand, and with the other lifted up the latch of the gate. The heavy door, creaking upon its hinges, reluctantly yielded to his hand; he applied his shoulder to it, and forced it open. He quitted it, and stepped forward; the door instantly shut with a thundering clap. His blood was chilled; he turned back to find the door, and it was long before his trembling hands could seize it; but his utmost strength could not open it again. After several ineffectual attempts, he looked behind him, and beheld, across a hall, a pale bluish flame, that cast a dismal gleam of light around. He again summoned forth his courage, and advanced toward it; it retired. He came to the foot of the stairs; and, after a moment's deliberation, ascended. He went slowly up, the flame retiring before him, till he came to a wide gallery. The flame proceeded along it, and he followed in silent horror, treading lightly, for the echo of his footsteps startled him. It led him to the foot of another staircase, and then vanished; at the same instant another toll sounded from the turret. Sir Bertrand felt it strike upon his heart. He was now in total darkness; and, with his arms extended, began to ascend the second stair-case. A dead cold hand met his left hand, and grasped it, drawing him forcibly forward; he endeavored to disengage himself, but could not; he made a furious blow with his sword, and instantly a loud shriek pierced his ears, and the dead hand was left powerless in his. He dropped it, and ran forward with a desperate valor.

The stairs were narrow and winding, and interrupted by frequent breaches and loose fragments of stones. The stair-case descended narrower and narrower, and at length terminated in a low iron grate. Sir Bertrand pushed it open; it led to an intricate winding passage, just large enough to admit a person upon his hands and knees. A faint glimmering of light served to show the nature of the place. Our knight entered; a deep hollow groan resounded from a distance through the vault. He went forward; and, proceeding beyond the first turning, discovered the same blue flame which had before conducted him. He followed it. The vault at length suddenly opened into a lofty gallery, in the midst of which a figure appeared, completely armed, with a terrible frown and a menacing gesture, brandishing a sword in his hand. Sir Bertrand undauntedly sprang forward; and, aiming a fierce blow at the figure, it instantly vanished, letting fall a massy iron key. The flame now rested upon a pair of ample folding doors at the end of the gallery. Our hero went to it, and applied the key to a brazen lock. With difficulty he turned the bolt; instantly the doors flew open, and discovered a large apartment, at the end of which was a coffin rested upon a bier, with a taper burning on each side of it. Along the room on both sides were gigantic statues of black marble, attired in the Moorish habit, and holding enormous sabres in their hands. Each of them reared its arm, and advanced one leg forward, as the knight entered; at the same moment the lid of the coffin flew open, and the bell tolled. The flame still glided forward; and Sir Bertrand resolutely followed, till he arrived within six paces of the coffin. Suddenly, a lady in a shroud and black veil rose up in it and stretched out her arms toward him; at the same time the statues clashed their sabres, and advanced. He flew to the lady, and clasped her in his arms; she threw up her veil, and kissed his lips; when instantly the whole building shook as with an earthquake, and fell asunder with a horrible crash.

Sir Bertrand was thrown into a sudden trance; and, on recovering, found himself seated on a velvet sofa, in the most magnificent room he had ever seen, lighted with innumerable tapers in lustres[1] of pure crystal. A sumptuous banquet was set in the middle. The doors opening to soft music, a lady of incomparable beauty, attired with amazing splendor, entered, surrounded by a troop of gay nymphs more fair than the graces. She advanced to the knight; and, falling on her knees, thanked him as her deliverer. The nymphs put a garland of laurel upon his head; and the lady led him by the hand to the banquet, and sat beside him. The nymphs placed themselves at the table; and a numerous train of servants entered, who served up the feast, delicious music playing all the time.

Sir Bertrand could not speak for astonishment; he could only return their honors by courteous looks and gestures. After the banquet was finished, all retired but the lady; who, leading the knight back to the sofa, addressed him in these words:—

"Sir Knight. — The grateful remembrance of my delivery from the iron hand of the Moorish tyrant, who in dying bequeathed his soul to the prince of the air for the horrid purpose of confining me in this my patrimonial estate, shall never be erased from my memory. And if to you I own his power over me, it was but transient, and of short duration. With horror I view the remains of his now extinguished fascination; and though years have rolled after years, and involved in their course the fate of my venerable ancestors, yet I have at last the consolation to find myself by your valor free from the machinations of Almanzor (for that was the name of the Moorish prince, whom our valiant King Edward brought over with him on his return from the crusades). My father approved of my union with him; but alas! I never beheld him without horror. His dark insidious looks, compared to the open and undisguised mein of him I had lately lost in the troubles of the times, made me shudder. In an unlucky moment I was induced to sign, in obedience to my father's will, a covenant with Almanzor, which he pretended would place me next heir to the Moorish throne. Each signature was made with our blood, and a requiem was afterward sung for the success of our union. But, alas! minds are not so easily transferred. My soul owed allegiance to Sir Walter, a generous knight of this country, and whom this horrid eastern tyrant had destroyed in conflict; and because I peremptorily refused to drink his blood, this monster swore he would invoke every power to confine me until some more valorous knight should arrive to release me from his hands. How long I have been enchanted, I do not know; but this I can declare, that from that time to the present I have not been free from horrid dreams like those which are said to infest the wicked in their graves."

So saying, she rose up; and taking Sir Bertrand by the hand, led him to the couch, where he took his repose for a few hours. Early in the morning he took his departure, promising to return soon. He was as good as his word; and, in a few days, the priest united them for ever. The marriage was attended with great pomp, both of ecclesiastic and military men, who all bestowed the most liberal benedictions upon this happy pair.

Notes

Text: *Gothic Stories*, S. Fisher, London, 1804.
1 Chandeliers.

COUSIN MARY

Mary Russell Mitford

Mary Russell Mitford (1787–1855), poet, sketch-writer, short-story writer and dramatist, was born in Hampshire. She won a £20,000 lottery at the age of 10, enabling her father to build a house near Reading and to educate her at the prestigious Hans Place School in London. Her first publications were volumes of poetry (1810, 1812 and 1813). The family moved to a cottage in a small Berkshire village after her father's compulsive gambling had reduced the family to poverty again. In 1819 she began publishing 'sketches' of village life in the *Lady's Magazine*. Hugely successful (the magazine's sales were increased from 250 to 2,000), these were collected in five volumes as *Our Village* (1824–32). Several similar works followed, as well as a number of plays, but none of her work equalled the continuing success of *Our Village*. She never married, but had a large circle of literary friends, with whom she carried on a lively correspondence. One of her last works was *Recollections of a Literary Life* (1852).

Further reading

Blain *et al.* (1990); Edwards (1988); Hunter (1984); L'Estrange (1870, 1882); Miller (1954); Shattock (1993); Sutherland (1988).

Cousin Mary

About four years ago, passing a few days with the highly educated daughters of some friends in this neighbourhood, I found domesticated in the family a young lady, whom I shall call as they called her, Cousin Mary. She was about eighteen, not beautiful, perhaps, but lovely certainly to the fullest extent of that loveliest word—as fresh as a rose; as fair as a lily; with lips like winter berries; dimpled, smiling lips; and eyes of which nobody could tell the colour, they danced so incessantly in their own gay light. Her figure was tall, round, and slender; exquisitely well proportioned it must have been, for in all attitudes (and in her innocent gaiety she was scarcely ever two minutes in the same) she was grace itself. She was, in short, the very picture of youth, health, and happiness. No one could see her without being prepossessed in her favour. I took a fancy to her the moment she entered the room and it increased every hour in spite of, or rather perhaps for, certain deficiencies, which caused poor Cousin Mary to be held exceedingly cheap by her accomplished relatives.

She was the youngest daughter of an officer of rank, dead long ago; and his sickly widow having lost by death, or that other death, marriage, all her children but this, could not, from very fondness, resolve to part with her darling for the purpose of acquiring the commonest instruction. She talked of it, indeed, now and then, but she only talked; so that, in this age of universal education, Mary C. at eighteen exhibited the extraordinary phenomenon of a young woman of high family, whose acquirements were limited to reading, writing, needle-work, and the first rules of arithmetic. The effect of this let-alone system, combined with a careful seclusion from all improper society, and a perfect liberty in her country rambles, acting upon a mind of great power and activity, was very reverse of what might have been predicted. It had produced not merely a delightful freshness and originality of manner and character, a piquant ignorance of those things of which one is tired to death, but knowledge, positive, accurate, and various knowledge. She was, to be sure, wholly unaccomplished; knew nothing of quadrilles, though her every motion was dancing; nor a note of music, though she used to warble like a bird sweet snatches of old songs, as she skipped up and down the house; nor of painting, except as her taste had been formed by a minute acquaintance with nature into an intense feeling of art. She had that real extra sense, an eye for colour, too, as well as an ear for music. Not one in twenty—not one in a hundred of our sketching and copying ladies could love and appreciate a picture where there was colour and mind, a picture by Claude, or by our English Claudes, Wilson and Hoffland,[1] as she could—for she loved landscape best, because she understood it best—it was a portrait of which she knew the original. Then her needle was in her hands almost a pencil. I never knew such an embroidress—she would sit "printing her thoughts on lawn," till the delicate creation vied with the snowy tracery, the fantastic carving of hoar frost, the richness of Gothic architecture, or of that which so much resembles it, the luxuriant fancy of old point lace. That was her only accomplishment, and a rare artist she was—muslin and net were her canvass. She had no French either, not a word; no Italian; but then her English was racy, unhackneyed, proper to the thought to a degree that only original thinking could give. She had not much reading, except of the Bible, and Shakspeare, and Richardson's novels,[2] in which she was learned; but then her powers of observation were sharpened and quickened, in a very unusual degree, by the leisure and opportunity afforded for their development at a time of life when they are most acute. She had nothing to distract her mind. Her attention was always awake and alive. She was an excellent and curious naturalist, merely because she had gone into the fields with her eyes open; and knew all the details of rural management, domestic or agricultural, as well as the peculiar habits and modes of thinking of the peasantry, simply because she had lived in the country, and made use of her ears. Then she was fanciful, recollective, new; drew her images from the real objects, not from their shadows in books. In short, to listen to her, and the young ladies her companions, who, accomplished to the height, had trodden the education-mill till they all moved in one step, had lost sense in sound, and ideas in words, was enough to make us turn masters and governesses out of doors, and leave our daughters and grand-daughters to Mrs. C.'s system of non-instruction. I should have liked to meet with another specimen, just to ascertain whether the peculiar charm and advantage arose from the quick and active mind of this fair Ignorant, or was really the natural and inevitable result of the training; but, alas! to find more than one unaccomplished young lady, in this accomplished age, is not to be hoped for. So I admired and envied; and her fair kinswomen pitied and scorned, and tried to teach; and Mary, never made a learner, and as full of animal spirits as a schoolboy in the holidays, sang, and laughed, and skipped about from morning till night.

It must be confessed, as a counter-balance to her other perfections, that the dear Cousin Mary was, as far as great natural modesty and an occasional touch of shyness would let her, the least in the world of a romp![3] She loved to toss about children, to jump over stiles, to scramble through hedges, to climb trees; and some of her knowledge of plants and birds may certainly have arisen from her delight in these boyish amusements. And which of us has not found that the strongest, the healthiest, and most flourishing acquirement has arisen from pleasure or accident, has been in a manner self-sown, like an oak of the forest?—Oh, she was a sad romp; as skittish as a wild colt, as uncertain as a butterfly, as uncatchable as a swallow! But her great personal beauty, the charm, grace, and lightness of her movements, and, above all, her evident innocence of heart, were bribes of indulgence which no one could withstand. I never heard her blamed by any human being. The perfect unrestraint of her attitudes, and the exquisite symmetry of her form, would have rendered her an invaluable study for a painter. Her daily doings would have formed a series of pictures. I have seen her scudding through a shallow rivulet, with her petticoats caught up just a little above the ankle, like a young Diana,[4] and a bounding, skimming, enjoying motion, as if native to the element, which might have become a Naiad.[5] I have seen her on the topmost round of a ladder, with one foot on the roof of a house, flinging down the grapes that no one else had nerve enough to reach, laughing, and garlanded, and crowned with vine-leaves, like a Bacchante.[6] But the prettiest combination of circumstances under which I ever saw her, was driving a donkey-cart up a hill, one sunny windy day in September. It was a gay party of young women, some walking, some in open carriages of different descriptions, bent to see a celebrated prospect from a hill called the Ridges. The ascent was by a steep narrow lane, cut deeply between sand-banks, crowned with high, feathery hedges. The road and its picturesque banks lay bathed in the golden sunshine, whilst the autumnal sky, intensely blue, appeared at the top as through an arch. The hill was so steep that we had all dismounted, and left our different vehicles in charge of the servants below; but Mary, to whom, as incomparably the best charioteer, the conduct of a certain non-descript machine, a sort of donkey curricle, had fallen, determined to drive a delicate little girl, who was afraid of the walk, to the top of the eminence. She jumped out for the purpose, and we followed, watching and admiring her as she won her way up the hill: now tugging at the donkeys in front, with her bright face towards them and us, and springing along backwards—now pushing the chaise from behind—now running by the side of her steeds, patting and caressing them—now soothing the half-frightened child—now laughing, nodding, and shaking her little whip at us—darting about like some winged creature—till at last she stopped at the top of the ascent, and stood for a moment on the summit, her straw bonnet blown back, and held on only by the strings; her brown hair playing on the wind in long natural ringlets; her complexion becoming every moment more splendid from exertion, redder and whiter; her eyes and her smile brightening and dimpling; her figure in its simple white gown, strongly relieved by the deep blue sky, and her whole form seeming to dilate before our eyes. There she stood under the arch formed by two meeting elms, a Hebe, a Psyche,[7] a perfect goddess of youth and joy. The Ridges are very fine things altogether, especially the part to which we were bound, a turfy breezy spot, sinking down abruptly like a rock into a wild fore-ground of heath and forest, with a magnificent command of distant objects;—but we saw nothing that day like the figure on the top of the hill.

After this I lost sight of her for a long time. She was called suddenly home by the dangerous illness of her mother, who, after languishing for some months, died; and Mary went to live with a sister much older than herself, and richly married, in a manufacturing town, where she languished in smoke, confinement, dependence, and display, (for her sister was a match-making lady, a manœuvrer,) for about a twelvemonth. She then left her house and went into Wales—as a governess! Imagine the astonishment caused by this intelligence amongst us all; for I myself, though admiring the untaught damsel almost as much as I loved her, should certainly never have dreamed of her as a teacher. However, she remained in the rich baronet's family where she had commenced her employment. They liked her apparently,—there she was; and again nothing was heard of her for many months, until, happening to call on the friends at whose house I had originally met her, I espied her fair blooming face, a rose amongst roses, at the drawing-room window,— and instantly with the speed of light was met and embraced by her at the hall-door.

There was not the slightest perceptible difference in her deportment. She still bounded like a fawn, and laughed and clapped her hands like an infant. She was not a day older, or graver, or wiser, since we parted. Her post of tutoress had at least done *her* no harm, whatever might have been the case with her pupils. The more I looked at her the more I wondered; and after our mutual expressions of pleasure had a little subsided, I could not resist the temptation of saying,—"So you are really a governess?"—"Yes."—"And you continue in the same family?"—"Yes."—"And you like your post?"—"O yes! yes!"—"But, my dear Mary, what could induce you to go?"—"Why, they wanted a governess, so I went."—"But what could induce them to keep you?" The perfect gravity and earnestness with which this question was put set her laughing, and the laugh was echoed back from a group at the end of the room, which I had not before noticed—an elegant man in the prime of life showing a portfolio of rare prints to a fine girl of twelve, and a rosy boy of seven, evidently his children. "Why did they keep me? Ask them," replied Mary, turning towards them with an arch smile. "We kept her to teach her ourselves," said the young lady. "We kept her to play cricket with us," said her brother. "We kept her to marry," said the gentleman, advancing gaily to shake hands with me. "She was a bad governess, perhaps; but she is an excellent wife—that is her true vocation." And so it is. She is, indeed, an excellent wife; and assuredly a most fortunate one. I never saw happiness so sparkling or so glowing; never saw such devotion to a bride, or such fondness for a step-mother, as Sir W. S. and his lovely children show to the sweet Cousin Mary.

Notes

Text: *Our Village: Sketches of Rural Character and Scenery*, Whittaker, London, 1824–32

1 Claude Lorrain (1600–62), influential French landscape painter; Andrew Wilson (1718–92) and Thomas Hofland (1777–1843), British landscape painters.
2 Samuel Richardson, *Pamela* (1740–1), *Clarissa* (1747–8), *Sir Charles Grandison* (1753–4).
3 Tomboy.
4 Roman goddess of hunting, chastity and the moon.
5 Water nymph (Greek myth).
6 Reveller, follower of Bacchus, Roman god of wine.
7 Hebe, daughter of Zeus, goddess of youth and spring; Psyche, a beautiful girl loved by Eros, personification of the soul (Greek myth).

THE THREE DAMSELS

David Lynsay

'David Lynsay' (Mary Diana Dods) (c. 1790–?1845), short-story writer, dramatist. Reputed to be the daughter of the 15th Earl of Morton. A friend of Mary Shelley, she lived in Paris from 1827, wearing men's clothes and using the name Walter Sholto Douglas. She specialised in gothic tales, and several of her stories, all published under her pseudonym, appeared in *Blackwood's*. She published a collection, *Tales of the Wild and Wonderful*, in 1825, and contributed stories to various annuals.

Further reading

Bennett (1980–8, 1991).

The Three Damsels

'Come hither, my beautiful Jean, and my fairy Lilias,' said the venerable Countess of Moray to her laughing, happy grand-daughters – 'come hither, my children, and spend your Halloween with me. I have not prepared the charms of the night, nor am I ready to join you in the incantations of the season, but I have a tale may suit it well; and you will not like it the less because the grey head tell you with her own lips the story of her day, when her locks were as bright as the berry, and her eyes as beaming as your own'.

'That, in truth, shall we not noble grandam', said the sparkling Lillias; 'but yet would I have the charm of Halloween. Ah, little canst thou dream how dear this night is to the expecting maiden! – Let us perform the rites of the even, and tomorrow, grandam, thy tale shall find us most attentive listeners'.

'Ah, true Scots !' said the Countess, 'thus clinging to the wonderful, and seeking to peep into futurity: but try not the charm, my children, if you love me. Alas! I think not of it without tears and a sorrow unspoken of till now, for the fate of a friend, dear to my early youth, gushes into my bosom. Sit, my children, and my story shall repay you for this loss of your time; me it will also please to speak of the things gone by: and if it convince you, as I trust it will, of the folly of these superstitions, I shall have more than gained my purpose. Will my children listen?' 'What is there we can refuse you, noble grandam?' said the lovely Jean, burying her locks of amber amid the snowy curls of the venerable Countess. 'Speak on, then; you have made us listeners already – and hark! wind, and rain, and snow – a goodly night for a tale. Tell on, dear grandam; the fire is bright, the lamp is clear, and we are seated gravely, our thoughts composed to attention – now for thy wondrous tale!'

'It was on this very eve, many years since,' began the noble lady to her auditors, 'that the three lovely daughters of a noble house assembled together in a dreary wood to try the charm of the night, which if successful was to give to their earnest sight the phantom form of the lover who was afterwards to become the husband. Their powerful curiosity had stifled their fear (for they were as timid as beautiful) on their first setting out on this expedition; but, on finding themselves alone in the dark and melancholy wood, some touches of cowardice and compunction assailed them together, and they determined by a somewhat holy beginning to sanctify the purpose which had brought them thither. They were too young to laugh at this mock compact between God and the Devil, and therefore when Catherine, the eldest sister, began, in an audible voice, to recite the prayer against witchcraft, the others joined in it most devoutly. Now then, fortified against evil, their courage rose with every additional sentence; and when the soft voice of the young Agnes, the loveliest and youngest of the three, steadily responded the 'amen', they were as courageous as was necessary, and no longer fearful of the power of the evil one. I know not, my children, all the forms used upon this occasion; but Catherine, after repeating certain words in a solemn voice, advanced before her sisters, and quietly placed upon the ground her offering to the shade she had invoked, as by his conduct towards it she was to judge of her future prospects. It was a beautiful rose-tree which she had chosen, and the flowers were full and many; and the sisters were contemplating from a little distance the rich hue, when they were startled by the clashing of arms and the loud outcries of men in fierce contention, breaking upon the stillness of the night. For a moment they hesitated whether to fly or remain concealed, when their doubts were decided by the rapid approach of a stern and stately Highland chief, who, brandishing his broad sword, swept on to the rose-tree as if he would annihilate from the earth its fair and fragile beauty. Suddenly his arm was no longer raised to destroy – the weapon drooped gently down beside the tree – and they saw his blue eye look mildly and kindly on the flowers as, bending down to gather them, he faded from their sight in the action. Catherine was by no means displeased with her fortune, and the appearance of her handsome bridegroom gave courage to the other two to hasten the coming of theirs. Marian, the second sister, removed the rose, placed a lily bough in its stead, and then, with a beating heart and wandering eye, repeated the charm. Again the silence was broken, as the quick but steady tramp of a warrior's horse struck upon the ear, and the shade of a noble cavalier, dismounting from his phantom steed, advanced slowly, very slowly, towards the lily: his face was beautiful, but sad – beyond expression sad; and they saw a tear fall upon the flower as he pressed it to his lips and deposited it gently in his bosom. He too had faded like a dream, when the beautiful Agnes advanced to perform her part in the witcheries of the night. She trembled, but she would not recede, and faintly repeating the charm, hung her white handkerchief on the branch of a distant tree. This time there was no sound, but a dread and solemn silence slowly ushered in her unexpected fate. From the wood came a long and sable procession of horse and foot, following a coffin, that was steadily borne towards them; many were the ghastly attendants supporting the pall, and many were the shadowy mourners who followed. Agnes watched with breathless attention the march of the phantom dead: they advanced slowly and steadily till they came under the tree, where her white offering fluttered lightly in the air; it was seen suspended a moment above them, then dropped amidst the cavalcade, and Agnes beheld the pale fingers of the chief mourner clutch at the offering as it fell.

'Days, weeks, months, passed away, and still found Agnes drooping over her blighted hopes, and expecting the death of which the omen of the forest had assured her; but still she died not, and was every succeeding month astonished that she yet lived. She now began to doubt the truth of the omen, more especially as the Highlander had not yet wedded her sister, who was betrothed to, and about to become the wife of, a favourite of the king, who had earnestly sought her hand. Agnes thought she too might now listen to a tale of love; and such a one as was told her by a noble lover, and of her sovereign's blood, she listened to with pleasure. Walter was now her all, and the omen of the forest was forgotten.

The marriage of Catherine was appointed to take place at a country residence of her affianced husband, and Agnes, with her betrothed, was invited to be present. Marian too was there, and no happiness could have been more complete than that of the bridal party; but a dark night set upon this brilliant morning: ere they could reach the church which was to be the scene of their union, the Highlanders had descended in force from their mountains and assailed the unarmed guests. 'The Camerons come!' cried the shrieking maidens, and flew in all directions from their sight; the bridegroom fell in the conflict; and the bride, as she rushed to the side of her dying husband, was clasped in the arms of the insolent chief, and borne away to *his* bridal bed. Marian escaped the tumult, and Walter preserved his adored by the effects of his desperate valour, cutting with his sword a passage through his foes, and encouraging the armed men, who now came to their assistance, to drive the invaders from their hold. They were successful; and silence, though accompanied by sorrow, again reigned in the hall of the young and hapless bridegroom.

'But the greatest evil resulting from this cruel inroad was the effect it had upon the mind of Agnes. Her belief in the omens of the forest again returned; her confidence in her prospects was shaken; and with the same feeling that bids the giddy wretch throw himself at once from the precipice over which he fears he shall fall, she determined to hasten the destiny which she now firmly believed to await her. Convinced by the fate of her sister of the certain fulfilment of her own, she resolved to spare her lover the anguish of beholding her expire; and, for this purpose, suddenly broke off connection with him, and refused to admit him to presence. Walter's hope still struggled with his despair; he made some earnest appeals to her tenderness, her reason, and her gratitude. Agnes was deaf to all; she believed herself destined to fall an early victim to death, and that that bridegroom would snatch her from an earthly one, even at the altar's foot. Walter, heartbroken, retired from his home, and joining the cavalier army of the king, sought in the tumult of military life forgetfulness of the wound his calmer days had given. In the intervals of his visits to his family Marian became interested in his welfare: she saw him frequently, spoke to him of Agnes, soothed his sufferings by her compassion, and gratified his pride by her admiration. He had no thought for any other: and though he loved not Marian, yet she became his trusted friend, his companion, and finally his wife. It was her will, not his: and what woman ever failed in her determination over the mind of man! They wedded and were wretched. The heart of Walter had not been interested, and the temper of Marian was not such as to acquire its delicate preference. She became jealous, irritable, perverse, and soon taught her hapless husband the difference between herself and the gentle Agnes. Such a course could have but one termination: stretched at length on that sick bed which was to be her last, she sent to desire the attendance of her younger sister. Agnes obeyed the mandate, but only arrived in time to meet the funeral procession which conducted the hapless Marian to her early grave. The widower instantly recognised, from a distance, his young heart's love, and rapidly flew to meet her; and as she shed tears of unfeigned sorrow for his loss, he took the white handkerchief she held and tenderly dried them away. O! at that moment, how deeply Agnes sighed! She beheld in this scene the fulfilment of the omen, and wept to think she had thus wasted some of the best years of her life, and trifled with her lover's happiness and her own. 'Ah, silly delusion!' she exclaimed in bitterness of heart, 'of what hast thou not bereaved me!' After the period of mourning had expired, she gave her hand to Walter, and endeavoured, in making his days tranquil, to forget the felicity she had lost.'

'But they were wedded, grandam dear', said the beautiful Lilias, laughing – 'what more would the people have had?' 'Youth, and its love, and its hope, and all its bright and gracious feeling,' said the venerable Countess: '*they* had all fled with time, and nothing but their remembrance remained with Agnes and her Walter, which made their lot more bitter. He was at their wedlock past even manhood's prime; she was no longer young; and though not wretched, yet they were not happy; and it was only in their descendants they looked for felicity. Agnes has found it truly, but for Walter –'

'Grandam, it is your own tale you tell and our grand-sire's, I am certain, by the tears which roll down your face,' replied Lilias. 'Ah, I will wait Heaven's own good time for a husband, and try these charms no more. Kiss me, noble grandam: your Lilias will never forget the Tale of Halloween.' The bright maiden threw herself into the arms of her venerable ancestress and at that moment it was scarcely possible to decide which was the nobler object, the damsel in the glory of her brilliant youth, or the Countess in the calmness of her majestic age.

Notes

Text: *Forget-me-Not; A Christmas and New Year's Present*, Ackerman, London, 1827.

LADY EVELYN SAVILE'S THREE TRIALS

Being an extract from the diary of Mr. S. of Charlcote-Park

Catherine Gore

Catherine Gore, née Moody (1799–1861), novelist, short-story writer and dramatist, was born in Nottinghamshire. She was brought up in London and educated mainly at home. Married to a captain of the Life Guards and the mother of ten children, she started publishing her witty, socially acute fiction in 1823. Her first success came with *Women as they Are; or The Manners of the Day* (1830), admired by George IV. She wrote approximately seventy other novels and numerous short stories, mostly of the so-called 'silver-fork' school of romances of fashionable life. Most were published anonymously, and in one week in 1841 she brought out two novels in deliberate rivalry with each other. She wrote several novels dealing with the theme of money, including the admired *The Banker's Wife* (1843). She came into a £20,000 inheritance in 1850, but was defrauded of it five years later by her guardian, Sir John Dean Paul, who was later imprisoned for embezzlement. She also wrote several dramas, among them a comedy, *Quid Pro Quo*, which won a £500 prize in 1843. Her husband's ill-health led to a move to France in 1832, where she supported the family by writing. She lost her sight towards the end of her life (though she continued to write), and returned to live in England. Only two of her children survived her.

Further reading

Adburgham (1983); Anderson (1976); Blain *et al.* (1990); Horne (1844); Rosa (1936); Shattock (1993); Sutherland (1988).

Lady Evelyn Savile's Three Trials

Charlcote, May, 1827. – How well I recollect my poor mother assuring me, among her parting exhortations on my leaving her for Christchurch,[1] that unless I exerted myself to subdue the wayward and sensitive irritability of my character, I should live to become the most miserable of human beings, and to alienate the regard of all my friends. I should not have endured such an accusation from any one but herself; but a presentiment at that very moment warned me she was in the right, and experience is beginning to confirm the lesson. Why – why can I not be satisfied with the events of life as I find them, – with the feelings I excite and see excited, without examining too curiously into their nature and origin? – Why should I care for aught beyond the surface of things in this most superficial world? – Because my spirit is endued with a tone of refinement, and my bosom nerved to a degree of morbid sensibility, which is at once the most exquisite and the most painful inheritance of nature. The thrill of ecstacy derived from the spectacle of a noble landscape, – from the attunement of a fine anthem pealing among the arches of an ancient cathedral, or the still more delicious music of a generous sentiment uttered by lips which are dear to us, – from an atmosphere laden with the fragrance of summer, – from a beautiful countenance or graceful figure, – is, after all, a poor compensation for the impatience arising from the every day monotony of life; for the disappointment of baffled affections, and the irritating doubts of an insatiable attachment.

Have I a right to be thus discontented? – Rich as I am in all those tangible gifts of Providence which limit the ambition of ordinary men, have I an excuse for murmuring? – Could I, with all my selfish indolence, have braved a life of hardship, or endured a compulsory association with the low-minded and the mercenary? – Well, well, – after all I believe I *have* some reason to congratulate myself on the possession of Charlcote, with its park and forest, – its library and picture-gallery, – its conservatories and fountains; and above all, with its rent-roll, and the ancient and honourable name which renders these things my own.

And yet – fool that I am! – it was the extent of these very possessions which first moved my misgivings, and prompted my ungenerous doubts of the motives and characters of other people. My old guardian, Sir Horace Savile, even before I quitted Eton, was perpetually reminding me that a man – and still more, – a *boy* – with an estate of forty thousand a year, is predestined to the snares of designing companions; and took care that every book he placed in my hands should confirm the precept. Would to heaven he had left me to become a dupe! What would have been the sacrifice of half my fortune, compared with the jealous caution and anxiety he succeeded in instilling into my mind? Companion after companion, associate after associate, was I tempted to dismiss from my regard, under an apprehension that my horses and hounds, my equipages, and preserves, and comfortable quarters at Charlcote, formed the secret inducement of their predilection for my society; and boyhood which, with all its guileless impulses and ready adoption of the pleasures and follies of the hour, is usually a season of so much spontaneous enjoyment, was to *me* embittered by a premature mistrust of myself and those by whom I was surrounded, such as pertains of right to the callous epoch of middle age.

But, alas! what were these sacrifices, – what was my reserve towards my fox-hunting companions and Oxford friends, – compared with the vexatious alarms I was soon to derive from the still more wary admonitions of my poor mother? Little did she suspect, when I parted from her at Charlcote to pass my first season in town a few months previous to her own decease, how fatally her counsels were calculated to embitter my future destiny; while *she* thought only of unveiling to my knowledge the artifices of her sex, and warning me against the sordid ambition actuating the conduct of half the women in the world – or rather *of* the world! Experience would have taught me such wisdom soon enough; and in a manner which, while it disgusted me with the sordid egotism of a single object, might have left me free to hope that there still existed pure and gentle hearts to be wooed, – frank and honourable hands to be won. As it was, arriving in London with a prepossession that every mother at Almack's[2] was on the watch to entangle the young owner of Charlcote and its thousands for some daughter or niece educated and brought out for the express purpose of forming a good establishment and strengthening the family interest, I taught myself to overlook the charms even of the loveliest face, and to despise the fascinations of some of the most high-minded women in England. I was convinced, for instance, that Lady Mary Blair, the sister of one of my chosen Oxford friends, was exerting all the arts of coquetry to make Charlcote-Park her own; when, as I afterwards discovered, she had been for many years betrothed to an absent cousin: and during the whole season I amused myself with tantalizing the expectation and exciting the hopes of pretty little Charlotte Howard by a violent flirtation, with the idea of driving her to despair by the eventual disappointment of her speculation, without once suspecting that she was using *me* as a mere screen to disguise from her family her attachment and engagement to poor Charles Rawdon, of the Guards.

It was however this very mistrust of the manœuvres to which I was exposed, that carried me to the feet of my dear Evelyn. The world was pleased to assert, with its ordinary liberality, that my addresses to Lady Rydal's daughter were prompted by the ambition of allying myself with the premier earl of the kingdom; but my real inducements, although scarcely less selfish, were of a very different nature. I knew that Evelyn, educated in all the gorgeous splendours of Castle Rydal, was unconscious of any other mode of existence than the brilliant profusion of her father's house; that her total ignorance of the world and its ways confirmed the natural disinterestedness of her character; and the very pride which might have been expected to deter me from an alliance far above my own degree, was in fact the original motive of my attachment to the young and lovely Lady Evelyn Beaufort. What were to her the caskets and settlements I had it in my power to offer? – A mansion, a thousand-fold more magnificently appointed than mine, – diamonds a thousand times more precious than those of the Savile family, had been glittering in her eyes from infancy; and I knew and felt with a most bewildering throb of triumph when first I pressed her to my bosom, that the concession was bestowed upon Edward Savile for his own and single sake, – not upon the proprietor of Charlcote. Another point, too, was strong in confirmation of the involuntary and fervent nature of Evelyn's affection. She loved me not only in spite of herself, but in spite of her parents; she, who had been from her birth the most submissive of children, ventured to brave and finally succeeded in overcoming Lady Rydal's reluctance to the match. Who – who could have withstood the tears of Evelyn? Even her authoritative mother found them irresistible; and while the voice of society accused Lady Rydal of withholding her consent from her daughter's marriage "with a commoner," that daughter honestly confided to me that my own jealousy of temper and waywardness of character were the true source of the disapprobation of her family.

They are mistaken, I can assure these Beauforts, if they fancy that *their* opposition is likely to school me into a more gentle frame of mind.

And yet I do not think I have given poor Evelyn *much* cause to regret the consent which her persevering attachment wrung from her parents: comparing myself with the generality of husbands, I cannot fancy that I have displayed *much* perverseness of temper or inattention to her wishes. From the day I first beheld her taming down the sportive vivacity of her footsteps to the sober pace of the stately countess among the shrubberies of Rydal Castle, I registered a vow within my heart that I would render her future life an uninterrupted tissue of prosperity and joy; – that I would make her the envy of the world, and the glory of my own existence, – and I trust I have fulfilled the promise. – I ask only in return, – is it too much? – an unqualified feeling of acknowledgment that her happiness is derived from me, and me only; and a degree of tenderness which would induce her to abandon all things – home, country, parents, friends, associates – for the sake of her husband. Such is the law of God in the institution of wedlock – such should be the law of man! – But although I may congratulate myself on having attained this paramount influence over her feelings, it sometimes occurs to me that Lady Evelyn is less cheerful and unconstrained in my presence than she used to be;

and that although her will is a law at Charlcote, where my hourly efforts are devoted to the forestalment of her wishes, she is occasionally tempted to regret its distance from Castle Rydal. What can she find to like in that grim, obscure old place? – What has it to offer in comparison with the modern elegance and luxurious refinement of her own abode? – Does she miss the noisy round of country hospitality in which Lord R. delights to take refuge from the nothingness of his own mind? – or is it – *can* it be – that she pines after the soothing idolatry of her doting mother?

Let me strive to recall the occasion on which I first noted an expression of sadness on her countenance. – Yes! it was on our wedding-day! – that sweetest holiday, – that brightest respite from the cares of life, – which ought to be unclouded as the luxurious sky of an eastern climate – unruffled as the glassy waves which sleep beneath. I had prepared for that morning a surprise which I expected would excite the eager delight and gratitude of my Evelyn. She has often asked me for my picture; and I, with my accustomed contrariety, had as often affected to decline the task of sitting for a portrait, although a celebrated artist was at that very moment engaged in the accomplishment of her request. Day after day I had seen her turn with indifference from the strings of pearls and sparkling gems collected by my ostentatious vanity as marriage gifts, and already I luxuriated in an anticipation of the rapture with which my last and simplest offering would be welcomed; when, half an hour previous to the ceremony which was to make her mine for ever, I sent to demand a private interview. How angrily did my heart recoil from the common-place worldliness of the reply! – "Lady Rydal's compliments, and Lady Evelyn Beaufort was engaged with her hair-dresser." I could have crushed the fellow who delivered the message; and was half inclined to jump into my travelling-carriage and quit Castle-Rydal for ever. I contented myself, however, with whispering to my beautiful bride when I led her into the castle chapel, "And can you venture, Evelyn, to pronounce a solemn marriage vow in the presence of God and man, after the frivolous manner in which you have prepared yourself for so sacred an institution? Had you *really* loved me, you would have been contented to approach this altar with tresses less trimly arrayed, rather than wound the heart of your future husband by such untimely levity." Even amidst the tears which burst from her eyes, and the sighs which escaped her lips, I could distinguish the words, "Forgive me, Edward! – it was my mother!" And I *did* forgive her; – but I could not so easily pardon myself when, on seeking her to press our departure for Charlcote an hour or two after the ceremony, I found her in the favourite boudoir of her beloved home, – her hair dishevelled, her crown of snow-white roses cast upon the ground, and tears streaming from her eyes. No, No! – there should not have been a tear on Evelyn's cheek upon her wedding-day; it should have been bright as the dawning of summer sunshine! And as we passed the lodge-gates of Charlcote on our entrance into her new residence, I whispered, in my turn, "Forgive *me*, dearest, – forgive my petulance this morning!"

"I do, I do!" she faltered, taking the miniature from her bosom, as if it offered an apology for all my faults; "but remember, love, this has been *your Evelyn's first trial.*"

Charlcote, January, 1829. – How strange that I cannot get a single order attended to in my own house. There are bonfires enough blazing yonder on the Wrottesmore Hills to bring all the county hither with their fulsome congratulations; and yet it is full an hour since I despatched a messenger on horseback to stop the ringing of the bells in the village. I have no doubt the blockheads are fully aware of my vexation at finding my hopes frustrated, and are triumphing in an opportunity of insulting me. But thank Heaven! though Charlcote has lost its heir, my Evelyn still lives – my poor, patient, tender, suffering Evelyn! – thank Heaven, I have yet years in store which will enable me to atone for my rash harshness towards her.

That a few short hours should have sufficed to crush the precious expectations I have so long, so vainly cherished! It is all Lady Rydal's doing. Had she not interfered with her officious parade of maternal solicitude, I should certainly have attended to Evelyn's suggestions; but I have no idea of being hectored into submission on any point of domestic arrangements, either by Lord Rydal or his consequential countess. I fancied, too, that from the first they evinced an unreasonable and groundless disinclination to my standing for the county.[3] Was it *their* affair if I chose to expend fifteen or twenty thousand pounds on the acquirement of a distinction which has become almost hereditary in the Savile family? The interests of their daughter and her unborn child could not be materially affected by such a trifle; and in allying myself with the Beaufort family, I never covenanted to subject either my financial projects or my political principles to their authority. What, too, could be more natural than that I should desire my lovely, my sympathizing Evelyn to witness and adorn my triumph? – How worthless and importunate would have been the plaudits of the multitude, or the gratulations of cordial friends, had I not been certain that they reached *her* ear! Lady Rydal, with her old woman's tales of fatigue and agitation, and the delicacy of her daughter's constitution, only moved my impatience; and when I replied to Evelyn's own confessions of alarm, that I should consider her absence on such an occasion a proof of the decline of her affection for her husband, I spoke with a sincere conviction that their terrors originated in the mere nervous susceptibility of fine ladyism.

Still it was the duty of that accursed coachman to forewarn me how imperfectly broken was the new set of horses sent down for the occasion by my inconsiderate friend Lord Blair. He *must* have been aware that they were totally unfit to stand the tumult of an election riot, – the flags, and streamers, and drums, and all the other intolerable nuisances attendant on such an occasion. I own I entertained not the slightest apprehension; and although on passing the carriage on our progress to the hustings, I noticed that Lady Evelyn amid all he smiles looked deadly pale, I attributed her emotion to the over-excitement of her sympathy in my success. Great God! – I shall never forget the tumult of my feelings, when a messenger first contrived to render himself audible to my ear through the uproar of the scene, in order to acquaint me that the Charlcote carriage had been seen dashing at full speed along the High-street, and that an accident was apprehended! It was full a quarter of an hour before the intelligence reached me; another had nearly expired before I could disentangle myself from the mob, and obtain a horse. I beheld nothing – I heard nothing till I reached the outskirts of the town; but when at length I *did* attain the private road leading towards Charlcote-Park, I distinctly saw the bank broken down by the violence with which the carriage had been dragged along by the infuriated horses. Agonized by the spectacle, I put mine to its full speed; till three miles further on I was stopped by an importunate tenant, who pointed out to me the spot where my coachman had been thrown from the box, and a neighbouring cottage where *his body* was lying.

"And the carriage – Lady Evelyn?"

"The carriage kept the road towards the hall: we have heard nothing yet of my lady."

I galloped on – I reached the lodge – I saw the broken carriage lying against the iron gates. – Again I breathed the name of my wife.

"Her ladyship had been carried up insensible to the hall."

Never did the park I had to traverse appear so extensive to me before; but when at last I came in sight of the house, and obtained a full view of Evelyn's chamber-windows, it seemed to my impatient bosom that the least consideration for my feelings would have induced Lady Rydal, or one of the family, to exhibit some ostensible token for the state of things, – of the life or death of all that was dearest to me in existence. As if any one had leisure to think of *me* at all in such a crisis! – unless, indeed, as the perverse author of the evil which had befallen.

A single question burst from my lips, when the house-steward, with a face as pale as ashes, met me in the vestibule – "*Was she alive?*"

"Her ladyship is still living, sir; but – "

I heard no more, – the shock was too much for me, – and on recovering my consciousness I found myself seated in a hall chair beside the window, surrounded by a herd of wondering servants; and had scarcely sufficient strength to support myself up the great staircase, and crawl along the corridor leading to Evelyn's apartments. A dim light was admitted into my wife's chamber, and a low moan of pain was the first sound which struck me as I entered: but that light was sufficient to show me the touching smile which overspread her ghastly countenance on beholding me, and that mournful tone of anguish proceeded at least from the lips of my living wife. I drew nearer to her bedside, and saw that she was surrounded by strange faces; that, extended on the coverlid, beside her swollen arm which had been broken and mangled in the recent accident, lay the body of a dead infant, which she was caressing;

and as I stooped over her, and mingled my tears with the damp dews that hung on her discoloured brow, she whispered, "He would have been the image of my dear Edward – the lips, the forehead, are exactly like your own; – but I must not talk – I must not exhaust myself. Remember, dearest, this is *your Evelyn's second trial*!"

February, 1829. – Surely there never was any thing so tediously protracted as Lady Evelyn's recovery; surely so much caution and seclusion is neither customary nor necessary on such occasions. I am convinced Lady Rydal has managed the affair so as to prolong all the mischief of the case before my eyes, and afford me what she considers a useful lesson. Not an annoyance nor a mortification has she spared me; – one day exhibiting letters of condolence from an intended royal sponsor; – another, ostentatiously laying aside some of the splendid preparations for this unfortunate babe; and at all hours and seasons lamenting over its loss as if it were the first and last of her family. She says she *had* hoped to look upon a child of her darling Evelyn's previous to her own decease, – but that it is now too late; and although *I* can see no symptoms of disease of decay about this tiresome pragmatical old woman, I own the thoughts of possessing my dear Evelyn beyond all further reach of her mother's interference and influence would have afforded an additional joy to the birth of our child. But the triumph of proving me to have been in the wrong, and of finding her prognostications fulfilled, will doubtless suffice to recover Lady Rydal from all her imaginary ailments.

It is now six weeks since the unfortunate occurrence, and she has enjoyed the luxury of sullen resentment ever since. This is the day we had set apart for the christening of our firstborn; and it was to have been solemnized by prodigious rejoicings among the tenantry, and by the opening of two school-houses erected under Evelyn's auspices in the village. Of this latter part of the ceremony it would have been impossible to defraud the horde of wondering wide-mouthed savages of the liberties of Charlcote: – were half my family exterminated, they would still think it high treason against their rights that a few score of their ragged urchins should be compelled to rehearse their alphabets and catechisms for another half-year in the old cottages. But if Evelyn possessed a particle of that warm sensibility for which I formerly gave her credit, she would not have selfishly left me to go through this odious ceremonial alone. She must have been fully aware of the exaggerated regrets and sympathy which would be poured upon me on such an occasion, and which her presence would have sufficed to silence. I went among these blockheads to perform an act of munificence towards them positively with the air of a culprit; and all because Lady Rydal thought proper to assert that the damp air of one of the finest spring mornings that ever shone would prove too much for her daughter! – There is such a parade of sensibility and solicitude between them! – Evelyn is perpetually desponding over the declining state of her mother's health; and I am scarcely ever left for half an hour alone with Lady Rydal, that she does not take occasion to beseech I will watch carefully over my wife after her departure; and to predict that, without the most vigilant attention, Evelyn will fall a sacrifice to the consequences of this disastrous affair. Was ever any thing more absurd! One would think, as old Lord Lindesay says in "The Abbot,"[4] that "woman's flesh were grown as tender as new-fallen snow."

I fancy, however, I have at last discovered a method of silencing the old raven's forebodings. Yesterday morning as Lady Evelyn was slowly approaching us through the conservatory, pausing to take breath at every step, (and had not that *exigeante*[5] Lady Rydal been sitting near me in the saloon how eagerly should I have rushed forward to tender her the support of my arm!) Lady R. thought proper to whisper the thrice-told tale of her maternal alarms lest my wife should never wholly recover her youthful strength and spirits; hinting that there was a pulmonary affection hereditary in the Beaufort family.

"Does your ladyship really apprehend any thing of hectic symptoms?"[6] I inquired. "In that case I shall give up my seat in the House without a moment's hesitation. Italy is our only resource; and we should lose no time in setting off, that we may avoid the inconvenience of travelling during the summer heats."

I shall never forget the shudder with which Lady Rydal recoiled from me at this unexpected announcement. "No!" she replied, in a concentrated whisper, "you could not be so inhuman; – *even you* could not be so inhuman as to separate an only child from a dying parent! My physicians have acknowledged to me, Mr. Savile, that I have not six months to live. Do not render my last moments desolate; – do not provoke on her deathbed the malediction of a bereaved mother!"

Lady Evelyn's entrance put a period to the conversation; and I trust I have also terminated Lady Rydal's groundless predictions: but I may yet find occasion to make her atone for those insolent words, "*even you* could not be so inhuman!"

July, 1829. – How delightful to date my diary once more from Charlcote; – to find myself once more in my own old familiar home; to look up to its towering oaks and massive chesnuts, and remember the day-dreams which I first learnt to cherish beneath their deep and impressive shade! *Here*, too, she is mine again! – The world cannot reach her here; – society cannot surround her with its contaminating whispers, nor that endless tribe of haughty Beauforts intrude their importunate claims on her time and regard. Here I shall have her for my own. We shall ride, walk, read, converse in the same solitary union which blest the first months of our marriage. Evelyn will sing to me, listen to me, chide me, love me, with all the intensity of her early affection! – What a summer of joy and enjoyment is before me!

During the tedious season we have been passing in town how little have I seen of my wife! Lady Rydal's real or fancied indisposition has been the means of drawing her daughter incessantly from home; and whenever she could be released from her attendance on her mother, there were drawing-rooms to be attended, or family connexions to be kept up by formal heca-tombs[7] of hospitality, or some high mightiness of the tribe to be propitiated by the endurance of a stupid concert or ball. But Heaven be thanked it is over. We can now live exclusively for ourselves, or rather for each other; – we can now exist as if the world were but a name. And such should ever be the destiny of *love*. Less than all is nothing to its insatiable exactions. For my own part I recognise no gradation in its impulses between the intense and absorbing ardour of passion, and the coldest torpor of indifference. I feel myself capable of passing from the utmost bigotry of religion, the holiest inspirations of a martyr, to the darkness of atheism: – I know no medium in such things. –

An express from Castle Rydal! Is it not too irritating? Must I resign all my precious schemes of happiness in favour of the caprices of that fantastical old woman? I see how it is – they will positively drive me from England, that I may enjoy Lady Evelyn's society unmolested. Is it not written that a woman shall leave father and mother and cleave to her husband? – and must my own hearth be deserted, and my own feelings set at nought, every time Lady Rydal's finger chooses to ache? – Yes, she shall go: on this occa-sion, and for the last time, I will overcome my own wishes: but I warn them that our return to Charlcote shall only be the signal for Evelyn's departure for Italy.

Beauvais, September 4th. – Thank Heaven I am at last released from the house of bondage! – thank Heaven my own efforts have at length unclasped the embrace of that clinging Old Man of the Sea![8] – I really began to fear that I had promised myself too much in undertaking our departure; but perseverance – ay, or obstinacy, or obduracy, or whatever Lady Rydal pleases to call it – has effected my purpose. And now the Garden of Eden lies before us; and more than all the happiness and triumph I ever anticipated in the confiding union of domestic life will be mine, while I devote myself to guiding my beloved Evelyn through the noble scenery of Italy – that laby-rinth teeming with the treasures of art which enraptured me even when I wandered amid its fascinations in all the uncompanionable dreariness of my earlier years: – there she will insensibly recover her health, her animation, her tenderness towards that husband who swears to devote his every thought and every moment to the task of aiding her recovery. No! she shall have no occasion to regret those endearing solicitudes of Lady Rydal's which she has taught herself to prize so highly.

I can scarcely fancy we are within a day's journey of Paris. Never did I approach that city before without feeling, and observing in my companions, a degree of excitement and exhilaration such as the vicinity of no other spot, no other city, is capable of affording; and now I not only perceive that Evelyn is oppressed by the prospect of mingling in its giddy scenes, but, were it not that I have so determinately formed my plans for introducing her to all its beauties and diversions, I could myself be well content to pass on at once to the South. Perhaps it is that my spirits were over harassed by all the scenes I had to endure at Castle Rydal – all Lord R.'s remonstrances and hypo-critical allusions to the desolation which would fall on his gray hairs on the approaching loss of his wife and during the absence of his child. I scarcely ever heard persons advanced in years allude to their own "gray hairs," unless for some cajoling purpose; and as to Lady R.'s danger, I am convinced she indulges in all sorts of exaggerations for the sole purpose of proving to the world how insensible I have shown myself to her distress, and to the feelings of Lady Evelyn. But the struggle is now over! – I can hold my wife to my bosom in unwatched and unmolested affection; and her mother, deprived of all motive for further dissembling, will gradually recover, and persuade her fashionable toady of a physician to reverse the fatal decree she had bespoken for herself.

Lausanne, October. – It is very strange, – but the nearer we approach the south, the more Lady Evelyn's debility increases. She takes no interest in the new objects which force themselves on her attention; and although, in answer to the allusions by which I strive to attract her notice and divert her from her silent reflections, she labours to appear more cheerful, and occasion-ally utters some constrained inquiry, it is evident that her thoughts are far away. On arriving in any new town or city, her first question is concerning the English post. I wish she would learn to dress her artificial smiles with somewhat of a less melancholy expression; – she *must* be aware that at pres-ent they convey daggers to my bosom. Such, however, is the perversity of woman's nature, even in the exercise of her best affections! It is not that she fractiously or unnecessarily complains – let me do her justice – but that in those involuntary bursts of tenderness which once rendered our exclusive companionship so enchanting to my soul, she no longer attempts to disguise her conviction that our union is drawing to a close. Last night, on returning from a dinner party at the villa of her cousin, Lord B., which she had excused herself from attending on the plea of indisposition, I found the saloon des-erted, and stole softly into Evelyn's room, believing that she had retired to rest; but I found her seated beside the window, with the curtains drawn aside and her eyes fixed in eager contemplation on the clear depths of the starry autumnal sky.

"I am trying to interpret yonder omens," she whispered, while I pressed my lips gently to her cheek. "I am trying to decipher in their mysterious aspect whether it is appointed to me to become an orphan – whether my dear mother will pass before me into the sanctuary."

"And your husband, Evelyn?" I exclaimed, interrupting her; "has he no claims on your consideration, that you indulge in this unreasonable depression?"

"Hush!" she faltered, laying her delicate hand on my lips; "this is too sacred an hour for chiding. I tell you, dearest Edward, that my doom is sealed. I feel it – I know it. Nothing is left for me but the grave – and, alas! a *foreign grave*! I shall not lie in the tomb of my fathers; I shall not rest where my beloved, and those he will in future learn to love, repose together in the dust. Alone – desolate – forgotten – the withered leaves of a strange country will come fluttering down on the turf that covers the broken heart of Evelyn."

There is something in her countenance at all seasons, but more especially when she indulges in these wild bursts of emotion, so bright beyond all human expression, so irradiated with the impulses of an immortal nature, that the harsh words of reproof I premeditate often become silenced on my lips as I gaze upon her face: yet on this occasion I ventured to reproach her with want of generosity towards me, even while she concealed her face in my bosom, with the tears of her ill-required tenderness stealing down her cheeks.

"Trust me," she murmured between her broken sobs, "trust me, dearest, these warnings are not spoken in bitterness. I wish but to say a few words – a *very* few words – which may linger in your memory when I shall be at rest. Edward – my own Edward! – when you shall wed again, and *that* time in spite of your incredulity will surely come, let it not be with the child of living parents – with the idol of a numerous family. Let your future wife be one who has experienced no domestic happiness such as you can suppose her capable of comparing with that you are inclined to bestow; and sometimes, – sometimes amid the transports of this new passion, think upon your poor lost Evelyn – upon her early faith, her early death – think upon her counsels, Edward, and do justice to the truth and tenderness of her love!"

My heart was too full to admit of my uttering more than a few incoherent sentences in reply; and probably they appeared harsher than I could have wished, – for I was apprehensive that by giving way to my feelings I might afford a confirmation of her presentiments.

Lausanne, 19*th.* – The physicians strenuously recommend that Lady Evelyn should pass the winter at Naples, while *she* is as obstinately bent on remaining here. Her connexion with the family of Lord B., whose brother has recently been appointed ambassador at Paris, ensures her a more constant communication with England than she could command elsewhere. It appears that poor Lady Rydal is about to undergo an operation of some danger; and her daughter is ill prepared to endure at such a crisis the delays and uncertainties attendant on all foreign correspondence. Yesterday, when she found that I had already set on foot the preparations for departure, she threw herself into my arms, and implored me to delay our journey towards Naples. "Do not, do not take me hence!" she exclaimed, with convulsive anguish. "Believe me I shall not much longer tax your patience. A few days – a week – a fortnight at furthest, will bring me the intelligence of my poor mother's safety or release. Should she recover this terrible effort, trust me your Evelyn will require no southern climate to expedite her recovery: should she *perish*, do not condemn me to encounter *my third trial* among aliens and strangers. No! do not compel me to quit Lausanne." I cannot however sacrifice the precious health of my wife, perhaps her very life, to such idle presentiments. The English physicians assure me I have not a day to lose; but I will suffer her to accuse me of caprice and unkindness rather than give her the slightest reason to suspect the truth.

Domo D'Ossola. – Again, and for the thousandth time, I recognise the impotency of human wishes, – the vanity of earthly prospects. Instead of enjoying side by side with the object of my idolatry, the glorious scenery amidst which we have been loitering, I rejoice only that the Simplon[9] is passed, and that we have proceeded thus far in safety. Standing once more upon the threshold of Italy, I begin to miss the charm with which I once found it invested; and the atmosphere positively affects me with a more baleful charm than even that of Castle Rydal. There is a feeling of oppression in the air, and a degree of languid torpor in my own frame, as if the Genius of Misfortune were wandering abroad to menace or destroy; and although I sometimes express my displeasure at Evelyn's ill-concealed despondency, I own I am beginning to acknowledge a similar influence. In a few days we shall be among the lakes which in times of old excited such pleasurable emotions in my bosom; and before I quitted Paris I promised Sommariva to pass a day or two with Evelyn at Isola Bella. If any local influence can dissolve the fatal spell enwoven round our journey, it will be the aspect of that enchanting spot.

Isola Bella, October 26th. – Yes! here indeed we find that balminess of nature which Milton assures us is

"Able to cure all sadness but despair."[10]

Never did I behold a scene so exquisite, never inhale an atmosphere so musky with the fragrance of the departing summer, as that which greeted us on reaching the island this morning. Yonder mountains maintain their rugged dignity as if in contrast to the ornate and luxurious cultivation of the oasis lying at their feet: – the nearer hills, – clothed with mournful olive groves relieving the bright foliage of the chesnut, the mulberry, and the wandering vines which unite them into a bower of verdure, – and enlivened by the spires of countless villages; – while the lake reflects as on a crystal mirror the skiffs which traffic between the Toccia, the Tesino, and its beautiful shores. But who can describe the charm of our approach to Isola Madre – with its palm-trees extending their mysterious foliage as if to invite us towards a refuge from the fervour of the autumnal sun, – its exotics flinging up their masses of blossom from amid the fissures of the rocks into the brightness of day, and seeming to exult in the consciousness of beauty? – Drawing aside the awning of our boat, that Lady Evelyn might enjoy with me the aspect of the unruffled lake and the bright Borromean gems[11] which seem to float upon its surface, I pointed out to her admiration the clear deep blue of the heavens, and felt satisfied that even her depression of spirit must give way to joyful emotions at such an hour in such a spot. But instead of replying to my enthusiasm, she extended her pale thin hand towards a single cloud, – a solitary dark speck on the verge of the horizon. –

"This is mere waywardness, –" I began, in an angry voice, while, with a mournful smile, she motioned me to silence.

"I love the sunshine," she faltered, "for it is for my beloved; – I welcome the cloud, for it is for Evelyn."

"Is this a scene for discontent?" I exclaimed: "think you that affliction can find its way to a seclusion so bright as this?"

"Yet even here," she replied, "must your Evelyn encounter her third trial – her last." I turned away – I would no longer listen to her peevish forebodings. –

27*th*. – Do I live to write it? – Yes! it is fitting that such records should not pass away. – Let me subdue the anguish of my heart till all is told, – and then – no matter!

We stood – *we* – O word of agony, which I must breathe no more! – on the marble terrace of the villa, watching the vessels as they wandered like living things upon its waves. She leant heavily on my arm – she raised her hand to my shoulder – she pointed out to me an approaching boat, apparently steered by the peasants of the country. –

"It bears my destiny!" she murmured. "I can discern Lord B.'s confidential servant seated in the stern. He promised to forward to me at this place the first letters that might arrive from England. Edward, Edward, – he would not have despatched that man, had not the news been fatal! – All is over!" –

I prayed her to be calm, but her agitation increased as the felucca[12] approached the landing-place. For a moment she became rigid and motionless as marble in my arms, – while the steward of Lord B., stepping from the boat, placed a letter in my hands. – It was sealed with black! – In another moment I was covered with the life's blood of my Evelyn; – and that throbbing heart was at peace!

And now she is mine again – mine only and for ever! – O what a refuge is the grave!

Notes

Text: *The Keepsake for MDCCCXXXIII*, ed. F. M. Reynolds, Longman, Rees, Orme, Brown and Longman, London, 1832.
 1 College of Oxford University.
 2 Club and gaming-rooms in London, founded by William Almack in 1764.
 3 As a member of parliament.
 4 Walter Scott, *The Abbott* (1820).

5 Unreasonable, over-particular.
6 Indications of tuberculosis.
7 Ceremonies.
8 Heavy burden, person impossible to shake off (from the story of Sinbad, in the *Arabian Nights*, who was forced to carry the sea-god on his shoulders for many days and nights).
9 Mountain pass dividing Switzerland and Italy.
10 Milton, *Paradise Lost* 4: 155–6.
11 Islands in Lake Maggiore, Italy.
12 Small narrow boat.

THE MORTAL IMMORTAL

Mary Shelley

Mary Shelley, née Godwin (1797–1851), novelist, editor, reviewer, essayist, short-story writer. Her mother, the feminist writer Mary Wollstonecraft, died ten days after her birth, and she was brought up, and formidably well educated, by her father, the philosopher William Godwin. She eloped with the poet Shelley in 1814, and married him in 1816 after his first wife's suicide. Only one of their four children survived. Her most famous work, begun when she was 18, is *Frankenstein; or The Modern Prometheus* (1818). After Shelley's death in 1822 she largely supported her son through Harrow and Cambridge by her writing. She published four further novels: *The Last Man* (1826), *Perkin Warbeck* (1830), *Lodore* (1835) and *Falkner* (1837) (a fifth novel, *Matilda*, dealing with a father's incestuous desire for his daughter, was completed in 1819 but not published until 1959). She also wrote numerous stories, essays and reviews, and contributed to Lardner's *Cabinet Cyclopedia*. Her editions of Shelley's *Poetical Works* (1839) and of his *Essays, Letters from Abroad, Translations and Fragments* (1840) remain standard today. Her interest in, and doubts about, scientific experimentation, and her fascination with Promethean, or Faustian, 'over-reaching' (evident in *Frankenstein*) are reflected in *The Mortal Immortal*.

Further reading

Bennett (1980–8); Behrendt in Feldman and Kelley (1995); Blain *et al.* (1990); Blumberg (1993); Crook (1995–); Feldman and Kilvert (1987); Jump (1997); Mellor (1988); Robinson (1976); Shattock (1993)

The Mortal Immortal

JULY 16, 1833. – This is a memorable anniversary for me; on it I complete my three hundred and twenty-third year!

The Wandering Jew?[1] – certainly not. More than eighteen centuries have passed over his head. In comparison with him, I am a very young Immortal.

Am I, then, immortal? This is a question which I have asked myself, by day and night, for now three hundred and three years, and yet cannot answer it. I detected a gray hair amidst my brown locks this very day – that surely signifies decay. Yet it may have remained concealed there for three hundred years – for some persons have become entirely white-headed before twenty years of age.

I will tell my story, and my reader shall judge for me. I will tell my story, and so contrive to pass some few hours of a long eternity, become so wearisome to me. For ever! Can it be? to live for ever! I have heard of enchantments, in which the victims were plunged into a deep sleep, to wake, after a hundred years, as fresh as ever: I have heard of the Seven Sleepers[2] – thus to be immortal would not be so burthensome: but, oh! the weight of never-ending time – the tedious passage of the still-succeeding hours! How happy was the fabled Nourjahad![3] – But to my task.

All the world has heard of Cornelius Agrippa.[4] His memory is as immortal as his arts have made me. All the world has also heard of his scholar,[5] who, unawares, raised the foul fiend during his master's absence, and was destroyed by him. The report, true or false, of this accident, was attended with many inconveniences to the renowned philosopher. All his scholars at once deserted him – his servants disappeared. He had no one near him to put coals on his ever-burning fires while he slept, or to attend to the changeful colours of his medicines while he studied. Experiment after experiment failed, because one pair of hands was insufficient to complete them: the dark spirits laughed at him for not being able to retain a single mortal in his service.

I was then very young – very poor – and very much in love. I had been for about a year the pupil of Cornelius, though I was absent when this accident took place. On my return, my friends implored me not to return to the alchymist's abode. I trembled as I listened to the dire tale they told; I required no second warning; and when Cornelius came and offered me a purse of gold if I would remain under his roof, I felt as if Satan himself tempted me. My teeth chattered – my hair stood on end: – I ran off as fast as my trembling knees would permit.

My failing steps were directed whither for two years they had every evening been attracted, – a gently bubbling spring of pure living waters, beside which lingered a dark-haired girl, whose beaming eyes were fixed on the path I was accustomed each night to tread. I cannot remember the hour when I did not love Bertha; we had been neighbours and playmates from infancy – her parents, like mine, were of humble life, yet respectable – our attachment had been a source of pleasure to them. In an evil hour, a malignant fever carried off both her father and mother, and Bertha became an orphan. She would have found a home beneath my paternal roof, but, unfortunately, the old lady of the near castle, rich, childless, and solitary, declared her intention to adopt her. Henceforth Bertha was clad in silk – inhabited a marble palace – and was looked on as being highly favoured by fortune. But in her new situation among her new associates, Bertha remained true to the friend of her humbler days; she often visited the cottage of my father, and when forbidden to go thither, she would stray towards the neighbouring wood, and meet me beside its shady fountain.

She often declared that she owed no duty to her new protectress equal in sanctity to that which bound us. Yet still I was too poor to marry, and she grew weary of being tormented on my account. She had a haughty but an impatient spirit, and grew angry at the obstacles that prevented our union. We met now after an absence, and she had been sorely beset while I was away; she complained bitterly, and almost reproached me for being poor. I replied hastily, –

"I am honest, if I am poor! – were I not, I might soon become rich!"

This exclamation produced a thousand questions. I feared to shock her by owning the truth, but she drew it from me; and then, casting a look of disdain on me, she said –

"You pretend to love, and you fear to face the Devil for my sake!"

I protested that I had only dreaded to offend her; – while she dwelt on the magnitude of the reward that I should receive. Thus encouraged – shamed by her – led on by love and hope, laughing at my late fears, with quick steps and a light heart, I returned to accept the offers of the alchymist, and was instantly installed in my office.

A year passed away. I became possessed of no insignificant sum of money. Custom had banished my fears. In spite of the most painful vigilance, I had never detected the trace of a cloven foot; nor was the studious silence of our abode ever disturbed by demoniac howls. I still continued my stolen interviews with Bertha, and Hope dawned on me – Hope – but not perfect joy; for Bertha fancied that love and security were enemies, and her pleasure was to divide them in my bosom. Though true of heart, she was somewhat of a coquette in manner; and I was jealous as a Turk. She slighted me in a thousand ways, yet would never acknowledge herself to be in the wrong. She would drive me mad with anger, and then force me to beg her pardon. Sometimes she fancied that I was not sufficiently submissive, and then she had some story of a rival, favoured by her protectress. She was surrounded by silk-clad youths – the rich and gay – What chance had the sad-robed scholar of Cornelius compared with these?

On one occasion, the philosopher made such large demands upon my time, that I was unable to meet her as I was wont. He was engaged in some mighty work, and I was forced to remain, day and night, feeding his furnaces and watching his chemical preparations. Bertha waited for me in vain at the fountain. Her haughty spirit fired at this neglect; and when at last I stole out during the few short minutes allotted to me for slumber, and hoped to be consoled by her, she received me with disdain, dismissed me in scorn, and vowed that any man should possess her hand rather than he who could not be in two places at once for her sake. She would be revenged! – And truly she was. In my dingy retreat I heard that she had been hunting, attended by Albert Hoffer. Albert Hoffer was favoured by her protectress, and the three passed in cavalcade before my smoky window. Methought that they mentioned my name – it was followed by a laugh of derision, as her dark eyes glanced contemptuously towards my abode.

Jealousy, with all its venom, and all its misery, entered my breast. Now I shed a torrent of tears, to think that I should never call her mine; and, anon, I imprecated a thousand curses on her inconstancy. Yet, still I must stir the fires of the alchymist, still attend on the changes of his unintelligible medicines.

Cornelius had watched for three days and nights, nor closed his eyes. The progress of his alembics[6] was slower than he expected: in spite of his anxiety, sleep weighed upon his eyelids. Again and again he threw off drowsiness with more than human energy; again and again it stole away his senses. He eyed his crucibles wistfully. "Not ready yet," he murmured; "will another night pass before the work is accomplished? Winzy,[7] you are vigilant – you are faithful – you have slept, my boy – you slept last night. Look at that glass vessel. The liquid it contains is of a soft rose-colour: the moment it begins to change its hue, awaken me – till then I may close my eyes. First, it will turn white, and then emit golden flashes; but wait not till then; when the rose-colour fades, rouse me." I scarcely heard the last words, muttered, as they were, in sleep. Even then he did not quite yield to nature. "Winzy, my boy," he again said, "do not touch the vessel – do not put it to your lips; it is a philter – a philter to cure love; you would not cease to love your Bertha – beware to drink!"

And he slept. His venerable head sunk on his breast, and I scarce heard his regular breathing. For a few minutes I watched the vessel – the rosy hue of the liquid remained unchanged. Then my thoughts wandered – they visited the fountain, and dwelt on a thousand charming scenes never to be renewed – never! Serpents and adders were in my heart as the word "Never!" half formed itself on my lips. False girl! – false and cruel! Never more would she smile on me as that evening she smiled on Albert. Worthless, detested woman! I would not remain unrevenged – she should see Albert expire at her feet – she should die beneath my vengeance. She had smiled in disdain and triumph – she knew my wretchedness and her power. Yet what power had she? – the power of exciting my hate – my utter scorn – my – oh, all but indifference! Could I attain that – could I regard her with careless eyes, transferring my rejected love to one fairer and more true, that were indeed a victory!

A bright flash darted before my eyes. I had forgotten the medicine of the adept; I gazed on it with wonder: flashes of admirable beauty, more bright than those which the diamond emits when the sun's rays are on it, glanced from the surface of the liquid; an odour the most fragrant and grateful stole over my sense; the vessel seemed one globe of living radiance, lovely to the eye, and most inviting to the taste. The first thought, instinctively inspired by the grosser sense, was, I will – I must drink. I raised the vessel to my lips. "It will cure me of love – of torture!" Already I had quaffed half of the most delicious liquor ever tasted by the palate of man, when the philosopher stirred. I started – I dropped the glass – the fluid flamed and glanced along the floor, while I felt Cornelius's gripe at my throat, as he shrieked aloud, "Wretch! you have destroyed the labour of my life!"

The philosopher was totally unaware that I had drunk any portion of his drug. His idea was, and I gave a tacit assent to it, that I had raised the vessel from curiosity, and that, frighted at its brightness, and the flashes of intense light it gave forth, I had let it fall. I never undeceived him. The fire of the medicine was quenched – the fragrance died away – he grew calm, as a philosopher should under the heaviest trials, and dismissed me to rest.

I will not attempt to describe the sleep of glory and bliss which bathed my soul in paradise during the remaining hours of that memorable night. Words would be faint and shallow types of my enjoyment, or of the gladness that possessed my bosom when I woke. I trod air – my thoughts were in heaven. Earth appeared heaven, and my inheritance upon it was to be one trance of delight. "This it is to be cured of love," I thought; "I will see Bertha this day, and she will find her lover cold and regardless; too happy to be disdainful, yet how utterly indifferent to her!"

The hours danced away. The philosopher, secure that he had once succeeded, and believing that he might again, began to concoct the same medicine once more. He was shut up with his books and drugs, and I had a holiday. I dressed myself with care; I looked in an old but polished shield, which served me for a mirror; methought my good looks had wonderfully improved. I hurried beyond the precincts of the town, joy in my soul, the beauty of heaven and earth around me. I turned my steps towards the castle – I could look on its lofty turrets with lightness of heart, for I was cured of love. My Bertha saw me afar off, as I came up the avenue. I know not what sudden impulse animated her bosom, but at the sight, she sprung with a light fawn-like bound down the marble steps, and was hastening towards me. But I had been perceived by another person. The old high-born hag, who called herself her protectress, and was her tyrant, had seen me, also; she hobbled, panting, up the terrace; a page, as ugly as herself, held up her train, and fanned her as she hurried along, and stopped my fair girl with a "How, now, my bold mistress? whither so fast? Back to your cage – hawks are abroad!"

Bertha clasped her hands – her eyes were still bent on my approaching figure. I saw the contest. How I abhorred the old crone who checked the kind impulses of my Bertha's softening heart. Hitherto, respect for her rank had caused me to avoid the lady of the castle; now I disdained such trivial considerations. I was cured of love, and lifted above all human fears; I hastened forwards, and soon reached the terrace. How lovely Bertha looked! her eyes flashing fire, her cheeks glowing with impatience and anger, she was a thousand times more graceful and charming than ever – I no longer loved – Oh! no, I adored – worshipped – idolized her!

She had that morning been persecuted, with more than usual vehemence, to consent to an immediate marriage with my rival. She was reproached with the encouragement that she had shown him – she was threatened with being turned out of doors with disgrace and shame. Her proud spirit rose in arms at the threat; but when she remembered the scorn that she had heaped upon me, and how, perhaps, she had thus lost one whom she now regarded as her only friend, she wept with remorse and rage. At that moment I appeared. "O, Winzy!" she exclaimed, "take me to your mother's cot; swiftly let me leave the detested luxuries and wretchedness of this noble dwelling – take me to poverty and happiness."

I clasped her in my arms with transport. The old lady was speechless with fury, and broke forth into invective only when we were far on our road to my natal cottage. My mother received the fair fugitive, escaped from a gilt cage to nature and liberty, with tenderness and joy; my father, who loved her, welcomed her heartily; it was a day of rejoicing, which did not need the addition of the celestial potion of the alchymist to steep me in delight.

Soon after this eventful day, I became the husband of Bertha. I ceased to be the scholar of Cornelius, but I continued his friend. I always felt grateful to him for having, unawares, procured me that delicious draught of a divine elixir, which, instead of curing me of love (sad cure! solitary and joyless remedy for evils which seem blessings to the memory), had inspired me with courage and resolution, thus winning for me an inestimable treasure in my Bertha.

I often called to mind that period of trance-like inebriation with wonder. The drink of Cornelius had not fulfilled the task for which he affirmed that it had been prepared, but its effects were more potent and blissful than words can express. They had faded by degrees, yet they lingered long – and painted life in hues of splendour. Bertha often wondered at my lightness of heart and unaccustomed gaiety; for, before, I had been rather serious, or even sad, in my disposition. She loved me the better for my cheerful temper, and our days were winged by joy.

Five years afterwards I was suddenly summoned to the bedside of the dying Cornelius. He had sent for me in haste, conjuring my instant presence. I found him stretched on his pallet, enfeebled even to death; all of life that yet remained animated his piercing eyes, and they were fixed on a glass vessel, full of a roseate liquid.

"Behold," he said, in a broken and inward voice, "the vanity of human wishes! a second time my hopes are about to be crowned, a second time they are destroyed. Look at that liquor – you remember five years ago I had prepared the same, with the same success; – then, as now, my thirsting lips expected to taste the immortal elixir – you dashed it from me! and at present it is too late."

He spoke with difficulty, and fell back on his pillow. I could not help saying, –

"How, revered master, can a cure for love restore you to life?"

A faint smile gleamed across his face as I listened earnestly to his scarcely intelligible answer.

"A cure for love and for all things – the Elixir of Immortality. Ah! if now I might drink, I should live for ever!"

As he spoke, a golden flash gleamed from the fluid; a well-remembered fragrance stole over the air; he raised himself, all weak as he was – strength seemed miraculously to re-enter his frame – he stretched forth his hand – a loud explosion startled me – a ray of fire shot up from the elixir, and the glass vessel which contained it was shivered to atoms! I turned my eyes towards the philosopher; he had fallen back – his eyes were glassy – his features rigid – he was dead!

But I lived, and was to live for ever! So said the unfortunate alchymist, and for a few days I believed his words. I remembered the glorious drunkenness that had followed my stolen draught. I reflected on the change I had felt in my frame – in my soul. The bounding elasticity of the one – the buoyant lightness of the other. I surveyed myself in a mirror, and could perceive no change in my features during the space of the five years which had elapsed. I remembered the radiant hues and grateful scent of that delicious beverage – worthy the gift it was capable of bestowing – I was, then, IMMORTAL!

A few days after I laughed at my credulity. The old proverb, that "a prophet is least regarded in his own country,"[8] was true with respect to me and my defunct master. I loved him as a man – I respected him as a sage – but I derided the notion that he could command the powers of darkness, and laughed at the superstitious fears with which he was regarded by the vulgar. He was a wise philosopher, but had no acquaintance with any spirits but those clad in flesh and blood. His science was simply human; and human science, I soon persuaded myself, could never conquer nature's laws so far as to imprison the soul for ever within its carnal habitation. Cornelius had brewed a soul-refreshing drink – more inebriating than wine – sweeter and more fragrant than any fruit: it possessed probably strong medicinal powers, imparting gladness to the heart and vigor to the limbs; but its effects would wear out; already were they diminished in my frame. I was a lucky fellow to have quaffed health and joyous spirits, and perhaps long life, at my master's hands; but my good fortune ended there: longevity was far different from immortality.

I continued to entertain this belief for many years. Sometimes a thought stole across me – Was the alchymist indeed deceived? But my habitual credence was, that should meet the fate of all the children of Adam at my appointed time – a little late, but still at a natural age. Yet it was certain that I retained a wonderfully youthful look. I was laughed at for my vanity in consulting the mirror so often, but consulted it in vain – my brow was untrenched – my cheeks – my eyes – my whole person continued as untarnished as in my twentieth year.

I was troubled. I looked at the faded beauty of Bertha – I seemed more like her son. By degrees our neighbours began to make similar observations, and I found at last that I went by the name of the Scholar bewitched. Bertha herself grew uneasy. She became jealous and peevish, and at length she began to question me. We had no children; we were all in all to each other; and though, as she grew older, her vivacious spirit became a little allied to ill-temper, and her beauty sadly diminished, I cherished her in my heart as the mistress I had idolized, the wife I had sought and won with such perfect love.

At last our situation became intolerable: Bertha was fifty – I twenty years of age. I had, in very shame, in some measure adopted the habits of a more advanced age; I no longer mingled in the dance among the young and gay, but my heart bounded along with them while I restrained my feet; and a sorry figure I cut among the Nestors[9] of our village. But before the time I mention, things were altered – we were universally shunned; we were – at least, I was – reported to have kept up an iniquitous acquaintance with some of my former master's supposed friends. Poor Bertha was pitied, but deserted. I was regarded with horror and detestation.

What was to be done? We sat by our winter fire – poverty had made itself felt, for none would buy the produce of my farm; and often I had been forced to journey twenty miles, to some place where I was not known, to dispose of our property. It is true we had saved something for an evil day – that day was come.

We sat by our lone fireside – the old-hearted youth and his antiquated wife. Again Bertha insisted on knowing the truth; she recapitulated all she had ever heard said about me, and added her own observations. She conjured me to cast off the spell; she described how much more comely gray hairs were than my chestnut locks; she descanted on the reverence and respect due to age – how preferable to the slight regard paid to mere children: could I imagine that the despicable gifts of youth and good looks outweighed disgrace, hatred, and scorn? Nay, in the end I should be burnt as a dealer in the black art, while she, to whom I had not deigned to communicate any portion of my good fortune, might be stoned as my accomplice. At length she insinuated that I must share my secret with her, and bestow on her like benefits to those I myself enjoyed, or she would denounce me – and then she burst into tears.

Thus beset, methought it was the best way to tell the truth. I revealed it as tenderly as I could, and spoke only of a *very long life*, not of immortality – which representation, indeed, coincided best with my own ideas. When I ended, I rose and said,

"And now, my Bertha, will you denounce the lover of your youth? – You will not, I know. But it is too hard, my poor wife, that you should suffer from my ill-luck and the accursed arts of Cornelius. I will leave you – you have wealth enough, and friends will return in my absence. I will go; young as I seem, and strong as I am, I can work and gain my bread among strangers, unsuspected and unknown. I loved you in youth; God is my witness that I would not desert you in age, but that your safety and happiness require it."

I took my cap and moved towards the door; in a moment Bertha's arms were round my neck, and her lips were pressed to mine. "No, my husband, my Winzy," she said, "you shall not go alone – take me with you; we will remove from this place, and, as you say, among strangers we shall be unsuspected and safe. I am not so very old as quite to shame you, my Winzy; and I dare say the charm will soon wear off, and, with the blessing of God, you will become more elderly-looking, as is fitting; you shall not leave me."

I returned the good soul's embrace heartily. "I will not, my Bertha; but for your sake I had not thought of such a thing. I will be your true, faithful husband while you are spared to me, and do my duty by you to the last."

The next day we prepared secretly for our emigration. We were obliged to make great pecuniary sacrifices – it could not be helped. We realised a sum sufficient, at least, to maintain us while Bertha lived; and, without saying adieu to any one, quitted our native country to take refuge in a remote part of western France.

It was a cruel thing to transport poor Bertha from her native village, and the friends of her youth, to a new country, new language, new customs. The strange secret of my destiny rendered this removal immaterial to me; but I compassionated her deeply, and was glad to perceive that she found compensation for her misfortunes in a variety of little ridiculous circumstances. Away from all tell-tale chroniclers, she sought to decrease the apparent disparity of our ages by a thousand feminine arts – rouge, youthful dress, and assumed juvenility of manner. I could not be angry – Did not I myself wear a mask? Why quarrel with hers, because it was less successful? I grieved deeply when I remembered that this was my Bertha, whom I had loved so fondly, and won with such transport – the dark-eyed, dark-haired girl, with smiles of enchanting archness and a step like a fawn – this mincing, simpering, jealous old woman. I should have revered her gray locks and withered cheeks: but thus! – It was my work, I knew; but I did not the less deplore this type of human weakness.

Her jealousy never slept. Her chief occupation was to discover that, in spite of outward appearances, I was myself growing old. I verily believe that the poor soul loved me truly in her heart, but never had woman so torment-ing a mode of displaying fondness. She would discern wrinkles in my face and decrepitude in my walk, while I bounded along in youthful vigour, the youngest looking of twenty youths. I never dared address another woman: on one occasion, fancying that the belle of the village regarded me with favour-ing eyes, she bought me a gray wig. Her constant discourse among her acquaintances was, that though I looked so young, there was ruin at work within my frame; and she affirmed that the worst symptom about me was my apparent health. My youth was a disease, she said, and I ought at all times to prepare, if not for a sudden and awful death, at least to awake some morning white-headed, and bowed down with all the marks of advanced years. I let her talk – I often joined in her conjectures. Her warnings chimed in with my never-ceasing speculations concerning my state, and I took an earnest, though painful, interest in listening to all that her quick wit and excited imagination could say on the subject.

Why dwell on these minute circumstances? We lived on for many long years. Bertha became bed-rid and paralytic: I nursed her as a mother might a child. She grew peevish, and still harped upon one string – of how long I should survive her. It has ever been a source of consolation to me, that I performed my duty scrupulusly towards her. She had been mine in youth, she was mine in age, and at last, when I heaped the sod over her corpse, I wept to feel that I had lost all that really bound me to humanity.

Since then how many have been my cares and woes, how few and empty my enjoyments! I pause here in my history – I will pursue it no further. A sailor without rudder or compass, tossed on a stormy sea – a traveller lost on a wide-spread heath, without landmark or star to guide him – such have I been: more lost, more hopeless than either. A nearing ship, a gleam from some far cot, may save them; but I have no beacon except the hope of death.

Death! mysterious, ill-visaged friend of weak humanity! Why alone of all mortals have you cast me from your sheltering fold? O, for the peace of the grave! the deep silence of the iron-bound tomb! that thought would cease to work in my brain, and my heart beat no more with emotions varied only by new forms of sadness!

Am I immortal? I return to my first question. In the first place, is it not more probable that the beverage of the alchymist was fraught rather with longevity than eternal life? Such is my hope. And then be it remembered, that I only drank *half* of the potion prepared by him. Was not the whole necessary to complete the charm? To have drained half the Elixir of Immortality is but to be half immortal – my For-ever is thus truncated and null.

But again, who shall number the years of the half of eternity? I often try to imagine by what rule the infinite may be divided. Sometimes I fancy age advancing upon me. One gray hair I have found. Fool! do I lament? Yes, the fear of age and death often creeps coldly into my heart; and the more I live, the more I dread death, even while I abhor life. Such an enigma is man – born to perish – when he wars, as I do, against the established laws of his nature.

But for this anomaly of feeling surely I might die: the medicine of the alchymist would not be proof against fire – sword – and the strangling waters. I have gazed upon the blue depths of many a placid lake, and the tumultuous rushing of many a mighty river, and have said, peace inhabits those waters; yet I have turned my steps away, to live yet another day. I have asked myself, whether suicide would be a crime in one to whom thus only the portals of the other world could be opened. I have done all, except presenting myself as a soldier or duellist, an object of destruction to my – no, *not* my fellow-mortals, and therefore I have shrunk away. They are not my fellows. The inextinguisbable power of life in my frame, and their ephemeral existence, place us wide as the poles asunder. I could not raise a hand against the meanest or the most powerful among them.

Thus I have lived on for many a year – alone, and weary of myself – desirous of death, yet never dying – a mortal immortal. Neither ambition nor avarice can enter my mind, and the ardent love that gnaws at my heart never to be returned – never to find an equal on which to expend itself – lives there only to torment me.

This very day I conceived a design by which I may end all – without self-slaughter, without making another man a Cain[10] – an expedition, which mortal frame can never survive, even endued with the youth and strength that inhabits mine. Thus I shall put my immortality to the test, and rest for ever – or return, the wonder and benefactor of the human species.

Before I go, a miserable vanity has caused me to pen these pages. I would not die, and leave no name behind. Three centuries have passed since I quaffed the fatal beverage: another year shall not elapse before, encountering gigantic dangers – warring with the powers of frost in their home – beset by famine, toil, and tempest – I yield this body, too tenacious a cage for a soul which thirsts for freedom, to the destructive elements of air and water – or, if I survive, my name shall be recorded as one of the most famous among the sons of men; and, my task achieved. I shall adopt more resolute means, and, by scattering and annihilating the atoms that compose my frame, set at liberty the life imprisoned within, and so cruelly prevented from soaring from this dim earth to a sphere more congenial to its immortal essence.

Notes

Text: *The Keepsake for MDCCCXXXIV*, ed. F.M. Reynolds, Longman, Rees, Orme, Brown and Longman, London, 1833.

1 Legendary figure who, having mocked Christ at the Crucifixion, was condemned to wander the world eternally.
2 Seven youths of Ephesus, said to have slept in a cave for several hundred years to escape persecution.
3 Presumably Nourjehan, wife of the seventeenth-century Moghul Emperor Jehangir, who built the Taj Mahal for her after her death.
4 Heinrich Cornelius Agrippa von Nettesheim (1486–1535), German occultist, philosopher and alchemist, author of the notorious Renaissance work on magic, *De Occulta Philosophia*.
5 Faust, the semi-legendary dealer in the black arts, who is said to have sold his soul to the devil in exchange for knowledge.
6 Vessels used by alchemists for distillation and purification.
7 Derived from the Scottish term 'winze', meaning curse: an appropriate name for the protagonist, who is cursed with eternal life.
8 Matthew 13:57.
9 Wise old men (from Nestor, the oldest and wisest Greek in the Trojan war).
10 Son of Adam and Eve, murderer of his brother Abel (Genesis 4:1–16).

SEFTON CHURCH

Laetitia E. Landon

Laetitia Elizabeth Landon ('L.E.L.'), later Maclean (1802–38), poet, short-story writer, novelist, editor, reviewer. A prolific and immensely successful writer, she published seven volumes of poetry, a number of novels, including the historical *Ethel Churchill* (1837), and edited and contributed to *Fisher's Drawing Room Scrapbook* (1832–9), *Heath's Book of Beauty* (1833) and the *New Juvenile Keepsake* (1838), as well as reviewing for the *Literary Gazette* and the *Monthly Magazine*. An attractive, lively and independent young woman, living on her own in London, she was surrounded by gossip and scandal, possibly unfounded, and her engagement to Dickens' future biographer John Foster ended following a rumoured affair. She married George Maclean, Governor of Cape Coast Castle (now Ghana) in 1838. A few months later she was found dead in their house in Africa, a bottle of prussic acid in her hand, though whether by accident, suicide or murder has never been established. Her poetry has often been dismissed as sentimental, although it is beginning to be taken more seriously. Her prose writing, of which 'Sefton Church' is representative, is sharply witty, intelligent and perceptive. Written to accompany a somewhat bland engraving of Sefton Church in Lancashire (supplied to her in advance by the publisher of *Fisher's Drawing-Room Scrapbook*), the story illustrates Landon's sceptical and subversive sense of humour.

Further reading

Armstrong *et al.* (1996); Ashton (1936); Blanchard (1841); Hickok (1984); Jerdan (1852–3); Leighton (1992, 1995); Mellor (1993); Shattock (1993); Stephenson (1995); Sutherland (1988).

Sefton Church

There are very many devices wherewith we delude ourselves – indeed, human life has never seemed to me anything more than a series of mistakes. It is a mistake to be born – another to live – and a third to die. However, there is one other mistake, more absurd than all the three – and that is marrying – and which is made worse by the fact, that the other three we cannot very well help, but the last we can. I say nothing of your matches of convenience, for I do not understand how any thing in existence can be other than inconvenient; nor of your marriage for money, as money, like patriotism, is an excuse for every thing; but I speak of your love matches. Now, a love match is like that childish toy which consists of various boxes enclosed one within another, and yet contains nothing, after all. I wonder where Experience got its reputation? – it has been very easily obtained – but it does not deserve it: they say, that it teaches fools; it may teach them, but they do not learn. Every year, one sees a young woman in a white gown, and a young man in a blue coat, adventuring on what is called 'the happiest day of one's life;' so called, perhaps, as they are never very particularly happy afterwards. Equally, every year, does one witness couples who, in like manner, begin in blue and white, continuing in – green and yellow melancholy: yet no one takes warning by the example; all seem to expect a miracle from fate, in their own favour – what business they have to expect it, I don't know; but we do flatter ourselves strangely. I must, however, do fate the justice to acknowledge its strict impartiality – all are disappointed alike. I hold that, in marriage, love augments the evil: contrast in such cases is an aggravation of ennui; it is so peculiarly provoking, to reflect how much pleasanter you used to be to each other. Hope and Love are the passions of the heart; the difference between them is, that Hope does not come to an end, but Love does. Love has two terminations; it concludes either in profound indifference, or in intense hate. Now, in the general run of human natures, there is not energy for hate; therefore, the usual finale is profound indifference; the most insipid state of existence that can be devised. No wonder that the household gods, like the images on a chimney-piece, often get broken. Quarrels are only the refreshing necessities of married life: but for their valuable aid, a whole city, like that in the *Arabian Nights* might get up some fine summer morning, and find itself turned into stone. It being the universal, therefore laudable fashion, on the principle of that never sufficiently to be commended concentration of the whole doctrine of expediency, that 'whatever is, is right'; to destroy all

delusions, whether of piety, poetry, or loyalty; and the universal demand
being for facts, I hold, that the vain lights thrown round 'the temple of
Hymen'[1] ought to be put out, as only false meteors luring to the slough of
despond,[2] taking the *ignis fatuus*[3] shapes of white gloves, silver favours, wedding excursions, and wedding cakes. I have seen many young people immol-
ate love on the shrine of mutual affection – but it is the reckless sacrifice I
have witnessed this morning, that has induced my thoughts to take the more
tangible shape of words. One goes out visiting for pleasure; a fallacy belonging to that melancholy mania for change which has recourse to stage-coaches,
and steam-boats, as if change of scene were change of self. For the last week I
have been made, if not exactly miserable, very uncomfortable; and the only
difference between them is, that the last wants dignity, – 'wearied with
sameness of perpetual talk'[4] about the marriage of a Miss Merton. She could
not be more glad when the wedding day came than I was – once over, the ifs
and buts, the whys and wherefores, of this eternal marriage, would subside
into silence. But the worst was yet to come – I love lying in bed, am an
invalid, and like the world to be thoroughly aired before I venture into it; yet
up was I dragged at seven o'clock, and a rainy morning, merely because my
friends were quite sure I should like to see Miss Merton married. What right
have people to be sure of any thing in this life? Of course we had no breakfast; nobody seemed to think of it but myself. Off we set through the rain,
and arrived in church just by eight o'clock – the bride, though, was before
us. There she sat, smiling in ignorant happiness; but what woman could put
on a new white bonnet, with orange flowers, a *gros des Indes brodé en colonnes*,[5]
and a blonde veil, and not feel –

Let what will come, I have been blest.[6]

I found the time very long, and myself very chilly: even as I had wished for
the arrival of the wedding day, did I now wish for the arrival of the bridegroom. Nine o'clock struck, every body counted it in silence, then a little
talk recommenced – some persons have such spirits! I read the inscription on
a marble monument (marble enough in it for three chimney pieces – very
extravagant,) erected to the memory of a major killed in the American war; it
informed us, that a grateful country would long preserve his name – I cannot
say that the information was correct: then I walked up and down the aisle,
endeavouring to remember all the happy couples I could; at last I recollected
one, and they were very happy indeed; she lived at Amsterdam, and he in
Demerara; they used to write each other such affectionate letters! Ten o'clock
struck; every body counted it again. Dead silence was succeeded by a thun-
derstorm of words – one mentioned an interesting fact how a bridegroom
had overslept himself one morning, and shot himself the next; another recollected, that a friend of *his* had been thrown from his gig, and had broken his
neck; while a third stated, that his gardener had been detained too long

shaving, and, when the damsel rejected him in consequence, made a vow he would never shave again, and 'has now a beard worthy a Jew or a Turk, excepting, that it is red.'

The misfortunes of others beguiled the time, as they always do. Eleven o'clock struck; the matter now became serious – the very youngest of the bridesmaids ceased to laugh – the bride herself began to cry. At length, a piece of advice I had been offering for the last two hours was taken – a messenger was sent to the inn where the bridegroom was staying. I augured ill, from the rapidity with which he returned – good news stops to take breath on the road; bad news never requires it. The recreant lover had taken fright and post horses, and had set off at six that morning 'over the hills, and far away'. We shall now go home to breakfast, thought I: but there was still a deal to be done; all surrounded the lady, and, as the most effective method of consoling her, began to abuse the departed – a common custom the world over. More effectual comfort was, however, at hand: a young lieutenant in the navy – a handsome young man he was, too – stepped forward, and addressed her thus – 'Madam, I never could bear to see a lady disappointed, that is, if she was pretty. Mr. – (hang the fellow, I forget his name, and you will forget it, too), he is off, but I am ready to take his place; and I have been in love with you a long time, though I did not know it till this morning.' The lady looked at the clergymen, then at the lieutenant, and then on the folds of her white veil. 'Well,' said she, 'it is a pity to be drest for nothing – I shall be very happy.' And married they were. True, that at last I got home to breakfast; but, that over, my feelings needed the relief of expression. I must protest against the outrageous recklessness of the young sailor – what can he expect from the future?

> Needs must the chariot wheels of destiny
> Crush one who flings him in its onward path
> Patient and prostrate.[7]

Notes

Text: *Fisher's Drawing Room Scrapbook for 1834*, ed. L. E. Landon, London, 1833.
1 Greek and Roman god of marriage.
2 Valley of despair through which the travellers have to pass in Bunyan, *The Pilgrim's Progress* (1678).
3 Delusive, alluring object (from the pale phosphorescent flame appearing over marshy land, sometimes called will-o'-the-wisp, believed to lure travellers to their doom).
4 Unidentified.
5 Wedding dress of embroidered heavy silk.
6 Byron, *The Giour*, I:1114, slightly misquoted.
7 Unidentified.

THE MANCHESTER MARRIAGE

Elizabeth Gaskell

Elizabeth Cleghorn Gaskell, née Stevenson (1810–65), novelist, short-story writer, biographer, was born in London, but was brought up by an aunt in Knutsford, Cheshire (which she later fictionalised in *Cranford* (1855)), following her mother's death when she was a year old. She was happily married to William Gaskell, a Unitarian minister, and lived in Manchester, where much of her fiction (notably the industrial novels *Mary Barton* (1848) and *North and South* (1855)) is set. Her other novels include the controversial *Ruth* (1853), the story of an unmarried mother, *Sylvia's Lovers* (1863) and *Cousin Phyllis* (1864). Her numerous short stories frequently deal with unorthodox subjects: *Lizzie Leigh* (1850) tackles prostitution, for example. She befriended Charlotte Brontë in 1850, and published her much-admired *Life of Charlotte Brontë* in 1857. She died suddenly before completing her final novel, *Wives and Daughters* (1865). *The Manchester Marriage* demonstrates her keen and humanitarian observation of human behaviour, especially that of the inhabitants of the industrial north, as well as her celebrated gift for story-telling.

Further reading

Blain *et al.* (1990); Chapple and Pollard (1966); Easson (1979, 1985, 1991); Gallagher (1986); Gaskell (1983, 1987, 1989, 1992, 1995a, 1995b, 1997); Lansbury (1975); Nestor (1985); Shattock (1993); Spencer (1993); Stoneman (1987); Sutherland (1988); Uglow (1993).

The Manchester Marriage

Mr and Mrs Openshaw came from Manchester to settle in London. He had been, what is called in Lancashire, a salesman for a large manufacturing firm, who were extending their business, and opening a warehouse in the city; where Mr Openshaw was now to superintend their affairs. He rather enjoyed the change; having a kind of curiosity about London, which he had never yet been able to gratify in his brief visits to the metropolis. At the same time, he had an odd, shrewd contempt for the inhabitants, whom he always pictured to himself as fine, lazy people, caring nothing but for fashion and aristocracy, and lounging away their days in Bond Street, and such places; ruining good English, and ready in their turn to despise him as a provincial. The hours that the men of business kept in the city scandalized him too, accustomed as he was to the early dinners of Manchester folk and the consequently far longer evenings. Still, he was pleased to go to London, though he would not for the world have confessed it, even to himself, and always spoke of the step to his friends as one demanded of him by the interests of his employers, and sweetened to him by a considerable increase of salary. This, indeed, was so liberal that he might have been justified in taking a much larger house than the one he did, had he not thought himself bound to set an example to Londoners of how little a Manchester man of business cared for show. Inside, however, he furnished it with an unusual degree of comfort, and, in the winter-time, he insisted on keeping up as large fires as the grates would allow, in every room where the temperature was in the least chilly. Moreover, his northern sense of hospitality was such that, if he were at home, he could hardly suffer a visitor to leave the house without forcing meat and drink upon him. Every servant in the house was well warmed, well fed, and kindly treated; for their master scorned all petty saving in aught that conduced to comfort; while he amused himself by following out all his accustomed habits and individuals ways, in defiance of what any of his new neighbours might think.

His wife was a pretty, gentle woman, of suitable age and character. He was forty-two, she thirty-five. He was loud and decided; she soft and yielding. They had two children; or rather, I should say, she had two; for the elder, a girl of eleven, was Mrs Openshaw's child by Frank Wilson, her first husband. The younger was a little boy, Edwin, who could just prattle, and to whom his father delighted to speak in the broadest and most unintelligible Lancashire dialect, in order to keep up what he called the true Saxon accent.

Mrs Openshaw's Christian name was Alice, and her first husband had been her own cousin. She was the orphan niece of a sea-captain in Liverpool; a quiet, grave little creature, of great personal attraction when she was fifteen or sixteen, with regular features and a blooming complexion. But she was very shy, and believed herself to be very stupid and awkward; and was frequently scolded by her aunt, her own uncle's second wife. So when her cousin, Frank Wilson, came home from a long absence at sea, and first was kind and protective to her; secondly, attentive; and thirdly, desperately in love with her, she hardly knew how to be grateful enough to him. It is true, she would have preferred his remaining in the first or second stages of behaviour; for his violent love puzzled and frightened her. Her uncle neither helped nor hindered the love affair, though it was going on under his own eyes. Frank's stepmother had such a variable temper, that there was no knowing whether what she liked one day she would like the next, or not. At length she went to such extremes of crossness that Alice was only too glad to shut her eyes and rush blindly at the chance of escape from domestic tyranny offered her by a marriage with her cousin; and, liking him better than any one in the world, except her uncle (who was at this time at sea), she went off one morning and was married to him, her only bridesmaid being the housemaid at her aunt's. The consequence was that Frank and his wife went into lodgings, and Mrs Wilson refused to see them, and turned away Norah, the warm-hearted housemaid, whom they accordingly took into their service. When Captain Wilson returned from his voyage he was very cordial with the young couple, and spent many an evening at their lodgings, smoking his pipe and sipping his grog; but he told them, for quietness' sake, he could not ask them to his own house; for his wife was bitter against them. They were not, however, very unhappy about this.

The seed of future unhappiness lay rather in Frank's vehement, passionate disposition, which led him to resent his wife's shyness and want of demonstrativeness as failures in conjugal duty. He was already tormenting himself, and her too in a slighter degree, by apprehensions and imaginations of what might befall her during his approaching absence at sea. At last, he went to his father and urged him to insist upon Alice's being once more received under his roof; the more especially as there was now a prospect of her confinement while her husband was away on his voyage. Captain Wilson was, as he himself expressed it, 'breaking up,' and unwilling to undergo the excitement of a scene; yet he felt that what his son said was true. So he went to his wife. And before Frank set sail, he had the comfort of seeing his wife installed in her old little garret in his father's house. To have placed her in the one best spare room was a step beyond Mrs Wilson's powers of submission or generosity. The worst part about it, however, was that the faithful Norah had to be dismissed. Her place as housemaid had been filled up; and, even if it had not, she had forfeited Mrs Wilson's good opinion for ever. She comforted her young master and mistress by pleasant prophecies of the time when they would have a household of their own; of which, whatever service she might be in meanwhile, she should be sure to form a part. Almost the last action Frank did, before setting sail, was going with Alice to see Norah once more at her mother's house; and then he went away.

Alice's father-in-law grew more and more feeble as winter advanced. She was of great use to her stepmother in nursing and amusing him; and although there was anxiety enough in the household, there was, perhaps, more of peace than there had been for years, for Mrs Wilson had not a bad heart, and was softened by the visible approach of death to one whom she loved, and touched by the lonely condition of the young creature expecting her first confinement in her husband's absence. To this relenting mood Norah owed the permission to come and nurse Alice when her baby was born, and to remain and attend on Captain Wilson.

Before one letter had been received from Frank (who had sailed for the East Indies and China), his father died. Alice was always glad to remember that he had held her baby in his arms, and kissed and blessed it before his death. After that, and the consequent examination into the state of his affairs, it was found that he had left far less property than people had been led by his style of living to expect; and what money there was, was settled all upon his wife, and at her disposal after her death. This did not signify much to Alice, as Frank was now first mate of his ship, and, in another voyage or two, would be captain. Meanwhile he had left her rather more than two hundred pounds (all his savings) in the bank.

It became time for Alice to hear from her husband. One letter from the Cape she had already received. The next was to announce his arrival in India. As week after week passed over, and no intelligence of the ship having got there reached the office of the owners, and the captain's wife was in the same state of ignorant suspense as Alice herself, her fears grew most oppressive. At length the day came when, in reply to her inquiry at the shipping office, they told her that the owners had given up hope of ever hearing more of the *Betsy-Jane*, and had sent in their claim upon the underwriters. Now that he was gone for ever, she first felt a yearning, longing love for the kind cousin, the dear friend, the sympathizing protector, whom she should never see again; – first felt a passionate desire to show him his child, whom she had hitherto rather craved to have all to herself – her own sole possession. Her grief was, however, noiseless and quiet – rather to the scandal of Mrs Wilson who bewailed her stepson as if he and she had always lived together in perfect harmony, and who evidently thought it her duty to burst into fresh tears at every strange face she saw; dwelling on his poor young widow's desolate state, and the helplessness of the fatherless child, with an unction as if she liked the excitement of the sorrowful story.

So passed away the first days of Alice's widowhood. By and by things subsided into their natural and tranquil course. But, as if the young creature was always to be in some heavy trouble, her ewe-lamb began to be ailing, pining, and sickly. The child's mysterious illness turned out to be some affection of the spine, likely to affect health but not to shorten life – at least, so the doctors said. But the long, dreary suffering of one whom a mother loves as Alice loved her only child, is hard to look forward to. Only Norah guessed what Alice suffered; no one but God knew.

And so it fell out, that when Mrs Wilson, the elder, came to her one day, in violent distress, occasioned by a very material diminution in the value of the property that her husband had left her – a diminution which made her income barely enough to support herself, much less Alice – the latter could hardly understand how anything which did not touch health or life could cause such grief; and she received the intelligence with irritating composure. But when, that afternoon, the little sick child was brought in, and the grandmother – who, after all, loved it well – began a fresh moan over her losses to its unconscious ears – saying how she had planned to consult this or that doctor, and to give it this or that comfort or luxury in after years, but that now all chance of this had passed away – Alice's heart was touched, and she drew near to Mrs Wilson with unwonted caresses, and, in a spirit not unlike to that of Ruth,[1] entreated that, come what would, they might remain together. After much discussion in succeeding days, it was arranged that Mrs Wilson should take a house in Manchester, furnishing it partly with what furniture she had, and providing the rest with Alice's remaining two hundred pounds. Mrs Wilson was herself a Manchester woman, and naturally longed to return to her native town; some connexions of her own, too, at that time required lodgings, for which they were willing to pay pretty handsomely. Alice undertook the active superintendence and superior work of the household; Norah – willing, faithful Norah – offered to cook, scour, do anything in short, so that she might but remain with them.

The plan succeeded. For some years their first lodgers remained with them, and all went smoothly – with the one sad exception of the little girl's increasing deformity. How that mother loved that child, it is not for words to tell!

Then came a break of misfortune. Their lodgers left, and no one succeeded to them. After some months, it became necessary to remove to a smaller house; and Alice's tender conscience was torn by the idea that she ought not to be a burden to her mother-in-law, but to go out and seek her own maintenance. And leave her child! The thought came like the sweeping boom of a funeral-bell over her heart.

By and by, Mr Openshaw came to lodge with them. He had started in life as the errand-boy and sweeper-out of a warehouse; had struggled up through all the grades of employment in it, fighting his way through the hard, striving Manchester life with strong, pushing energy of character. Every spare moment of time had been sternly given up to self-teaching. He was a capital accountant, a good French and German scholar, a keen, far-seeing tradesman – understanding markets and the bearing of events, both near and distant, on trade; and yet, with such vivid attention to present details, that I do not think he ever saw a group of flowers in the fields without thinking whether their colour would, or would not, form harmonious contrasts in the coming spring muslins and prints. He went to debating societies, and threw himself with all his heart and soul into politics; esteeming, it must be owned, every man a fool or a knave who differed from him, and overthrowing his opponents rather by the loud strength of his language than the calm strength of his logic. There was something of the Yankee in all this. Indeed, his theory ran parallel to the famous Yankee motto[2] – 'England flogs creation, and Manchester flogs England.' Such a man, as may be fancied, had had no time for falling in love, or any such nonsense. At the age when most young men go through their courting and matrimony, he had not the means of keeping a wife, and was far too practical to think of having one. And now that he was in easy circumstances, a rising man, he considered women almost as encumbrances to the world, with whom a man had better have as little to do as possible. His first impression of Alice was indistinct, and he did not care enough about her to make it distinct. 'A pretty, yea-nay kind of woman,' would have been his description of her, if he had been pushed into a corner. He was rather afraid, in the beginning, that her quiet ways arose from a listlessness and laziness of character, which would have been exceedingly discordant to his active, energetic nature. But, when he found out the punctuality with which his wishes were attended to, and her work was done; when he was called in the morning at the very stroke of the clock, his shaving-water scalding hot, his fire bright, his coffee made exactly as his peculiar fancy dictated (for he was a man who had his theory about everything based upon what he knew of science, and often perfectly original) – then he began to think: not that Alice had any particular merit, but that he had got into remarkably good lodgings; his restlessness wore away, and he began to consider himself as almost settled for life in them.

Mr Openshaw had been too busy, all his days, to be introspective. He did not know that he had any tenderness in his nature; and if he had become conscious of its abstract existence he would have considered it as a manifestation of disease in some part of him. But he was decoyed into pity unawares; and pity led on to tenderness. That little helpless child – always carried about by one of the three busy women of the house, or else patiently threading coloured beads in the chair from which, by no effort of its own, could it ever move – the great grave blue eyes, full of serious, not uncheerful, expression, giving to the small delicate face a look beyond its years – the soft plaintive voice dropping out but few words, so unlike the continual prattle of a child – caught Mr Openshaw's attention in spite of himself. One day – he half scorned himself for doing so – he cut short his dinner-hour to go in search of some toy, which should take the place of those eternal beads. I forget what he bought; but, when he gave the present (which he took care to do in a short abrupt manner, and when no one was by to see him), he was almost thrilled by the flash of delight that came over that child's face, and he could not help, all through that afternoon, going over and over again the picture left on his memory, by the bright effect of unexpected joy on the little girl's face. When he returned home, he found his slippers placed by his sitting-room fire; and even more careful attention paid to his fancies than was habitual in those model lodgings. When Alice had taken the last of his tea-things away – she had been silent as usual till then – she stood for an instant with the door in her hand. Mr Openshaw looked as if he were deep in his book, though in fact he did not see a line; but was heartily wishing the woman would go, and not make any palaver of gratitude. But she only said:

'I am very much obliged to you, sir. Thank you very much,' and was gone, even before he could send her away with a 'There, my good woman, that's enough!'

For some time longer he took no apparent notice of the child. He even hardened his heart into disregarding her sudden flush of colour and little timid smile of recognition, when he saw her by chance. But, after all, this could not last for ever; and, having a second time given way to tenderness, there was no relapse. The insidious enemy having thus entered his heart, in the guise of compassion to the child, soon assumed the more dangerous form of interest in the mother. He was aware of this change of feeling – despised himself for it – struggled with it; nay, internally yielded to it and cherished it, long before he suffered the slightest expression of it, by word, action, or look to escape him. He watched Alice's docile, obedient ways to her step-mother; the love which she had inspired in the rough Norah (roughened by the wear and tear of sorrow and years); but, above all, he saw the wild, deep, passionate affection existing between her and her child. They spoke little to any one else, or when any one else was by; but, when alone together, they talked, and murmured, and cooed, and chattered so continually, that Mr Openshaw first wondered what they could find to say to each other, and next became irritated because they were always so grave and silent with him. All this time he was perpetually devising small new pleasures for the child. His thoughts ran, in a pertinacious way, upon the desolate life before her; and often he came back from his day's work loaded with the very thing Alice had been longing for, but had not been able to procure. One time, it was a little chair for drawing the little sufferer along the streets; and, many an evening that following summer, Mr Openshaw drew her along himself, regardless of the remarks of his acquaintances. One day in autumn, he put down his newspaper, as Alice came in with the breakfast, and said, in as indifferent a voice as he could assume:

'Mrs Frank, is there any reason why we two should not put up our horses together?'

Alice stood still in perplexed wonder. What did he mean? He had resumed the reading of his newspaper, as if he did not expect any answer; so she found silence her safest course, and went on quietly arranging his breakfast, without another word passing between them. Just as he was leaving the house, to go to the warehouse as usual, he turned back and put his head into the bright, neat, tidy kitchen, where all the women breakfasted in the morning:

'You'll think of what I said, Mrs Frank' (this was her name with the lodgers), 'and let me have your opinion upon it to-night.'

Alice was thankful that her mother and Norah were too busy talking together to attend much to this speech. She determined not to think about it at all through the day; and, of course, the effort not to think made her think all the more. At night she sent up Norah with his tea. But Mr Openshaw almost knocked Norah down as she was going out at the door, by pushing past her and calling out, 'Mrs Frank!' in an impatient voice, at the top of the stairs.

Alice went up, rather than seem to have affixed too much meaning to his words.

'Well, Mrs Frank,' he said, 'what answer? Don't make it too long; for I have lots of office work to get through to-night.'

'I hardly know what you meant, sir,' said truthful Alice.

'Well! I should have thought you might have guessed. You're not new at this sort of work, and I am. However, I'll make it plain this time. Will you have me to be thy wedded husband, and serve me, and love me, and honour me, and all that sort of thing? Because, if you will, I will do as much by you, and be a father to your child – and that's more than is put in the Prayer-book. Now, I'm a man of my word; and what I say, I feel; and what I promise, I'll do. Now, for your answer!'

Alice was silent. He began to make the tea, as if her reply was a matter of perfect indifference to him; but, as soon as that was done, he became impatient.

'Well?' said he.

'How long, sir, may I have to think over it?'

'Three minutes!' (looking at his watch). 'You've had two already – that makes five. Be a sensible woman, say Yes, and sit down to tea with me, and we'll talk it over together; for, after tea, I shall be busy; say No' (he hesitated a moment to try and keep his voice in the same tone), 'and I shan't say another word about it, but pay up a year's rent for my rooms to-morrow, and be off. Time's up! Yes or no?'

'If you please, sir – you have been so good to little Ailsie –'

'There, sit down comfortably by me on the sofa, and let's have our tea together. I am glad to find you are as good and sensible as I took you for.'

And this was Alice Wilson's second wooing.

Mr Openshaw's will was too strong, and his circumstances too good, for him not to carry all before him. He settled Mrs Wilson in a comfortable house of her own, and made her quite independent of lodgers. The little that Alice said with regard to future plans was in Norah's behalf.

'No,' said Mr Openshaw. 'Norah shall take care of the old lady as long as she lives; and, after that, she shall either come and live with us, or, if she likes it better, she shall have a provision for life for your sake, missus. No one who has been good to you or the child shall go unrewarded. But even the little one will be better for some fresh stuff about her. Get her a bright, sensible girl as a nurse; one who won't go rubbing her with calf's-foot jelly as Norah does; wasting good stuff outside that ought to go in, but will follow doctors' directions; which, as you must see pretty clearly by this time, Norah won't; because they give the poor little wench pain. Now, I'm not above being nesh[3] for other folks myself. I can stand a good blow, and never change colour; but, set me in the operating room in the infirmary, and I turn as sick as a girl. Yet, if need were, I would hold the little wench on my knees while she screeched with pain, if it were to do her poor back good. Nay, nay, wench! keep your white looks for the time when it comes – I don't say it ever will. But this I know, Norah will spare the child and cheat the doctor, if she can. Now, I say, give the bairn a year or two's chance, and then, when the pack of doctors have done their best – and, maybe, the old lady has gone – we'll have Norah back or do better for her.'

The pack of doctors could do no good to little Ailsie. She was beyond their power. But her father (for so he insisted on being called, and also on Alice's no longer retaining the appellation of Mamma, but becoming henceforward Mother), by his healthy cheerfulness of manner, his clear decision of purpose, his odd turns and quirks of humour, added to his real strong love for the helpless little girl, infused a new element of brightness and confidence into her life; and, though her back remained the same, her general health was strengthened, and Alice – never going beyond a smile herself – had the pleasure of seeing her child taught to laugh.

As for Alice's own life, it was happier than it had ever been before. Mr Openshaw required no demonstration, no expressions of affection from her. Indeed, these would rather have disgusted him. Alice could love deeply, but could not talk about it. The perpetual requirement of loving words, looks, and caresses, and misconstruing their absence into absence of love, had been the great trial of her former married life. Now, all went on clear and straight, under the guidance of her husband's strong sense, warm heart, and powerful will. Year by year their worldly prosperity increased. At Mrs Wilson's death, Norah came back to them as nurse to the newly-born little Edwin; into which post she was not installed without a pretty strong oration on the part of the proud and happy father, who declared that if he found out that Norah ever tried to screen the boy by a falsehood, or to make him nesh either in body or mind, she should go that very day. Norah and Mr Openshaw were not on the most thoroughly cordial terms; neither of them fully recognizing or appreciating the other's best qualities.

This was the previous history of the Lancashire family who had now removed to London.

They had been there about a year, when Mr Openshaw suddenly informed his wife that he had determined to heal long-standing feuds, and had asked his uncle and aunt Chadwick to come and pay them a visit and see London. Mrs Openshaw had never seen this uncle and aunt of her husband's. Years before she had married him, there had been a quarrel. All she knew was, that Mr Chadwick was a small manufacturer in a country town in South Lanca-shire. She was extremely pleased that the breach was to be healed, and began making preparations to render their visit pleasant.

They arrived at last. Going to see London was such an event to them, that Mrs Chadwick had made all new linen fresh for the occasion – from night-caps downwards; and as for gowns, ribbons, and collars, she might have been going into the wilds of Canada where never a shop is, so large was her stock. A fortnight before the day of her departure for London, she had formally called to take leave of all her acquaintance; saying she should need every bit of the intermediate time for packing up. It was like a second wedding in her imagination; and, to complete the resemblance which an entirely new ward-robe made between the two events, her husband brought her back from Manchester, on the last market-day before they set off, a gorgeous pearl and amethyst brooch, saying, 'Lunnon should see that Lancashire folks knew a handsome thing when they saw it.'

For some time after Mr and Mrs Chadwick arrived at the Openshaws' there was no opportunity for wearing this brooch; but at length they obtained an order to see Buckingham Palace, and the spirit of loyalty demanded that Mrs Chadwick should wear her best clothes in visiting the abode of her sovereign. On her return she hastily changed her dress; for Mr Openshaw had planned that they should go to Richmond, drink tea, and return by moonlight. Accordingly, about five o'clock, Mr and Mrs Openshaw and Mr and Mrs Chadwick set off.

The housemaid and cook sat below, Norah hardly knew where. She was always engrossed in the nursery in tending her two children, and in sitting by the restless, excitable Ailsie till she fell asleep. By and by the housemaid Bessy tapped gently at the door. Norah went to her, and they spoke in whispers.

'Nurse! there's some one downstairs wants you.'

'Wants me! who is it?'

'A gentleman –'

'A gentleman? Nonsense!'

'Well! a man, then, and he asks for you, and he rang at the front-door bell, and has walked into the dining-room.'

'You should never have let him,' exclaimed Norah. 'Master and missus out –'

'I did not want him to come in; but, when he heard you lived here, he walked past me, and sat down on the first chair, and said, "Tell her to come and speak to me." There is no gas lighted in the room, and supper is all set out.'

'He'll be off with the spoons!' exclaimed Norah, putting the housemaid's fear into words, and preparing to leave the room; first, however, giving a look to Ailsie, sleeping soundly and calmly.

Downstairs she went, uneasy fears stirring in her bosom. Before she entered the dining-room she provided herself with a candle, and, with it in her hand, she went in, looking around her in the darkness for her visitor.

He was standing up, holding by the table. Norah and he looked at each other; gradual recognition coming into their eyes.

'Norah?' at length he asked.

'Who are you?' asked Norah, with the sharp tones of alarm and incredulity. 'I don't know you'; trying, by futile words of disbelief, to do away with the terrible fact before her.

'Am I so changed?' he said pathetically. 'I dare say I am. But, Norah, tell me!' he breathed hard, 'where is my wife? Is she – is she alive?'

He came nearer to Norah, and would have taken her hand; but she backed away from him; looking at him all the time with staring eyes, as if he were some horrible object. Yet he was a handsome, bronzed, good-looking fellow, with beard and moustache, giving him a foreign-looking aspect; but his eyes! there was no mistaking those eager, beautiful eyes – the very same that Norah had watched not half an hour ago, till sleep stole softly over them.

'Tell me, Norah – I can bear it – I have feared it so often. Is she dead?' Norah still kept silence. 'She is dead!' He hung on Norah's words and looks, as if for confirmation or contradiction.

'What shall I do?' groaned Norah. 'Oh, sir! why did you come? how did you find me out? where have you been? We thought you dead, we did indeed!' She poured out words and questions to gain time, as if time would help her.

'Norah! answer me this question straight, by yes or no – Is my wife dead?'

'No, she is not!' said Norah, slowly and heavily.

'Oh, what a relief! Did she receive my letters? But perhaps you don't know. Why did you leave her? Where is she? Oh, Norah, tell me all quickly!'

'Mr Frank!' said Norah at last, almost driven to bay by her terror lest her mistress should return at any moment and find him there – unable to consider what was best to be done or said – rushing at something decisive, because she could not endure her present state: 'Mr Frank! we never heard a line from you, and the shipowners said you had gone down, you and every one else. We thought you were dead, if ever man was, and poor Miss Alice and her little sick, helpless child! Oh, sir, you must guess it,' cried the poor creature at last, bursting out into a passionate fit of crying 'for indeed I cannot tell it. But it was no one's fault. God help us all this night!'

Norah had sat down. She trembled too much to stand. He took her hands in his. He squeezed them hard, as if, by physical pressure, the truth could be wrung out.

'Norah.' This time his tone was calm, stagnant as despair. 'She has married again!'

Norah shook her head sadly. The grasp slowly relaxed. The man had fainted.

There was brandy in the room. Norah forced some drops into Mr Frank's mouth, chafed his hands, and – when mere animal life returned, before the mind poured in its flood of memories and thoughts – she lifted him up, and rested his head against her knees. Then she put a few crumbs of bread taken from the supper-table, soaked in brandy, into his mouth. Suddenly he sprang to his feet.

'Where is she? Tell me this instant.' He looked so wild, so mad, so desperate, that Norah felt herself to be in bodily danger; but her time of dread had gone by. She had been afraid to tell him the truth, and then she had been a coward. Now, her wits were sharpened by the sense of his desperate state. He must leave the house. She would pity him afterwards; but now she must rather command and upbraid; for he must leave the house before her mistress came home. That one necessity stood clear before her.

'She is not here: that is enough for you to know. Nor can I say exactly where she is' (which was true to the letter if not to the spirit). 'Go away, and tell me where to find you to-morrow, and I will tell you all. My master and mistress may come back at any minute, and then what would become of me, with a strange man in the house?'

Such an argument was too petty to touch his excited mind.

'I don't care for your master and mistress. If your master is a man, he must feel for me – poor shipwrecked sailor that I am – kept for years a prisoner amongst savages, always, always, always thinking of my wife and my home – dreaming of her by night, talking to her though she could not hear, by day. I loved her more than all heaven and earth put together. Tell me where she is, this instant, you wretched woman, who salved over her wickedness to her, as you do to me!'

The clock struck ten. Desperate positions require desperate measures.

'If you will leave the house now, I will come to you to-morrow and tell you all. What is more, you shall see your child now. She lies sleeping upstairs. Oh, sir, you have a child, you do not know that as yet – a little weakly girl – with just a heart and soul beyond her years. We have reared her up with such care! We watched her, for we thought for many a year she might die any day, and we tended her, and no hard thing has come near her, and no rough word has ever been said to her. And now you come and will take her life into your hand, and will crush it. Strangers to her have been kind to her; but her own father – Mr Frank, I am her nurse, and I love her, and I tend her, and I would do anything for her that I could. Her mother's heart beats as hers beats; and, if she suffers a pain, her mother trembles all over. If she is happy, it is her mother that smiles and is glad. If she is growing stronger, her mother is healthy: if she dwindles, her mother languishes. If she dies – well, I don't know; it is not every one can lie down and die when they wish it. Come upstairs, Mr Frank, and see your child. Seeing her will do good to your poor heart. Then go away, in God's name, just this one night; to-morrow, if need be, you can do anything – kill us all if you will, or show yourself a great, grand man, whom God will bless for ever and ever. Come, Mr Frank, the look of a sleeping child is sure to give peace.'

She led him upstairs; at first almost helping his steps, till they came near the nursery door. She had wellnigh forgotten the existence of little Edwin. It struck upon her with affright as the shaded light fell over the other cot; but she skilfully threw that corner of the room into darkness, and let the light fall on the sleeping Ailsie. The child had thrown down the coverings, and her deformity, as she lay with her back to them, was plainly visible through her slight nightgown. Her little face, deprived of the lustre of her eyes, looked wan and pinched, and had a pathetic expression in it, even as she slept. The poor father looked and looked with hungry, wistful eyes, into which the big tears came swelling up slowly and dropped heavily down, as he stood trembling and shaking all over. Norah was angry with herself for growing impatient of the length of time that long lingering gaze lasted. She thought that she waited for full half an hour before Frank stirred. And then – instead of going away – he sank down on his knees by the bedside, and buried his face in the clothes. Little Ailsie stirred uneasily. Norah pulled him up in terror. She could afford no more time, even for prayer, in her extremity of fear; for surely the next moment would bring her mistress home. She took him forcibly by the arm; but, as he was going, his eye lighted on the other bed: he stopped. Intelligence came back into his face. His hands clenched.

'His child?' he asked.

'Her child,' replied Norah. 'God watches over him,' she said instinctively; for Frank's looks excited her fears, and she needed to remind herself of the Protector of the helpless.

'God has not watched over me,' he said, in despair; his thoughts apparently recoiling on his own desolate, deserted state. But Norah had no time for pity. To-morrow she would be as compassionate as her heart prompted. At length she guided him downstairs, and shut the outer door, and bolted it – as if by bolts to keeps out facts.

Then she went back into the dining-room, and effaced all traces of his presence, as far as she could. She went upstairs to the nursery and sat there, her head on her hand, thinking what was to come of all this misery. It seemed to her very long before her master and mistress returned; yet it was hardly eleven o'clock. She heard the loud, hearty Lancashire voices on the stairs; and, for the first time, she understood the contrast of the desolation of the poor man who had so lately gone forth in lonely despair.

It almost put her out of patience to see Mrs Openshaw come in, calmly smiling, handsomely dressed, happy, easy, to inquire after her children.

'Did Ailsie go to sleep comfortably?' she whispered to Norah.

'Yes.'

Her mother bent over her, looking at her slumbers with the soft eyes of love. How little she dreamed who had looked on her last! Then she went to Edwin, with perhaps less wistful anxiety in her countenance, but more of pride. She took off her things, to go down to supper. Norah saw her no more that night.

Beside having a door into the passage, the sleeping-nursery opened out of Mr and Mrs Openshaw's room, in order that they might have the children more immediately under their own eyes. Early the next summer's morning, Mrs Openshaw was awakened by Ailsie's startled call of 'Mother! mother!' She sprang up, put on her dressing-gown, and went to her child. Ailsie was only half awake, and in a not unusual state of terror.

'Who was he, mother? Tell me!'

'Who, my darling? No one is here. You have been dreaming, love. Waken up quite. See, it is broad daylight.'

'Yes,' said Ailsie, looking round her; then clinging to her mother, 'but a man was here in the night, mother.'

'Nonsense, little goose. No man has ever come near you!'

'Yes, he did. He stood there. Just by Norah. A man with hair and a beard. And he knelt down and said his prayers. Norah knows he was here, mother' (half angrily, as Mrs Openshaw shook her head in smiling incredulity).

'Well! we will ask Norah when she comes,' said Mrs Openshaw, soothingly. 'But we won't talk any more about him now. It is not five o'clock; it is too early for you to get up. Shall I fetch you a book and read to you?'

'Don't leave me, mother,' said the child, clinging to her. So Mrs Openshaw sat on the bedside talking to Ailsie, and telling her of what they had done at Richmond the evening before, until the little girl's eyes slowly closed and she once more fell asleep.

'What was the matter?' asked Mr Openshaw, as his wife returned to bed.

'Ailsie wakened up in a fright, with some story of a man having been in the room to say his prayers – a dream, I suppose.' And no more was said at the time.

Mrs Openshaw had almost forgotten the whole affair when she got up about seven o'clock. But, by and by, she heard a sharp altercation going on in the nursery – Norah speaking angrily to Ailsie, a most unusual thing. Both Mr and Mrs Openshaw listened in astonishment.

'Hold your tongue, Ailsie! let me hear none of your dreams; never let me hear you tell that story again!'

Ailsie began to cry.

Mr Openshaw opened the door of communication, before his wife could say a word.

'Norah, come here!'

The nurse stood at the door, defiant. She perceived she had been heard, but she was desperate.

'Don't let me hear you speak in that manner to Ailsie again,' he said sternly, and shut the door.

Norah was infinitely relieved; for she had dreaded some questioning; and a little blame for sharp speaking was what she could well bear, if cross-examination was let alone.

Downstairs they went, Mr Openshaw carrying Ailsie; the sturdy Edwin coming step by step, right foot foremost, always holding his mother's hand. Each child was placed in a chair by the breakfast-table, and then Mr and Mrs Openshaw stood together at the window, awaiting their visitors' appearance and making plans for the day. There was a pause. Suddenly Mr Openshaw turned to Ailsie, and said:

'What a little goosy somebody is with her dreams, wakening up poor, tired mother in the middle of the night, with a story of a man being in the room.'

'Father! I'm sure I saw him,' said Ailsie, half-crying. 'I don't want to make Norah angry; but I was not asleep, for all she says I was. I had been asleep – and I wakened up quite wide awake, though I was so frightened. I kept my eyes nearly shut, and I saw the man quite plain. A great brown man with a beard. He said his prayers. And then looked at Edwin. And then Norah took him by the arm and led him away, after they had whispered a bit together.'

'Now, my little woman must be reasonable,' said Mr Openshaw, who was always patient with Ailsie. 'There was no man in the house last night at all. No man comes into the house, as you know, if you think; much less goes up into the nursery. But sometimes we dream something has happened, and the dream is so like reality, that you are not the first person, little woman, who has stood out that the thing has really happened.'

'But, indeed, it was not a dream!' said Ailsie, beginning to cry.

Just then Mr and Mrs Chadwick came down, looking grave and discomposed. All during breakfast-time they were silent and uncomfortable. As soon as the breakfast things were taken away, and the children had been carried upstairs, Mr Chadwick began, in an evidently preconcerted manner, to inquire if his nephew was certain that all his servants were honest; for, that Mrs Chadwick had that morning missed a very valuable brooch, which she had worn the day before. She remembered taking it off when she came home from Buckingham Palace. Mr Openshaw's face contracted into hard lines; grew like what it was before he had known his wife and her child. He rang the bell, even before his uncle had done speaking. It was answered by the housemaid.

'Mary, was any one here last night, while we were away?'

'A man, sir, came to speak to Norah.'

'To speak to Norah! Who was he? How long did he stay?'

'I'm sure I can't tell, sir. He came – perhaps about nine. I went up to tell Norah in the nursery, and she came down to speak to him. She let him out, sir. She will know who he was, and how long he stayed.'

She waited a moment to be asked any more questions, but she was not, so she went away.

A minute afterwards Mr Openshaw made as though he were going out of the room; but his wife laid her hand on his arm.

'Do not speak to her before the children,' she said, in her low, quiet voice. 'I will go up and question her.'

'No! I must speak to her. You must know,' said he, turning to his uncle and aunt, 'my missus has an old servant, as faithful as ever woman was, I do believe, as far as love goes, – but at the same time, who does not speak truth, as even the missus must allow. Now, my notion is, that this Norah of ours has been come over by some good-for-nothing chap (for she's at the time o' life when they say women pray for husbands – "any, good Lord, any") and has let him into our house, and the chap has made off with your brooch, and m'appen many another thing beside. It's only saying that Norah is soft-hearted and doesn't stick at a white lie – that's all, missus.'

It was curious to notice how his tone, his eyes, his whole face was changed, as he spoke to his wife; but he was the resolute man through all. She knew better than to oppose him; so she went upstairs, and told Norah that her master wanted to speak to her, and that she would take care of the children in the meanwhile.

Norah rose to go, without a word. Her thoughts were these:

'If they tear me to pieces, they shall never know through me. He may come – and then, just Lord have mercy upon us all! for some of us are dead folk to a certainty. But *he* shall do it; not me.'

You may fancy, now, her look of determination, as she faced her master alone in the dining-room; Mr and Mrs Chadwick having left the affair in their nephew's hands, seeing that he took it up with such vehemence.

'Norah! Who was that man that came to my house last night?'

'Man, sir!' As if infinitely surprised; but it was only to gain time.

'Yes; the man that Mary let in; that she went upstairs to the nursery to tell you about; that you came down to speak to; the same chap, I make no doubt, that you took into the nursery to have your talk out with; the one Ailsie saw, and afterwards dreamed about; thinking, poor wench! she saw him say his prayers, when nothing, I'll be bound, was further from his thoughts; the one that took Mrs Chadwick's brooch, value ten pounds. Now, Norah! Don't go off. I'm as sure as my name's Thomas Openshaw that you knew nothing of this robbery. But I do think you've been imposed on, and that's the truth. Some good-for-nothing chap has been making up to you, and you've been just like all other women, and have turned a soft place in your heart to him; and he came last night a-lovyering, and you had him up in the nursery, and he made use of his opportunities, and made off with a few things on his way down! Come, now, Norah; it's no blame to you, only you must not be such a fool again! Tell us,' he continued, 'what name he gave you, Norah. I'll be bound, it was not the right one; but it will be a clue for the police.'

Norah drew herself up. 'You may ask that question, and taunt me with my being single, and with my credulity, as you will, Master Openshaw. You'll get no answer from me. As for the brooch, and the story of theft and burglary; if any friend ever came to see me (which I defy you to prove, and deny), he'd be just as much above doing such a thing as you yourself, Mr Openshaw – and more so, too; for I'm not at all sure as everything you have is rightly come by, or would be yours long, if every man had his own.' She meant, of course, his wife; but he understood her to refer to his property in goods and chattels.

'Now, my good woman,' said he, 'I'll just tell you truly, I never trusted you out and out; but my wife liked you, and I thought you had many a good point about you. If you once begin to sauce me, I'll have the police to you, and get out the truth in a court of justice, if you'll not tell it me quietly and civilly here. Now, the best thing you can do is quietly to tell me who the fellow is. Look here! a man comes to my house; asks for you; you take him upstairs; a valuable brooch is missing next day; we know that you, and Mary, and cook, are honest; but you refuse to tell us who the man is. Indeed, you've told me one lie already about him, saying no one was here last night. Now, I just put it to you, what do you think a policeman would say to this, or a magistrate? A magistrate would soon make you tell the truth, my good woman.'

'There's never the creature born that should get it out of me,' said Norah. 'Not unless I choose to tell.'

'I've a great mind to see,' said Mr Openshaw, growing angry at the defiance. Then, checking himself, he thought before he spoke again:

'Norah, for your missus' sake I don't want to go to extremities. Be a sensible woman, if you can. It's no great disgrace, after all, to have been taken in. I ask you once more – as a friend – who was this man that you let into my house last night?'

No answer. He repeated the question in an impatient tone. Still no answer. Norah's lips were set in determination not to speak.

'Then there is but one thing to be done. I shall send for a policeman.'

'You will not,' said Norah, starting forward. 'You shall not, sir! No policeman shall touch me. I know nothing of the brooch, but I know this: ever since I was four-and-twenty, I have thought more of your wife than of myself: ever since I saw her, a poor motherless girl, put upon in her uncle's house, I have thought more of serving her than of serving myself! I have cared for her and her child, as nobody ever cared for me. I don't cast blame on you, sir, but I say it's ill giving up one's life to any one; for, at the end, they will turn round upon you, and forsake you. Why does not my missus come herself to suspect me? Maybe, she is gone for the police? But I don't stay here, either for police, or magistrate, or master. You're an unlucky lot. I believe there's a curse on you. I'll leave you this very day. Yes! I'll leave that poor Ailsie, too. I will! No good ever will come to you!'

Mr Openshaw was utterly astonished at this speech; most of which was completely unintelligible to him, as may easily be supposed. Before he could make up his mind what to say, or what to do, Norah had left the room. I do not think he had ever really intended to send for the police to this old servant of his wife's; for he had never for a moment doubted her perfect honesty. But he had intended to compel her to tell him who the man was, and in this he was baffled. He was, consequently, much irritated. He returned to his uncle and aunt in a state of great annoyance and perplexity, and told them he could get nothing out of the woman; that some man had been in the house the night before; but that she refused to tell who he was. At this moment his wife came in, greatly agitated, and asked what had happened to Norah; for that she had put on her things in passionate haste, and left the house.

'This looks suspicious, said Mr Chadwick. 'It is not the way in which an honest person would have acted.'

Mr Openshaw kept silence. He was sorely perplexed. But Mrs Openshaw turned round on Mr Chadwick, with a sudden fierceness no one ever saw in her before.

'You don't know Norah, uncle! She is gone because she is deeply hurt at being suspected. Oh, I wish I had seen her – that I had spoken to her myself. She would have told me anything.' Alice wrung her hands.

'I must confess,' continued Mr Chadwick to his nephew, in a lower voice, 'I can't make you out. You used to be a word and a blow, and oftenest the blow first; and now, when there is every cause for suspicion, you just do nought. Your missus is a very good woman, I grant; but she may have been put upon as well as other folk, I suppose. If you don't send for the police, I shall.'

'Very well,' replied Mr Openshaw, surlily. 'I can't clear Norah. She won't clear herself, as I believe she might if she would. Only I wash my hands of it; for I am sure the woman herself is honest, and she's lived a long time with my wife, and I don't like her to come to shame.'

'But she will then, be forced to clear herself. That, at any rate, will be a good thing.'

'Very well, very well! I am heart-sick of the whole business. Come, Alice, come up to the babies; they'll be in a sore way. I tell you, uncle,' he said, turning round once more to Mr Chadwick, suddenly and sharply, after his eye had fallen on Alice's wan, tearful, anxious face, 'I'll have no sending for the police, after all. I'll buy my aunt twice as handsome a brooch this very day; but I'll not have Norah suspected, and my missus plagued. There's for you!'

He and his wife left the room. Mr Chadwick quietly waited till he was out of hearing, and then said to his wife, 'For all Tom's heroics, I'm just quietly going for a detective, wench. Thou need'st know nought about it.'

He went to the police-station and made a statement of the case. He was gratified by the impression which the evidence against Norah seemed to make. The men all agreed in his opinion, and steps were to be immediately taken to find out where she was. Most probably, as they suggested, she had gone at once to the man, who, to all appearance, was her lover. When Mr Chadwick asked how they would find her out, they smiled, shook their heads, and spoke of mysterious but infallible ways and means. He returned to his nephew's house with a very comfortable opinion of his own sagacity. He was met by his wife with a penitent face.

'Oh, master, I've found my brooch! It was just sticking by its pin in the flounce of my brown silk, that I wore yesterday. I took it off in a hurry, and it must have caught in it; and I hung up my gown in the closet. Just now, when I was going to fold it up, there was the brooch! I am very vexed, but I never dreamt but what it was lost!'

Her husband, muttering something very like 'Confound thee and thy brooch too! I wish I'd never given it thee,' snatched up his hat, and rushed back to the station, hoping to be in time to stop the police from searching for Norah. But a detective was already gone off on the errand.

Where was Norah? Half mad with the strain of the fearful secret, she had hardly slept through the night for thinking what must be done. Upon this terrible state of mind had come Ailsie's questions, showing that she had seen the Man, as the unconscious child called her father. Lastly came the suspicion of her honesty. She was little less than crazy as she ran upstairs and dashed on her bonnet and shawl; leaving all else, even her purse, behind her. In that house she would not stay. That was all she knew or was clear about. She would not even see the children again, for fear it should weaken her. She dreaded above everything Mr Frank's return to claim his wife. She could not tell what remedy there was for a sorrow so tremendous, for her to stay to witness. The desire of escaping from the coming event was a stronger motive for her departure, than her soreness about the suspicions directed against her; although this last had been the final goad to the course she took. She walked away almost at headlong speed; sobbing as she went, as she had not dared to do during the past night for fear of exciting wonder in those who might hear her. Then she stopped. An idea came into her mind that she would leave London altogether, and betake herself to her native town of Liverpool. She felt in her pocket for her purse as she drew near the Euston Square station with this intention. She had left it at home. Her poor head aching, her eyes swollen with crying, she had to stand still, and think, as well as she could, where next she should bend her steps. Suddenly the thought flashed into her mind that she would go and find out poor Mr Frank. She had been hardly kind to him the night before, though her heart had bled for him ever since. She remembered his telling her, when she inquired for his address, almost as she had pushed him out of the door, of some hotel in a street not far distant from Euston Square. Thither she went: with what intention she scarcely knew, but to assuage her conscience by telling him how much she pitied him. In her present state she felt herself unfit to counsel, or restrain, or assist, or do aught else but sympathize and weep. The people of the inn said such a person had been there; had arrived only the day before; had gone out soon after arrival, leaving his luggage in their care; but had never come back. Norah asked for leave to sit down, and await the gentleman's return. The landlady – pretty secure in the deposit of luggage against any probable injury – showed her into a room, and quietly locked the door on the outside. Norah was utterly worn out, and fell asleep – a shivering, starting, uneasy slumber, which lasted for hours.

The detective, meanwhile, had come up with her some time before she entered the hotel, into which he followed her. Asking the landlady to detain her for an hour or so, without giving any reason beyond showing his authority (which made the landlady applaud herself a good deal for having locked her in), he went back to the police-station to report his proceedings. He could have taken her directly; but his object was, if possible, to trace out the man who was supposed to have committed the robbery. Then he heard of the discovery of the brooch; and consequently did not care to return.

Norah slept till even the summer evening began to close in. Then started up. Some one was at the door. It would be Mr Frank; and she dizzily pushed back her ruffled grey hair, which had fallen over her eyes, and stood looking to see him. Instead, there came in Mr Openshaw and a policeman.

'This is Norah Kennedy,' said Mr Openshaw.

'Oh, sir,' said Norah, 'I did not touch the brooch; indeed I did not. Oh, sir, I cannot live to be thought so badly of'; and very sick and faint, she suddenly sank down on the ground. To her surprise, Mr Openshaw raised her up very tenderly. Even the policeman helped to lay her on the sofa; and, at Mr Openshaw's desire, he went for some wine and sandwiches; for the poor gaunt woman lay there almost as if dead with weariness and exhaustion.

'Norah,' said Mr Openshaw, in his kindest voice, 'the brooch is found. It was hanging to Mrs Chadwick's gown. I beg your pardon. Most truly I beg your pardon, for having troubled you about it. My wife is almost broken-hearted. Eat, Norah – or, stay, first drink this glass of wine,' said he, lifting her head, and pouring a little down her throat.

As she drank, she remembered where she was, and who she was waiting for. She suddenly pushed Mr Openshaw away, saying, 'Oh, sir, you must go. You must not stop a minute. If he comes back, he will kill you.'

'Alas, Norah! I do not know who "he" is. But some one is gone away who will never come back: some one who knew you, and whom I am afraid you cared for.'

'I don't understand you, sir,' said Norah, her master's kind and sorrowful manner bewildering her yet more than his words. The policeman had left the room at Mr Openshaw's desire, and they two were alone.

'You know what I mean, when I say some one is gone who will never come back. I mean that he is dead!'

'Who?' said Norah, trembling all over.

'A poor man has been found in the Thames this morning – drowned.'

'Did he drown himself?' asked Norah, solemnly.

'God only knows,' replied Mr Openshaw, in the same tone. 'Your name and address at our house were found in his pocket; that, and his purse, were the only things that were found upon him. I am sorry to say it, my poor Norah; but you are required to go and identify him.'

'To what?' asked Norah.

'To say who it is. It is always done, in order that some reason may be discovered for the suicide – if suicide it was. I make no doubt, he was the man who came to see you at our house last night. It is very sad, I know.' He made pauses between each little clause, in order to try and bring back her senses, which he feared were wandering – so wild and sad was her look.

'Master Openshaw,' said she, at last, 'I've a dreadful secret to tell you – only you must never breathe it to any one, and you and I must hide it away for ever. I thought to have done it all by myself, but I see I cannot. Yon poor man – yes! the dead, drowned creature is, I fear, Mr Frank, my mistress's first husband!'

Mr Openshaw sat down, as if shot. He did not speak; but, after a while, he signed to Norah to go on.

'He came to me the other night, when – God be thanked! – you were all away at Richmond. He asked me if his wife was dead or alive. I was a brute, and thought more of your all coming home than of his sore trial; I spoke out sharp, and said she was married again, and very content and happy. I all but turned him away: and now he lies dead and cold.'

'God forgive me!' said Mr Openshaw.

'God forgive us all!' said Norah. 'Yon poor man needs forgiveness, perhaps, less than any one among us. He had been among the savages – shipwrecked – I know not what – and he had written letters which had never reached my poor missus.'

'He saw his child!'

'He saw her – yes! I took him up, to give his thoughts another start; for I believed he was going mad on my hands. I came to seek him here, as I more than half promised. My mind misgave me when I heard he never came in. Oh, sir, it must be him!'

Mr Openshaw rang the bell. Norah was almost too much stunned to wonder at what he did. He asked for writing materials, wrote a letter, and then said to Norah:

'I am writing to Alice, to say I shall be unavoidably absent for a few days; that I have found you; that you are well, and send her your love, and will come home to-morrow. You must go with me to the police court; you must identify the body; I will pay high to keep names and details out of the papers.'

'But where are you going, sir?'

He did not answer her directly. Then he said:

'Norah! I must go with you, and look on the face of the man whom I have so injured – unwittingly, it is true; but it seems to me as if I had killed him. I will lay his head in the grave as if he were my only brother: and how he must have hated me! I cannot go home to my wife till all that I can do for him is done. Then I go with a dreadful secret on my mind. I shall never speak of it again, after these days are over. I know you will not, either.' He shook hands with her; and they never named the subject again, the one to the other.

Norah went home to Alice the next day. Not a word was said on the cause of her abrupt departure a day or two before. Alice had been charged by her husband, in his letter, not to allude to the supposed theft of the brooch: so she, implicitly obedient to those whom she loved both by nature and habit, was entirely silent on the subject, only treated Norah with the most tender respect, as if to make up for unjust suspicion.

Nor did Alice inquire into the reason why Mr Openshaw had been absent during his uncle and aunt's visit, after he had once said that it was unavoidable. He came back grave and quiet; and from that time forth was curiously changed. More thoughtful, and perhaps less active; quite as decided in conduct, but with new and different rules for the guidance of that conduct. Towards Alice he could hardly be more kind than he had always been; but he now seemed to look upon her as some one sacred, and to be treated with reverence, as well as tenderness. He throve in business, and made a large fortune, one half of which was settled upon her.

Long years after these events – a few months after her mother died – Ailsie and her 'father' (as she always called Mr Openshaw) drove to a cemetery a little way out of town, and she was carried to a certain mound by her maid, who was then sent back to the carriage. There was a headstone, with F. W. and a date upon it. That was all. Sitting by the grave, Mr Openshaw told her the story; and for the sad fate of that poor father whom she had never seen, he shed the only tears she ever saw fall from his eyes.

Notes

Text: *Right at Last and Other Tales*, Samson Low, London, 1860. First published in Extra Christmas Number of *Household Words* for 1858.
1 In the Old Testament book bearing her name, left her own people to live with Naomi, her mother-in-law.
2 Probably: 'Pa's the boss of Ma, Ma's the boss of me, and I'm the boss of the dog – and boy, is he going to get it!' (traditional family proverb).
3 Fearful, cowardly.

EVELINE'S VISITANT

Mary Elizabeth Braddon

Mary Elizabeth Braddon, later Maxwell (1835–1915), novelist, short-story writer and magazine editor, was born in London but spent part of her childhood in Sussex after her mother deserted her feckless journalist father. She began to write at the age of 8, and by her early twenties was attempting to support her family by writing for the magazines. After a short period as an actress, she wrote her first novel, *Three Times Dead; or The Secret of the Heath*. A meeting with the publisher John Maxwell led to the publication of a number of stories and then to her hugely successful 'sensation' novel *Lady Audley's Secret* (1862). The 'bigamy novel', *Aurora Floyd*, followed in 1863. Altogether she published eighty novels (the later ones less sensational and more psychological), numerous short stories and edited *Belgravia* (1866–76), *The Belgravia Annual* (1867–76), and *The Mistletoe Bough* (which she founded in 1878). She caused a scandal by living unmarried for a number of years with John Maxwell, bringing up his five children and six more of her own, until they were able to marry in 1874 following the death of his institutionalised wife. Her short stories range from ghost stories to comedies: *Eveline's Visitant* has been much admired, and shows her interest in France and in history as well as demonstrating her lively writing style and her attraction to themes of murder, illicit desire and retribution.

Further reading

Blain *et al.* (1990); Maxwell (1937); Hughes (1980); Pykett (1992, 1994); Shattock (1993); Sutherland (1988); Wolff (1979)

Eveline's Visitant

It was a masked ball at the Palais Royal that my fatal quarrel with my first cousin André de Brissac began. The quarrel was about a woman. The women who followed the footsteps of Philip of Orleans[1] were the causes of many such disputes; and there was scarcely one fair head in all that glittering throng which, to a man versed in social histories and mysteries, might not have seemed bedabbled with blood.

I shall not record the name of her for love of whom André de Brissac and I crossed one of the bridges, in the dim August dawn on our way to the waste ground beyond the church of Saint-Germain des Prés.

There were many beautiful vipers in those days, and she was one of them. I can feel the chill breath of that August morning blowing in my face, as I sit in my dismal chamber at my château of Puy Verdun tonight, alone in the stillness, writing the strange story of my life. I can see the white mist rising from the river, the grim outline of the Châtelet, and the square towers of Notre Dame black against the pale-grey sky. Even more vividly can I recall André's fair young face, as he stood opposite me with his two friends – scoundrel's both, and like eager for that unnatural fray. We were a strange group to be seen in a summer sunrise, all of us fresh from the heat and clamour of the Regent's saloons – André in a quaint hunting-dress copied from a family portrait at Puy Verdun, I costumed as one of Law's Mississippi Indians,[2] the other men in like garish frippery, adorned with broideries and jewels that looked wan in the pale light of dawn.

Our quarrel had been a fierce one – a quarrel which could have but one result, and that the direst. I had struck him; and the welt raised by my open hand was crimson upon his fair, womanish face as he stood opposite to me. The eastern sun shone on the face presently, and dyed the cruel mark with a deeper red; but the sting of my own wrongs was fresh, and I had not yet learned to despise myself for that brutal outrage.

To André de Brissac such an insult was most terrible. He was the favourite of Fortune, the favourite of woman; and I was nothing – a rough soldier who had done my country good service, but in the boudoir of a Parabère a mannerless boor.

We fought, and I wounded him mortally. Life had been very sweet to him; and I think that a frenzy of despair took possession of him when he felt the life-blood ebbing away. He beckoned me to him as he lay on the ground. I went, and knelt at his side.

"Forgive me, André!" I murmured.

He took no more heed of my words than if that piteous entreaty had been the idle ripple of the river near at hand.

"Listen to me, Hector de Brissac," he said. "I am not one who believes that a man has done with earth because his eyes glaze and his jaw stiffens. They will bury me in the old vault at Puy Verdun; and you will be master of the château. Ah, I know how lightly they take things in these days, and how Dubois will laugh when he hears that *Ça* has been killed in a duel. They will bury me, and sing masses for my soul; but you and I have not finished our affair yet, my cousin. I will be with you when you least look to see me – I, with this ugly scar upon the face that women have praised and loved. I will come to you when your life seems brightest. I will come between you and all that you hold fairest and dearest. My ghostly hand shall drop a poison in your cup of joy. My shadowy form shall shut the sunlight from your life. Men with such iron will as mine can do what they please, Hector de Brissac. It is my will to haunt you when I am dead."

All this in short, broken sentences he whispered into my ear. I had need to bend my ear close to his dying lips; but the iron will of André de Brissac was strong enough to do battle with Death, and I believe he said all he wished to say before his head fell back upon the velvet cloak they had spread beneath him, never to be lifted again.

As he lay there, you would have fancied him a fragile stripling, too fair and frail for the struggle called life; but there are those who remember the brief manhood of André de Brissac, and who can bear witness to the terrible force of that proud nature.

I stood looking down at the young face with that foul mark upon it, and God knows I was sorry for what I had done.

Of these blasphemous threats which he had whispered in my ear I took no heed. I was a soldier, and a believer. There was nothing absolutely dreadful to me in the thought that I had killed this man. I had killed many men on the battlefield; and this one had done me a cruel wrong.

My friends would have had me cross the frontier to escape the consequences of my act; but I was ready to face those consequences, and I remained in France. I kept aloof from the court, and received a hint that I had best confine myself to my own province. Many masses were chanted in the little chapel of Puy Verdun for the soul of my dead cousin, and his coffin filled a niche in the vault of our ancestors.

His death had made me a rich man; and the thought that it was so made my newly acquired wealth very hateful to me. I lived a lonely existence in the old château, where I rarely held converse with any but the servants of the household, all of whom had served my cousin, and none of whom liked me.

It was a hard and bitter life. It galled me, when I rode through the village, to see the peasant children shrink away from me. I have seen old women cross themselves stealthily as I passed by. Strange reports had gone forth about me;

and there were those who whispered that I had given my soul to the Evil One as the price of my cousin's heritage. From my boyhood I had been dark of visage and stern of manner; and hence, perhaps no woman's love had ever been mine. I remembered my mother's face in all its changes of expression; but I can remember no look of affection that ever shone on me. The other woman, beneath whose feet I laid my heart, was pleased to accept my homage, but she never loved me; and the end was treachery.

I had grown hateful to myself, and had well-nigh begun to hate my fellow-creatures, when a feverish desire seized upon me, and I pined to be back in the press and throng of the busy world once again. I went back to Paris, where I kept myself aloof from the court, and where an angel took compassion on me.

She was the daughter of an old comrade, a man whose merits had been neglected, whose achievements had been ignored, and who sulked in his shabby lodging like a rat in a hole, while all Paris went mad with the Scotch Financier,[3] and gentlemen and lackeys were trampling one another to death in the Rue Quincampoix. The only child of this little cross-grained old captain of dragoons was an incarnate sunbeam, whose mortal name was Eveline Duchalet.

She loved me. The richest blessings of our lives are often those which cost us least. I wasted the best years of my youth in the worship of a wicked woman, who jilted and cheated me at last. I gave this meek angel but a few courteous words – a little fraternal tenderness – and lo, she loved me. The life which had been so dark and desolate grew bright beneath her influence; and I went back to Puy Verdun with a fair young bride for my companion.

Ah, how sweet a change there was in my life and in my home! The village children no longer shrank appalled as the dark horseman rode by, the village crones no longer crossed themselves; for a woman rode by his side – a woman whose charities had won the love of all those ignorant creatures, and whose companionship had transformed the gloomy lord of the château into a loving husband and gentle master. The old retainers forgot the untimely fate of my cousin, and served me with cordial willingness, for love of their young mistress.

There are no words which can tell the pure and perfect happiness of that time. I felt like a traveller who had traversed the frozen seas of an arctic region, remote from human love or human companionship, to find himself all of a sudden in the bosom of a verdant valley, in the sweet atmosphere of home. The change seemed too bright to be real; and I strove in vain to put away from my mind the vague suspicion that my new life was but some fantastic dream.

So brief were those halcyon hours, that, looking back on them now, it is scarcely strange if I am still half inclined to fancy the first days of my married life could have been no more than a dream.

Neither in my days of gloom nor in my days of happiness had I been troubled by the recollection of André's blasphemous oath. The words which with his last breath he had whispered in my ear were vain and meaningless to me. He had vented his rage in those idle threats, as he might have vented it in idle execrations. That he will haunt the footsteps of his enemy after death is the one revenge which a dying man can promise himself; and if men had power thus to avenge themselves the earth would be peopled with phantoms.

I had lived for three years at Puy Verdun; sitting alone in the solemn midnight by the hearth where he had sat, pacing the corridors that had echoed his footfall; and in all that time my fancy had never so played me false as to shape the shadow of the dead. Is it strange, then, if I had forgotten André's horrible promise?

There was no portrait of my cousin at Puy Verdun. It was the age of boudoir art, and a miniature set in the lid of a gold bonbonnière,[4] or hidden artfully in a massive bracelet, was more fashionable than a clumsy life-size image, fit only to hang on the gloomy walls of a provincial château rarely visited by its owner. My cousin's fair face had adorned more than one bonbonnière, and had been concealed in more than one bracelet; but it was not among the faces that looked down from the pannelled walls of Puy Verdun.

In the library I found a picture which awoke painful associations. It was the portrait of a de Brissac, who had flourished in the time of Francis the First,[5] and it was from this picture that my cousin André had copied the quaint hunting dress he wore at the Regent's ball. The library was a room in which I spent a good deal of my life; and I ordered a curtain to be hung before this picture.

We had been married three months, when Eveline one day asked: "Who is the lord of the château nearest to this?"

I looked at her in astonishment.

"My dearest," I answered, "do you not know that there is no other château within forty miles of Puy Verdun?"

"Indeed!" she said. "That is strange."

I asked her why the fact seemed strange to her; and after much entreaty I obtained from her the reason of her surprise.

In her walks about the park and woods during the last month she had met a man who, by his dress and bearing, was obviously of noble rank. She had imagined that he occupied some château near at hand, and that his estate adjoined ours. I was at a loss to imagine who this stranger could be; for my estate at Puy Verdun lay in the heart of a desolate region, and unless when some traveller's coach went lumbering and jingling through the village, one had little more chance of encountering a gentlemen than of meeting a demigod.

"Have you seen this man often, Eveline?" I asked.

She answered, in a tone which had a touch of sadness: "I see him every day."

"Where, dearest?"

"Sometimes in the park, sometimes in the wood. You know the little cascade, Hector, where there is some old neglected rock-work that forms a kind of cavern. I have taken a fancy to that spot, and have spent many mornings there reading. Of late I have seen the stranger there every morning."

"He has never dared to address you?"

"Never. I have looked up from my book, and have seen him standing at a little distance, watching me silently. I have continued reading; and when I have raised my eyes again I have found him gone. He must approach and depart with a stealthy tread, for I never hear his footfall. Sometimes I have almost wished that he would speak to me. It is so terrible to see him standing silently there."

"He is some insolent peasant who seeks to frighten you."

My wife shook her head.

"He is no peasant," she answered. "It is not by his dress alone I judge, for that is strange to me. He has an air of nobility which it is impossible to mistake."

"Is he young or old?"

"He is young and handsome."

I was much disturbed by the idea of this stranger's intrusion on my wife's solitude; and I went straight to the village to enquire if any stranger had been seen there. I could hear of no one. I questioned the servants closely, but without result. Then I determined to accompany my wife in her walks, and to judge for myself of the rank of the stranger.

For a week I devoted all my mornings to rustic rambles with Eveline in the park and woods; and in all that week we saw no one but the occasional peasant in *sabos*,[6] or one of our own household returning from a neighbouring farm.

I was a man of studious habits, and those summer rambles disturbed the even current of my life. My wife perceived this, and entreated me to trouble myself no further.

"I will spend my mornings in the pleasaunce, Hector," she said; "the stranger cannot intrude upon me there."

"I began to think the stranger is only a phantasm of your own romantic brain," I replied, smiling at the earnest face lifted to mine. "A châtelaine who is always reading romances may well meet handsome cavaliers in the woodlands. I dare say I have Mademoiselle Scuderi[7] to thank for this noble stranger, and that he is only the great Cyrus in modern costume."

"Ah, that is the point which mystifies me, Hector," she said. "The stranger's costume is not modern. He looks as an old picture might look if it could descend from its frame."

Her words pained me, for they reminded me of that hidden picture in the library, and the quaint hunting costume of orange and purple, which André de Brissac wore at the Regent's ball.

121

After this my wife confined her walks to the pleasaunce; and for many weeks I heard no more of the nameless stranger. I dismissed all thought of him from my mind, for a graver and heavier care had come upon me. My wife's health began to droop. The change in her was so gradual as to be almost imperceptable to those who watched her day by day. It was only when she put on a rich gala dress which she had not worn for months that I saw how wasted the form must be on which the embroidered bodice hung so loosely, and how wan and dim were the eyes which had once been brilliant as the jewels she wore in her hair.

I sent a messenger to Paris to summon one of the court physicians; but I knew that many days must needs elapse before he could arrive at Puy Verdun.

In the interval I watched my wife with unutterable fear.

It was not her health only that had declined. The change was more painful to behold than any physical alteration. The bright and sunny spirit had vanished, and in the place of my joyous young bride I beheld a woman weighed down by rooted melancholy. In vain I sought to fathom the cause of my darling's sadness. She assured me that she had no reason for sorrow or discontent, and that if she seemed sad without a motive, I must forgive her sadness, and consider it as a misfortune rather than a fault.

I told her that the court physician would speedily find some cure for her despondency, which needs must arise from physical causes, since she had no real ground for sorrow. But although she said nothing, I could see she had no hope or belief in the healing powers of medicine.

One day, when I wished to beguile her from that pensive silence in which she was wont to sit an hour at a time, I told her, laughing, that she appeared to have forgotten her mysterious cavalier in the wood, and it seemed also as if he had forgotten her.

To my wonderment, her pale face became a sudden crimson; and from crimson changed to pale again in a breath.

"You have never seen him since you deserted your woodland grotto?" I said.

She turned to me with a heart-rending look.

"Hector," she cried, "I see him every day; and it is that which is killing me."

She burst into a passion of tears when she had said this. I took her in my arms as if she had been a frightened child, and tried to comfort her.

"My darling, this is madness," I said. "You know that no stranger can come to you in the pleasaunce. The moat is ten feet wide and always full of water, and the gates are kept locked day and night by old Massou. The châtelaine of a medieval fortress need fear no intruder in her antique garden."

My wife shook her head sadly.

"I see him every day," she said.

On this I believed that my wife was mad. I shrank from questioning her more closely concerning her myserious visitant. It would be ill, I thought, to give form and substance to the shadow that tormented her, by too close inquiry about its looks and manner, its coming and going.

I took care to assure myself that no stranger to the household could by any possibility penetrate to the pleasaunce. Having done this, I was fain to await the coming of the physician.

He came at last. I revealed to him the conviction which was misery. I told him that I believed my wife to be mad. He saw her – spent an hour alone with her, and then came to me. To my unspeakable relief he assured me of her sanity.

"It is just possible that she may be affected by one delusion," he said; "but she is so reasonable upon all other points that I can scarcely bring myself to believe her the subject of a monomania[8]. I am rather inclined to think that she really sees the person of whom she speaks. She described him to me with a perfect minuteness. The descriptions of scenes or individuals given by patients afflicted with monomania are always more or less disjointed; but your wife spoke to me as clearly and calmly as I am now speaking to you. Are you sure there is no one who can approach her in that garden where she walks?"

"I am quite sure."

"Is there any kinsman of your steward, or hanger-on of your household – a young man with a fair, womanish face, very pale and rendered remarkable by a crimson scar, which looks like the mark of a blow?"

"My God!" I cried, as the light broke in upon me all at once. "And the dress – the strange, old-fashioned dress?"

"The man wears a hunting costume of purple and orange," answered the doctor.

I knew then that André de Brissac had kept his word, and that in the hour when my life was brightest his shadow had come between me and happiness.

I showed my wife the picture in the library, for I would fain assure myself that there was some error in my fancy about my cousin. She shook like a leaf when she beheld it, and clung to me convulsively.

"This is witchcraft Hector," she said. "The dress in that picture is the dress of the man I see in the pleasaunce; but the face is not his."

Then she described to me the face of the stranger; and it was my cousin's face line for line – André de Brissac, whom she had never seen in the flesh. Most vividly of all did she describe the cruel mark upon his face, the trace of a fierce blow from an open hand.

After this I carried my wife away from Puy Verdun. We wandered far – through the southern provinces, and into the very heart of Switzerland. I thought to distance the ghastly phantom, and I fondly hoped that change of scene would bring peace to my wife.

It was not so. Go where we would, the ghost of André de Brissac followed us. To my eyes that fatal shadow never revealed itself. *That* would have been too poor a vengeance. It was my wife's innocent heart which André made the instrument of his revenge. The unholy presence destroyed her life. My constant companionship could not shield her from the horrible intruder. In vain did I watch her; in vain did I strive to comfort her.

"He will not let me be at peace," she said. "He comes between us, Hector. He is standing between us now. I can see his face with the red mark upon it plainer than I see yours."

One fair moonlight night, when we were together in a mountain village in the Tyrol, my wife cast herself at my feet, and told me she was the worst and vilest of women. "I have confessed all to my Director," she said; "from the first I have not hidden my sin from heaven. But I feel that death is near me; and before I die I would fain reveal my sin to you."

"What sin, my sweet one?"

"When first the stranger came to me in the forest, his presence bewildered and distressed me, and I shrank from him as from something strange and terrible. He came again and again; by and by I found myself thinking of him, and watching for his coming. His image haunted me perpetually; I strove in vain to shut his face out of my mind. Then followed an interval in which I did not see him; and, to my shame and anguish, I found that life seemed dreary and desolate without him. After that came the time in which he haunted the pleasaunce; and – oh, Hector, kill me if you will, for I deserve no mercy at your hands! – I grew in those days to count the hours that must elapse before his coming, to take no pleasure save in the sight of that pale face with the red brand upon it. He plucked all old familiar joys out of my heart, and left in it but one weird, unholy pleasure – the delight of his presence. For a year I lived but to see him. And now curse me, Hector; for this is my sin. Whether it comes of the baseness of my heart, or is the work of witchcraft, I know not; but I know that I have striven against this wickedness in vain."

I took my wife to my breast, and forgave her. In sooth, what had I to forgive? Was the fatality that overshadowed us any work of hers? On the next night she died, with her hand in mine; and at the very last she told me, sobbing and affrighted, that *he* was by her side.

Notes

Text: *Ralph the Bailiff and Other Tales*, Maxwell, London, 1867.
1 Phillip, Duke of Orleans (1674–1723), Regent of France, had a (probably well-founded) reputation for debauchery.
2 John Law (1671–1729), founder of the Mississippi Scheme for the development of Louisiana (1717). Law is also the 'Scotch Financier' referred to below: his Banque Générale, the first bank established in France, failed in 1720, causing him to flee from France.

3 See note 2 above.
4 Box made to contain sweetmeats.
5 King of France (1494–1547).
6 Wooden clogs.
7 Madeleine de Scudery (1607–91), author of fashionable and influential French romances, including *Artamène, ou le Grand Cyrus* (10 vols, 1649–53).
8 Excessive mental preoccupation with one idea.

SISTER JOHANNA'S STORY

Amelia Edwards

Amelia Blandford Edwards (1831–92), novelist, short-story writer, journalist, Egyptologist, was born in London. She supported her family after her banker father's financial failure by writing numerous short stories for magazines and periodicals, including *Household Words* and *All the Year Round*. Her ghost stories were admired, and many were collected in *Miss Carew* (1865) and *Monsieur Maurice* (3 vols, 1873). She published eight novels, including *My Brother's Wife* (1855), *Barbara's History*, a 'bigamy' novel (1864), *Half a Million of Money* (1865), *Debenham's Vow* (1870), and *Lord Brackenbury* (1880), each of which apparently took two years to write owing to the meticulous research she put into them. A journey to Egypt in 1873 set in motion a life-long involvement with, and passion for, Egyptian antiquities. Her meticulously researched *A Thousand Miles up the Nile* (1877) described Egyptian civilization and recorded her discovery of many monuments and treasures. She never married, and died a few months after a woman friend with whom she had lived for twenty-eight years. She had become England's most important Egyptologist, and left her Egyptian collection and library to University College, London.

Further reading

Blain *et al.* (1990); Sergeant (1897); Shattock (1993); Sutherland (1988).

Sister Johanna's Story

If you have ever heard of the Grödner Thal,[1] then you will also have heard of the village of St Ulrich, of which I, Johanna Riederer, am a native. And if, as is more likely, you have never heard of either, then still, without knowing it, many of you have, even from your earliest childhood, been familiar with the work by which, for many generations, we have lived and prospered. Your rocking-horse, your Noah's ark, your first doll, came from St Ulrich – for the Grödner Thal is the children's paradise, and supplies the little ones of all Europe with toys. In every house throughout the village – I might almost say in every house throughout the valley – you will find wood-carving, painting, or gilding, perpetually going on; except only in the hay-making harvest-time, when all the world goes up to the hills to mow and reap, and breathe the mountain air. Nor do our carvers carve only grotesque toys. All the crucifixes that you see by the wayside, all the carved screens and tabernacles,[2] all the painted and gilded saints decorating screens and side altars in our Tyrolean churches, are the work of their hands.

After what I have said, you will no doubt have guessed that ours was a family of wood-carvers. My father, who died when my sister and I were quite little children, was a wood-carver. My mother was also a wood-carver, as were her mother and grandmother before her, and Katrine and I were of course brought up by her to the same calling. But, as it was necessary that one should look after the home duties, and as Katrine was always more delicate than myself, I gradually came to work less and less at the business; till at last, what with cooking, washing, mending, making, spinning, gardening, and so forth, I almost left it off altogether. Nor did Katrine work very hard at it either; for, being so delicate, and so pretty, and so much younger than myself, she came, of course, to be a good deal spoiled and to have her own way in everything. Besides, she grew tired, naturally, of cutting nothing but cocks, hens, dogs, cats, cows, and goats; which were all our mother had been taught to make, and, consequently, all she could teach her children.

'If I could carve saints and angels, like Ulrich, next door', Katrine used sometimes to say; 'or if I might invent new beasts out of my own head, or if I might cut caricature nutcrackers of Herr Pürger and Don Wian, I shouldn't care if I worked hard all day; but I hate the cocks and hens, and I hate the dogs and cats, and I hate all the birds and beasts that ever went into the ark – and I only wish they had all been drowned in the Deluge, and not one left for a pattern!'

And then she would fling her tools away, and dance about the room like a wild creature, and mimic the Herr Pürger, who was the great wholesale burgher[3] of all our St Ulrich ware, till even our mother, grave and sober woman as she was, could not help laughing, till the tears ran down her cheeks.

Now the Ulrich who lived next door, of whom our little Katrine used to speak, was the elder of two brothers named Finazzer, and he lived in the house adjoining our own; for at St Ulrich, as in some of the neighbouring villages, one frequently sees two houses built together under one roof, with gardens and orchards surrounded by a common fence. Such a house was the Finazzer's and ours; or, I should rather say, both houses were theirs, for they were our landlords, and we rented our cottage from them year by year.

Ulrich, named after the patron saint of our village, was a tall, brown, stalwart man, very grave, very reserved, very religious, and the finest wood-carver in all the Grödner Thal. No Madonnas, no angels, could compare with his for heavenly grace and tenderness; and as for his Christs, a great foreign critic who came to St Ulrich some ten or twelve years ago said that no modern artist with whose works he was acquainted could treat that subject with anything like the same dignity and pathos. But then, perhaps, no other modern artist went to his work in the same spirit, or threw into it, not only the whole force of a very noble and upright character, but all the loftiest aspirations of a profoundly religious nature.

His younger brother, Alois, was a painter – fair-haired, light-hearted, pleasure-loving; as unlike Ulrich, both in appearance and disposition, as it is possible to conceive. At the time of which I am telling you, he was a student in Venice and had already been three years away from home. I used to dream dreams, and weave foolish romances, about Alois and my little Katrine, picturing to myself how he would some day come home, in the flush, perhaps, of his first success, and finding her so beautiful and a woman grown, fall in love with her at first sight, and she with him; and the thought of this possibility became at last such a happy certainty in my mind, that when things began to work round in quite the other way, I could not bring myself to believe it. Yet so it was, and, much as I loved my darling, and quick-sighted as I had always been in everything that could possibly concern her, there was not a gossip in St Ulrich who did not see what was coming before I even suspected it.

When, therefore, my little Katrine came to me one evening in the orchard and told me, half laughing, half crying, that Ulrich Finazzer had that day asked her to be his wife, I was utterly taken by surprise.

'I never dreamed that he would think of me, dear', she said, with her head upon my bosom. 'He is so much too good and too clever for such a foolish birdie as poor little Katrine'.

'But – but my birdie loves him?' I said, kissing her bright hair.

She half lifted her head, half laughed through her tears, and said with some hesitation:

'Oh, yes, I love him. I – I think I love him – and then I am quite sure he loves me, and that is more than enough'.

'But, Katrine –'

She kissed me, to stop the words upon my lips.

'But you know quite well dear, that I could never love any lover half as much as I love you; and he knows it, too, for I told him so just now, and now please don't look so grave, for I want to be very happy tonight, and I can't bear it'.

And I also wanted her to be very happy, so I said all the loving things I could think of, and when we went into supper we found Ulrich Finazzer waiting for us.

'Dear Johanna', he said, taking me by both hands, 'you are to be my sister now'.

And then he kissed me on the forehead. The words were few; but he had never spoken to me or looked at me so kindly before, and somehow my heart seemed to come into my throat, and I could not answer a word.

It was now the early summer time, and they were to be married in the autumn. Ulrich, meanwhile, had his hands full, as usual, and there was, besides, one important task which he wanted to complete before his wedding. This task was a Christ, larger than life, which he designed as a gift to our parish church, then undergoing complete restoration. The committee of management had invited him in the first instance to undertake the work as an order, but Ulrich would not accept a price for it. He preferred to give it as a free-will offering, and he meant it to be the best piece of wood-sculpture that had ever left his hand. He had made innumerable designs for it both in clay and on paper, and separate studies from life for the limbs, hands, and feet. In short, it was to be no piece of mere conventional Grödner Thal work, but a work of art in the true sense of the word. In the meantime he allowed no one to see the figure in progress – not even Katrine – but worked upon it with closed doors, and kept it covered with a linen cloth whenever his workshop was open.

So the Summer time wore on, and the roses bloomed abundantly in our little garden, and the corn yellowed slowly on the hill-sides, and the wild white strawberry blossoms turned to tiny strawberries, ruby-red, on every mossy bank among the fir-forests of the Seisser Alp. And still Ulrich laboured on his great work, and sculptured many a gracious saint besides; and still the one object of his earthly worship was Katrine.

Whether it was that, being so grave himself, and she so gay, he loved her the better for the contrast, I cannot tell; but his affection for her seemed to deepen daily. I watched it as one might watch the growth of some rare flower, and I wondered sometimes if she prized it as she ought. Yet I scarcely know how, child that she was, she should ever have risen to the heights or sounded the depths of such a nature as his. That she could not appreciate him, however, would have mattered little, if she had loved him more. There was the pity of it. She had accepted him, as many a very young girl accepts her first lover, simply because he was her first. She was proud of his genius – proud of his preference – proud of the house, and the lands, and the worldly goods that were soon going to be hers; but for that greater wealth of love, she held it all too lightly.

Seeing this day after day, with the knowledge that nothing I could say would make things better, I fell, without being conscious of it, into a sad and silent way that arose solely out of my deep love for them both, and had no root of selfishness in it, as my own heart told me then, and tells me to this day.

In the midst of this time, so full of happiness for Ulrich, so full of anxiety for me, Alois Finazzer came home suddenly. We had been expecting him in a vague way ever since the Spring, but the surprise when he walked in unannounced was as great as if we had not expected him at all.

He kissed us all on both cheeks, and sat down as if he had not been away for a day.

'What a rich fellow I am!' he said, joyously. 'I left only a grave elder brother when I went to Venice, and I come back to find two dear little sisters to welcome me home again.'

And then he told us that he had just taken the gold medal at the Academy, that he had sold his prize picture for two hundred florins, and that he had a pocketful of presents for us all – a necklace for Katrine, a spectacle-case for our mother, and a housewife[4] for myself. When he put the necklace round my darling's neck he kissed her again, and praised her eyes, and said he should one day put his pretty little sister into one of his pictures.

He was greatly changed. He went away a curly-headed lad of eighteen; he came back a man, bearded and self-confident.

Three years, at certain turning-points on the road of life, work with us more powerfully, whether for better or worse, than would ten years at any other period. I thought I liked Alois Finazzer better when he was three years younger.

Not so Katrine, however – not so our mother – not so the St Ulrich folk, all of whom were loud in his praise. Handsome, successful, gay, generous, he treated the men, laughed with the girls, and carried all before him.

As for Ulrich, he put his work aside, and cleared his brow, and made holiday for two whole days, going round with his brother from house to house, and telling every one how Alois had taken the great gold medal in Venice. Proud and happy as he was, however, he was prouder and happier still when, some three or four days later, at a meeting of the Church Committee of management, the Commune formally invited Alois to paint an altar-piece for the altar of San Marco at the price of three hundred florins.

That evening Ulrich invited us to supper, and we drank Alois's health in a bottle of good Barbera wine. He was to stay at home now, instead of going back to Venice, and he was to have a large room at the back of Ulrich's workshop for a studio.

'I'll bring your patron saint into my picture if you will sit for her portrait, Katrine', said Alois, laughingly.

And Katrine blushed and said 'Yes'; and Ulrich was delighted; and Alois pulled out his pocket-book, and began sketching her on the spot.

'Only you must try to think of serious things, and not to laugh when you are sitting for a saint, my little Mädchen',[5] said Ulrich, tenderly; whereupon Katrine blushed still more deeply, and Alois, without looking up from his drawing, promised they would both be as grave as judges whenever the sittings were going on.

And now there began for me a period of such misery that even at this distance of time I can scarcely bear to speak or think of it. There, day after day, was Alois painting in his new studio, and Katrine sitting to him for Santa Catarina, while Ulrich, unselfish, faithful, trustful, worked on in the next room, absorbed in his art, and not only unconscious of treachery, but incapable of conceiving it as a possibility. How I tried to watch over her, and would fain have watched over her still more closely if I could, is known to myself alone. My object was to be with her through all those fatal sittings; Alois's object was to make the appointments for hours when my household duties compelled me to remain at home. He soon found out that my eyes were opened. From that moment it was a silent, unacknowledged fight between us, and we were always fighting it.

And now, as his work drew nearer completion, Ulrich seemed every day to live less for the people and things about him, and more for his art. Always somewhat over-silent and reserved, he now seemed scarcely conscious, at times, of even the presence of others. He spoke and moved as if in a dream; went to early mass every morning at four; fasted three days out of seven; and, having wrought himself up to a certain pitch of religious and artistic excitement, lived in a world of his own creation, from which even Katrine was for the time excluded. Things being thus, what could I do but hold my peace? To speak to Ulrich would have been impossible at any time; to speak to my darling (she being, perhaps, wholly unconscious) might be to create the very peril I dreaded; to appeal to Alois, I felt beforehand, would be worse than useless. So I kept my trouble to myself, and prayed that the weeks might pass quickly, and bring their wedding-day.

Now, just about this time of which I am telling (that is, towards the middle of August) came round the great annual fair, or Sagro, as we call it, at Botzen; and to this fete Katrine and I had for some years been in the habit of going – walking to Atzwang the first day by way of Castelruth; sleeping near Atzwang in the house of our aunt, Maria Bernhard, whose husband kept the Gasthaus called the Schwarzen Alder; taking the railway next morning from Atzwang to Botzen, and there spending the day at the Sagro; and returning in the same order as we came. This year, however, having the dread of Alois before my eyes, and knowing that Ulrich would not leave his work, I set my face against the Botzen expedition, and begged my little sister, since she could not have the protection of her betrothed husband, to give it up. And so I think she would have done at first, but that Alois was resolute to have us go; and at last even Ulrich urged it upon us, saying that he would not have his little Mädchen balked of her fiesta simply because he was too busy to take her himself. Would not Johanna be there to take care of her, Alois to take care of them both? So my protest was silenced, and we went.

It is a long day's walk from St Ulrich to Atzwang, and we did not reach my aunt's house till nearly supper-time; so that it was quite late before we went up to our room. And now my darling, after being in wild spirits all day, became suddenly silent, and instead of going to bed, stayed by the window, looking at the moon.

'What is my birdie thinking of?' I said, putting my arm about her waist.

'I am thinking', she said, softly, 'how the moon is shining now at St Ulrich on our mother's bedroom window, and on our father's grave!'

And with this she laid her head down upon my shoulder, and cried as if her heart would break.

I have reproached myself since for letting that moment pass as I did. I believe I might have had her confidence if I had tried, and then what a world of sorrow might have been averted from us all!

We reached Botzen next morning in time for the six o'clock mass; went to high mass again at nine, and strolled among the booths between the services. Here Alois, as usual, was very free with his money, buying ribbons and trinkets for Katrine, and behaving in every way as if he, and not Ulrich, were her acknowledged lover. At eleven, having met some of our St Ulrich neighbours, we made a party and dined all together at a Gasthaus[6] in the Silbergasse; and after dinner the young men proposed to take us to see an exhibition of rope-dancers and tumblers. Now I knew that Ulrich would not approve of this, and I entreated my darling for his sake, if not for mine, to stay away. But she would not listen to me.

'Ulrich, Ulrich!', she repeated, pettishly. 'Don't tease me about Ulrich; I am tired of his very name!'

The next moment she had taken Alois's arm, and we were in the midst of the crowd.

Finding she would go, I of course went also, though sorely against my inclination; and one of our St Ulrich friends gave me his arm, and got me through. The crowd, however, was so great that I lost sight somehow of Alois and Katrine, and found myself landed presently inside the booth and sitting on a front seat next to the orchestra, alone with the St Ulrich people. We kept seats for them as long as we could, and stood upon the bench to look for them, till at last the curtain rose, and we had to sit down without them.

I saw nothing of the performance. To this day I have no idea how long it lasted, or what it consisted of. I remember nothing but the anxiety with which I kept looking towards the door, and the deadly sinking at my heart as the minutes dragged by. To go in search of them was impossible, for the entrance was choked, and there was no standing-room in any part of the booth, so that even when the curtain fell we were fully another ten minutes getting out.

You have guessed it, perhaps, before I tell you. They were not in the market-place; they were not at the Gasthaus; they were not in the Cathedral.

'The tall young man in a grey and green coat, and the pretty girl with a white rose in her hair?' said a bystander. 'Tush, my dear, don't be uneasy. They are gone home; I saw them running towards the station more than half an hour ago'.

So we flew to the station, and there one of the porters, who was an Atzwang man and knew us both, confirmed the dreadful truth. They were gone indeed, but they were not gone home. Just in time to catch the Express, they had taken their tickets through to Venice, and were at this moment speeding southwards.

How I got home – not stopping at all at Atzwang, but going straight away on foot in the broiling afternoon sun – never resting till I reached Castelruth, a little after dusk – lying down outside my bed and sobbing all the night – getting up at the first glimmer of dawn and going on before the sun was up – how I did all this, faint for want of food, yet unable to eat; weary for want of rest yet unable to sleep – I know not. But I did it, and was home again at St Ulrich, kneeling beside our mother's chair, and comforting her as best I could, before seven.

'How is Ulrich to be told?'

It was her first question. It was the question I had been asking myself all the way home. I knew well, however, that I must be the one to break it to him. It was a terrible task, and I put it from me as long as possible.

When at last I did go, it was past midday. The workshop door stood open – the Christ, just showing a vague outline through the folds, was covered with a sheet, and standing up against the wall. Ulrich was working on the drapery of a St Francis, the splinters from which were flying off rapidly in every direction.

Seeing me on the threshold, he looked up and smiled.

'So soon back, leibe[7] Johanna?' he said. 'We did not expect you till evening'.

Then, finding I made no answer, he paused in his work, and said, quickly: –

'What is the matter? Is she ill?'

I shook my head.

'No', I said, 'she is not ill'.

'Where is she, then?'

'She is not ill', I said again, 'but she is not here'.

And then I told him.

He heard me out in dead silence, never moving so much as a finger, only growing whiter as I went on. Then, when I had done, he went over to the window, and remained standing with his back toward me for some minutes.

'And you?' he said, presently, still without turning his head. 'And you – through all these weeks – you never saw or suspected anything?'

'I feared – I was not sure –'

He turned to me with a terrible pale anger in his face.

'You feared – you were not sure!' he said, slowly. 'That is to say, you saw it going on, and let it go on, and would not put out your hand to save us all! False! false! false! – all false together – false love, false brother, false friend!'

'You are not just to me, Ulrich', I said; for to be called false by him was more than I could bear.

'Am I not just? Then I pray that God will be more just to you, and to them, than I can ever be; and that his justice may be the justice of vengeance – swift, and terrible, and without mercy'.

And saying this he laid his hand on the veiled Christ, and cursed us all three with a terrible, passionate curse, like the curse of a prophet of old.

For one moment my heart stood still and I felt as if there was nothing left for me but to die – but it was only for that one moment; for I knew, even before he had done speaking, that no words of his could harm either my poor little erring Katrine or myself. And then, having said so as gently as I could, I formally forgave him in her name and mine, and went away.

That night Ulrich Finazzer shut up his house and disappeared, no one knew whither. When I questioned the old woman who lived with him as a servant, she said he had paid and dismissed her a little before dusk; that she then thought he was looking very ill, and that she had observed how, instead of being as usual hard at it all day in the workshop, he had fetched his gun out of the kitchen about two o'clock, and carried it up to his bedroom, where, she believed, he had spent nearly all the afternoon cleaning it. This was all she had to tell; but it was more than enough to add to the burden of my terrors.

Oh the weary, weary time that followed – the long, sad, solitary days – the days that became weeks – the weeks that became months – the Autumn that chilled and paled as it wore on towards Winter – the changing wood – the withering leaves – the snow that whitened daily on the great peaks round about! Thus September and October passed away, and the last of the harvest was gathered in, and November came with bitter winds and rain; and save for a few hurried lines from Katrine, posted in Perugia, I knew nothing of the fate of all whom I had loved and lost.

'We were married', she wrote, 'in Venice, and Alois talks of spending the winter in Rome. I should be perfectly happy if I knew that you and Ulrich had forgiven us'.

This was all. She gave me no address; but I wrote to the Poste Restante, Perugia, and again to the Poste Restante, Rome; both of which letters, I presume, lay unclaimed till destroyed by the authorities, for she never replied to either.

And now the Winter came on in earnest, as Winter always comes in our high valleys, and Christmas-time drew round again; and on the eve of St Thomas, Ulrich Finazzer returned to his house as suddenly and silently as he had left it.

Next door neighbours as we were, we should not have known of his return but for the trampled snow upon the path, and the smoke going up from the workshop chimney. No other sign of life or occupation was to be seen. The shutters remained unopened. The doors, both front and back, remained fast locked. If any neighbour knocked, he was left to knock unanswered. Even the old woman, who used to be his servant, was turned away by a stern voice from within, bidding her begone and leave him at peace.

That he was at work was certain; for we could hear him in the workshop by night as well as by day. But he could work there as in a tomb, for the room was lighted by a window in the roof.

Thus St Thomas's day, and the next day which was the fourth Sunday in Advent, went by; and still he who had ever been so constant at mass showed no sign of coming out amongst us. On Monday our good curé[8] walked down, all through the fresh snow (for there had been a heavy fall in the night), on purpose to ask if we were sure that Ulrich was really in his house; if we had yet seen him; and if we knew what he did for food, being shut in there quite alone. But to these questions we could give no satisfactory reply.

That day when we had dined, I put some bread and meat in a basket and left it at his door; but it lay untouched all through the day and night, and in the morning I fetched it back again, with the food still in it.

This was the fourth day since his return. It was very dreadful – I cannot tell you how dreadful – to know that he was so near, yet never even to see his shadow on the blind. As the day wore on, my suspense became intolerable. Tonight, I told myself, would be Christmas Eve; tomorrow Christmas Day. Was it possible that his heart would not soften if he remembered our happy Christmas of only last year, when he and Katrine were not yet betrothed; how he supped with us, and how we all roasted nuts on the hearth, and sang part-songs after supper?

Then again, it seemed incredible that he should not go to church on Christmas Day.

Thus the day went by, and the evening dusk came on, and the village choir came round singing carols from house to house, and still he made no sign.

Now what with the suspense of knowing him to be so near, and the thought of my little Katrine far away in Rome, and the remembrance of how he – whom I had honoured and admired above all the world my whole life long – had called down curses on us both the very last time that he and I had stood face to face – what with all this, I say, and what with the season and all its associations, I had such a great restlessness and anguish upon me that I sat up trying to read my Bible long after my mother had gone to bed. But my thoughts wandered continually from the text, and at last the restlessness so gained upon me that I could sit still no longer, and so got up and walked about the room.

And now suddenly, while I was pacing to and fro, I heard, or fancied I heard, a voice in the garden calling to me by name. I stopped – I listened – I trembled. My very heart stood still! Then, hearing no more, I opened the window and outer shutters, and instantly there rushed in a torrent of icy cold air and a flood of brilliant moonlight, and there, on the shining snow below, stood Ulrich Finazzer.

Himself, and yet so changed! Worn, haggard, grey.

I saw him, I tell you, as plainly as I see my own hand at this moment. He was standing close, quite close, under the window, with the moonlight full upon him.

'Ulrich!' I said, and my own voice sounded strange to me, somehow, in the dead waste and silence of the night – 'Ulrich, are you coming to tell me we are friends again?'

But instead of answering me he pointed to a mark on his forehead – a small dark mark, that looked at this distance and by this light like a bruise – cried aloud with a strange, wild cry, less like a human voice than a far off echo, 'The brand of Cain! the brand of Cain!'[9] and so flung up his arms with a despairing gesture, and fled away into the night.

The rest of my story may be told in a few words – the fewer the better. Insane with the desire of vengeance, Ulrich Finazzer had tracked the fugitives from place to place, and slain his brother at mid-day in the streets of Rome. He escaped unmolested, and was well nigh over the Austrian border before the authorities began to inquire into the particulars of the murder. He then, as was proved by a comparison of dates, must have come home by way of Mantua, Verona, and Botzen, with no other object, apparently, than to finish the statue that he had designed for an offering to the church. He worked upon it, accordingly, as I have said, for four days and nights incessantly, completed it to the last degree of finish, and then, being in who can tell how terrible a condition of remorse, and horror, and despair, sought to expiate his crime with his blood. They found him shot through the head by his own hand, lying quite dead at the foot of the statue upon which he had been working, probably, up to the last moment; his tools lying close by; the pistol still fast in his clenched hand, and the divine pitying face of the Redeemer whose law he had outraged, bending over him as if in sorrow and forgiveness.

Our mother has now been dead some years; strangers occupy the house in which Ulrich Finazzer came to his dreadful death; and already the double tragedy is almost forgotten. In the sad, faded woman, prematurely grey, who lives with me, ever working silently, steadily, patiently, from morning to night at our hereditary trade, few who had known her would now recognise my beautiful Katrine. Thus from day to day, from year to year, we journey on together, nearing the end.

Did I indeed see Ulrich Finazzer that night of his self-murder? If I did so with my bodily eyes and it was no illusion of the senses, then most surely I saw him not in life, for that dark mark which looked to me in the moonlight like a bruise was the bullet-hole in his brow.

But did I see him? It is a question I ask myself again and again, and have asked myself for years. Ah! who can answer it?

Notes

Text: *Monsieur Maurice, A New Novelette, and Other Tales*, 3 vols, Hurst and Blackett, London, 1873.
1 Valley in the Austrian Tyrol, close to the Italian border.
2 Carved niches or recesses holding statue of a saint.
3 Tradesman.
4 Container for sewing materials.
5 Maiden.
6 Inn.
7 Dear.
8 Priest.
9 Cain, son of Adam, was branded by God on the forehead after he murdered his brother Abel (Genesis 4:1–16).

THE MYSTERY AT NUMBER SEVEN

Ellen Wood

Ellen (Mrs Henry) Wood, née Price (1814–87), novelist, short-story writer, editor. Born in Worcester, the daughter of a glove manufacturer, she suffered from curvature of the spine and spent several years of her childhood bedridden. Despite her precarious health she supported her family after her banker husband's business failure. Her first novel, *Danesbury House* (1860), was written in less than a month and won a £100 prize offered by the Scottish Temperance League. It was followed by over thirty more novels, including her celebrated 'sensation' novel *East Lynne* (1861) and the less-known but equally sensational *Mrs Halliburton's Troubles* (1862), and more than 300 short stories. Most of her work appeared initially in her magazine *Argosy*, which she edited from 1867. Her political and religious conservatism is evident in her fiction. Her plots, including those of many of her admired 'Johnny Ludlow' stories, show a recurring interest in crime and detection: *The Mystery at Number Seven* is typical in this respect, although the somewhat melodramatic denouement recalls her earlier sensation novels.

Further reading

Blain *et al.* (1990); Eliott (1976); Hughes (1980); Mitchell (1984); Sergeant (1897); Shattock (1993).

The Mystery at Number Seven

"LET us go and give her a turn," cried the Squire.[1]

Tod laughed. "What, all of us?" said he.

"To be sure. All of us. Why not? We'll start to-morrow."

"Oh dear!" exclaimed Mrs. Todhetley, dismay in her mild tone. "Children and all?"

"Children and all: and take Hannah to see them," said the Squire. "You don't count, Joe: you will be off elsewhere."

"We could never be ready," said the Mater, looking the image of perplexity. "To-morrow's Friday. Besides, there would be no time to write to Mary."

"*Write to her!*" cried the Squire, turning sharply on his heel as he paced the room in his nankeen morning coat. "And who do you suppose is going to write to her? Why, it would cause her to make all sorts of preparation; put her to no end of trouble. A pretty conjurer you'd make! We will take her by surprise: that's what we will do."

"But, if, when we got there, we should find her rooms are let, sir?" said I, the doubt striking me.

"Then we'll go into others, Johnny. A spell at the seaside will be a change for us."

This conversation, and the Squire's planning-out, arose through a letter we had just received from Mary Blair – poor Blair's widow, if you have not forgotten him, who went to his end through that gazette of Jerry's. After a few ups and downs, trying at this thing for a living, trying at that, Mrs. Blair had now settled in a house at the seaside and opened a day-school. She hoped to get on in it in time, she wrote, especially if she could be so fortunate as to let her drawing-room to visitors. The squire, always impulsive and good-hearted, at once cried out that *we* would go and take it.

"It will be doing her a good turn, you see," he ran on, "and when we leave I daresay she'll find other people to go in. Let's see" – picking up the letter to refer to the address: "No. 6, Seabord Terrace, Montpellier-by-Sea. Whereabouts is Montpellier-by-Sea?"

"Never heard of it in my life," cried Tod. "Don't believe there is such a place."

"Be quiet, Joe. I fancy it lies somewhere towards Saltwater."

Tod flung back his head. "Saltwater! A nice common place that is!"

"Hold your tongue, sir. Johnny, fetch me the railway guide."

Upon looking at the guide, it was found there, "Montpellier-by-Sea," the

143

last station before getting to Saltwater. As to Saltwater, it might be common, as Tod said; for it was crowded by all sorts of people, but it was lively and healthy.

Not on the next day, Friday, for it was impossible to get ready in such a heap of a hurry, but on the following Tuesday we started. Tod had left on the Saturday for Gloucestershire. His own mother's relatives lived there, and they were always inviting him.

"Montpellier-by-Sea?" cried the railway clerk in a doubting tone as we were getting the tickets. "Let's see? Where is that?"

Of course that set the Squire exploding: what right had clerks to pretend to issue tickets unless they knew their business? The clerk in question coolly ran his finger down the railway list he had turned to, and then gave us the tickets.

"It is a station not much frequented, you see," he civilly observed. "Travellers mostly go on to Saltwater."

But for the train being due, and our having to make a rush for the platform, the Squire would have waited to give the young man a piece of his mind. "Saltwater, indeed!" said he, "I wonder the fellow does not issue his edict as to where people shall go and where they sha'n't."

We arrived in due time at our destination. It was written up as large as life on a white board, "Montpellier-by-Sea." A small roadside station, open to the country around; no signs of sea or of houses to be seen; a broad rural district, apparently given over entirely to agriculture. On went the whistling train, leaving the group of us standing by our luggage on the platform. The Square was staring about him doubtfully.

"Can you tell me where Seabord Terrace is?"

"Seabord Terrace?" repeated the station-master. "No, sir, I don't know it. There's no terrace of that name hereabouts. For that matter there are no terraces at all; no houses in fact."

The Squire's face was a picture. He saw that (save a solitary farm homestead or two) the country was bare of dwelling places.

"This is Montpellier-by-Sea?" he questioned at last.

"Sure enough it is, sir. Munpler, it's called down here."

"Then Seabord Terrace must be *somewhere* in it – somewhere about. What a strange thing!"

"Perhaps the gentlefolks want to go to Saltwater?" spoke up one of the two porters employed at the little station. "There's lots of terraces there. Here, Jim!" – calling to his fellow – "come here a minute. He'll know, sir; he comes from Saltwater."

Jim approached, and settled the doubt at once. He knew Seabord Terrace very well indeed: it was at Saltwater; just out at the eastern end of it.

Yes, it was at Saltwater. And there were we, more than two miles off it, on a broiling hot day when walking was impracticable, with all our trunks about us, and no fly to be had, or other means of getting on. The Squire went into one of his passions, and demanded why people living at Saltwater should give their address as Montpellier-by-Sea.

He had hardly patience to listen to the station-master's explanation – who acknowledged that we were not the first travelling party that had been deluded in like manner. Munpler (as he and the rest of the natives persisted in calling it) was an extensive, straggling, rural parish, filled with farm lands; an arm of it extended as far as Saltwater, and the new buildings at that end of Saltwater had rechristened themselves Montpellier-by-Sea, deeming it more aristocratic than the common old name. Had the Squire been able to transport the new buildings, builders and all, he had surely done it on the spot.

Well, we got on to Saltwater in the evening by another train, and to No. 6, Seaboard Terrace. Mary Blair was just delighted.

"If I had but known you were coming, if you had but written to me, I would have explained that it was Saltwater Station you must get out at, not Montpellier," she cried in deprecation.

"But, my dear, why on earth do you give in to a deceit?" stormed the Squire. "Why call your place Montpellier when it's Saltwater?"

"I do what other people do," she sighed; "I was told it was Montpellier when I came here. Generally speaking, I have explained when writing to friends, that it is really Saltwater, in spite of its fine name: I suppose I forgot it when writing to you – I had so much to say. The people really to blame are those who named it so."

"And that's true, and they ought to be shown up," said the Squire.

Seabord Terrace consisted of seven houses, built in front of the sea a little beyond the town. The parlours had bay windows; the drawing-rooms had balconies and verandahs. The two end houses, Nos. 1 and 7, were double houses, large and handsome, each of them being inhabited by a private family; the middle houses were smaller, most of them being let out in lodgings in the season. Mary Blair began talking that first evening as we sat together about the family who lived in the house next door to her, No. 7. Their name was Peahern, she said, and they had been so very, very kind to her since she took her house in March. Mr. Peahern had interested himself for her and got her several pupils; he was much respected at Saltwater. "Ah, he is a good man," she added; "but – "

"I'll call and thank him," interrupted the Squire. "I am proud to shake hands with such a man as that."

"You cannot," she said; "he and his wife are gone abroad. A great misfortune has lately befallen them."

"A great misfortune! what was it?"

I noticed a kind of cloud pass over Mary Blair's face, a hesitation in her manner before she replied. Mrs. Todhetley was sitting by her on the sofa; the Squire was in the arm-chair opposite them, and I at the table, as I had sat at our tea-dinner.

"Mr. Peahern was in business once; a wholesale druggist, I believe; but he

made a good fortune, and retired some years ago," began Mary. "Mrs. Peahern has poor health and is a little lame. She was very kind to me also; very
good and kind indeed. They had one son; no other children; I think he was
studying for the Bar; I am not sure; but he lived in London and came down
here occasionally. My young maid-servant, Susan, got acquainted with their
servants, and she gathered from their gossip that he, Edmund Peahern, a very
handsome young man, was in some way a trouble to his parents. He was
down at Easter, and stayed three weeks; and in May he came down again.
What happened I don't know; I believe there was some scene with his father
the day he arrived; anyway, Mr. Peahern was heard talking angrily to him:
and that night he – he died."

She had dropped her voice to a low whisper. The Squire spoke.

"Died! Was it a natural death?"

"No. A jury decided that he was insane; and he was buried here in the
churchyard. Such a heap of claims and debts came to light, it was said. Mr.
Peahern left his lawyer to pay them all, and went abroad with his poor wife
for change of scene. It has been a great grief to me. I feel so sorry for them."

"Then, is the house shut up?"

"No. Two servants are left in it; the two housemaids. The cook, who had
lived with them five-and-twenty years and was dreadfully affected at the
calamity, went with her mistress. Nice, good-natured young women, are
these two that are left, running in most days to ask if they can do anything
for me."

"It is good to have such neighbours," said the Squire. "And I hope you'll
get on, my dear. How came you at this place at all?"

"It was through Mr. Lockett," she answered: the clergyman who had been
so much with her husband before he died, and who had kept up a correspondence with her. Mr. Lockett's brother was in practice as a doctor at
Saltwater, and they thought she might perhaps do well if she came to it. So
Mary's friends had screwed a point or two[2] to put her into the house, and
gave her besides a ten-pound note to start with.

"I tell you what it is, young Joe: if you run and reve yourself into that scarlet
heat, you sha'n't come here with me again."

"But I like to race with the donkeys," replied young Joe. "I can run a'most
as fast as they, Johnny. I like to see the donkeys."

"Wouldn't it be better to ride a donkey, lad?"

He shook his head. "I have never had a ride but once," he answered: "I've
no sixpences for it. That once Matilda treated me. She brings me on the
sands."

"Who is Matilda?"

"Matilda at No. 7: Mr. Peahern's."

"Well, if you are a good boy, young Joe, and stay by me, you shall have a
ride as soon as the donkeys come back."

They were fine sands. I sat down on a bench with a book; little Joe strained his eyes to look after the donkeys in the distance, cantering off with some young shavers like himself on their backs, their nursemaids walking quickly after them. Poor little Joe! – he had the gentlest, meekest face in the world, with his thoughtful look and nice eyes – waited and watched in silent patience. The sands were crowded with people this afternoon; organs were playing, dancing dolls exhibiting; and vessels with their white sails spread glided smoothly up and down on the sparkling sea.

"And you will really pay the sixpence?" asked the little fellow presently. "They won't let me get on for less."

"Really and truly, Joe. I'll take you for a row in a boat some calm day, if mamma will allow you to go."

Joe looked grave. "I don't *much* like the water, please," said he, timidly. "Alfred Dale went on it in a boat and fell in, and was nearly drowned. He comes to mamma's school."

"Then we'll let the boats alone, Joe. There's Punch! He is going to set himself up yonder: wouldn't you like to run and see him?"

"But I might miss the donkeys," answered Joe.

He stood by me quietly, gazing in the direction taken by the donkeys: evidently they made his primary attraction. The other child, Mary, who was a baby when her father died (poor Baked Pie, as we boys used to call him at Frost's), was in Wales with Mrs. Blair's people. They had taken the child for a few months, until she saw whether she should get along at Saltwater.

But we thought she would get along. Her school was a morning school for little boys of good parentage, all of whom paid liberal terms: and she would be able to let her best rooms for at least six months in the year.

"There's Matilda! Oh, there's Matilda!"

It was quite a loud shout for little Joe. Looking up, I saw him rush to a rather good-looking young woman, neatly dressed in a black-and-white print gown and small shawl of the same, with black ribbons crossed on her straw bonnet. Servants did not dress fine enough to set the Thames on fire in those days. Joe pulled her triumphantly up to me. She was one of the housemaids at No. 7.

"It's Matilda," he said: and the young woman curtsied. "And I am going to have a donkey-ride, Matilda: Mr. Johnny Ludlow's going to give the sixpence for me!"

"I know you by sight, sir," observed Matilda to me. "I have seen you go in and out of No. 6."

She had a pale olive complexion, with magnificent, melancholy dark eyes. Many persons would have called her handsome. I took a sort of liking for the girl – if only for her kindness to poor little fatherless Joe. In manner she was particularly quiet, subdued, and patient.

"You had a sad misfortune at your house not long ago," I observed to her, at a loss for something to say.

147

"Oh sir, don't talk of it, please!" she answered with a sob of the breath. "I seem to have the shivers at times ever since. It was me that found him."

Up cantered the donkeys: and presently away went Joe on the back of one, Matilda attending him. The ride was just over and Joe beginning to enlarge on its delights to me, when another young woman, dressed precisely similar to Matilda, even to the zigzag white running pattern on the print gown, and the black cotton gloves, was seen making her way towards us. She was nice looking also in a different way; fair, with blue eyes, and a laughing, arch face.

"Why, there's Jane Cross!" exclaimed Matilda. "What in the world have you come out for, Jane? Have you left the house safe?"

"As if I should leave it unsafe!" lightly retorted the one they had called Jane Cross. "The back door's locked, and here's the key of the front – showing a huge key. Why shouldn't I go out if you do? – come, Matilda! The house is none so lively a one now, to stop in all alone."

"And that's true enough," was Matilda's quiet answer. "Little master Joe's here: he has been having a donkey-ride."

The two servants, fellow-housemaids, strolled off towards the sea, taking Joe with them. At the edge of the beach they encountered Hannah, who had just come on with our two children, Hugh and Lena. The maids sat down for a gossip, while the children took off their shoes and stockings to dabble in the gently-rising tide.

And that was my introductory acquaintanceship with the servant maids at No. 7. Unfortunately it did not end there.

Twilight was coming on. We had been out and about all day, had dined as usual at one o'clock (not to give unnecessary trouble) and had just finished tea in Mrs. Blair's parlour. It was where we generally took tea, and supper also. The Squire liked to sit in the open bay window and watch the passers-by as long as ever a glimmer of daylight lasted: and he could not see them so well as the drawing-room above. I was at the other corner of the bay window. The Mater and Mary Blair were on their favourite seat, the sofa, at the end of the room, both knitting. In the room at the back, Mary held her morning school.

I sat facing towards the end house, No. 7. And I must here say that during the last two or three weeks I had met the housemaids several times on the sands, and so had become quite at home with each of them. Both appeared to be thoroughly well-conducted, estimable young women; but, of the two, I liked Jane Cross best, she was always so lively and pleasant-mannered. One day, she told me why No. 7 generally called her by her two names – which I had thought rather odd. It appeared that when she entered her place two years before, the other housemaid was named Jane, so they took to call her by her full name, Jane Cross. That housemaid had left in about a twelvemonth, and Matilda had entered in her place. The servants were regarded as equals in the house, not one above the other, as is the case in many places. These details will probably be thought unnecessary and uncalled for, but you will soon see why I mention them. This was Monday. On the morrow we should have been three weeks at Saltwater, and the Squire did not yet talk of leaving. He was enjoying the free-and-easy life, and was as fond as a child of picking up shells on the sands and looking at Punch and the dancing dolls.

Well, we sat this evening in the bay window as usual, I facing No. 7. Thus sitting, I saw Matilda cross the strip of garden with a jug in her hand, and come out of the gate to fetch the beer for supper.

"There goes Jane Cross," cried the Squire, as she passed the window. "Is it not, Johnny?"

"No sir, it's Matilda." But the mistake was a very natural one, for the girls were about the same height and size, and were usually dressed alike, the same mourning having been supplied to both of them.

Ten minutes, or so, had elapsed when Matilda came back: she liked a gossip with the landlady of the Swan. She had her pint jug full of beer, and shut the iron gate of No. 7 after her. Putting my head as far out at the window as it would go, to watch her indoors, for no earthly reason but that I had nothing else to do, I saw her try the front door, and then knock at it. This knock she repeated three times over at intervals, each knock being louder than the last.

"Are you shut out, Matilda?" I called out.

"Yes, sir, it seems like it," she called back again, without turning her head. "Jane Cross must be gone to sleep."

Had she been a footman with a carriage full of ladies in court trains behind him, she could not have given a louder or longer knock than she gave now. There was no bell to the front door at No. 7. But he knock remained unanswered and the door unopened.

"Matilda at No. 7 is locked out," I said, laughing, bringing in my head and speaking to the parlour generally. "She has been to fetch the supper beer and can't get in again."

"The supper beer," repeated Mrs. Blair. "They generally go out, at the back gate to fetch that, Johnny."

"Anyhow, she took the front way to-night. I saw her come out."

Another tremendous knock. The Squire put his good old nose round the window-post; two boys and a lady, passing by, halted a minute to look on. It was getting exciting, and I ran out. She was still at the door, which stood in the middle of the house, between the sitting-rooms on each side.

"So you have got the key of the street, Matilda!"

"I can't make it out," she said: "what Jane Cross can be about, or why the door should be closed at all. I left it on the latch."

"Somebody has slipped in to make love to her. Your friend, the milkman, perhaps."

Evidently Matilda did not like the allusion to the milkman: catching a glimpse of her face by the street gas-lamp, I saw it had turned white. The milkman was supposed to be paying court at No. 7: but to which of the two maids gossip did not decide. Mrs. Blair's Susan, who knew them well, said it was Matilda.

"Why don't you try the back way?" I asked, after more waiting.

"Because I know the outer door is locked, sir. Jane Cross locked it just now, and that's why I came out this front way. I can try it."

She went round to the road that ran by the side of the house, and tried the door in the garden wall. It was fastened, as she had said. Seizing the bell-handle, she gave a loud peal. Another, and another.

"I say, it seems odd, though," I cried, beginning to find it so. "Do you think she can have gone out?"

"I'm sure I don't know, sir. But – no; it's not likely, Master Johnny. I left her laying the cloth for our supper."

"Was she in the house alone?"

"We are always alone, sir; we don't have visitors. Anyway, none have been with us this evening."

I looked at the upper windows of the house. No light was to be seen in any of them, no sign of Jane Cross. The lower windows were hidden from view by the wall – which was high.

"I think she must have dropped asleep, Matilda. Suppose you come in through Mrs. Blair's and get over the wall?"

I ran round to tell the news to our people. Matilda followed me slowly; I thought, reluctantly. Even in the dim twilight, as she stood at our gate in hesitation, I could see how white her face was.

"What are you afraid of?" I asked her, going out again to where she stood.

"I hardly know, Master Johnny. Jane Cross used to have fits. Perhaps she has been frightened into one."

"What should frighten her?"

The girl looked round in a scared manner before replying. Just then I found my jacket sleeve wet. Her trembling hands had shaken some drops of the ale upon it.

"If she – should have seen Mr. Edmund?" the girl brought out in a horri-fied whisper.

"Seen Mr. Edmund! Mr. Edmund who? – Mr. Edmund Peahern? Why! You don't surely mean his ghost?"

Her face was growing whiter. I stared at her in surprise.

"We have always been afraid of seeing something, she and me, since last May: we haven't liked the house at night-time. It has often been quite a scuffle which of us should fetch the beer, so as not to be the one left alone. Many a time I have stood right out at the back door while Jane Cross has gone for it."

I began to think her an idiot. If Jane Cross was another, why perhaps she had scared herself into a fit. All the more reason that somebody should see after her.

"Come along, Matilda, don't be foolish: we'll get over the wall."

It was a calm, still summer evening, nearly dark now. All the lot of us went out to the back garden, I whispering to them what the girl had said to me.

"Poor thing!" said Mrs. Todhetley, who had a kind of fellow-feeling for ghosts. "It has been very lonely for the young women: and if Jane Cross is subject to fits, she may be lying in one."

The wall between the gardens was nothing like as high as the outer one. Susan brought out a chair, and Matilda could have got over easily. But when she reached the top she stuck there.

"I can't go on by myself; I dare not," she said, turning her scared face towards us. "If Mr. Edmund is there – "

"Don't thee be a goose, girl!" interrupted the Squire, in doubt whether to laugh or scold. "Here, I'll go with you. Get on down. Hold the chair tight for me, Johnny."

We hoisted him over without damage. I leaped after him, and Susan, grinning with delight, came after me. She supposed that Jane Cross had slipped out somewhere during Matilda's absence.

The door faced the garden, and the Squire and Susan were the first to enter. There seemed to be no light anywhere, and the Squire went gingerly, picking his way. I turned round to look for Matilda, who had hung back, and found her with her hand on the trellis work of the porch, and the beer shaking over.

"I say, look here, Matilda: you must be a regular goose, as the Squire says, to put yourself into this fright before you know whether there's any cause for it. Susan says she has only stepped out somewhere."

She put up her hand and touched my arm, panting like mad. Her lips were the colour of chalk.

"Only last night that ever was, Mr. Johnny, as we were going up the staircase to bed, we heard a sound in the room as we passed it. It was just like a groan. Ask Jane Cross, else, sir."

"What room?"

"Mr. Edmund's: where he did it. She has heard him to-night, or seen him or something, and has got a fit."

The kitchen was on the right of the passage. Susan, knowing the ways of the house, soon lighted a candle. On a small round table was spread a white cloth, some bread and cheese, and two tumblers. A knife or two had seemingly been flung on it at random.

"Jane Cross! Jane Cross!" shouted the Squire, going forward towards the front hall, Susan following with a candle. It was a good-sized hall; I could see that; with a handsome well-staircase at this end of it.

"Halloa! What's this? Johnny! Susan! – all of you come here. Here's somebody lying here. It must be the poor girl. Goodness bless my heart! Johnny, help me to raise her."

Still and white she was lying, underneath the opening of the staircase.

Upon lifting her head, it fell back in a curious manner. We both backed a little. Susan held the candle nearer. As its light fell on the upturned face, the girl shrieked.

"She has got a fit," cried Matilda.

"God help her!" whispered the Squire. "I fear this is something worse than a fit. We must have a doctor."

Susan thrust the candlestick into my hand and ran out at the back door, saying she'd fetch Mr. Lockett. Back she came in a moment: the garden gate was locked and the key not in it.

"There's the front door, girl," stuttered the Squire in a passion, angry with her for returning, though it was no fault of hers. He was like one off his head, and his nose and cheeks had turned blue.

But there could be no more egress by the front door than the back. It was locked, and the key gone. Who had done these things? what strange mystery was here? Locking the poor girl in the house to kill her!

Matilda, who had lighted another candle, found the key of the back gate lying on the kitchen dresser. Susan caught it up, and flew away. It was a most uncomfortable moment: there lay Jane Cross, pale and motionless, and it seemed that we were helpless to aid her.

"Ask that stupid thing to bring a pillow or a cushion, Johnny. Ghosts, indeed! The idiots that women are!"

"What else has done it? – what else was there to hurt her?" remonstrated Matilda, bringing up the second candle. "She'd not go into a fit for nothing, sir."

And now that more light was present, we began to see other features of the scene. Nearly close to Jane Cross lay a work-basket, overturned: a flat open basket, a foot and a half square. Reels of cotton, scissors, tapes, small bundles of work tied up, and such like things, lay scattered around.

The Squire looked at these, and then at the opening above. "Can she have fallen down the well?" he asked, in a low tone. And Matilda, catching the words, gave a great cry of dismay, and burst into tears.

"A pillow, girl. A pillow, or a cushion."

She went into one of the sitting-rooms and brought out a thick sofa cushion. The Squire, going down on his knees, for he was not good at stooping, told me to slip it under while he raised the head.

A sound of stalking feet, a sudden flash of light from a bull's-eye,[3] and a policeman came upon the scene. The man was quietly passing on his beat when met by Susan. In her excitement she told him what had happened, and sent him in. We knew the man, whose beat lay at this end of Saltwater; a civil man, named Knapp. He knelt down where the Squire had just been kneeling, touching Jane Cross here and there.

"She's dead, sir," he said. "There can be no mistake about that."

"She must have fallen down the well of the staircase, I fear," observed the Squire.

"Well – yes; perhaps so," assented the man in a doubtful tone. "But what of this?"

He flung the great light on the front of poor Jane Cross's dress. A small portion of the gown-body, where it fastened in front, had been torn away; as well as one of the sleeve wristbands.

"It's no fall," said the man. "It is foul play – as I think."

"Goodness bless me!" gasped the Squire. "Some villains must have got in. This comes of that other one's having left the front door on the latch." But I am not sure that any of us, including himself, believed she could be really dead.

Susan returned with speed, and was followed by Mr. Lockett. He was a young man, thirty perhaps, pale and quiet, and much like what I remembered of his brother. Poor Jane Cross was certainly dead, he said: had been dead, he thought, an hour.

But this could scarcely have been – as we knew. It was not, at the very utmost, above twenty-five minutes since Matilda went out to fetch the beer, leaving her alive and well. Mr. Lockett looked again, but thought he was not mistaken. When a young doctor takes up a crotchet,[4] he likes to hold to it.

A nameless sensation of awe fell upon us all. Dead! In that sudden manner! The Squire rubbed up his head like a helpless lunatic; Susan's eyes were round with horror; Matilda had thrown her apron over her face to hide its grief and tears.

Leaving her for the present where she was, we turned to go upstairs. I stooped to pick up the overturned basket, but the policeman sharply told me to let all things stay as they were until he had time to look into them.

The first thing the man did, on reaching the landing above, was to open the room doors one by one, and throw his bull's-eye light into them. They were all right; unoccupied, straight and tidy. On the landing of the upper floor lay one or two articles, which seemed to indicate that some kind of struggle had taken place there. A thimble here, a bodkin there; also the bit that had been torn out of the girl's gown in front and the wristband from the sleeve. The balustrades were very handsome but very low; on this upper landing, dangerously low. These bedrooms were all in order; the one in which the two servants slept, alone showing signs of occupation.

Downstairs went Knapp again, carrying with him the torn-out pieces, to compare them with the gown. It was the print gown I had often seen Jane Cross wear: a black gown with white zigzag lines running down it. Matilda was wearing the fellow to it now. The pieces fitted in exactly.

"The struggle must have taken place upstairs: not here," observed the doctor.

Matilda, questioned and cross-questioned by the policeman, gave as succinct an account of the evening as her distressed state allowed. We stood round the kitchen while she told it.

Neither she nor Jane Cross had gone out at all that day. Monday was rather a busy day with them, for they generally did a bit of washing. After tea, which they took between four and five o'clock, they went up to their bedroom, it being livelier there than in the kitchen, the window looking down the side road. Matilda sat down to write a letter to her brother, who lived at a distance; Jane Cross sat at the window doing a job of sewing. They sat there all the evening, writing, working, and sometimes talking. At dusk, Jane remarked that it was getting Blindman's holiday,[5] and that she should go on downstairs and put the supper. Upon that, Matilda finished her letter quickly, folded and directed it, and followed her down. Jane had not yet laid the cloth, but was then taking it out of the drawer. "You go and fetch the beer, Matilda," she said: and Matilda was glad to do so. "You can't go that way: I have locked the gate," Jane called out, seeing Matilda turning towards the back; accordingly she went out at the front door, leaving it on the latch. Such was her account; and I have given it almost verbatim.

"On the latch," repeated the policeman, taking up the words. "Does that mean that you left it open?"

"I drew it quite to, so that it looked as if it were shut; it was a heavy door, and would keep so," was Matilda's answer. "I did it, not to give Jane the trouble to open it to me. When I got back I found it shut and could not get in."

The policeman mused. "You say it was Jane Cross who locked the back door in the wall?"

"Yes," said Matilda. "She had locked it before I got downstairs. We liked to lock that door early, because it could be opened from the outside – while the front door could not be."

"And she had not put these things on the table when you went out for the beer?" – pointing to the dishes.

"No: she was only then putting the cloth. As I turned round from taking the beer-jug from its hook, the fling she gave the cloth caused the air of it to whiffle in my face like a wind. She had not begun to reach out the dishes."

"How long were you away?"

"I don't know exactly," she answered, with a moan. "Rather longer than usual, because I took my letter to the post before going to the Swan."

"It was about ten minutes," I interposed. "I was at the window next door, and saw Matilda go out and come back."

"Ten minutes!" repeated the policeman. "Quite long enough for some ruffian to come in and fling her over the stairs."

"But who would do it?" asked Matilda, looking up at him with her poor pale face.

"Ah, that's the question; that's what we must find out," said Knapp. "Was the kitchen just as it was when you left it?"

"Yes – except that she had put the bread and cheese on the table. And the glasses, and knives," added the girl, looking round at the said table, which remained as we had found it, "but not the plates."

"Well now, to go to something else: Did she bring her work-basket down-stairs with her from the bedroom when she remarked to you that she would go and put the supper on?"

"No, she did not."

"You are sure of that?"

"Yes. She left the basket on the chair in front of her where it had been standing. She just got up and shook the threads from off her gown, and went on down. When I left the room the basket was there; I saw it. And I think," added the girl, with a great sob, "I think that while putting the supper she must have gone upstairs again to fetch the basket, and must have fallen against the banisters with fright, and overbalanced herself."

"Fright at what?" asked Knapp.

Matilda shivered. Susan whispered to him that they were afraid at night of seeing the ghost of Mr. Edmund Peahern.

The man glanced keenly at Matilda for a minute. "Did you ever see it?" he asked.

"No," she shuddered. "But there are strange noises, and we think it is in the house."

"Well," said Knapp, coughing to hide a comical smile, "ghosts don't tear pieces out of gowns – that ever I heard of. I should say it was something worse than a ghost that has been here to-night. Had this poor girl any sweetheart?"

"No," said Matilda.

"Have you one?"

"No."

"Except Owen the milkman."

A scarlet streak flashed into Matilda's cheeks. I knew Owen: he was Mrs. Blair's milkman also.

"I think Owen must be your sweetheart or hers," went on Knapp. "I've seen him, often enough, talking and laughing with you both when bringing the afternoon's milk round. Ten minutes at a stretch he has stayed in this garden, when he need not have been as many moments."

"There has been no harm: and it's nothing to anybody," said Matilda.

The key of the front door was searched for, high and low; but it could not be found. Whoever locked the door, must have made off with the key. But for that, and for the evidences of the scuffle above and the pieces torn out of the gown, we should have thought Matilda's opinion was correct: that Jane Cross had gone upstairs for her basket, and through some wretched accident had pitched over the balustrades. Matilda could not relinquish the notion.

"It was only a week ago that ever was; a week ago this very day; that Jane Cross nearly fell over there. We were both running upstairs, trying in sport which should get first into our bedroom; and, in jostling one another on the landing, she all but overbalanced herself. I caught hold of her to save her. It's true – if it were the last word I had to speak."

155

Matilda broke down, with a dreadful fit of sobbing. Altogether she struck me as being about as excitable a young woman as one could meet in a summer day's journey.

Nothing more could be made out of it this evening. Jane Cross had met her death, and some evil or other must have led to it. The police took possession of the house for the night: and Matilda, out of compassion, was brought to ours. To describe the Mater's shock and Mary Blair's, when they heard the news, would be beyond me.

All sorts of conjectures arose in the neighbourhood. The most popular belief was that some person must have perceived the front door open, and, whether with a good or an ill intention, entered the house; that he must have stolen upstairs, met Jane Cross on the top landing, and flung her down in a scuffle. That he must then have let himself out at the front door and locked it after him.

Against this theory there were obstacles. From the time of Matilda's leaving the house till her return, certainly not more than ten minutes had elapsed, perhaps not quite as much, and this was a very short space of time for what had been done in it. Moreover the chances were that I, sitting at the next window, should have seen anyone going in or out; though it was not of course certain. I had got up once to ring the bell, and stayed a minute or two away from the window, talking with Mary Blair and the Mater.

Some people thought the assassin (is it too much to call him so?) had been admitted by Jane Cross herself; or he might have been in hiding in the garden before she locked the door. In short, the various opinions would fill a volume.

But suspicion fell chiefly upon one person – and that was Thomas Owen the milkman. Though, perhaps, "suspicion" is too strong a word to give to it – I ought rather to say "doubt." These Owens were originally from Wales, very respectable people. The milk business was their own; and, since the father's death, which happened only a few months before, the son had carried it on in conjunction with his mother. He was a young man of three or four-and-twenty, with a fresh colour and open countenance, rather superior in his manner and education. The carrying out the milk himself was a temporary arrangement, the boy employed for it being ill. That he had often lingered at No. 7, laughing with the two young women, was well known; he had also been seen to accost them in the street. Only the previous day, he and Matilda had stayed talking in the churchyard after morning service when everybody else had left it; and he had walked up nearly as far as Seabord Terrace with Jane Cross in the evening. A notion existed that he had entered the house on the Monday evening, for who else was it likely to have been, cried everybody. Which was, of course logic. At last a rumour arose – arose on the Tuesday – that Owen had been *seen* to leave the house at dusk on the fatal evening; that this could be proved. If so, it looked rather black. I was startled, for I had liked the man.

The next day, Wednesday, the key was found. A gardener who did up the garden of the other end house, No. 1, every Wednesday, was raking the ground underneath some dwarf pines that grew close against the front railing, and raked out a big door-key. About fifteen people came rushing off with it to No. 7.

It was the missing key. It fitted into the door at once, locked and unlocked it. When the villain had made his way from the house after doing the mischief, he must have flung the key over amidst the pines, thinking no doubt it would lie hidden there.

The coroner and jury assembled; but they could not make more of the matter than we had made. Jane Cross had died of the fall down the well staircase, which had broken her neck; and it was pretty evident she had been flung down. Beyond the one chief and fatal injury, she was not harmed in any way; not by so much as a scratch. Matilda, whose surname turned out to be Valentine, having got over the first shock, gave her testimony with subdued composure. She was affected at parts of it, and said she would have saved Jane Cross's life with her own: and no one could doubt that she spoke the truth. She persisted in asserting her opinion that there had been no scuffle, in spite of appearances; but that the girl had been terrified in some way and had accidentally fallen over.

When Matilda was done with, Thomas Owen took her place. He was all in black, having dressed himself to come to the inquest and wearing mourning for his father; and I must say, looking at him now, you'd never have supposed he carried out milk-pails.

Yes, he had known the poor young woman in question, he readily said in answer to questions; had been fond of chaffing with the two girls a bit, but nothing more. Meant nothing by it, nothing serious. Respected both of them; regarded them as perfectly well-conducted young women. – Was either of them his sweetheart? Certainly not. Had not courted either of them. Never thought of either of them as his future wife: should not consider a servant eligible for that position – at least, his mother would not. Of the two, he had liked Jane Cross the best. Did not know anything whatever of the circumstances attending the death; thought it a most deplorable calamity, and was never more shocked in his life than when he heard of it.

"Is there any truth in the report that you were at the house on Monday evening?" asked the coroner.

"There is no truth in it."

"I see him come out o' No. 7: I see him come out o' the side door in the garden wall," burst forth a boy's earnest voice from the back of the room.

"You saw me *not* come out of it," quietly replied Thomas Owen, turning round to see who it was that had spoken. "Oh, it is you, is it, Bob Jackson! Yes, you came running round the corner just as I turned from the door."

"You *were* there then?" cried the coroner.

"No, sir. At the door, yes; that's true enough; but I was not inside it. What happened was this: on Monday I had some business at a farm-house near

Munpler, and set out to walk over there early in the evening. In passing down the side road by No. 7, I saw the two maids at the top window. One of them – I think it was Jane Cross – called out to ask me in a joking kind of way whether I was about to pay them a visit; I answered, not then, but I would as I came back if they liked. Accordingly, in returning, I rang the bell. It was not answered, and I rang again with a like result. Upon that, I went straight home to my milk books, and did not stir out again, as my mother can prove. That is the truth, sir, on my oath; and all the truth."

"What time was this?"

"I am not quite sure. It was getting dusk."

"Did you see anything of the young women this second time?"

"Not anything."

"Or hear anything? – Any noise?"

"None whatever. I supposed that they would not come to the door to me because it was late: I thought nothing else. I declare, sir, that this is all I know of the matter."

There was a pause when he concluded. Knapp, the policeman, and another one standing by his side, peered at Owen from under their eyebrows, as if they did not put implicit faith in his words: and the coroner recalled Matilda Valentine.

She readily confirmed the statement of his having passed along the side road, and Jane Cross's joking question to him. But she denied having heard him ring on his return, and said the door-bell had not rung at all that night. Which would seem to prove that Owen must have rung during the time she had gone out for the beer.

So, you perceive, the inquest brought forth no more available light, and had to confess itself baffled.

"A fine termination this is to our pleasure," cried the Squire, gloomily. "I don't like mysteries, Johnny. And of all the mysteries I have come across in my life, the greatest mystery is this at No. 7."

But mysteries, like murder, will "out" in time.

It was a grand sea to-day: one of the grandest that we had seen at Saltwater. The waves were dancing and sparkling like silver; the blue of the sky was deeper than a painter's ultramarine. But to us, looking on it from Mrs. Blair's house in Seabord Terrace, its brightness and beauty were dimmed.

"For you see, Johnny," observed the Squire to me, his face and tone alike gloomy – outward things take their impress from the mind – "with that dreadful affair at the next door jaundicing one's thoughts, the sea might as well be grey as blue, and the sky lowering with thunder-clouds. I repeat that I don't like mysteries: they act on me like a fit of indigestion."

More than a week had elapsed since the Monday evening when it took place, and poor Jane Cross now lay buried in the windy graveyard.

Matilda was to be pitied. The two young women had cared a good deal for one another, and the shock to Matilda was serious. The girl, now staying in our house, had worn a half-dazed look since, and avoided No. 7 as though it had the plague. Superstition in regard to the house had already been rife in both the servants' minds, in consequence of the unhappy death in it of their master's son, Edmund Peahern, some weeks back: and if Matilda had been afraid of seeing one ghost before (as she had been) she would now undoubtedly expect to see two of them.

On this same morning, as I stood with the Squire looking at the sea from the drawing-room window of No. 6, Matilda came in. Her large dark eyes had lost their former sparkle, her clear olive skin its freshness. She asked leave to speak to Mrs. Todhetley: and the Mater – who sat at the table adding up some bills, for our sojourn at Saltwater was drawing towards its close – told her, in a kind tone, to speak on.

"I am making bold to ask you, ma'am, whether you could help me to find a place in London," began Matilda, standing between the door and the table in her black dress. "I know, ma'am, you don't live in London, but a long way off it; Mrs. Blair has told me so, Master Johnny Ludlow also: but I thought perhaps you knew people there, and might be able to hear of something."

The Mater looked at Matilda without answering, and then round at us. Rather strange it was, a coincidence in a small way, that we had had a letter from London from Miss Deveen that morning, which had concluded with these lines of postscript: "Do you chance to know of any nice, capable young woman in want of a situation? One of my housemaids is going to leave."

Naturally this occurred to the Mater's mind when Matilda spoke. "What kind of situation do you wish for?" she asked.

"As housemaid, ma'am, or parlour-maid. I can do my duty well in either."

"But now, my girl," spoke up the Squire, turning from the window, "why need you leave, Saltwater? You'd never like London after it. This is a clear, fresh, health-giving place, with beautiful sands and music on them all day; London is nothing but smoke and fogs."

Matilda shook her head. "I could not stay here, sir."

"Nonsense, girl. Of course what has happened *has* happened, and it's very distressing; and you, of all people, must feel it so; but you will forget it in time. If you don't care to go back to No. 7 before Mr. and Mrs. Peahern come home – "

"I can never go back to No. 7, sir," she interrupted, a vehemence that seemed born of terror in her subdued voice. "Never in this world. I would rather die."

"Stuff and nonsense!" said the Squire, impatiently. "There's nothing the matter with No. 7. What has happened in it won't happen again."

"It is an unlucky house, sir; a haunted house," she contended with suppressed emotion. "And it's true that I would rather die outright than go to live in it; for the terror of being there would slowly kill me. And so, ma'am," she added quickly to Mrs. Todhetley, evidently wishing to escape the subject, "I should like to go away altogether from Saltwater; and if you can help me to hear of a place in London, I shall be very grateful."

"I will consider of it, Matilda," was the answer. And when the girl had left the room the Mater asked us what we thought about recommending her to Miss Deveen. We saw no reason against it – not but what the Squire put the girl down as an idiot on the subject of haunted houses – and Miss Deveen was written to.

The upshot was, that on the next Saturday, Matilda bade farewell to Saltwater and departed for Miss Deveen's, the Squire sarcastically assuring her that *that* house had no ghosts in it. We should be leaving, ourselves, the following Tuesday.

But, before that day came, it chanced that I saw Owen, the milkman. It was on the Sunday afternoon. I had taken little Joe Blair for a walk across the fields as far as Munpler (their Montpellier-by-Sea, you know), and in return-ing met Thomas Owen. He wore his black Sunday clothes, and looked a downright fine fellow, as usual. There was something about the man I could not help liking, in spite of the doubt attaching to him.

"So Matilda Valentine is gone, sir," he observed, after we had exchanged a few sentences.

"Yes, she went yesterday," I answered, putting my back against the field fence, while young Joe went careering about in chase of a yellow butterfly. "And for my part, I don't wonder at the girl's not liking to stay at Saltwater. At least, in Seabord Terrace."

"I was told this morning that Mr. and Mrs. Peahern were on their road home," he continued.

"Most likely they are. They'd naturally want to look into the affair for themselves."

"And I hope with all my heart they will be able to get some light out of it," returned Owen, warmly. "I mean to do *my* best to bring out the mystery sir; and I sha'n't rest till it's done."

His words were fair, his tone was genuine. If it was indeed himself who had been the chief actor in the tragedy, he carried it off well. I hardly knew what to think. It is true I had taken a bit of a fancy to the man, according to my customary propensity to take a fancy, or the contrary; but I did not know much of him, and not anything of his antecedents. As he spoke to me now, his tone was marked, rather peculiar. It gave me a notion that he wanted to say more.

"Have you any idea that you will be able to trace it out?"

"For my own sake I should like to get the matter cleared up," he added, not directly answering my question. "People are beginning to turn the cold shoulder my way: one woman asked me to my face yesterday whether I did it. No, I told her, I did not do it, but I'd try and find out who did."

"You are sure you heard and saw nothing suspicious that night when you rang at the bell and could not get in, Owen?"

"Not then, sir; no. I saw no light in the house and heard no noise."

"You have not any clue to go by, then?"

"Not much, sir, yet. But I can't help thinking somebody else has."

"Who is that?"

"Matilda."

"Matilda!" I repeated, in amazement. "Surely you can't suspect that she — that she was a party to any deed so cruel and wicked!"

"No, no, sir, I don't mean that; the young women were too good friends to harm one another: and whatever took place, took place while Matilda was out of the house. But I can't help fancying that she knows, or suspects, more of the matter than she will say. In short, that she is screening some one."

To me it seemed most unlikely. "Why do you judge so, Owen?"

"By her manner, sir. Not by much else. But I'll tell you something that I saw. On the previous Wednesday when I left the afternoon milk at that tall house just beyond Seabord Terrace, the family lodging there told me to call in the evening for the account, as they were leaving the next day. Accordingly I went; and was kept waiting so long before they paid me that it was all but night when I came out. Just as I was passing the back door at No. 7, it was suddenly drawn open from the inside, and a man stood in the opening, whispering with one of the girls. She was crying, for I heard her sobs, and he kissed her and came out, and the door was hastily shut. He was an ill-looking man; so far at least as his clothes went; very shabby. His face I did not see, for he pulled his slouching round hat well over his brows as he walked away rapidly, and the black beard he wore covered his mouth and chin."

"Which of the maids was it?"

"I don't know, sir. The next day I chaffed them a bit about it, but they both declared that nobody had been there but the watchmaker, Mr. Renninson, who goes every Wednesday to wind up the clocks, and that it must have been him that I saw, for he was late that evening. I said no more; it was no business of mine; but the man I saw go out was just about as much like Renninson as he was like me."

"And do you fancy — "

"Please wait a minute, sir," he interrupted, "I haven't finished. Last Sunday evening, upon getting home after service, I found I had left my prayer-book in church. Not wishing to lose it, for it was the one my father always used, I went back for it. However, the church was shut, so I could not get in. It was a fine evening, and I took a stroll round the churchyard. In the corner of it, near to Mr. Edmund Peahern's tomb, they had buried poor Jane Cross but two days before — you know the spot, sir. Well, on the flat square of earth that covers her grave, stood Matilda Valentine, the greatest picture of distress you can imagine, tears streaming down her cheeks. She dried her eyes when she saw me, and we came away together. Naturally I fell to talking of Jane

Cross and the death. 'I shall do as much as lies in my power to bring it to light,' I said to Matilda; 'or people may go on doubting me to the end. And I think the first step must be to find out who the man was that called in upon you the previous Wednesday night.' Well, sir, with that, instead of making any answering remark as a Christian would, or a rational being, let us say, Matilda gives a smothered, sobbing shriek, and darts away out of the church-yard. I couldn't make her out; and all in a minute a conviction flashed over me, though I hardly know why, that she knew who was the author of the calamity, and was screening him; or any rate that she had her suspicions, if she did not actually know. And I think so still, sir."

I shook my head, not seeing grounds to agree with Owen. He resumed:

"The next morning, between nine and ten, I was in the shop, putting a pint of cream which had been ordered into a can, when to my surprise Matilda walked in, cool and calm. She said she had come to tell me that the man I had seen leave the house was her brother. He had fallen into trouble through having become security for a fellow workman, had had all his things sold up, including his tools, and had walked every step of the way – thirty miles – to ask her if she could help him. She did help him as far as she could, giving him what little money she had by her, and Jane Cross had added ten shillings to it. He had got in only at dusk, she said, had taken some supper with them, and left again afterwards, and that she was letting him out at the gate when I must have been passing it. She did not see me, for her eyes were dim with crying: her heart felt like to break in saying farewell. That was the truth, she declared, and that her brother had had no more to do with Jane's death than she or I had; he was away again out of Saltwater the same night he came into it."

"Well? Did you not believe her?"

"No, sir," answered Owen, boldly. "I did not. If this was true, why should she have gone off into that smothered shriek in the churchyard when I men-tioned him, and rush away in a fright?"

I could not tell. Owen's words set me thinking.

"I did not know which of the two girls it was who let the man out that Wednesday night, for I did not clearly see; but, sir, the impression on my mind at the moment was, that it was Jane Cross. Jane Cross, and not Matilda. If so, why does she tell me this tale about her brother, and say it was herself?"

"And if it was Jane Cross?"

Owen shook his head. "All sorts of notions occur to me, sir. Sometimes I fancy that the man might have been Jane's sweetheart, that he might have been there again on the Monday night, and done the mischief in a quarrel; and that Matilda is holding her tongue because it is her brother. Let the truth be what it will, Matilda's manner convinces me of one thing: that there's something she is concealing, and that it is half frightening her wits out of her. – You are going to leave Saltwater, I hear, sir," added the young man in a different tone, "and I am glad to have the opportunity of saying this, for I should not like you to carry away any doubt of me. I'll bring the matter to light if I can."

Touching his hat, he walked onwards, leaving my thoughts all in a whirligig.

Was Owen right in drawing these conclusions? – or was he purposely giving a wrong colouring to facts, and seeking craftily to throw suspicion off himself? It was a nice question, one I could make neither top nor tail of. But, looking back to the fatal evening, weighing this point, sifting that, I began to see that Matilda showed more anxiety, more terror, than she need have shown *before* she knew that any ill had happened. Had she a prevision, as she stood at the door with the jug of ale in her hand, that some evil might have chanced? Did she leave some individual in the house with Jane Cross when she went to the Swan to get the ale? – and was it her brother? Did she leave OWEN in the house, and was she screening him?

"Why, Matilda! Is it you?"

It was fourteen months later, and autumn weather, and I had just arrived in London at Miss Deveen's. My question to Matilda, who came into my dressing-room with some warm water to wash off the travelling dust, was not made in surprise at seeing *her*, for I supposed she was still in service at Miss Deveen's, but at seeing the change in her. Instead of the healthy and, so to say, handsome girl known at Saltwater, I saw a worn, weary, anxious-looking shadow, with a feverish fire in her wild dark eyes.

"Have you been ill, Matilda?"

"No, sir, not at all. I am quite well."

"You have grown very thin."

"It's the London air, sir. I think everybody must get thin that lives in it."

Very civilly and respectfully, but yet with an unmistakable air of reticence, spoke she. Somehow the girl was changed and greatly changed. Perhaps she had been grieving after Jane Cross? Perhaps the secret of what had happened (if in truth Matilda knew it) lay upon her with too heavy a weight?

"Do you find Matilda a good servant?" I asked of Miss Deveen, later, she and I being alone together.

"A very good servant, Johnny. But she is going to leave me."

"Is she? Why?"

Miss Deveen only nodded, in answer to the first query, passing over the last. I supposed she did not wish to say.

"I think her so much altered."

"In what way, Johnny?"

"In looks: looks and manner. She is just a shadow. One might say she had passed through a six months' fever. And what a curious light there is in her eyes!"

"She has always impressed me with the idea of having some great care upon her. None can mistake that she is a sorrowful woman. I hear that the other servants accuse her of having been 'crossed in love,'" added Miss Deveen, with a smile.

"She is thinner even than Miss Cattledon."

"And that, I daresay you think, need not be, Johnny! Miss Cattledon, by the way, is rather hard upon Matilda just now: calls her a 'demon.'"

"A demon! Why does she?"

"Well, I'll tell you. Though it is but a little domestic matter, one that perhaps you will hardly care to hear. You must know (to begin with) that Matilda has never made herself sociable with the other servants here; in return they have become somewhat prejudiced against her, and have been ready to play her tricks, tease her, and what not. But you must understand, Johnny, that I knew nothing of the state of affairs below; such matters rarely reach me. My cook, Hall, was especially at war with Matilda: in fact, I believe there was no love lost between the two. The girl's melancholy – for at times she does seem very melancholy – was openly put down by the rest to the assumption that she must have had some love affair in which the swain had played her false. They were continually plaguing her on this score, and it no doubt irritated Matilda; but she rarely retorted, preferring rather to leave them and take refuge in her room."

"Why could they not let her alone?"

"People can't let one another alone, as I believe, Johnny. If they did, the world would be pleasanter to live in."

"And I suppose Matilda got tired at last, and gave warning?"

"No. Some two or three weeks back it appears that, by some means or other, Hall obtained access to a small trunk; one that Matilda keeps her treasures in, and has cautiously kept locked. If I thought Hall had opened this trunk with a key of her own, as Matilda accuses her of doing, I would not keep the woman in my house another day. But she declares to me most earnestly – for I had her before me here to question her – that Matilda, called suddenly out of her chamber, left the trunk open there, and the letter, of which I am about to tell you, lying, also open, by its side. Hall says that she went into the room – it adjoins her own – for something she wanted, and that all she did – and she admits this much – was to pick up the letter, carry it downstairs, read it to the servants, and make fun over it."

"What letter was it?"

"Strictly speaking, it was only part of a letter: one begun but not concluded. It was in Matilda's own hand, apparently written a long while ago, for the ink was pale and faded, and it began 'Dearest Thomas Owen. The – '"

"Thomas Owen!" I exclaimed, starting in my chair. "Why, that is the milkman at Saltwater."

"I'm sure I don't know who he is, Johnny, and I don't suppose it matters. Only a few lines followed, three or four, speaking of some private conversation that she had held with him on coming out of church the day before, and of some reproach that she had then made to him respecting Jane Cross. The words broke suddenly off there, as if the writer had been interrupted. But why Matilda did not complete the letter and send it, and why she should have kept it by her all this while, must be best known to herself."

"Jane Cross was her fellow-servant at Mr. Peahern's. She who was killed by falling down the staircase."

"Yes, poor thing, I remembered the name. But, to go on. In the evening, after the finding of this letter, I and Miss Cattledon were startled by a disturbance in the kitchen. Cries and screams, and loud, passionate words. Miss Cattledon ran down; I stayed at the top of the stairs. She found Hall, Matilda, and one of the others there, Matilda in a perfect storm of fury, attacking Hall like a maniac. She tore handfuls out of her hair, she bit her thumb until her teeth met in it: Hall, though by far the bigger person of the two, and I should have thought the stronger, had no chance against her; she seemed to be as a very reed in her hands, passion enduing Matilda with a strength perfectly unnatural. George, who had been out on an errand, came in at the moment, and by his help the women were parted. Cattledon maintains that Matilda, during the scene, was nothing less than a demon; quite mad. When it was over, the girl fell on the floor utterly exhausted, and lay like a dead thing, every bit of strength, almost of life, gone out of her."

"I never could have believed it of Matilda."

"Nor I, Johnny. I grant that the girl had just cause to be angry. How should we like to have our private places rifled, and their contents exhibited to and mocked at by the world; contents which to us seem sacred? But to have put herself into that wild rage was both unseemly and unaccountable. Her state then, and her state immediately afterwards, made me think – I speak it with all reverence, Johnny – of the poor people in holy writ from whom the evil spirits were cast out."

"Ay. It seems to be just such a case, Miss Deveen."

"Hall's thumb was so much injured that a doctor had to come daily to it for nine or ten days," continued Miss Deveen. "Of course, after this climax, I could not retain Matilda in my service; neither would she have remained in it. She indulged a feeling of the most bitter hatred to the women servants, to Hall especially – she had not much liked them before, as you may readily guess – and she said that nothing would induce her to remain with them, even had I been willing to keep her. So she has obtained a situation with some acquaintances of mine who live in this neighbourhood, and goes to it next week. That is why Matilda leaves me, Johnny."

In my heart I could not help being sorry for her, and said so. She looked so truly, sadly unhappy!

"I am very sorry for her," assented Miss Deveen. "And had I known the others were making her life here uncomfortable, I should have taken means to stop their pastime. Of the actual facts, with regard to the letter, I cannot be at any certainty – I mean in my own mind. Hall is a respectable servant, and I have never had cause to think her untruthful during the three years she has lived with me: and she most positively holds to it that the little trunk was standing open on the table and the letter lying open beside it. Allowing that it was so, she had, of course, no right to touch either trunk or letter, still less to take the letter downstairs and exhibit it to the others, and I don't defend her conduct: but yet it is different from having rifled the lock of the trunk and filched the letter out."

"And Matilda accuses her of doing that?"

"Yes: and, on her side, holds to it just as positively. What Matilda tells me is this: On that day it chanced that Miss Cattledon had paid the women servants their quarter's wages. Matilda carried hers to her chamber, took this said little trunk out of her large box, where she keeps it, unlocked it, and put the money into it. She disturbed nothing in the trunk; she says she had wrapt the sovereigns in a bit of paper, and she just slipped them inside, touching nothing else. She was shutting down the lid when she heard herself called to by me on the landing below. She waited to lock the box but not to put it up, leaving it standing on the table. I quite well remembered calling to the girl, having heard her run upstairs. I wanted her in my room."

Miss Deveen paused a minute, apparently thinking.

"Matilda has assured me again and again that she is quite sure she locked the little trunk, that there can be no mistake on that point. Moreover, she asserts that the letter in question was lying at the bottom of the trunk beneath other things, and that she had not taken it from thence or touched it for months and months."

"And when she went upstairs again – did she find the little trunk open or shut?"

"She says she found it shut: shut and locked just as she had left it; and she replaced it in her large box, unconscious that anybody had been to it."

"Was she long in your room, Miss Deveen?"

"Yes, Johnny, the best part of an hour. I wanted a little sewing done in a hurry, and told her to sit down there and then and do it. It was during this time that the cook, going upstairs herself, saw the trunk, and took the opportunity to do what she did do."

"I think I should feel inclined to believe Matilda. Her tale sounds the more probable."

"I don't know that, Johnny. I can hardly believe that a respectable woman, as Hall undoubtedly is, would deliberately unlock a fellow-servant's box with a false key. Whence did she get the key to do it? Had she previously provided herself with one? The lock is of the most simple description, for I have seen the trunk since, and Hall might possess a key that would readily fit it: but if so, as the woman herself says, how could she know it? In short, Johnny, it is one woman's word against another's: and, until this happened, I had deemed each of them to be equally credible."

To be sure there was reason in that. I sat thinking.

"Were it proved to have been as Matilda says, still I could not keep her," resumed Miss Deveen. "Mine is a peaceable, well-ordered household, and I should not like to know that one, subject to insane fits of temper, was a member of it. Though Hall in that case would get her discharge also."

"Do the people where Matilda is going know why she leaves?"

"Mrs. and Miss Soames. Yes. I told them all about it. But I told them at the same time, what I had then learnt – that Matilda's temper had doubtlessly been much tried here. It would not be tried in their house, they believed, and took her readily. She is an excellent servant, Johnny, let who will get her."

I could not resist the temptation of speaking to Matilda about this, an opportunity offering that same day. She came into the room with some letters just left by the postman.

"I thought my mistress was here, sir," she said, hesitating with the tray in her hand.

"Miss Deveen will be here in a minute: you can leave the letters. So you are going to take flight, Matilda! I have heard all about it. What a silly thing you must be to put yourself into that wonderful tantrum!"

"She broke into my box, and turned over its contents, and stole my letter to mock me," retorted Matilda, her fever-lighted eyes taking a momentary fierceness. "Who, put in my place, would not have gone into a tantrum, sir?"

"But she says she did not break into it."

"As surely as that is heaven's sun above us, she *did it*, Mr. Johnny. She has been full of spite towards me for a long time, and she thought she would pay me out. I did but unlock the box, and slip the little paper of money in, and I locked it again instantly and brought the key away with me: I can never say anything truer than that, sir: to make a mistake about it is not possible."

No pen could convey the solemn earnestness with which she spoke. Somehow it impressed me. I hoped Hall would get served out.

"Yes, the wrong has triumphed for once. As far as I can see, sir, it often does triumph. Miss Deveen thinks great things of Hall, but she is deceived in her; and I daresay she will find her out sometime. It was Hall who ought to have been turned away instead of me. Not that I would stay here longer if I could."

"But you like Miss Deveen?"

"Very much indeed, sir; she is a good lady and a kind mistress. She spoke very well indeed of me to the new family where I am going, and I daresay I shall do well enough there. – Have you been to Saltwater lately, sir?" she added, abruptly.

"Never since. Do you get news from the place?"

She shook her head. "I have never heard a word from any soul in it. I have written to nobody, and nobody has written to me."

"And nothing more has come out about poor Jane Cross. It is still a mystery."

"And likely to be one," she replied, in a low tone.

"Perhaps so. Do you know what Owen the milkman thought?"

She had been speaking the last sentence or two with her eyes bent, fiddling with the silver waiter. Now they were raised quickly.

"Owen thought that you could clear up the mystery if you liked, Matilda. At least, that you possessed some clue to it. He told me so."

"Owen as good as said the same to me before I left," she replied, after a pause. "He is wrong, sir; but he must think it if he will. Is he – is he at Saltwater still?"

"For all I know to the contrary. This letter, that the servants here got at, was one you were beginning to write to Owen. Did – "

"I would rather not talk of that letter, Mr. Johnny: my private affairs concern myself only," she interrupted – and went out of the room like a shot.

Had anyone told me that during this short visit of mine in London I should fall across the solution of the mystery of that tragedy enacted at No. 7, I might have been slow to credit it. Nevertheless, it was to be so.

Have you ever noticed, in going through life, that events seem to carry a sequence in themselves almost as though they bore in their own hands the guiding thread that connects them from beginning to end? For a time this thread will seem to be lost; to lie dormant, as though it had snapped, and the course of affairs it was holding to have disappeared for good. But lo! up peeps a little end when least expected, and we catch hold of it, and soon it grows into a handful; and what we had thought lost is again full of activity, and gradually works itself out. Not a single syllable, good or bad, had we heard of that calamity at Saltwater during the fourteen months which had passed since. The thread of it lay dormant. At Miss Deveen's it began to steal up again: Matilda, and her passion, and the letter she had commenced to Thomas Owen were to the fore: and before that visit of mine came to an end, the thread had, strange to say, unwound itself.

I was a favourite of Miss Deveen's: you may have gathered that from past papers. One day, when she was going shopping, she asked me to accompany her and not Miss Cattledon: which made that rejected lady's face all the more like vinegar. So we set off in the carriage.

"Are we going to Regent Street, Miss Deveen."

"Not do-day, Johnny. I like to encourage my neighbouring tradespeople and shall buy my new silk here. We have excellent shops not far off."

After a few intricate turnings and windings, the carriage stopped before a large linendraper's, which stood amidst a colony of shops nearly a mile from Miss Deveen's. George came round to open the door.

"Now what will you do, Johnny?" said Miss Deveen. "I daresay I shall be half an hour in here, looking at silks and calico; and I won't inflict that penalty on you. Shall the carriage take you for a short drive the while, or will you wait in it? – or walk about?"

"I will wait in the street here," I said, "and come in to you when I am tired. I like looking at shops." And I do like it.

The next shop to the linendraper's was a carver and gilder's: he had some nice pictures displayed in his window; at any rate, they looked nice to me: and there I took up my station to begin with.

"How do you do, sir? Have you forgotten me?"

The words came from a young man who stood at the next door, close to me, causing me to turn quickly to him from my gaze at the pictures. No, I had not forgotten him. I knew him instantly. It was Owen, the milkman.

After a few words had passed, I went inside. It was a spacious shop, well fitted up with cans and things pertaining to a milkman's business. The window-board was prettily set off with moss, ferns, a bowl containing gold and silver fish, a miniature fountain, and a rush basket of fresh eggs. Over the door was his own name, Thomas Owen.

"You are living here, Owen?"

"Yes, sir."

"But why have you left Saltwater?"

"Because, Mr. Johnny, the place looked askance at me. People, in their own minds, set down that miserable affair at No. 7 to my credit. Once or twice I was hooted at by the street boys, asking what I had done with Jane Cross. My mother couldn't stand that, and I couldn't stand it, so we just sold our business at Saltwater, and bought this one here. And a good change it has been, in a pecuniary point of view: this is an excellent connection, and grows larger every day."

"I'm sure I am glad to hear it."

"At first, mother couldn't bear London: she longed for the pure country air and the green fields: but she is reconciled to it now. Perhaps she'll have an opportunity soon of going back to see her own old Welsh mountains, and of staying there if it pleases her."

"Then I should say you are going to be married, Owen."

He laughed and nodded. "You'll wish me good luck, won't you, sir? She's the only daughter at the next door, the grocer's."

"That I will. Have you discovered any more of that mysterious business, Owen?"

"At Saltwater? No, sir: not anything at all that could touch the matter itself. But I have heard a good bit that bears upon it."

"Do you still suspect that Matilda could tell if she chose?"

"I suspect more than that, sir?"

The man's words were curiously significant. He had a bit of fern in his hand, and his fresh, open, intelligent face was bent downwards, as if he wanted to see what the leaf was made of.

"I am not sure, sir. It is but suspicion at the best: but it's an uncommonly strong one."

"Won't you tell me what you mean? You may trust me."

"Yes, I am sure I may," he said, promptly. "And I think I will tell you – though I have never breathed it to mortal yet. I think Matilda did it herself."

Backing away from the counter in my surprise, I upset an empty milk-can. "Matilda!" I exclaimed, picking up the can.

"Mr. Johnny, with all my heart I believe it to have been so. I have believed it for some time now."

"But the girls were too friendly to harm one another. I remember you said so yourself, Owen."

"And I thought so then, sir. No suspicion of Matilda had occurred to me, but rather of the man I had seen there on the Wednesday. I think she must have done it in a sudden passion; not of deliberate purpose."

"But now, what are your reasons?"

"I told you, sir, as I daresay you can recall to mind, that I should do what lay in my power to unravel the mystery – for it was not at all agreeable to have it laid at my door. I began, naturally, with tracing out the doings of that night as connected with No. 7. Poor Jane Cross had not been out of doors that night, and so far as I knew had spoken to no one, save to me from the window; therefore of her there seemed nothing to be traced: but of Matilda there was. Inquiring here and there, I, bit by bit, got a few odds and ends of facts together. I traced out the exact time, almost to a minute, that I rang twice at the door-bell at No. 7, and was not answered; and the time that Matilda entered the Swan to get the supper beer. Pretty nearly half an hour had elapsed between the first time and the second."

"Half an hour!"

"Not far short of it. Which proved that Matilda must have been indoors when I rang, though she denied it before the coroner, and it was taken for granted that I had rung during her absence to fetch the beer. And you knew, sir, that her absence did not exceed ten minutes. Now why did not Matilda answer my ring? Why did she not candidly say that she had heard the ring, but did not choose to answer it? Well, sir, that gave rise to the first faint doubt of her: and when I recalled and dwelt on her singular manner, it appeared to me that the doubt might pass into grave suspicion. Look at her superstitious horror of No. 7. She never would go into the house afterwards!"

I nodded.

"Two or three other little things struck me, all tending to strengthen my doubts, but perhaps they are hardly worth naming. Still, make the worst of it, it was only suspicion, not certainty, and I left Saltwater, holding my tongue."

"And is this all, Owen?"

"Not quite, sir. Would you be so good as to step outside, and just look at the name over the grocer's door?"

I did so, and read Valentine. "John Valentine." The same name as Matilda's.

"Yes, sir, it is," Owen said, in answer to me. "After settling here we made acquaintance with the Valentines, and by and by learnt that they are cousins of Matilda's. Fanny – my wife that is to be – has often talked to me about Matilda; they were together a good bit in early life; and by dint of mentally sifting what she said, and putting that and that together, I fancy I see daylight."

"Yes. Well?"

"Matilda's father married a Spanish woman. She was of a wild, ungovernable temper, subject to fits of frenzy; in one of which fits she died. Matilda has inherited this temper; she is liable to go into frenzies that can only be compared to insanity. Fanny has seen her in two only; they occur but at rare intervals; and she tells me that she truly believes the girl is mad – mad, Mr. Johnny – during the few minutes that they last."

The history I had heard of her mad rage at Miss Deveen's flashed over me. Temporarily insane they had thought her there.

"I said to Fanny one day when we were talking of her," resumed Owen, "that a person in that sort of uncontrollable passion, might commit any crime; a murder, or what not. 'Yes,' Fanny replied, 'and not unlikely to do it, either: Matilda has more than once said that she should never die in her bed.' Meaning – "

"Meaning what?" I asked, for he came to a pause.

"Well, sir, meaning, I suppose, that she might sometime lay violent hands upon herself, or upon another. I can't help thinking that something must have put her into one of these rages with Jane Cross, and that she pushed or flung the poor girl over the stairs."

Looking back, rapidly recalling signs and tokens, I thought it might have been so. Owen interrupted me.

"I shall come across her sometime, Mr. Johnny. These are things that don't hide themselves for ever: at least, not often. And I shall tax her with it to her face."

"But – don't you know where she is?"

"No, I don't, sir. I wish I did. It was said that she came up to take a situation in London, and perhaps she is still in it. But London's a large place, I don't know what part of it she was in, and one might as well look for a needle in a bundle of hay. The Valentines have never heard of her at all since she was at Saltwater."

How strange it seemed; – that she and they were living so near one another, and yet not to be aware of it. Should I tell Owen? Only for half a moment did the question cross me. *No*: most certainly not. It might be as he suspected; and, with it all, I could only pity Matilda. Of all unhappy women, she seemed the unhappiest.

Miss Deveen's carriage bowled past the door to take her up at the linen-draper's. Wishing Owen good-day, I was going out, but drew back to make room for two people who were entering: an elderly woman in a close bonnet, and a young one with a fair, pretty, and laughing face.

"My mother and Fanny, sir," he whispered.

"She is very pretty, very nice, Owen," I said, impulsively. "You'll be sure to be happy with her."

"Thank you, sir; I think I shall. I wish you had spoken a word or two to her, Mr. Johnny: you'd have seen how nice she is."

"I can't stay now, Owen. I'll come again."

Not even to Miss Deveen did I speak of what I had heard. I kept thinking of it as we drove round Hyde Park, and she told me I was unusually silent.

The thread was unwinding itself more and more. Once it had set on a lengthening, I suppose it could not stop. Accident led to an encounter between Matilda and Thomas Owen. Accident? No, it was this same thread of destiny. There's no such thing as accident in the world.

During the visit to the linendraper's, above spoken of, Miss Deveen bought a gown for Matilda. Feeling in her own heart sorry for the girl, thinking she had been somewhat hardly done by in her house, what with Hall and the rest of them, she wished to make her a present on leaving, as a token of her good-will. But the quantity of stuff bought proved not to be sufficient: Miss Deveen had had her doubts upon the point when it was cut off, and she told Matilda to go herself and get two yards more. This it was, this simple incident, that led to the meeting with Owen. And I was present at it.

The money-order office of the district was situated amidst this colony of shops. In going down there one afternoon to cash an order, I overtook Matilda. She was on her way to buy the additional yards of stuff.

"I suppose I am going right, sir?" she said to me. "I don't know much about this neighbourhood."

"Not know much about it! What, after having lived in it more than a year!"

"I have hardly ever gone out; except to church on a Sunday," she answered. "And what few articles I've wanted in the dress line, I have mostly bought at the little draper's shop round the corner."

Hardly had the words left her lips, when we came face to face with Thomas Owen. Matilda gave a kind of smothered cry, and stood stock still, gazing at him. What they said to one another in that first moment, I did not hear. Matilda had a scared look, and was whiter than death. Presently we were walking together towards Thomas Owen's, he having invited Matilda to go and see his home.

But there was another encounter first. Standing at the grocer's door was pretty Fanny Valentine. She and Matilda recognised each other, and clasped hands. It appeared to me that Matilda did it with suppressed reluctance, as though it gave her no pleasure to meet her relatives. She must have known how near they lived to Miss Deveen's, and yet she had never sought them out. Perhaps the very fact of not wishing to see them had kept her from the spot.

They all sat down in the parlour behind the shop – a neat room. Mrs. Owen was out; her son produced some wine. I stood up by the bookcase, telling them I must be off the next minute to the post-office. But the minutes passed, and I stayed on.

How he led up to it, I hardly know; but, before I was prepared for anything of the kind, Thomas Owen had plunged wholesale into the subject of Jane Cross, recounting the history of that night, in all its minute details, to Fanny Valentine. Matilda, sitting back on the far side of the room in an armchair, looked terror-stricken: her face seemed to be turning into stone.

"Why do you begin about that, Thomas Owen?" she demanded, when words at length came to her. "It can have nothing to do with Fanny."

"I have been wishing to tell it her for some little time, and this seems to be a fitting opportunity," he answered, coolly resolute. "You, being better acquainted with the matter than I, can correct me if I make any blunders. I don't care to keep secrets from Fanny: she is going to be my wife."

Matilda's hands lifted themselves with a convulsive movement and fell again. Her eyes flashed fire.

"Your wife?"

"If you have no objection," he replied. "My dear old mother goes into Wales next month, and Fanny comes here in her place."

With a cry, faint and mournful as that of a wounded dove, Matilda put her hands before her face and leaned back in her chair. If she had in truth loved Thomas Owen, if she loved him still, the announcement must have caused her cruel pain.

He resumed his narrative; assuming as facts what he had in his own mind conceived to have been the case, and by implication, but not directly, charging Matilda with the crime. It had a dreadful effect upon her; her agitation increased with every word. Suddenly she rose up in the chair, her arms lifted, her face distorted. One of those fits of passion had come on.

We had a dreadful scene. Owen was powerful, I of not much good, but we could not hold her. Fanny ran sobbing into her own door and sent in two of the shopmen.

It was the climax in Matilda Valentine's life. One that perhaps might have been always looked for. From that hour she was an insane woman, her ravings being interspersed with lucid intervals. During one of these, she disclosed the truth.

She had loved Thomas Owen with a passionate love. Mistaking the gossip and the nonsense that the young man was fond of chattering to her and Jane Cross, she believed her love was returned. On the day preceding the tragedy, when talking with him after morning service, she had taxed him with paying more attention to Jane Cross than to herself. Not a bit of it, he had lightly answered; he would take her for a walk by the sea-shore that evening if she liked to go. But, whether he had meant it, or not, he never came, though Matilda dressed herself to be in readiness. On the contrary, he went to church, met Jane there, and walked the best part of the way home with her. Matilda jealously resented this; her mind was in a chaos; she began to suspect that it was Jane Cross he liked, not herself. She said a word or two upon the subject to Jane Cross on the next day, Monday; but Jane made sport of it –

laughed it off. So the time went on to the evening, when they were upstairs together, Jane sewing, Matilda writing. Suddenly Jane Cross said that Thomas Owen was coming along, and Matilda ran to the window. They spoke to him as he passed, and he said he would look in as he returned from Munpler. After Matilda's letter to her brother was finished, she began a note to Thomas Owen, intending to reproach him with not keeping his promise to her and for joining Jane Cross instead. It was the first time she had ever attempted to write to him; and she stuck her work-box with the lid open behind the sheet of paper that Jane Cross might not see what she was doing. When it got dusk, Jane Cross remarked that it was blind man's holiday and that she would go on down and put the supper. In crossing the room, work-basket in hand, she passed behind Matilda, glanced at her letter, and saw the first words of it, "Dearest Thomas Owen." In sport, she snatched it up, read the rest where her own name was mentioned, and laughingly began, probably out of pure fun, to plague Matilda. "Thomas Owen your sweet-heart!" she cried, running out on the landing. "Why, he is mine. He cares more for my little finger than for – " Poor girl! She never finished her sentence. Matilda, fallen into one of those desperate fits of passion, had caught her up and was clutching her like a tiger-cat, tearing her hair, tearing pieces out of her gown. The scuffle was but brief: almost in an instant Jane Cross was falling headlong down the well of the staircase, pushed over the very low balustrades by Matilda, who threw the work-basket after her.

The catastrophe sobered her passion. For a while she lay on the landing in a sort of faint, all strength and power taken out of her as usual by the frenzy. Then she went down to look after Jane Cross.

Jane was dead. Matilda, not unacquainted with the aspect of death, saw that at once, and her senses pretty nearly deserted her again with remorse and horror. She had never thought to kill Jane Cross, hardly to harm her, she liked her too well: but in those moments of frenzy she had not the slightest control over her actions. Her first act was to run and lock the side door in the garden wall, lest anyone should come in. How she lived through the next half hour, she never knew. Her superstitious fear of seeing the dead Edmund Peahern in the house was strong – and now there was another one! But, with all her anguish and her fear, the instinct of self-preservation was making itself heard. What must she do? How could she throw the suspicion off herself? She could not run out of the house and say, "Jane Cross has fallen accidentally over the stairs; come and look to her" – for no one would have believed it to be an accident. And there were the pieces, too, she had clutched out of the gown! While thus deliberating, the gate bell rang, putting her into a state of the most intense terror. It rang again. Trembling, panting, Matilda stood cowering in the kitchen, but it did not ring a third time. This was, of course, Thomas Owen.

Necessity is the mother of invention. Something she *must* do, and her brain hastily concocted the plan she should adopt. Putting the cloth and the bread-and-cheese on the table, she took the jug and went out at the front door to fetch the usual pint of ale. A moment or two she stood at the front door, peering up and down the road to make sure that no one was passing. Then she slipped out, locking the door softly; and, carrying the key concealed in the hollow of her hand, she threw it amidst the shrubs at No. 1. *Now* she could not get into the house herself; she would not have entered it alone for the world: people must break it open. All along the way to the post-office, to which she really did go, and then to the Swan, she was mentally rehearsing her tale. And it succeeded in deceiving us all, as the reader knows. With regard to the visit of her brother on the Wednesday, she had told Thomas Owen the strict truth; though, when he first alluded to it in the churchyard, her feelings were wrought up to such a pitch that she could only cry out and escape. But how poor Matilda contrived to live on and carry out her invented story, how she bore the inward distress and repentance that lay upon her, we shall never know. A distress, remorse, repentance that never quitted her, night or day; and which no doubt contributed to gradually unhinge her mind, and to throw it finally off its balance.

Such was the true history of the affair at No. 7, which had been so great a mystery to Saltwater. The truth was never made public, save to the very few who were specially interested in it. Matilda Valentine is in the asylum, and likely to remain there for life; while Thomas Owen and his wife flourish in sunshine, happy as a summer's day.

Notes

Text: *The Argosy*, January–February 1877.

1 The characters in this story, one of EW's popular 'Johnny Ludlow' tales, are Johnny's extended family: Squire Todhetley is his stepfather, Mrs Todhetley his mother, and Tod (called Joe by the Squire) is the Squire's son by his first marriage.
2 Exerted pressure to bring the price down.
3 Lantern casting a long beam.
4 Espouses a notion.
5 The hour just before twilight when it is too dark to work.

A RAILWAY JOURNEY

Lady Margaret Majendie

Lady Margaret Majendie, née Lindsay (1850–1912), short-story writer, novelist. Little is known of her, except that she was the wife of Lewis Ashurst Majendie, J.P. She contributed several stories to *Blackwood's Magazine*, and published at least seven novels: *Dita* (1877); *Fascination* (1880); *The Turn of the Tide* (1881); *Out of their Element* (1884); *Sisters in Law* (1885); *Precautions* (1887); *Past Forgiveness* (1889) and *Tom's Wife* (1890).

A Railway Journey

A CLOSE cab laden with luggage drove up to Euston Station in time for the 7.30 a.m. train for the north. While the porters surrounded the boxes, the occupants of the cab passed straight through on to the platform, looking rather nervously about them. They were two – a very pretty girl in a most fascinating travelling costume of blue serge and fur, and an elderly woman, who, from her appearance, might have been her nurse.

"Sit here, and don't move, Miss Edith, while I take your ticket: now, mind you don't stir;" and she deposited her on a bench.

"Are you the young lady as has ordered a through carriage reserved?" asked a guard, with official abruptness.

"Yes."

"Then come along of me, miss."

"No, no; I must wait," and Edith, who was quite unused to travelling, grasped her bag and did not move. The guard looked astonished, but only shrugged his shoulders and walked off. Presently he came back.

"You'll be late, miss," he said, not encouragingly. "Train 'ill be off in another minute." Edith looked at him in despair. Should she leave her post? Would Jenkins never come back? A loud aggressive bell began to ring. Edith started up; she seized all the things Jenkins had put under her charge – rugs, carpet-bag, umbrella-case, loose shawl, and provision-basket – and was trying to stagger away under the load, when Jenkins came back very hot and flurried, seized half the packages, and hurried her to the train. The guard unlocked the special carriage and put her in.

"No hurry, ma'am," he said; "four minutes still."

"I don't at all like it, now it has come to the point, Jenkins," said Edith, leaning out of the window.

"Nor I, miss; and how your mamma could let you go all alone like this, passes me; but I have spoken to the guard and written to the station-master, and you've a good bit to eat, and not a blessed soul to get into the carriage from end to end; so don't be afraid, my dear, and I make no doubt that your dear uncle will meet you at the other end."

"I have no doubt that one of my uncles will – I hope Uncle John, as I have never seen Uncle George."

"Everything you want, miss?" said an extra porter. "I have put in all the rugs and a hot-water tin, and the luggage is all right in the van just behind."

"All right, all right!" said Mrs Jenkins.

"Thank you, ma'am," said the porter, pocketing a shining half-crown.

A gentleman suddenly came running on to the platform; the train was just about to start. "Here, porter, take my portmanteau; quick – smoking carriage!"

"All full, sir! quick, sir, please!"

"It's Mr George!" cried Jenkins, suddenly. Edith started forward. "Oh!"

The gentleman caught sight of Jenkins. "Here, guard, guard! put me in here!"

"Can't sir – special."

"Quick; let me in! it's – it's my niece!"

The train began to move.

"Confound you, be quick!"

The door was opened just in time, and Edith, as excited as Mr George, seized him with both hands by the coat-sleeves, and pulled him in with all her might into the carriage. They were off.

Mr George sat down opposite to Edith with a sigh of relief.

"I am so glad to see you, Uncle George," said Edith, timidly; "for though I am generally bold enough, I was rather afraid of this long journey."

"I will take care of you," said the uncle. "I am very glad to make your acquaintance, my dear." The "my dear" sounded a little strained, as though it were not a common expression on Uncle George's lips, and Edith looked up at him. She had not expected her uncle to be so young in appearance; but she had often heard her mother say that he was the youngest-looking man of his age she had ever known; and now she quite agreed, – for though she knew him to be really about fifty-eight years of age, he might from his appearance be taken for five-and-twenty, or even less. He was remarkably good-looking – more so than she had expected – and his eyes looked very young, and frank, and blue. There was a twinkle in them also; she was sure that he was fond of fun. Edith felt quite fond of her uncle; she was not one bit afraid of him – his face was so open, and good, and kindly.

"Now we must make ourselves comfortable," said Uncle George, and he proceeded to set to work. He put the rugs and baskets into the nets, he pushed the carpet-bag and portmanteau under the seat, took off his hat, put on a very becoming Turkish fez, extracted newspapers from his pocket, spread a shawl over Edith's knees, and then wriggled himself comfortably into a corner seat.

"How well old Jenkins wears!" he said. "She looks like a young dairy-maid."

"Oh!" said Edith, a little shocked by his irreverence.

"I remember how she used to feed me with dried fruit and macaroons out of the store-room."

"Really! surely she is not old enough for that?"

"Oh, ah! I forget her age; but the fact was, I wasn't of course a boy."

"Of course not. Why, I think mamma said that you and Jenkins were born the same day – or was she the eldest?"

"Oh, I was the eldest."

"No, you were not; I remember she was three weeks older than you, and it was because she was your foster-sister that she always was so fond of you. Indeed, mamma said that she wanted to leave her to go to you and Aunt Maria when your eldest children were born, even out to India."

"My eldest children! what do you mean? Oh! by the by, yes; they are dead."

"Dead! my cousin George dead?"

"Yes, yes, my dear."

"Poor little Addie? was it true that George never got over her loss?"

"Don't!" said Uncle George, abruptly; and he held up a newspaper upside down.

Edith touched his arm very gently.

"I am so sorry, Uncle George," she said, sweetly. "If I had known that you had lost them both, I would not have said anything; please forgive me. And poor Aunt Maria, too! Oh, I beg your pardon."

Uncle George threw down his paper and looked smilingly at her.

"Does your mamma ever speak of me?"

"Constantly, perpetually," said Edith, her voice still a little choked.

"And what does she say of me?"

"She says that you are the dearest, kindest, warmest-hearted, most sweet-dispositioned old gentleman existing; she says you have been a gallant officer, and a loyal, true-hearted soldier." Edith's eyes kindled. "And I have heard how you distinguished yourself in India, and I – I am very glad to see you, Uncle George."

"Yes, yes, he is all that," said he, with enthusiasm.

"What? who?" asked Edith, confused.

"My father – I – I – I mean my son."

"Poor George! he was a most distinguished soldier also. I wish I had known him. No, Uncle George, I won't speak so – I do not want to pain you."

"I like to hear all you tell me about him, my dear."

"I have only heard how good a soldier he was, and that he was so handsome and so good."

"And had he faults and defects?"

Edith looked surprised.

"I used to hear that he was conceited."

"No, no," said Uncle George, hastily; "he never was that. He was proud, I grant – perhaps too proud – but never conceited."

"Poor George!" sighed Edith; "I had so looked forward to knowing him."

"Had you really?"

"Yes; I never had a companion of my own age. Do tell me, shall I like my cousins at Hatton?"

"I think so, some of them: do you mean Uncle John's daughters, or his step-children?"

"Both."

"I think you will like Mary, tolerate Susan, abhor Agatha, admire Jane, and adore Alice."

"Alice is the adorable one, is she?" said Edith, laughing; "and is she the one they say is so pretty?"

"Oh no; poor Alice is deformed, and can never leave the sofa; but she has the sweetness of an angel and the courage of a martyr; she is not in the least pretty."

"Oh, what a trial! always on the sofa!"

"What a sweet little thing this is!" thought Uncle George, but he said nothing.

"How comes it that you know none of your cousins?" said he, suddenly.

"Why do you want me to tell you what you know so much better than I do, Uncle George?"

"Yes, yes, of course; but naturally I want to know your side of the story. Have you never been at Hatton?"

"Never; and I thought it so very kind of you to induce Uncle John to persuade mamma to let me go."

"Yes; I thought, you know, that a few companions of your own age would do you good. How old are you?"

"Did you not get mamma's letter, in which she told you that I was to be eighteen to-morrow?"

"No; it must have been late. I never heard of it."

"How very unfortunate! Then no one will know I am coming. She asked you to tell Uncle John about the trains and things."

"Oh, ah! *that* letter! oh, of course, that is all right. I don't – I – I sometimes don't read letters through."

Edith laughed.

"I will tell you one version of my story. Mamma being papa's widow, and papa having been the eldest son, had to leave Hatton when I was born and turned out to be a stupid little girl; and she went abroad because she was so delicate, and became a Roman Catholic."

"Holloa!"

"What is it, Uncle George?"

"You are not one, I hope?"

Edith looked rather indignant. "It is *very* odd of you to say that," she said, "when you know as well as I do all that you did about it; indeed I shall never forget your kindness. I was very unhappy when mamma wanted me to change; and Uncle John's letters and all Aunt Maria wrote made it worse than ever, only your letters made all smooth; and mamma was so much touched by the one you wrote to her about papa's trust in her, and my not being hers only, and all that, that, indeed, I have always loved you – you have seemed to me like my own dear father."

"I am very glad, my dear child, and I hope that in future you will be guided by my advice."

"I hope I shall see a great deal of you, Uncle George, for I know how fond I shall be of you, for my mother loves you dearly."

"It is very kind of her."

"And do you know, since we came to live in England, I have never paid a single visit, or been for one week away from home. Oh, it is such fun going to Hatton! Do my cousins ride?"

"Yes, a great deal; are you fond of it?"

"I love it; there is nothing in the world to me like a good gallop. Ah, it was the greatest trial of all my life when Queen Mab was sold!"

"When was that?"

"Mamma made me give up riding, or rather I gave it up of myself, because it made her so nervous."

"What else do you care for? – dancing?"

"Oh, I love it; but I have never been to a ball in my life."

"There are to be two at Hatton next week, and you must promise me the first valse at each."

"Do *you* valse?"

"Oh yes. You see I am not such an old fogy as you expected."

"No; nobody would believe you to be fifty-eight, except for one thing."

"What is that?"

But Edith blushed and would not answer.

"You need not mind, child – I never was at all sensitive; and alas! now my memory is not what it was."

"That's it," said Edith, eagerly; "only I did not like to say it. Here we are at a station."

It was now ten o'clock; Uncle George bought the 'Times' and 'Daily News,' and they both began to read. About twelve o'clock the pangs of hunger began to assail Edith, and she exclaimed –

"Uncle George, it is only twelve o'clock, and I must eat to live."

"I have been existing merely for the last hour with the greatest difficulty, but I have got nothing wherewith to refresh exhausted nature; I calculated on a bun at Carlisle."

"Hours hence! No, I am amply provided. Will you have beef or chicken sandwiches, or cold partridge, or what?"

They made a very good lunch, and uncle and niece grew hourly better acquainted.

"I believe we ought to look out of the window," said he, presently. "My father said that the country about here was quite beautiful."

"That must have been before the days of railways," said Edith, gravely. "Those coaching days must have been quite delightful."

"They were."

"Mamma has told me about that extraordinary adventure you and papa had on the Aberdeen coach."

"It was extraordinary."

"Papa caught the branch of a tree, did he not?"

"Yes; and do you remember what I did?"

"You jumped out just as the coach upset, and sat on all the horses' heads."

"And a most uneasy seat it must have been; and did Uncle Arthur – I mean your papa – remain suspended in mid-air?"

"No, he swung into the tree. I have often heard of your climbing exploits, and that when you were young you could climb any tree."

"I have not lost the power," said Uncle George, stretching himself. "Holloa!"

"What is the matter?" said Edith, startled.

"Nothing – nothing – sit still!"

But she followed the direction of his eyes. The train (a very long one) was going round a sharp curve, they were in one of the last carriages, and to her horror and terror, she saw, about a hundred yards in front of the train, a whole herd of cows on and off the line – two or three frantically galloping.

All heads were stretched out of the windows, clamouring tongues and even cries resounded from the other carriages, but neither Edith nor George uttered a sound, only she put back her hand and caught his; he seized it very tightly in the suspense, knowing well that a terrible accident might be impending. It was hardly a second, but it seemed a lifetime. The frantic cattle rushed off the line in a body, all but one unfortunate beast. The guards put on the very heaviest brakes, but the impetus was so great that the slackening was hardly perceptible. It may have been fortunate that it was so, for instead of upsetting the train, the cow was tossed off the line utterly destroyed, and the engine rushed on in safety.

George and Edith sat down opposite to each other; both were very pale.

"Thank God!" said Edith, and she covered her face with one hand. George did not speak, but he took off his cap and looked out of the window for one minute.

"Now I shall give you some sherry," he said, suddenly. "You are the pluckiest little brick I ever came across. Any other girl would have screamed."

"I never scream," said Edith, indignantly; "and I don't want any sherry."

"I am your uncle, and I say you are to have some – drink it up."

"I hate wine," she said, giving back the flask.

"There, good child, to do as you are told."

At the next station a perfect crowd of passengers was waiting for the up train. A great *fête* was going on in the next town for the visit of some royal personage, and the train was filled to overflowing. Presently the civil guard came up to the special carriage and said most deprecatingly that there was one gentleman who couldn't find a place anywhere; and as he was only going to the next station, would they admit him just for that twenty minutes? Uncle George consented very discontentedly, and very grudgingly moved his long legs to admit of the entry of a very stout old gentleman, who sat heavily down, and received into his ample lap a perfect pile of packages and baskets, and a brace of hares and a rabbit tied by the legs which he had dexterously suspended by a string round his neck.

"Not worth while, indeed, my dear madam," he said, as Edith began to make room for his things. "Only twenty minutes – no inconvenience, I assure you."

The heavily-weighted train moved off. The old gentleman now began a series of playful bows which made the hares and rabbit dance up and down.

"It really was too good of you to admit an old fogy like me," he said, blandly; "for of course with half an eye I can see the tender situation."

A deep growl from Uncle George. He gave a little start and went on to himself –

"Sweet young couple! just wedded, eh?"

Edith felt half choked with laughter, but she managed to say convulsively –

"Will you give me my book, Uncle George?"

The old gentleman started, cocked his head as a blackbird does when he perceives a very fat worm, and muttered –

"Impossible!"

Edith and George were wrapped in their respective novels. The old gentleman fidgeted, sighed, and arranged his features into a most sanctimonious expression. There was dead silence till he reached his station, where he descended. The departure bell was ringing, when his head suddenly reappeared at the window, the hares and rabbit streaming wildly from the back of his neck.

"My children," he said, "take my advice – go back to your friends. This – "
A little shriek ended his discourse; the train was going on; and he, being borne along on the step involuntarily, two stout porters rushed to the rescue and lifted him off. Edith and George laughed till the tears ran down their cheeks.

"I could eat again, with a little persuasion," said George, presently.

"Why, what o'clock is it?"

"Just five, and we shall not get in till eight-thirty. Remember that we had our luncheon at twelve."

"Very well." And they proceeded to eat.

The sun had gone down, and the whole sky was gorgeous with gold and crimson light, on which great black clouds floated prophetically.

"What a grand sky!" said Edith.

"Magnificent! Nowhere does one see such clouds as in England."

"Were you very fond of India?"

"Of course I am; my work lies there, my hopes, my future."

Edith looked astonished. "I should have thought," she said, "that *now* you would have been content to rest at home; but I admire you for loving work. Shall you go out again?"

"That depends very much upon circumstances. It would be a great grief to me to give up my profession."

"It is very odd, but I certainly thought that mamma told me you had given up your profession."

"She was mistaken," said Uncle George, shortly.

"I have often longed to go to India," cried Edith.

"Have you?" said George, very eagerly.

"Oh yes, beyond anything; life there gives everybody a chance. I mean, heroic men and great characters are formed in India, and men have great responsibilities and development for quite a different class of most desirable qualities there."

"That is quite true; and you are just the sort of woman to help a man to do anything."

"I am so glad you think so, Uncle George," she said, laughing and blushing.

At seven o'clock they reached a very large station, where the train had half an hour to wait. They got a cup of tea, and then, both being rather cold, they began to walk vigorously up and down to the very end of the terminus. It was quite dark at the far end, and they stood side by side, looking up into the mouth of the great station with its mighty arch. Trains rushed past, or heavily moved away with a harsh, discordant whistle. Great red lamps loomed out of the darkness like dragons' eyes. George drew Edith hastily on one side that she might not be struck by the chain of a huge carthorse which passed close by them, on its way to bring up a coal-truck. It was very cold, and they stamped up and down, and George enjoyed a fragrant cigar.

"Take your seats!" shouted the porter. "Take your seats!" And they resumed their places.

"Them's a bride and bridegroom," said a stout country-woman to a friend; and the loud guttural "Lor!" with which the news was received reached the ears of the travellers.

A blazing lamp was in the carriage, and under its yellow light Edith tried to read.

"Don't read, Edith," said the young uncle, suddenly. "Talk instead."

She shut up her book.

"To tell you the truth, Uncle George," she said, "we are getting so near that I am beginning to feel ridiculously nervous."

He looked at his watch, and suddenly started.

"So late," he said. "We shall be there in ten minutes."

"Oh!"

"And the fact is," he began, restlessly fidgeting; "the fact is – a – a – I have got a confession to make to you."

"To me! oh, Uncle George!"

"D – n Uncle George!"

Edith looked startled beyond measure.

"The fact is, Edith, I am not my father."

"What do you mean?"

"I mean I am my son."

"But he is dead."

"No, no; only, what was a fellow to say when you pressed me so hard? I am your cousin George."

"Oh!"

"And we have been such friends, you won't be angry? Are you vexed, Edith?" and he took both her hands.

"No; only astonished. I think – on the whole, I am rather – glad."

"That's all right; for, do you know, Edith, I seem to have known you for years! You have shown to-day every good quality a woman can possibly possess."

"Don't spoil me by such sayings."

"And Edith, dear Edith, do you know – confound it! here we are!" – only this, I should like to go on travelling with you, like this, for ever and ever – and –

Hatton! Hatton! tickets, please. Hatton!

"Here, Jones! take Miss Edith's bag. Is the carriage up?"

"Yes, sir."

"And a cart? there is a heap of luggage."

"All right sir."

"Come along, Edith? here we are, and my father is in the carriage."

Notes

Text: *Blackwood's Magazine,* Blackwood, Edinburgh, April 1877.

THE END OF HER JOURNEY

Lucy Clifford

(Sophia) Lucy Clifford, née Lane (1853–1929), novelist, playwright, and short-story writer, was born in the West Indies. She married mathematician and philosopher William Kingdon Clifford in 1875. He died suddenly four years later, leaving her with two young children. Her fiction typically presents women protagonists who are alone and struggling. Her first novel, *Mrs Keith's Crime* (1882), the story of a dying widow who kills her child to prevent her being left alone, was her most successful and controversial, although she wrote at least eight others, including *Aunt Anne* (1892), which describes the marriage of a woman of sixty-eight with a man forty years her junior. A friend of both Mary Braddon and Henry James, she wrote a number of plays in addition to her novels and stories. The most popular was *The Likeness of the Night* (1900), a dramatization of *The End of Her Journey*.

Further reading

Blain *et al.* (1990); Edel (1971); Shattock (1993); Sutherland (1988); Wolff (1979).

The End of Her Journey

Chapter I

Mrs Edward Archerson was not an attractive little woman, but she had a thousand a-year of her own, and people generally supposed that that was why 'Teddy A.', as his friends called him, had rather suddenly married her. He was known to be hard up and tolerably in debt, he had done nothing at the Bar, and it seemed unlikely that he ever would do much. At Cambridge he had been exceedingly popular, played an excellent hand at whist, and took a very mild degree. After he came to London, his rooms being pretty and his landlady obliging, he felt that it would be utter folly not to entertain; so he entertained a good deal. There was a bailiff downstairs one evening, while Teddy upstairs was giving one of his most successful parties, and after that things came to a crisis.

'Something will have to be done, or I shall bust up,' he said to himself. 'Must turn over a new leaf and be respectable, for this sort of thing can't go on.' And it didn't go on. He turned over the new leaf, to a certain extent, and became moderately respectable, openly laughing at himself all the time. Then, perhaps, thinking it was no use doing things by halves, he suddenly became very respectable indeed, married Mildred Benson after a short engagement, and settled down to hard work, routine, and the ways of domesticity. His wife was a good gentle little soul with a pale face, rather pathetic grey eyes, and a quantity of dull fair hair done up in very neat plaits. In manner she was quiet, seldom talked much, and was perhaps a little too tame; for it was absolutely certain – and that you knew directly you looked at her – that she would never make herself disagreeable to any one, come what might. Moreover, she was one of those women who weep when they would do wiser to scorn. She was immoderately in love with Teddy when she married him, that was quite evident to every one, except perhaps to Teddy – a clinging worshipping love that expected little, exacted nothing, and satisfied itself in giving all, consciously asking no return. Teddy, it was also equally evident, was only very moderately in love with her, and, as a natural consequence, took her love for him as a fact that was pleasant but not of much importance. Still he was an attentive husband, he thought it good form to be attentive to his wife; besides, he was a gentleman, and there are some little evidences of being a gentleman that he thought a man should never forget to give. So on the whole they got

191

on very well together, and if there was not much billing and cooing there was never any bickering.

At first after their marriage they went out a great deal. Teddy took his wife to parties, and sometimes to a theatre; but he never noticed what she wore, or with whom she talked, or took much interest in what she did or said. Once they spent a day on the river – a whole day; but it was so long before evening time he would never repeat the experiment, though she enjoyed it enormously, so she said.

'The river is all very well, but it doesn't do with your wife,' Teddy thought to himself. 'She is horribly in the way, and makes everything feel played out.' After a time Teddy said he was tired of parties, and made excuses. It also became known in the family that he was disappointed at not having any little ones, for he had always been devoted to children; but he got over that after a few years. Then almost suddenly he took to staying a good deal at his club, and encouraging his wife to have her pretty cousin on a visit.

'It will be more fun for you to take Amy about than to go alone,' he said, 'and a relief to me; for I may often have to stay late at chambers for the next few months. I hate to feel that you are waiting when I can't get back to dinner or in time to take you out anywhere.'

'But I would always rather stay at home when you can't go out,' his wife answered. 'I only care for parties for the pleasure of going with you.'

'Yes, dear; but it looks better for one of us to be seen about – shows we are in the swim, and gives an air of prosperity to the house. Besides, I like to think that you are enjoying yourself and not moping at home while I am wiring away[1] over some difficult business.'

'Could you not bring your work home sometimes, Teddy?' It was quite a bright idea, she thought; but he gave his head a good professional shake.

'Oh, no, my dear, that would never do. Be as bad as a woman's home-made gown, which Charlie's wife said she could tell at a glance, do you remember? No, Millie, go and enjoy yourself, and don't trouble your head about me, there's a good girl.' After that Mrs Archerson always went about alone, or with her pretty cousin Amy, and Teddy's evenings were free.

It was astonishing how well and quickly Teddy got on; perhaps his wife's money helped, but his quick eyes and charming manner probably did a great deal more. No one knew how it was, but in less than no time, as things go in his profession, all manner of good work fell to him; he was a busy man, prosperous and rising. Yet, in spite of his increasing means, he steadily refused to add to his expenditure, or to launch out in any way. And still he let his wife go out as much as she pleased (though she only pleased because he wished it), while he spent his evenings at his chambers or his club. Sometimes he stayed so late at the club that he did not return till next morning. Then Guy Forbes, Teddy's particular friend, set up a bachelor establishment at Richmond, and Teddy took to going to him once a week, always dining and sleeping, so that his wife did not see him at all till the next evening. It did him good, he said, the air of Richmond was quite different from that of Kensington, which had never really agreed with him; he was afraid he might get headaches if he did not have an occasional change. She bore it very well, but a time came in which the little woman's lip would sometimes quiver and her eyes fill with tears – nay, she would now and then shut herself up, and when she reappeared it looked very much as if she had been having a good cry.

'Don't you wish Edward would come out with us a little oftener, Mildred?' Amy asked one day. 'I know I shouldn't like it if I had a husband, and he left me to my own devices every evening.'

'He has so much to do – it is very difficult to leave his work; and when he can he finds whist a greater rest than parties, especially when he can get change of air too. It is very good of him to let us go about together as we do, dear Amy. Some husbands expect their wives to stay at home.'

'That is all very well; but I should like a man who enjoyed taking me about himself.'

'He doesn't care for parties. He said the other day that he had quite outgrown them.'

'Was he very much in love when you were married?' Amy asked presently. Mrs Archerson reflected for a moment, and did not appear to like the question, for she answered, a little distantly:

'Oh, I don't know. I suppose so, or he would not have married me. Let us talk of something else, dear – people don't always show what they feel, or how much they feel. At any rate, they can't be always showing it, you know; it would be very tiresome and undignified.'

That evening, after dinner, Amy wanted to write a letter for the late post – rather a long one, she said – and went upstairs to begin it. The Archersons stayed in the dining-room, lingering over the dessert; and something made Mrs Archerson ask her husband:

'Did you love me very much when you married me, Teddy?' He got up rather quickly, and went to the fire-place to light a cigarette.

'Yes, I suppose so, dear. What on earth makes you suddenly ask?' She got up and stood beside him on the hearthrug

'I was thinking – Amy told me to-day that Kate gets a letter from Herbert every morning. You used only to write to me once a week.'

'Not a letter-writing man,' he laughed, with an air of relief.

She looked up at him with a long, tender look, and an expression in her grey eyes that for the moment made her whole face different. Then she spoke in a low voice, that almost trembled:

'I know you – liked me, of course,' she said, humbly; 'but – were you ever really in love with me – were you – '

'Yes, dear, of course,' he interrupted, looking at the end of his cigarette; 'don't get nervous about it. Don't you remember how we used to hang about in the woods, at Chilworth?'

'Yes I do,' she answered; and his words carried conviction enough to her simple heart. 'But do you care for me still – for me at all?' she went on nervously, determined to have the matter out and her fears set at rest; 'or are you tired – '

He turned round, put down his cigarette, and looked back at her, into her eyes.

'What do you mean?' he asked, in an anxious, eager voice, as though he knew of some reason for her questioning. But her manner changed suddenly, she was so unused to excitement; she had always despised it. And now she felt foolish, almost guilty of something – she did not know of what.

'You don't seem to care much,' she said softly. 'You never seem to like being with me. You never take me out – '

'Too busy, my dear child. Lots of men make their wives do the going-out alone, while they grind at their work.'

'Ah, but you never seem to care what I do or say, or anything about me. You are very kind in many ways, I know; but you never seem to – to – I sometimes wonder if I were very, very ill, whether you – ' But she broke down helplessly in what she wanted to say; she was not good at making out a case.

'You silly little woman,' he laughed, and put his arm round her waist and kissed her in a kindly affectionate manner that had nothing of the lover in it – 'what is the matter? I expect very few people spoon[2] after five or six years of marriage,' he added.

'It is not that,' she answered hurriedly, half-ashamed; 'but if I could only know that you ever loved me, that you really love me still?' She said it almost as an entreaty, longing for his answer. He looked at her again – at her eyes, that had a strange fear and tenderness in them tonight; he remembered swiftly how often they were dull and expressionless, and wondered at it – at her pale face and thin commonplace figure. An almost sad look came over him for a moment, while he answered:

'I should be a brute if I did not love you, Mildred. You are a good little soul – a thousand times too good for me.' And then Teddy smoked his cigarette intently, as if to steady himself after what he felt had been almost a scene. 'I'll tell you what,' he said, when he had enjoyed a few minutes' thoughtful smoking, 'I'll get stalls and take you both to the play to-morrow, you and Amy. It is a long time since we went anywhere; a little spree will cheer us up and do us good, eh?' He went back to the table and helped himself to the claret, and she followed him mechanically. She had a way of 'pattering' after him, as he called it, that worried him sometimes; it was like a cat, a gentle, affectionate cat, but still it worried him. They both sat down to the table again; she considering the question about the play.

'I thought you were going to Richmond to-morrow?' she said.

'Never mind; I'll throw Guy over for once. Some claret, darling?' It was quite an age since he had called her darling; it made her heart feel like a feather as she heard it. What a goose she had been! He was just as fond of her as other men were of their wives, only he was not demonstrative. Dear Teddy, he was so much taken up with his work that he had little time to think of other things; and when he had, it was so natural that he should try to get as thorough a change as possible. She pushed her glass towards him.

'Yes, some claret' – and then a servant entered.

'If you please, sir,' the maid said, 'a man has come with this card-case; he says he found it in Sisterton Road, Clapham, last night.' Teddy knocked the claret jug against his wife's glass, and stained the tablecloth.

'Yes – well – how does he know it's mine?'

'He says he found the address on the cards inside; and he wants to know if there's any reward?'

'But you were not at Clapham last night, Edward, were you?' Mrs Archerson asked. She generally called him Edward before the servants; she thought it sounded better.

'Here's half-a-crown – far more than it's worth – an old card-case and half-a-dozen pasteboards.³ Confound him! No, dear,' he said when the servant had left the room. 'I suppose it was picked up at the club or somewhere, and dropped again there.'

'Yes, that must have been it. But how odd that it should have been lost twice in one day,' she answered innocently.

'Perhaps the beggar who found it first was disgusted at its not being something better, and threw it away.'

'Yes, perhaps that was it,' she laughed. 'Do you know, Teddy dear, your hand quite trembled when Jane brought it in. That was how you spilt the wine.'

'Too many cigarettes, they make one nervous. I am glad we are going to the play to-morrow. We might have a little dinner somewhere first, be a treat for Amy. What do you say?'

'Yes,' she answered gratefully.

Then he looked at her again. She was a good little soul, he thought; but it was impossible to help being a little bored by her, she was so curiously lacking in charm.

'Then that's agreed. Now I must go out, unfortunately.' He looked at his watch, and there was a tone of relief in his voice. 'Don't sit up for me, dear. Good-night.' As if he reproached himself for his critical thoughts of a minute before, or as if some half-tender remembrance overtook him, he stopped for a moment by the doorway and looked back at her. 'Don't be foolish again,' he said. 'I would do anything to make you happy, Millie dear.'

Chapter II

Nearly a year had passed. It was the end of October, and the Archersons had come back to town. Teddy Archerson was more devoted than ever to his work, his whist, and his bachelor friend at Richmond. He had been thoroughly restless in the North; even the shooting when it began did not engross him as it had formerly. The fact was, he told his wife, that, in spite of its being vacation-time, there were many things that needed his presence in town – things concerning the great case of Willoughby v. Conyers, on which he was among the junior counsel retained, and so on. Once or twice he grew so anxious about his work that he ran up to town for a few days, and left Mildred down in Fifeshire. It was a very wet season, and she could stay indoors and do needlework; but he grew impatient in a country-house in bad weather, and a little spell of work would do him good, he said.

After they were back at Kensington again he seemed to care less and less for society, his friends almost lost sight of him, except in a professional sense. Even when those with whom he had formerly been most intimate asked him and his wife to cosy little winter-season dinners he generally made excuses, though he was always glad when Mildred found courage to go alone. He was very good to her. He was getting on so well, was so successful in all he undertook, that he made their single-horse a pair, and gave her a brougham[4] as a supplement to the victoria[5] she had always had; it was much nicer than jobbing,[6] he said, especially as she went about a good deal alone. On her birthday, too, he gave her quite a beautiful diamond bracelet; and his manner was always gentle, it was sometimes oddly deferential. But he never seemed happy, nay, even content, to be much in her society. Anything he could do for her comfort, anything she wanted, or he fancied she wanted, he was ready enough to give her, though he always refused to take a larger house or to live on a more expensive scale; but being with her made him impatient or restless or absent – in short, he always seemed as if he wished he were somewhere else. At last, in spite of his presents and gentleness, try as she would, it was no good, she could not satisfy herself with her own excuses and arguments any longer, she grew restless and unhappy. Other women's husbands could take them out or stay at home contented and happy; and why not hers? She was not very pretty or clever or fascinating, but Edward had known what she was when he married her. Besides, lots of women not one whit better than she had devoted husbands. She felt that he was anxious, over-anxious, to be kind; she could not remember that he had ever said a single cross word to her; but virtually she lived alone.

She sat and thought it over for the thousandth time one afternoon early in December. She looked round the room – a trim, well-kept room, with everything in its place, everything pretty and carefully arranged, and yet that somehow lacked coziness. It looked as if it had never been untidy, as if no one had ever sat there dreaming a day-dream or dozing in the twilight, or telling little confidential stories over its crackling fire. She wondered why Teddy always looked so uncomfortable, so like a stranger in it. She could not tell. Beside her was a little tea-table, and on it a tray with a cup and saucer and a plate with two slices of thin bread-and-butter. It told much to discerning eyes. No charming woman has one solitary cup brought in for her afternoon tea; she knows how unlikely it is that she will drink it alone, and a second cup is put ready. Somebody is sure to come – some merry little married woman whose husband will not be at home that day; some happy girl who has been shopping, or forlorn bachelor who remembers that her tea is sure to be good, her talk bright, and her sympathy certain, and who thinks how pleasantly she will make an hour pass before he betakes himself to his club. But cosy chats of this sort were unknown to Mrs Archerson. She was a little dull to the married woman, she had no attraction for girls, and men felt strange and awkward with her. They never quite knew what to talk about; she did not care for books or politics, she never contrived to be in the swing of the gossip of the moment; moreover she had some old-fashioned prejudices she felt it a duty to stand by, that made her rather difficult to get along with. Just as people were trying to be a little intimate with her they found they had to pick and choose carefully their subjects of conversation. It was told of her by a cousin of Teddy's that she had stated openly that she seldom read books, unless they were religious, when it was a duty to read them; or historical, when it was instructive. Poetry she did not care for unless it rhymed and flowed very easily; and novels as a rule she considered immoral. Was not the 'Vicar of Wakefield'[7] a story of seduction? and were the scenes between the Knight and the Jewess in 'Ivanhoe'[8] fit for modest women to read? If she had had daughters they would have read neither till matrimony had overtaken them. As for modern novels, she left them alone, perhaps to her profit, and certainly to the development of her natural gravity.

At parties, where she saw most of life and gathered the majority of her ideas, she merely stood in a crowd with the rest, saying now and then a word or two to this person or that, noticing the gowns of her friends, and wondering how it was that others contrived to look so much more lively than herself. Altogether she had little enough material to form lively talk for her own tea-table. The result was that at five o'clock Mrs Archerson was generally alone. Her callers left cards or came early, and having stayed a quarter of an hour went away with an air of having fulfilled a duty. There are some people who seem born to put others through minor moral exercises; Mildred was one of them. And yet meanwhile deaf and dumb the woman's soul lived within its prison, unconsciously beating against its bars, longing to escape, wondering and weeping at its own limits, its own blindness, its own incapacity, having no power at all except to suffer without seeing the reason of it, or knowing any remedy.

But it was not yet time for her lonely tea; never did she allow herself to venture upon it before five. She felt that the mistress of a household had no business to humour herself, for upon her depended the examples of method and punctuality that were so important to every member of it. And yet, how dull and weary she felt! And how much – for women are comforted by small things – a cup of tea, and a cosy creeping nearer to the fire, or perhaps a love-story, or the playing of a few snatches on the piano, would have brightened things. But this never dawned upon her. She sat, and dreamily waited – for nothing; her thoughts dwelling on the one subject that engrossed them always now, going over it again and again, always coming to a *cul de sac*, and turning wearily back once more. Presently, woman-like, she looked down at her dress; it was good enough, but not too well made: another woman would probably have called it dowdy. At her throat there was some soft lace, badly arranged; it had not the picturesque touch that other fingers would have given it, or the prim fashioning that would have suited her perfectly, if she had but known how to manage it. She raised her eyes to the mantel-shelf; there was a tiny Dresden china clock on it. She thought for a moment vaguely of the housemaid, and wished she dusted more carefully. There were some little cut crystal vases full of yellow roses, though it was winter-time. She had told Teddy once, in a longing voice, that she had seen a bowl of them at Christmas-time at Mrs Stanley's; and the next day he had ordered a florist to send her some every week. It was very good of him; but she remembered how once, a few months after they were married, he had brought her home half-a-dozen snowdrops, and she had kissed them every morning when she changed the water. It was not possible to kiss flowers sent from a florist's. And then her eyes fell on Teddy's portrait, smiling down on her as he himself never smiled. Her breast swelled, a lump rose in her throat, as she wondered of what it was that he had been thinking – of whom, that he had looked so happy, when that portrait was taken, so unconstrained, so thoroughly light-hearted. It had not been taken very long; yet it was years since she had seen that look on his face when he was alone with her. She felt as if she depressed him now, as if she were a duty, a part of his routine of life, a relation, a something he had to take care of and look after, but his sweetheart, his wife, the woman of his heart – no, never. It was all right, perhaps; many men grew absorbed in their work after they were married, and merely took their wives in with the matter-of-course part of their lives. And yet all the women she knew, even the women with far less easy-going generous husbands than hers, were on a better footing than she – a footing that meant greater happiness, that was altogether more satisfying to their hearts and their womanly dignity. She put her face down on her hands for a moment, and shutting out the room and the memory of the last few years, thought over the time of her engagement. It had been a very happy one, for she had been very much in love, and unsophisticated enough to take it for granted that Teddy was also. It never entered her head that her money could have had anything to do with her marriage. It simply never occurred to Mildred to suspect any one – much less her own husband – of meanness or untruth. Yet now, looking back, she felt as if he could not have cared very much; she remembered that he had not seemed very eager even when he proposed. He had written to her once a week – religiously once a week; but his letters had not been very full of endearment. They had satisfied her at the time, but now they seemed to have been almost cold; for since her marriage she had once or twice been shown other girls' love-letters – they were vastly different from Teddy's to her. She sat and wondered, then suddenly rose, went to the glass over the china shelf at the end of the room and looked at herself, long and sorrowfully. And then she dimly understood it all. She was a woman who would never win any man's intense love – a woman to marry for peace and quietness – one whom a man might be certain would never cause him a moment's uneasiness – but not a woman with whom to fall in love. She looked at her soft and yet dull grey eyes, her only tolerable complexion, her lips that lacked form and colour – at her slim figure that had no roundness, at her own youth that had none of the flush and sunniness of youth. For a moment something like despair overtook her, and then a quick thankfulness that Teddy was so engrossed with his work and whist. Perhaps it would never strike him, perhaps he would never see at all what she saw plainly. In future she would try to accept the inevitable, to be content with what she had; for she felt that it was impossible to get more, it was not in her to provoke it. It was perhaps lucky that Teddy did not go out oftener – did not care for women's society. Who knows but what, seeing the difference, he might – but she could not even think of that! If Teddy were to care for another woman she should die. His neglect, his carelessness, his scant love-making, his absorption in his work – all these she could endure. After all, was it not something to be his, to bear his name, to live beneath the same roof, to have all the affection and care he could spare time or remembered to give her? But if he had cared or were to care for any one else, it would kill her. It was a happy thing for her that women were not attractive to him, that he troubled so little about them.

It was five o'clock. She stopped her thinking as a matter of course, a little brass kettle was brought in, and after waiting a minute for the water to boil up over the spirit lamp, she made tea, then while it was drawing took up her knitting and worked, glad that some little part of the day's routine had claimed her attention. Suddenly there came a cheering sound that caused her to look up expectingly – the sound of the visitors' bell; and then there entered a pretty little woman, lively, and with plenty to say. It was quite a novelty to see anyone so late in the afternoon; Mildred's face almost brightened into a laugh, she was so glad and surprised.

'I thought I should find you,' Mrs Carew said, sitting down and preparing for a cosy chat. She had known Mildred for years – ever since her marriage; and had always rather gone out of her way to be cordial. 'Yes, I am longing for some tea,' she added, as the second cup was brought in. She pulled off her glove ready for some hot tea-cake, and then, seeing that there was none, put it on again. Tea-cake was just one of those things that Mrs Archerson would not have, Mrs Carew thought; but it was too cold for bread-and-butter. 'I have been shopping all the afternoon and am so tired,' she said, putting her two little feet on the fender – 'and so cold,' she added, with an apologetic laugh for making herself so much at home.

'Shopping is very tiring,' Mildred remarked.

'Oh dear, yes, very; and I always have to do mine in a hurry. I never have time for anything. I often wish our grandmothers could come back and see what busy lives women have nowadays. It would astonish them.'

'I suppose they went about less than we do,' Mildred said thoughtfully.

'Far less. It is a mere miracle that they did not get covered with moss, on the principle of the stone that never rolls. But they must have had an easy time. I wish I had been born a grandmother.'

'I dare say they found plenty to do, after all,' Mildred answered. 'They looked after their homes better than we do.'

'Made jam and dusted their own china. I am glad we don't. They took more trouble about their homes it is true, but with less success; and they took very little trouble about their dress.'

'But their dress was very pretty. Why, we copy it now!'

'Oh, yes, occasionally. But they always looked precisely the same, and all alike; and we are always looking different, which adds to our charm,' Mrs Carew laughed, 'and prevents our husbands from getting tired of us, as our grandpapas often did of our grandmammas.'

Mrs Archerson thought the remark was not a very nice one, but she was too much interested in the subject to mind.

'Do you think,' she asked slowly, 'that anything one wears or does has any effect on one's husband – say three years after marriage?'

'Of course it has. Three years! Why, it has an effect thirty years after. I often think that it is a woman's own fault if he changes or grows tired of her. It is terrible to a man always to see the same thing before his eyes. She should take care not to become monotonous, not even to herself, for fear of growing stupid!'

'But how is she to avoid growing monotonous to herself? She can't make herself into somebody else to avoid getting tired of herself,' Mildred said. She was becoming quite excited in the conversation, feeling as if every moment Mrs Carew might accidentally give her some recipe by which Teddy could be turned into a devoted husband.

'She can change – she can alter her dress, her amusements, her everything. Men grow tired of women who are always the same, just as they would tire of the same dinner every day. Besides, it would be so dull to one's self to be always the same; one would know so little, and be so narrow. Surely it is better to change with life, which is always changing?'

'I think men grow tired of their wives because they are there, and under their control – because with marriage all the romance and necessity for love-making comes to an end,' Mildred said.

'But wives are not entirely under their control,' Mrs Carew laughed. 'And the romance and all the rest of it does not come to an end with marriage – unless the woman chooses. Let us be thankful for our station in life, my dear. The men much lower down beat their wives; and the men a little lower down

– the second-rate men, and half-educated – have notions about keeping their wives in order, and treat them as puppets of which they must pull the strings. But that is over as far as the majority of us are concerned. I think wives now have a very good time; they do pretty much as they like. Men like pleasant companions; and if a woman only knows how to look nice and be nice, she has nothing to complain of.'

'I don't believe in Women's Rights,' Mildred said nervously.

'Neither do I,' answered Mrs Carew. 'But I believe in having a good time. And if we are only nice to our husbands, and take care not to be always the same, that's the fatal thing, we get an excellent time. I know I do – get my own way and fight Charlie as much as I like on various topics, and all the time am proud to feel that he is the stronger of the two, even if he does give way. We all like strong men, you know.'

'Yes – when they love us,' Mildred answered.

'Ah,' Mrs Carew said, with a little mock sigh – 'yes, when they love us. It is a terrible thing to reflect how much we women depend for happiness on our affections. If we are only well-loved all the world is ours, and anyone else who pleases may have fame and wealth and everything life has to give, but that is not worth sixpence to one of us, unless we have also love. It is horrible! Give me some more tea – may I have another cup?' And then poor Mildred's aching heart found courage to put the question she longed to ask all women she met.

'Is your husband as fond of you as ever – I don't mean is he kind only; but is he fond of you?'

'As much in love as the day we married – just. I mean him to remain so till the day I die.'

'But if he altered – if he grew careless?'

'Ah, I should nip that sort of thing in the bud, for fear of getting my heart broken,' she added.

'But how would you nip it in the bud?' asked Mrs Archerson eagerly.

'I can't tell you at this moment,' Mrs Carew said, with an air of consideration; 'but I should do it – or run away' – and seeing Mrs Archerson look shocked, she added 'or die'. There was nothing to shock her principles in the idea of dying, Mrs Carew thought.

'Teddy is so much taken up with his work,' Mrs Archerson said.

'He is getting on. How proud you must be!' And she looked up with a sympathetic glow on her pretty face, but it reflected none on Mildred's. 'His name is always in the paper now. What lovely roses! You must have some kind friend at Nice who sends them?'

'No; they came from the florist's'.

'How very extravagant! Charlie would give me a little wigging[9] if I indulged in such luxuries.'

'I don't; it is Teddy. He ordered them, and told Brooks to send enough every week to fill the glasses; he knows I like flowers.'

'I call that being an attentive husband,' Mrs Carew said, arranging her cloak-clasp and preparing to go.

'So he is,' Mildred answered in a grateful voice, while her heart reproached her with all her discontent – 'the best and the most generous in the world.'

'By-the-way, were you going on to the Palace yesterday?'

'No. Why?'

'Oh, Charlie said he saw you at Clapham.'

'At Clapham?' Mrs Archerson looked up in surprise.

'Yes, he saw Mr Archerson, and thought you were with him; but you had your back turned, and he only saw your bonnet – or hat, I think he said,' Mrs Carew answered, wondering vaguely, now that it was too late, whether she had been indiscreet; but still something made her go on. 'He said you were on the platform at Clapham, but he did not see you at the Palace, though he looked out for you. He went down to the meeting. Perhaps, after all, he was mistaken,' she added, trying to patch up any mischief she might have done.

'Perhaps so; or perhaps Teddy met some one he knew,' Mrs Archerson said, slowly and naturally enough. But swift as an arrow her thoughts went back to that evening, many months ago now, when the man brought the card-case he had found at Clapham – and from that moment Mrs Archerson was not only an unhappy but a jealous woman. With jealousy too there came its wisdom, or its artfulness. She said nothing to her friend – nay, she seemed to suddenly brighten – and was so lively that when Mrs Carew went home she told her husband Teddy A.'s wife was a nice little thing; it was a shame Teddy didn't take her about more.

'She's rather slow, you know, darling,' Mr Carew answered. 'And then, she always looks so dowdy.'

'I know,' his wife answered triumphantly. 'I tried to give her a hint of that to-day. I told her you men were all susceptible to pretty clothes.'

'Indeed! That's your sole reason for wearing them, I suppose?'

'Of course, and because I like you to admire me; and – oh, by-the-way, Charlie, she wasn't at Clapham yesterday. Are you certain there was some one with him?'

'Certain. You were not such a goose as to tell her so?'

'Yes, I did; but I don't think I made any mischief. She said he had probably met some one.'

'Well, perhaps he had. Teddy has toned down of late years. Still, when a man has married for money he is not always such a pattern of virtue as if – '

'As if he had married for love, as you did?'

'Precisely.'

'Then it is a great pity that she was not a pauper, as I was, poor thing.'

'Don't be too sure. You may have been an heiress unawares, and I may have known it beforehand.' At which his wife laughed, and said she only wished it were true. And then they went merrily down to their cosy little dinner, while Mrs Archerson at Kensington was looking blankly at her lonely meal, and wondering if she could get two or three mouthfuls down just to deceive the servants. Ten minutes before she had received a telegram saying that her husband was detained and could not be back to dinner.

Teddy came home late that night, but Mildred was still up – an unusual thing for her; she looked so pale and worn that he noticed it.

'You should have gone to bed,' he said anxiously. 'You know you are not strong enough to be up late at nights. Besides, it worries me to think you are waiting for me.'

'I wanted to finish my work. Besides, I don't see very much of you now, Edward.'

He winced a little. Moreover he always felt uneasy if she called him Edward when they were alone. It was absurd, but it gave him an idea that things were not quite right.

'No, you don't, I am afraid. Somehow I never have any time now.'

'Have you been at work all the evening?'

'Well – no, dear, not precisely at work; but I have been occupied.'

'Mrs Carew came to-day. She says you must be getting on, for she is always seeing your name in the papers.'

'That's all right,' he answered cheerfully.

'I looked for it this morning, but I did not see it. Were you in any case yesterday?'

'Yesterday – let me see. Well, no, not yesterday, dear. I was in chambers all day looking through a brief with Wilson.'

She looked up at him keenly.

'All day?' she asked, and saw him wince.

'Nearly all day. I had an engagement in the afternoon. Why do you ask?'

For a moment she hesitated, tempted to tell him her suspicions. But it is the curse of jealously that it cannot be straightforward, and she fenced. Something seemed to close her lips. She grew silent and miserable – so miserable that she became thin and pale, and more and more dejected. But tears and dejection, especially when they cannot be accounted for, win no man's heart; and Teddy, though he was sorry enough, and anxious too, felt his feet hurry faster and faster from her, day by day. At last she looked so ill he grew alarmed. 'She wants more excitement,' he thought. 'It's dull for her alone all day at Kensington.' He pondered over matters a bit, and then a bright thought struck him. 'I'll tell you what it is, Millie,' he said 'you want a thorough change. You ought to get away from all this fog and brick and mortar. How would you like to go to Rome for a month or two, or to Nice or Mentone? You were always fond of travelling.'

'With you, Edward?' she asked eagerly.

'Well, no. You see it would be utterly impossible for me to get away. Mrs Carew would miss my name in the paper every morning. But you might take Amy with you. I dare say she would be delighted. I should be rather on my beam ends at Nice or Mentone, though of course I could get over to Monte

Carlo every day; but I don't suppose you would approve of that, or care about staying there.'

'I should care about staying anywhere with you,' she answered quickly.

'Couldn't manage it, dear – not even for a day. Too many things coming on.'

'Then let me stay,' she said. 'I would far rather stay at home.'

'You shall do as you like; but I would rather that you went.'

'Do you want to get rid of me, Teddy?'

'No, of course not. Why should I want to get rid of you?' he asked. But after that he did not press her to go. 'She is only a little moped,'[10] he thought. 'I am away a good deal, and she hasn't many resources. I wish she would go to Mentone for a few months, it would do her a world of good; and I might be able to turn out and fetch her at Easter.'

But Mrs Archerson did not mean to go. She stayed at home with eyes that watched and ears that tried to hear, and a heart that ached sorely, with a feeling that a strange drama was being played almost in her presence, but the curtain of the theatre was down so that she could not see, and she was dazed and could not comprehend. She knew instinctively that the end would come of all this terrible suspense, that some day, some moment when she least expected it, the curtain would be thrust aside, and all things made plain. She waited, dreading what she might lift her eyes to see.

Chapter III

The great case of Willoughby v. Conyers came on in January. Teddy went off in good time on the morning of the trial. His wife remembered afterwards with a sort of dazed wondering that when he reached the street door he hesitated, and turning back looked in at her, saying 'Good-bye, Millie. Keep up your courage.' Courage for what? It was like the ringing of the prompter's bell to an actor about to play a part in an unknown play. She watched him out of sight, but he did not know, he never looked back; she knew that he forgot her as soon as the door that divided them closed behind him. It had never struck her before that when that door closed it left her a prisoner and made him a free man.

As Teddy vanished in the distance she went back to the fire, and sat thinking over the one ceaseless subject of all her thoughts. What did it mean, her husband's absences, his excuses, his almost elaborate efforts to be kind? She no longer for a moment supposed that he spent all his evenings at his chambers or his club, or went twice a week to see a bachelor friend at Richmond. There was some other woman. For a long time she did not dare to think it, but now she felt it and knew it – some woman who had won him from her. And the odd thing was, that she did not blame him much; it put a sick dread in her heart, while all things grew dim before her eyes; it made her unspeakably miserable, and yet hardly angry at all. Since that afternoon when she had looked hopelessly at her own face she had understood all that Teddy felt, struggle against it as he would; it said something for her courage that she dared thus far to face the truth. Besides, she loved Teddy too well to be angry with him – the great love was greater than all feelings of anger and pride, than all those that go to make up indignation and self-assertion. It was as a calamity, the greatest that could overtake her, that she dreaded what might come – there might be pain too great to bear, and yet she able to do nothing but bow her head. Other women who loved less might rage and storm with all the fury of jealousy and the burden of insult; it was not in her to do that – not yet, at any rate – as she sat there staring the idea of what might come blankly in the face. Before the reality all her feelings might change – she did not know, she could not tell. She only did know that if she might but have Teddy's deep true love, such as other men gave other women, for just one hour – just one hour to see his face and hear his voice all full of tender love for her – of lover's love, and not mere dutiful affection – if she might but feel his dear arms round her and rest her head on his shoulder for even one single moment, while he stooped whispering foolish love-words to her, and then she had to die, no matter how terrible and lonely a death, she could yet bless fate for its goodness and bountifulness to her. It was odd how the misery of the last few months had brought the unsuspected passion in her nature to the surface – passion she held down and hid, but could not kill. A little while since she had been an even-humoured, humdrum woman; but all the time hidden somewhere there had been in her heart a little spark of fire that lately had been fanned and fanned by cold and bitter winds until it had leaped into flame – flame that withal was subdued by the gentleness of her nature. She was stupid with going over and over and over the same thing again and again; she could think, even of it, actively no more, but sat by the fire, blankly staring at it, the everlasting subject on which she for ever speculated. She tried to rouse herself, and went to the window. The postman was in the street, she went back to her seat by the fire and listened to his knocks. They made her realize that she was very lonely; the simple homely sound seemed to come into an empty room, and to find just one woman sitting by the fire. She heard his footsteps faintly on the pavement, and followed him in thought from house to house. Then he stopped before the gate; she knew when he pushed it open; she heard him come up the steps and drop something into the letter-box. The servant would bring it in a moment – more than one letter, she thought, judging from the sound. She shivered and drew nearer to the fire; there is nothing so chilly as misery.

A note and two printed things – circulars, from the look of the wrappers – were brought in. She put them down on her lap and looked round the room again, as if to take farewell of the familiar objects before the play she had been waiting for ceased to be a play and turned into a living reality. Then she opened the note. It was a dinner invitation from the Paton-Greenes'. She wondered listlessly if Teddy would go, and began to think again. Presently she took up the circulars. One was about the Kensington Bazaar. She had been asked to assist in it. She would get Amy to make some things: perhaps Amy would like to come up for it and stay a bit. But no, she did not think just now that she could bear to have anyone staying with her. She wanted to be alone, to think over the great problem that was for ever perplexing her. She opened the other circular: it was about cottage homes for destitute children, an appeal for subscriptions, a list patrons and donors. She put it down and began to think once more. The Dresden clock struck ten. Teddy was in his wig and gown, looking bright and handsome. He would be a judge some day, of course. Already he talked of applying for silk,[11] and would probably do so in a couple of years. It was so certain that his career would be a triumph; how odd it was that she did not care! But she cared for nothing save that one thing that she felt was for ever denied her.

The fire was burning hollow. She stirred it, and made a blaze; and mechanically taking up the circular about cottage homes, began reading down the list of donors of small sums. Suddenly she started to her feet, her heart stood still, and quick as lightning it flashed through her that everything was about to be made plain. There, half-way down the page, was –

Mrs Edward Archerson, 3, Sisterton Road, Clapham. £3 3s.

Her own name, and at Clapham! It was in the Sisterton Road that the man had found the card-case; she remembered it perfectly. There were not two Mrs Edward Archersons, there could not be; there were no Archersons in London except themselves. Teddy had often said so in the first years of their marriage. Then suddenly it seemed as if a storm had overtaken the lonely woman standing there helpless and alone.

'Oh, what shall I do!' she cried – 'what shall I do! It will break my heart.' She walked about the room in a frenzy of misery, wringing her hands and wishing that she could die. She was mad, or blind, or foolish. It was a nightmare, an evil dream. She stopped quickly and snatched up the paper and looked at it again, half expecting to see that it had vanished. But no, it was clear enough, and she was wide awake. Oh, if Teddy would only come back – if she could but telegraph to him or devise some way of getting at him, to get him to clear up this mystery! She could not wait till evening time. Then, as if a wind had swept over her, the vehemence died away, the old quiet nature asserted itself, and she sat down calm and still, perhaps half-stunned, to think things over and decide what she would do. She folded her hands and looked blankly towards the window, as she had before the postman; she thought of him for a moment, and the difference his coming had made. She realized that she had regained the senses that had seemed to be going a few minutes since; but the calmness that was overtaking her was the calmness of despair. For before that story was told she knew what it was, and what the end must be. Once more she looked at the name and address. Yes, it was spelt properly – it was the same, the very same; there was no mistake at all. She put it, together with the one about the Kensington Bazaar, into her pocket. In every corner of the room the face of the unknown woman at Clapham seemed to be shaping itself in a blurred mocking manner. She could not see what it was like, only that there was a look upon it that would drive her out of the world. The clock struck half-past ten. Teddy was in Court, full of his case; and she – for a moment she put her hands over her face and shuddered.

'It is no good waiting or flinching,' she thought. 'I will know what it all means. I will see her. I must and will.'

She rang the bell, and waited nervously for it to be answered. It was the beginning of what she was going to do. She was curious to hear her own voice, to judge how she would play her part.

'I am going out,' she said to the servant. 'Tell Rice that I shall want the carriage in half-an-hour.'

She went upstairs and dressed, feeling as if she were a person in a dream pretending to be some one who was awake. She pushed her hair back from her forehead, and put on a veil that tied with two ends under her chin. When she was ready she sat down for a moment and considered. It was a desperate thing that she was about to do, but she was determined to have all doubts set at rest, and above all she was determined to see the woman who bore her name. As if she had decided on some plan of action, she got up after a few minutes and rang the bell again.

'Marks,' she said, 'I shall not want the carriage. I am going to walk.'

She was very calm. No one would have suspected that she was playing a part in a tragedy. Her face was merely the face of a woman setting about the commonplace routine of her daily life. She went slowly downstairs and out of the house. As she left it she turned to look back, and recognised with a quick throb how much she had loved her home. She had perhaps never wholly realised this before, it had merely been a part of her life; but now she felt that it was about to be wrenched away, to become a separate thing, a memory that would for ever be an ache and pain, a bit of the past that had nothing to do with the present.

She went on towards the Addison-road Station. She had never been to Clapham; she had thought of it as a junction at which everyone took fresh trains and no one knew whither the old ones went. Oh, yes! there was Clapham Common. Admiral Somers had once lived there. She remembered how, when he used to dine with her father, he always left at ten o'clock, always remarking in precisely the same tone that he had a long way to drive. How strange it was to think of him now, while she was walking perhaps to the end of the world – to the end of all it held for her. There was a cold wintry wind; she shuddered as it swept past her, it seemed as if it would bear off all the life left in her. Oh, if it could! if it would! If she had only died yesterday – last night, in that dream that kept coming back, all confused and broken, as if it were struggling to make itself clear, to show her that it had had some bearing on all this!

She tried to rouse herself a little, wondering if it were after all but an evil dream. Surely no waking woman could feel as she did – so strange and dazed that she could do and was doing she hardly knew what, but waited half-curiously to see. Afterwards, when the calm came in which she sat and thought all things over, it seemed to her that she had suffered more during that morning of uncertainty and dread than in all the after hours. It was pain so great that it stupefied all other sense, and drove her onwards without consideration of any sort.

There was a train ready to start from Addison Road; she found an empty carriage, and, incapable of thinking more, turned and looked aimlessly out of window. There were the squalid dreary backs of houses – she wondered if the people who lived within were ever happy? – the ugly unkept gardens, with the clothes hanging out to dry, or the crooked dirty lines, where they had been hung, left forgotten. The gardens were worse than the houses, and she looked up at the windows again. She could see into some of the rooms, corners of beds, backs of toilet-glasses, now and then a cheap ornament, and she recoiled a little. It was all so tawdry – the tawdriness of the lower middle-class, that knows not how to make the best of poverty as even the poorest poor of other countries do, and that never for a moment has dreamt of making itself picturesque. A path of green came, a bank of gravel, an open space, a few distant trees; she looked at them all, glad of the lull that had come into her heart, and speculating idly how long it would last.

A few minutes more and she was at Clapham Junction. It was quite odd to go outside the station and not down among the passages. She enquired of a porter for Sisterton Road. It was a long way off, he said; he didn't quite know how far. So she took a cab and told the man to drive her to it; and when at last he stopped at the end of the Road, she felt more than ever as if everything was a dream and the waking far away somewhere beyond the world. She walked slowly down the Road – No. 3 was at the other end. For a moment she almost stopped her dreamy state to wonder what to do next. But she was too intent on her object to trouble about details. Besides, she had the Bazaar circular; that would serve as an excuse. She was quite accustomed to going on charity missions, and was not likely to betray herself. There were some shops to pass; she saw herself reflected in one of the plate-glass windows. Her prim bonnet with the veil tied under her chin, the comfortable fur-trimmed cloak, the quiet self-possessed air – all helped to make her appear quite a model charitable lady out on a subscription-hunt.

She stopped before the house at last. There were some dark evergreens in boxes at the windows, a little shining brass knocker to the olive-green door. It looked like a cosy, well-kept house, and her heart sank as she beheld it. Even from the outside she fancied that it had an air of Teddy. A young maid-servant answered Mildred's knock, and stared at her in blank surprise, as though she were wholly unused to visitors. Yes, Mrs Archerson was at home.

'Will you ask if I can see her? I will not keep her long. It is on business,' she added hurriedly; for the servant hesitated.

'Well, I'll see.' And, half-unwillingly, she showed the way into a little drawing-room on the ground-floor – a pretty room, all curtains and flowers, brass ornaments, and Japanese screens with storks on them. And there, on a little table facing the doorway, in a crimson plush frame, was a portrait of Teddy. All hope died out of Mildred's life as she beheld it. It was true, then, true – true. On the mantel-shelf was another portrait – a little smiling one, like that she had at home. She understood now of what he had been thinking when the happy look came over his face, and for a moment she was bitterly angry and indignant. She would denounce him to the shameless woman for whose sake he had been so false, and leave the house; she felt that it was unfit for her feet to stand in, and – but, while she was still defiant, the door opened, and there appeared a woman with a slight round figure, and a face on which there was nothing shameless, nor any consciousness of wrong.

She was five or six-and-twenty, perhaps, the woman who entered, but she looked so young that Mildred, remembering her own two or three additional years, felt as if old age had suddenly fastened upon her. A girl, in fact, whom one only called a woman because there was about her a certain sedateness as of one who had domestic responsibilities, and a distinct and defined place in the world. She had blue eyes – tender eyes, with a dreamy look in them, as though they remembered much; and golden-brown hair, twisted in soft coils round her head, different enough from poor Mildred's dull plaits.

'You wanted to see me?' she asked. Mildred's lips quivered, but made no sound. For a moment it seemed as if she were tottering, though the calm face betrayed nothing. 'May I ask why you wish to see me?' There was some surprise in the voice, perhaps a little nervousness. Mildred, pulling the circular concerning the Bazaar from her pocket, tried to remember her part.

'I ought to apologise, but I believe you take an interest in things that help women and children; and there is to be a Bazaar – ' An air of relief spread over the other's face, a happy smile came to her lips, as she interrupted, almost gaily:

'Oh, yes, indeed I do, a great deal of interest; but I never go to Bazaars or take stalls, or do anything of the sort, if that is what you wish to ask.'

'No,' Mildred answered, 'I did not want that. I – ' She stopped almost with a gasp; but the girl, suspecting nothing, took the circular, and holding it between her two dimpled hands, glanced quickly down it. On the third finger of her left hand there was a pile of rings; the bottom one was a wedding-ring. It fascinated Mildred like a snake.

'But this is for Kensington. Why should you come to us at Clapham?'

'It does not matter where they live, if – ' She tried to think of the words to say, but they were like a lesson long forgotten, and impossible to repeat correctly.

'How did you get my address?' the girl asked, puzzled. 'And how did you know that I was interested in charities? I never did anything in public in my life, and I don't want to do anything. Do tell me how you got my name?'

'I found it in a list of donors to cottage homes for children,' Mildred said, looking at the face before her as though she would remember it through all eternity. It was such a happy face; it looked as if there could never have been a cloud on it, never a single tear in those soft eyes.

'Oh, yes, I know. I gave the money, but did not mean my name to appear; and I was so vexed when – ' She stopped, and followed the eyes that, with a sad, almost wild look in them, had turned from her face to Teddy's portrait on the table.

'Is that your husband?' Mildred asked slowly, in a low voice, with bated breath. The answer came quickly and firmly.

'Yes, that is my husband.'

'Mr Edward Archerson?'

'Yes.' The speaker looked up, and then her lips closed as if she were prepared to resent any more questions. For a moment they looked at each other in silence; then, with a faltering voice, Mildred spoke –

'I did – I did not know his wife lived here. I thought she lived elsewhere. Please forgive me,' she added hurriedly; for she saw the colour rising on the girl's face, and the idea was taking possession of her that Teddy might have been deceiving two women – that two would have to suffer. 'Please forgive me,' she repeated, 'I know him well. I have known him for years,' she added. The girl rose, and stood looking Mildred straight in the face.

'What do you mean? Did you come on purpose? What business have you to intrude here asking questions? Did you come on purpose?' she repeated, almost breathlessly.

'Yes, I came on purpose,' Mildred said, in the same low voice in which she had previously spoken; it seemed as if she had no strength to raise it.

'May I ask why?' The words were meant to be defiant, but there was a note of coming fear in her voice.

'Because there is one woman to whom this is a matter of life and death,' Mildred answered, so calmly that she might well be taken for a person outside the desperate scene that seemed to be going on somewhere else rather than in the room in which they stood – two women, each with a part that meant her life's whole history. They stood looking at each other for a moment gravely and silently. The girl's face had lost its flush, and slowly turned ashy white. But otherwise she took no notice of Mildred's answer. When she spoke again each word seemed to be dragged from her.

'You say you have known him for years,' she said. 'Did you know that – he – was married?'

'Yes, I knew that he was married.'

'Do you know his wife?' The question was almost whispered.

'Yes, I know his wife,' came the calm, unflinching answer. The girl waited a moment, but the inexplicable woman before her seemed like some strange automaton, and did not offer to speak of her own accord.

'Well? – do you know her well?' There was a change in Mildred's voice then.

'Yes, I know her well,' she said, bitterly; 'better than anyone else in the world knows her.'

'You are her friend?'

'Yes, I suppose so.'

'When did you find this out?'

'Just before I started – an hour ago.'

'Then she cannot know yet! Oh, don't tell her! don't tell her!' the woman who had taken Mildred's place cried, putting her hands out entreatingly. 'Don't tell her. He says she is so gentle and good, it would break her heart. I would rather die, I think, than that she should know;' and, suddenly resting her face down on the edge of the velvet-covered shelf, she sobbed bitterly. The words took Mildred altogether aback, but her heart grew cold and hard as she watched her rival – her rival, and no dupe – and, apart from all other feelings, the remembrance of a marriage ceremony with a choral service filled her full of indignation.

'You are very considerate,' she said, in a grinding voice; 'it is most kind.' The girl raised her head quickly, and brushed her tears away.

'You don't understand,' she said, almost fiercely. 'Wait, and in a moment I will tell you. You must let me get calm – you say you know him – and her?'

'Yes, I know them well.'

'Then you know that he married her for her money. He did not love her. She is very gentle and good, but he does not love her; he never did, and he always loved me – always.' She clasped her hands together, and said the last words with a tenderness of which Mildred knew her own voice to be incapable. In that tone alone lay half the reason of everything.

'Always?'

'Yes, always. He loved me before he had ever seen her.'

Mildred looked at her half-bewildered, incapable of taking in all the bitterness of those last words; but her thoughts went back to the early days of her married life, to all the little endearments and foolish names and sweet nonsense of the time. It had all been a make-believe, then – a sham, a mockery.

'Why did not he marry you, if he loved you before he even saw her?' she asked.

'I was poor, I had no money at all. I was just a little drawing-mistress, and he was poor too, and very much in debt. One day he told me that it was of no use going on, it couldn't be; that he must have money, and could only get it by marrying. I was angry, he wanted to go, and I let him. We were both wrong, for I let him go, though I knew he loved me; but what could I do?' she asked, still speaking eagerly, as though for dear life. 'I was alone too,' she went on; 'there was no one else in the world, and I was so very, very miserable

I thought my heart would break. And yet I was angry, too, and gave up all my pupils, and moved so that he might not find me. I only wanted never, never to see him again – '

'Well?'

'And then we met, and – and I had nearly died in the two years and more between. It was like Heaven meeting him again; and though he tried to hide it, it was no good – I saw that he loved me just the same. Oh, you cannot think what it was to meet – the misery, the joy of it; and he told me that his wife was good and gentle, but she had no lilt, no go – she loved him in an even, passionless manner, as a school-girl loves, not as I did, as I do! He is just my life!' she exclaimed, with flushed cheeks and eyes that had lost their dreaminess, and flashed as she looked up – 'just my life, and light, and love, and all the world, as I am his.'

'Yes,' Mildred said calmly, 'go on. It is better to tell me all. I know them both, remember.'

'And he had no child, and, try as he would to help it, his wife was so little to him, he could not take her into his life; his heart was empty save for me; it ached for me; and I was alone and loved him. We went on meeting and parting – it was maddening! and at last he made me come to him. "His wife should never know", he said. You must not think – you are her friend, that is why I wish you to know all this – that he does not care for her; he does. But he does not love her; it is just affection – '

'And for her money.'

'Her money was a great deal to him once – he married her for it; but now he is rich, and it is nothing to him. It is that he fears to grieve her; it is because he knows how gentle and good she is – '

'While he is unfaithful to her every hour of his life – ' Mildred said. She had listened to the story as if it were all a dream – a story that concerned some other person – some one she had known and remembered. She could not grasp the fact that it was her own history that she was hearing and living through. The girl looked up quickly at Mildred's last words, and spoke again, as she had all through, in a voice that came from the innermost depths of her soul.

'There are some people,' she said, and Mildred, looking back at her, thought while she listened how blue her eyes were. It was odd how Mildred dallied with her knowledge and her anguish that morning, though it wrecked all her happiness; dallied with it and put it a little way from her, and looked at it curiously as a thing for which she could put off grieving, though she knew that there would never be another hour in her life that would not bear the bitter fruit of this. 'There are some people,' the girl said, 'who have lives that go out to meet each other – ours did. They have met, and can never be parted. She lives there his wife in name and before the world by virtue of a marriage ceremony, but I am the wife of his heart, his soul, his innermost self; and as for wronging her – '

'Does he suppose she will never know?' Mildred asked. She had hardly heard the last words.

'She will never know if he can help it. How is she to know? I use his name, but that is all. I could not bear not to do that. I go nowhere, know no one, we seldom go out together; the name is not in the Directory, it is by the merest accident that it is in that list, and I shall instantly have it withdrawn; it is in no other place at all. How is she to know? We shall keep our secret. Oh, he would not let her know for the wide world.' She went forward a step or two and put her hand on Mildred's arm, but the latter shrank away. 'Oh, if you love her,' she pleaded, not heeding the movement, 'and have any regard for him; if you have a woman's heart, and know what it is to love – be silent. What good will telling her do? It will not make his heart go from me to her. You cannot love as you will. Remember that. Let her keep her poor happiness; she will never find out what a ghost it is. I, loving him, can understand, and dread to think what she would suffer if she knew – '

'You said she was cold.'

'Yes, she is cold – she has no fire, no abandon, no passion; but she is good and gentle, and loves him truly in her own way. Surely, knowing her, you understand; for I, who have never even seen her, can – '

'Oh, yes, I can understand,' Mildred said, with a long weary sigh, and eyes turned towards the door. For one moment she wondered foolishly if she would be a dead woman when she went out of that room. Then she asked one more question. 'Does it never strike you that you are making him wicked, dragging him down, the man you say you love so much better than she does – and that you are doing her a terrible wrong?'

'No, I am not making him wicked,' the girl answered gravely, in the tone of one who was certain; 'and I am not doing her a terrible wrong. He did her that when he married her for her money, and he knows it now. Yet, after all, remember her money bought her the man of her heart, though she does not know that that was the price of him. She will spend her life with him, possessing his affection and regard, bearing his name, sharing his public triumphs. That he never loved her she will never know. Is it not better than if she had never married, had not had the blessedness of being his, of seeing his face every day of her life?' There was something in her voice that was almost eloquence, that paralysed more and more the woman who listened, that seemed to send farther and farther away all the life left in her.

'But she is his wife.' It was a forlorn argument, but there was nothing else to say.

'No,' the other said, contradicting it as a statement she could not and would not allow; '*I* am his wife. Marriage is not a mere ceremony. It is the joining of two lives that for ever become one. I am the woman of his heart. That is my justification. If I were not I should be infamous. But I am not infamous; for I am his wife, body and soul, bound faster than any ceremony in all the world could bind. As for making him wicked' – and a smile that was almost scornful came for a moment to her face – 'I do not, I – oh, I wonder if you understand! Are you married? I do not even know your name. Tell me who you are, and –' The handle rattled for a moment, then the door opened, and there entered a little fair-haired child of two or three years old.

'Mammy, darling!' he said. 'Nurse says am I to go out?'

'Yes, darling; and baby too.'

'Baby's fast asleep,' he answered, looking at the strange lady. Mildred stared at him with a long fixed gaze, as one standing at the gate of hell might turn to see a far-off glimpse of the Heaven for ever denied her. Then she went a step forward towards the door, like some hunted creature seeking instinctively a hiding-place somewhere in the dark, away from everything. How she had longed for children – for a little one to hold in her arms while her husband stooped to kiss it; she knew, too, that he had longed for them. He had them now, and the woman before her was their mother.

'He is so like his father,' the girl said tenderly. 'Teddy, dear, do you love papa?'

'Yes, very much,' the child answered, never once taking his eyes off Mildred; and then shyly turning to avoid her, he ran out of the room. On his way he brushed against her dress, she shivered and shrank back – her husband's child, his and another woman's! The woman looked up as the door closed.

'Do you understand now?' she asked. 'You cannot take him from me, for I am a part of his life. She is a woman outside it.'

'Are you never jealous of her? Do you never wish that she were dead?' Mildred asked, desperately, looking back at her, for she still stood with her face towards the door.

'Dead! No, I could not be so cruel; for life is sweet, even at its worst. And jealous! Why should I be jealous?' the other answered, almost sadly. 'I do not think I am ever jealous. I have his life's best love; why should I grudge her poor heart the little happiness it sometimes gets?'

'May heaven forgive you!' Mildred said, with a sense of awakening life, of returning pain, and of what all this would mean to her.

'Tell me who you are!' the girl cried going forward and trying to see clearly the pale face and grey eyes of the strange woman who had wrung from her the story of her life. 'Tell me who you are! – *you* cannot be his wife! – you could not have borne this if you had been.'

'No, I am not his wife,' Mildred answered; and her whole soul felt the lie to be a truth.

'Do you love her so much, that you feel it thus keenly?'

'It is so terrible, so much worse than death for her.'

'She will never know, unless you tell her. If you are really her friend – if you know what love is – Are you married?' she asked, in her impatient, earnest voice.

'I – I am alone in the world, I think.'

'As I was till I loved him, and he me.'

'Had you no friends, no relations, no one to prevent – '

'No, no one. We came to England, my father and I, when I was little; he speculated, and I was left at school. He died, and I came to London and lived alone, giving lessons. That is my history. There is none to whom I need give account of myself, if that is what you mean. I am his, and he is all I have in the world – he and the children. But before you go,' she pleaded, putting her hand on the door to keep Mildred back for a moment, 'promise me you will not tell her. You will do no good; think how much misery you would cause her. I will make him entreat you too – ' Then Mildred hesitated.

'I will be silent on one condition,' she answered slowly – 'that you are, too – that you never tell him of this.'

'But I never had a secret from him yet in my life. I could not bear to have one. Remember, nothing can part us – not joy, or sorrow, or shame, or anything in the world; it is too late for that. You cannot part us; you will do no good by telling her.'

'Nor you by telling him,' Mildred said, and opened the door.

'If you will promise not to tell her – if that is the only price of your silence – then I will keep your visit a secret from him,' the girl said, giving way, since it was the only alternative.

'Very well. Now let me go,' Mildred answered, in a dreamy, miserable voice; and at last she dragged herself to the street-door. For a moment she stopped, wondering almost wildly where she could go. There was no place in the world for her. No one had any need of her. And while she still hesitated she heard the sound of the child's voice above, and the patter-patter of his footsteps coming down the stairs. She looked up once more, with a look of such unspeakable anguish that it wrung an exclamation from her rival.

'Oh, come back – ' she cried. But Mildred heard no more, only the sound of the child's joyous voice, as with a scared face she hurried into the street.

Chapter IV

Teddy came home to dinner that night. His case was going well, he was in excellent spirits, and ran gaily upstairs to the drawing-room. He felt that something had happened the moment he opened the door. Mildred was lying on the sofa, worn and white. She did not attempt to rise as he entered.

'Why what's the matter?' he asked. 'I thought you would be glad to see me back.'

'Yes,' she answered gently, 'but till half-an-hour ago I thought you were going to dine out. I am resting – it is only a headache,' she added. 'Why didn't you go to your dinner?'

'Had a telegram putting me off. So I instantly telegraphed to you. Did you get it?'

'Yes.'

'I thought you would be glad to see me,' he repeated, resenting mentally his dreary home-coming. 'You are generally glad when I dine at home.'

'Yes,' she said again. She could not say any more, for all the time she heard ringing in her ears, 'You cannot take him from me'; and the infinite pity of her heart kept adding, 'and there are the children.' The anger, the sense of insult, of injury, all that had died away. She was no coward, and unflinchingly faced the whole story. Above all, she saw its hopelessness. There was only one ending, and she knew it. She was like a woman waiting to die. She had a strange power of realising things from another's point of view; it was only from her own that she was narrow; but when mentally she looked from Teddy's she saw clearly, judged herself from it and understood, and did not wonder much. Only there was this great bitterness – it was all done in ignorance, a result of the strange fetters that seemed to bind her body and soul. If she could only once have broken away from them, and have found the voice that was never hers save in the secret recesses of her heart, where, as if in an iron chamber from which it gave no outward sign, a restless fire burnt that made a still agony of life – if just once she had dared to put into words that which she knew well she could never have said at all, for before it reached her lips it would have become distorted, and her voice uncertain and husky. It was no use. For ever before his eyes and in his thoughts she must be the woman she seemed, without charm, or passion, or excitement. His judgment was just; she knew and felt her own narrowness, the narrowness of her outward self, and had no power to help it. It was as if there dwelt in her some other soul besides the one she showed to the world and lived by – some soul that told her of the dullness of its mate, of the unattractiveness of her face and form, of the commonplaceness of her words and gestures, of the bands that bound down her heart, so that even from its depths there came only lukewarm utterances while it vainly longed to find the voice that should have been its natural one. Oh! it was terrible to have that absolute knowledge of self, with the consciousness of the uselessness and hopelessness of striving against it; to know that she had no power to be other than she seemed, to appear other than the woman she looked. A common thing enough, perhaps; for many have secret souls with which to feel, and working ones with which to make themselves felt and known. And if they are judged according to the latter, is it not fair enough in these days, in which it matters little what a man is, but only what he does?

'Have you been out to-day?' Teddy asked, looking round the room with a sense of some defect in its arrangement. It had not the air of restfulness that a woman strong in the characteristics of her sex makes the place to which her husband comes home after his work.

'Yes,' she said once more. There was something choking her, she could not talk. 'You cannot take him from me,' was still ringing in her ears. There were no other words in the world. But as she watched him round the room she thought it was true what her rival had said – she had 'no lilt, no go'. The

216

other woman would have run to meet him, and putting her arms round his neck, looked up into his face with loving eyes and tender words upon her lips. Never in her brightest days had Mildred had courage enough for that sort of thing; she had seemed indifferent, perhaps, but in reality she had been shy and awkward, even with Teddy. She realised this, too, now that all things were too late. Even if to-day had been a year ago, and all the terrible story she had heard untold, it would never have occurred to her to ask Teddy about his work; she had always waited meekly to be told what it pleased him to tell her. The other woman, she knew surely, and he remembered, would have asked him a dozen eager questions – would have lived through the case, laughing at the good points made on his side, vexed at those made on the other. To his wife Teddy hardly mentioned it at all, it never occurred to him that she would be interested in it. He put it away from him as much as possible, in order to talk to her in the manner he thought she would like best.

'By the way,' he said presently, 'I was lunching with Bolton to-day. He gave the medical evidence on our side. I told him about you – that I was anxious to see you regularly set up. He says the real thing for you is a sea-voyage.'

'Yes? To the end of the world?' she asked, getting up and standing listlessly by the fire.

'Well, no, we won't send you quite so far as that; but a brilliant idea struck me all at once to-day. You know George is at Malta. It is a nice place – not too far; you could always race back by Italy, if you were in a hurry to get home again. I should not mind your going out there alone, with Marks, in the P. & O. You would be all right once on board. It is not a long voyage – rather more than a week – but quite long enough to do you good. You would like Malta; there's plenty always going on there. You like George and his wife, and I know they would be awfully glad to see you.'

Teddy had evidently made up his mind that he had hit upon the right thing for her. George was his elder brother.

'Yes, it will do very well,' she answered. 'Let me go at once,' she added. 'I meant to tell you when you came home to-night that I wanted to go somewhere. I don't care where it is, so that it is a long way off. How soon can I go?' There was something in her words and tone that went to his guilty heart like a knife. It was the tone that might have been hers had she known all, and was breaking her heart, he thought. The fire blazed up, and he saw her face plainly. Either the firelight exaggerated its paleness and weariness, or she had altered much since yesterday.

'Is anything the matter? You look so ill – so different,' he said.

'Oh, I am neuralgic, I suppose.' But her voice trembled, her eyes filled with tears. He felt that he was somehow, though how he did not know, responsible for her sorrowfulness; that it was not all neuralgia or mere low spirits, as she would have him believe; and he hated himself for the part he had played. Had she not given him her all in the world – that poor little soul whom he had never once loved truly, but had used merely as a stepping-stone

217

to that which was his now, but a few years since had been far enough away. He felt that he was a scoundrel, and wished with all his heart that in days that were gone he had had courage enough to be honest.

'You will be better soon, dear,' he said gently. 'You want cheering up a bit; you have not been anywhere lately.' And going forward he stooped to kiss her. She pushed him away, almost with a shudder.

'Oh, don't, don't,' she cried, 'I cannot bear it – I cannot, indeed.' He looked at her in surprise. Usually she had been demurely eager for the caresses that he had half-grudged her.

'What is the matter, Mildred?' he asked, facing the worst.

'I am ill,' she answered, cowering away from him. 'I cannot go on living this life. Let me go away.' Then suddenly a flood of memories swept over her, as she looked at him bending down, as she felt his breath upon her cheek – her handsome, clever husband, of whom she had been so proud. She thought of the days they had spent together, days in which she had never dreamt of all that now must evermore divide them. She thought of all his tenderness and gentleness, for he had been very tender and gentle to her; and she divined that at heart he had been grateful and often self-reproachful. He need not have married her; but it was not his fault that he had not been in love with her. Did not many men marry for money, just as he had, and soon grow careless and callous? He had never done that. Perhaps it was all her fault. And yet it was not her fault; for she could not help not being pretty and lovable, like that other woman. She put her arms gently round his neck and kissed him. She had seldom had courage to do so much before uncoaxed, though he was her own husband. 'You must forgive me,' she said, in the low weary voice that had become natural to her, 'I am not well; let me go away, and soon, as soon as possible. I shall be better then. Now I am worn out, and tired of everything.'

'All right, dear,' he said, thankful that the scene was blowing over. 'You shall start for Malta as soon as we can get you off. Now we'll have dinner – there's the gong – so we have just made it up in time. We had better have some champagne to pick us up. Come along.' He pulled her arm through his, and almost dragged her downstairs, in laughing, good-humoured fashion. She would be better when she once got away, he thought. The voyage was an excellent idea. How lucky it was he had spoken to Bolton. She could not help this sort of thing, he supposed; still, it was trying when a man had been hard at work all day. But she had never been so foolish before; it was evident that she was out of health. It was very bad luck that the little girl at Clapham had telegraphed that she had a headache too, and was obliged to go to bed. He had so longed to go to her – and had been looking forward to it all day – his darling, his pretty one; and he thought of her even in that one moment with a love that outweighed all that he had ever felt for the fragile woman on his arm since the day when he had first set eyes on her.

*

Teddy and his wife were standing on board the P. & O. at Southampton. He had come down to see her off. They had lunched together downstairs, and Teddy had quite won over the captain, who knew him by reputation, and was delighted to make his acquaintance. There were a good many passengers, the captain said, and when they were within two or three days of Gibraltar Mrs Archerson would find everything delightful – weather warm, sea smooth, and every one friendly.

'By the way, you stop at Gibraltar, Millie, probably for a few hours,' Teddy said, as they took a last walk up and down the deck, 'so you may be able to go ashore and have a look at the big guns and the orange-trees. I remember George writing home when he stopped on his way to India, and saying it was all big guns and orange-trees.'

'Yes,' she answered. She could only think of him, just of him whom she was about to leave, and not of any place in the world. But he rattled on:

'Lucky little woman you are to get away into the sunshine, while your unfortunate husband stays behind, and slaves – ' She turned round quickly; it seemed as if some words rose to her lips, but if so, they were left unsaid. He misunderstood the action. 'Of course, I sha'n't slave really,' he said, consolingly. 'I dare say I shall manage to take things pretty easily.'

'Oh, yes,' she said, with a long sigh. She had no words to talk with, no thoughts that she dared put into words. She was living through a crisis in which everything but a silent struggle for self-control was impossible. She shivered suddenly – it was all so terrible, and she was so utterly alone in her suffering. He thought she was trembling, and, stopping, adjusted her furs closer round her neck, while she submitted half-bewildered. For a passing moment he vaguely guessed that she was going through some terrible ordeal, and his heart smote him. He pulled her hand through his arm and drew her a little closer to him as they resumed their walk.

'You will soon be in the sunshine,' he said. 'You will get rather too much of it at Malta. They say there isn't a bit of shade to be had, and not a tree higher than a gooseberry-bush.'

'Oh, I don't mind,' she cried; 'I don't mind anything.' She could not bear to hear him talking as lightly as if to-morrow's sun would not rise and find them far apart. Her voice betrayed plainly enough this time that she was suffering, and the knowledge gave him a dull gnawing pain.

'You must take care of yourself,' he said, looking into her grey eyes with a quaking conscience, thankful with a thankfulness that knew no bounds that she had never guessed his secret. He prayed in his heart that she might never know it. 'You don't look up to much now, poor child,' he said tenderly; 'but George and Nellie will take care of you, and cheer you up, and do you a world of good.'

'Yes,' she said, almost gratefully. It was odd how she understood all that was in his thoughts on that last walk they took together.

'You will come back strong and well.'

'If I die,' she said suddenly, 'you must marry again soon and be very happy – do you hear?'

'Nonsense!' and he tried to laugh – a sorry sort of laugh. 'You are not going to die; you must not get morbid.'

'I am not morbid,' she said gravely. Then, after a moment's pause, she went on: 'I wish I had been better to you, Teddy, brighter and more companionable, and more lovable – oh, I do!' she cried. 'I would give all the world to have been different.' The last words came almost in a whisper from her trembling lips. He stopped, and with a troubled face answered her earnestly:

'No one in the world could have been better – no one in the world. You are the gentlest woman alive, Millie; I wish I had been worthier of you.'

She could not speak, but for answer she stooped and kissed his coat-sleeve. It was unlike her, but it was the action by which he remembered her through all the after years.

They stopped by the stern for a moment. The wheel-house was there, and behind it, at the extreme end of the ship, there were two raised steps that formed a seat. It was the point from which the log was taken. Mildred looked at the place for a moment, and hesitated; then mounting the steps, looked down at the water beneath. 'I shall come and sit here when it is warm enough,' she said. 'I shall have my face towards home, and my back towards Malta.'

'Don't you want to go?' he asked, hating himself.

'Oh, yes; I couldn't have stayed longer in England.' She sat down on the steps for an instant, and looked out towards the distance.

'You must mind how you sit there,' he said, 'unless it is very calm. If the ship gave a lurch you would go over before you knew where you were, and not a soul have an inkling of it in time to pick you up.'

'Yes,' she answered slowly, 'if the ship gave a lurch I might go over.'

They went for one more turn along the deck, and then it was time for Teddy to go ashore. He turned back as he stood by the gangway.

'I'll send you a line to Gibraltar, though I am not sure that it will get there in time,' he said. 'But at any rate you can post me one from there, and tell me how you are getting on.' She nodded her head, she could not speak, but he understood. He waved his hand, and she stood watching him going farther and farther away. Just before he vanished altogether he turned and made one more sign of farewell.

'Good-bye,' she whispered to herself, 'good-bye,' and looked at the water – at the sea that already divided them.

Gibraltar, 27*th January*

DEAREST TEDDY,

We stay here about six hours, but I am not going ashore. There is no letter from you. They say it is impossible for one to arrive in time.

We have had lovely weather since Saturday, warm and soft; and I have gone to the little seat we found behind the wheel-house, and sat with my back to the ship and my face towards England, and watched the long line of foam we left behind as we came through the water. I have thought of you all the time; sometimes I have held out my arms to that long white line stretching and stretching between us, and felt as if I would die gladly for one more look at your dear face. I hope you are very happy, Teddy. I am always hoping that.

I do not know what has come to my fingers, I cannot write. I stop to think of one evening, years ago now – it was very soon after we were married – I met you in the hall, and you held me fast and kissed me. It felt as if I could never get away, as if you loved me. If I had only died then – my darling, my love, my husband, *mine*! Don't think that I have not loved you much or passionately because I have kept my heart hidden and my lips still. No woman has loved you nor ever will love you as I have, not if you live to be a thousand. Good-bye. Be happy, very, very happy. Your happiness is the thing I long for most in the world. Always remember that.

MILDRED

Teddy moved from the little house at Kensington before his second marriage, and took a better one nearer town. It was prettier and cosier as well as grander than the one over which poor Mildred had presided – more like a home to which a man hurries back from his work and is proud to ask his friends. He could not bear to spend an evening away from it; he had almost forgotten the short cuts to the club, he went there so seldom; and sometimes, when he was obliged to work in the evening, brought his papers home, and did it in the pretty drawing-room, while his wife sat near him. Many a time when he was absorbed in some legal problem, or framing some eloquent explanation of a difficult point, it helped him to look up and for a moment to see her face. It was like a gleam of sudden sunshine in a lawyer's office. He told her so once, and she laughed – that little merry laugh that seems to live in a happy life, like a bird in a wood – and said she should never have dreamt of calling him a lawyer's office. People said that she had been a widow, that Teddy had fallen head and ears in love with her, and was a wonderful step-father to her children. He and she laughed at the little deception sometimes. They laughed that night when George's letter came, saying that he was on his way home at last, and should be with them before the month was out.

'I wonder if he will be curious about Mr Grey?' Teddy said. 'I shall say you ill-used him, Mary; do you hear?' She was writing notes at a little table beside the fireplace. Her husband sat pretending to turn over a pile of new books, but in reality looking at her, and at all the prettinesses gathered round her. She had altered little since her interview with Mildred, nearly two years ago now. The idealism of youth still looked out of her eyes, and there was

221

more of the strength and passion of womanhood in the lines of her mouth and the tones of her voice. But she was girl-like still, though the white throat was a shade fuller, the sweet face a little graver, perhaps more thoughtful. She was even prettier – she might almost have been called beautiful. Teddy thought so as he looked at her – his sweetheart, his dear one, his wife of whom he was so proud. She had a knack of making her surroundings picturesque, too, and yet most thoroughly comfortable. He had never realised the happy restfulness of home till her hands had made one for him. She had raised in his eyes the whole value of women.

'Dear Mr Grey,' she said, holding out her hand to him. 'I wonder what he was like.' He stooped and kissed her fingers.

'A disagreeable sort of fellow, no doubt.'

'That is ungenerous,' she laughed. 'I wonder if he was fond of his wife?'

'Perhaps so, poor fellow.

'And why poor?'

'No doubt she killed him.'

'Your manners are positively shocking!' she said gaily; 'but I forgive you. I am so happy that I can afford to be generous,' she added, with a touch of gravity.

'Happier than – than before?' he asked.

She clasped her hands together, and answered, with a long sigh of content:

'Oh, a thousand times. I can breathe more freely, and look round and not feel ashamed.

'Ah, I thought Mr Grey was not so very delightful,' he said, trying to laugh away her seriousness. She understood him – she always did, almost instinctively – and tried to fall in with his humour.

'I was very fond of him,' she laughed. 'He was quite as nice as you are, Mr Vanity. Let us draw his portrait.' She took up a pencil and made a grotesque likeness of Teddy, at which he, leaning over her shoulder, laughed, then he looked down at her head and smoothed her hair.

'My pretty wife,' he said. 'Then you can breathe freely now?'

'Yes, but not altogether – it troubles even now to think of it.'

'Ah, you women put an enormous value on respectability,' he answered. He liked to provoke her a little; he thought his words would do it, and he was right. She got up quickly and looked at him.

'It isn't that,' she flashed – 'you know it isn't,' she cried passionately; 'but there are the children. Sometimes when I think of it I feel ashamed to look them in the face – not for what I did, but for what it may yet cause them to suffer.

He hardly listened. She was so pretty when she was roused, when her cheeks were flushed and her eyes sparkling. She knew how to make herself look pretty, too, and did it always for Teddy. He looked at her bright hair, at her trailing dress, at the lace ruffles at her elbows, leaving the white arms bare. There were some flowers in her bosom – he had brought them home that day – round her throat there was a twist of soft lace, fastened with a diamond arrow. He thought of the day when he had bought it and sold it to her for a kiss, while she had declared it was far too dear.

'My prettiest,' he exclaimed, 'how I love you! Don't think of the children – they can never suffer or know. Don't be foolish, my sweet,' and he caught her in his arms and kissed her. 'If I could only know that you would never hate me for it – Mary, I am a fool about you. I love you so, my darling.'

'Hate you!' she cried, 'how could I? And yet I wish it had been right,' she whispered. 'I usedn't to care, but I do now. I would give anything if we had waited. We called what we did fine names, and I felt them all to be true then; but now I seem to see more clearly how wrong it was. I wish we had waited. I remember reading somewhere once, "All sin is dogged; and though that which follows may lag, it never loses the track." Sometimes I feel as if that which follows were overtaking us. Just when I am happiest its shadow is in my heart.'

'Thank God *she* never knew, my darling.' He sat down on her chair by the writing-table as he spoke, and she kneeling beside him clasped her hands upon his shoulder.

'No, she never knew,' she said, with a sigh of thankfulness; 'but – did it ever strike you what a thin curtain sometimes divides us from the most terrible suffering? If she had known – oh, Teddy, what would she have done?'

'It would have broken her heart, I think,' he said, sadly. Then trying to shake off the subject, he played with the arrow at her throat. 'Sweet, would it break your heart if I were false to you?' he asked. The question was half a joke; for he knew how fast her chains bound him. She looked up. There was none of Mildred's patience in her. She was a woman to win love easily, but not easily to let it go.

'Yes, it would break my heart, too,' she answered. 'But first I would kill you.'

'Kill me! Why not kill her?'

'The woman for whose sake you were false? No, I would kill you. She would suffer more in living.'

'Mary, I am half afraid of you,' he said.

With one of her quick changes of mood she laughed, a happy, triumphant little laugh. She unclasped her hands from his shoulders. 'Are you?' she said. 'Then you are free. Go and love elsewhere, if you will.'

'You know I can't,' he said fervently.

'Nor I,' she whispered. 'I never did or could, right or wrong. But oh, how glad I am that it is right at last,' she added, with a sigh.

'So am I, my own – more thankful than I can say.'

'Teddy,' she whispered, 'I never dared say it before; but I wish that she had died naturally – that she had not been drowned.' He nodded his head. Many and many a time had the same thought come over him too. 'It is so strange, but in the twilight I can often see her face looking up from a grey sea to a grey sky, a dead white face.'

'Nonsense!' he shuddered.

'I am thankful that I never saw her,' she went on, with a little shiver – 'that I never even saw a portrait of her. I could not bear to shape her face, her real face, in my thoughts.'

'You shall never see a portrait of her, my darling,' he said. 'But let us shake this off; we are only making ourselves miserable.'

'I know,' she answered. 'Let us shake it off. If she had only not been drowned – it is what might have happened, had she known? She would not have killed you, as I should?'

'No, she would not have killed me. Yes, it is perhaps what she might have done, had she known.'

'Oh, Teddy! it would have killed me too. I should have shrank away from you for ever afterwards.' And even as she spoke she shuddered and drew back from him. 'I would never have let you kiss me again – never! I should have died too.'

'But she never did know, darling. Let us stop all this painful talk. Are we not happy together, in spite of all we did? And were we not happy even then?'

'Yes, oh yes!' she said; and putting her arms round his neck again she rested her face against his, and was silent for a minute. Then she spoke calmly. 'Teddy, dear,' she said, 'I want to tell you something. It is the only secret I ever had from you. It cost me so much at the time, but I promised not to tell, and a sort of superstition has kept me silent. Besides, I wanted to save you pain. I do not think there has been a day since – hardly an hour – in which I have not thought of it. Wait a minute.' She went back to the writing-table, and kneeling before it, took up her pencil, and began to draw some one from memory – some one in a bonnet, with a veil tied under her chin. Suddenly he, watching, started with an exclamation.

'Great Heaven!' he cried, 'it is Mildred!' She got up and stood facing him, holding out her hands as one blinded, while her lips grew white and trembled.

'Then she knew!' she cried, and stretched out her arms, but they did not reach him. 'She knew! oh, God! she knew!' she cried, shrinking as though she dreaded lest he should touch her. Slowly, with scared faces, they looked at each other, it seemed as if across a great space – as if between them flowed the sea.

He shut the door and locked it, feeling that if any one came near him he should go mad. With a shiver he looked round the chilly empty room, and towards the shadowy corners. Then going to the writing-table, with a hand he vainly tried to make steady he unlocked a drawer, and taking out her letter, read it once again. There was a line under the word *mine*, a thick line, blurred, as though a tear had fallen on it. He had wondered when it came – at its passionate tone, at its sadness, at the living something in it that had haunted him many a time since. He remembered the night it had all happened; how he in England had sat through the twilight before the fire talking to Mary. He closed his eyes and groaned as he thought of it; he could see her sitting at the ship's end on the little seat they had looked at together. He remembered that her maid had described how she had not gone down to dinner that night after the ship had left Gibraltar, she had wished to be left alone. He could see her watching the track of the white foam, while the shadows gathered round her, and through the open hatchments came the clink of glasses, the sound of voices, as the passengers dined and laughed in the saloon below. He could feel the cool breeze that swept over her face, could see her hold out her hands to him once more, could feel all the agony in her heart, the bitter, bitter loneliness, and then – ah, God! and the ship went on, and the white line stretched and stretched. And he had sat the while with his arms round another woman.

Notes

Text: *Temple Bar*, June–July 1887.
 1 Working energetically.
 2 Behave in a foolishly amorous way.
 3 Visiting cards.
 4 Carriage drawn by two horses.
 5 Carriage drawn by one horse.
 6 Hiring.
 7 Novel (1766) by Oliver Goldsmith.
 8 Novel (1819) by Walter Scott.
 9 Scolding.
10 Depressed.
11 Barristers appointed Queen's Counsel are entitled to wear a silk gown.

A WICKED VOICE

Vernon Lee

'Vernon Lee' (Violet Paget) (1856–1935), novelist, short-story writer and critic, was born in France and brought up in continental Europe. At 24 she published her most celebrated book, *Studies of the Eighteenth Century in Italy* (1880), adopting a male pseudonym in order to be taken more seriously. She visited England for the first time in 1881. She wrote several novels, of which *Ottilie* (1883), *Penelope Brantling* (1903) and *Louis Norbert* (1914) were historical, *Miss Brown* (1884) was a satire on aestheticism, and *A Phantom Lover* (1886) a fantasy. A number of short stories were collected as *Hauntings* (1890). Her travel writing was much admired, but her most significant works are those on aesthetics: *The Beautiful* (1913) and *The Handling of Words* (1923). Her drama, *Satan the Waster* (1920), drew criticism for its passionate pacifism. *A Wicked Voice* is typical of her short fiction in being an intense psychological study of the effects of evil.

Further reading

Blain *et al.* (1990); Gardner (1987); Gunn (1964); Mannocchi (1983, 1986); Shattock (1993); Sutherland (1988)

A Wicked Voice

They have been congratulating me again to-day upon being the only composer of our days – of these days of deafening orchestral effects and poetical
quackery – who has despised the newfangled nonsense of Wagner,[1] and
returned boldly to the traditions of Handel and Gluck and the divine
Mozart,[2] to the supremacy of melody and the respect of the human voice.

O cursed human voice, violin of flesh and blood, fashioned with the subtle
tools, the cunning hands, of Satan! O execrable art of singing, have you not
wrought mischief enough in the past, degrading so much noble genius, corrupting the purity of Mozart, reducing Handel to a writer of high-class
singing-exercises, and defrauding the world of the only inspiration worthy of
Sophocles and Euripedes,[3] the poetry of the great poet Gluck? Is it not
enough to have dishonoured a whole century in idolatry of that wicked and
contemptible wretch the singer, without persecuting an obscure young composer of our days, whose only wealth is his love of nobility in art, and perhaps
some few grains of genius?

And then they compliment me upon the perfection with which I imitate
the style of the great dead masters; or ask me very seriously whether, even if I
could gain over the modern public to this bygone style of music, I could
hope to find singers to perform it. Sometimes, when people talk as they have
been talking to-day, and laugh when I declare myself a follower of Wagner, I
burst into a paroxysm of unintelligible, childish rage, and exclaim, "We shall
see that some day!"

Yes; some day we shall see! For, after all, may I not recover from this
strangest of maladies? It is still possible that the day may come when all
these things shall seem but an incredible nightmare; the day when *Ogier the
Dane* shall be completed, and men shall know whether I am a follower of the
great master of the Future or the miserable singing-masters of the Past. I am
but half-bewitched, since I am conscious of the spell that binds, me. My old
nurse, far off in Norway, used to tell me that were-wolves are ordinary men
and women half their days, and that if, during that period, they become
aware of their horrid transformation they may find the means to forestall it.
May this not be the case with me? My reason, after all, is free, although my
artistic inspiration be enslaved; and I can despise and loathe the music I am
forced to compose and the execrable power that forces me.

Nay, is it not because I have studied with the doggedness of hatred this
corrupt and corrupting music of the Past, seeking for every little peculiarity

of style and every biographical trifle merely to display its vileness, is it not for this presumptuous courage that I have been overtaken by such mysterious, incredible vengeance?

And meanwhile, my only relief consists in going over and over again in my mind the tale of my miseries. This time I will write it, writing only to tear up, to throw the manuscript unread into the fire. And yet, who knows? As the last charred pages shall crackle and slowly sink into the red embers, perhaps the spell may be broken, and I may possess once more my long-lost liberty, my vanished genius.

It was a breathless evening under the full moon, that implacable full moon beneath which, even more than beneath the dreamy splendour of noontide, Venice seemed to swelter in the midst of the waters, exhaling, like some great lily, mysterious influences, which make the brain swim and the heart faint – a moral malaria, distilled, as I thought, from those languishing melodies, those cooing vocalisations which I had found in the musty music-books of a century ago. I see that moonlight evening as if it were present. I see my fellow-lodgers of that little artists' boarding-house. The table on which they lean after supper is strewn with bits of bread, with napkins rolled in tapestry rollers, spots of wine here and there, and at regular intervals chipped pepper-pots, stands of toothpicks, and heaps of those huge hard peaches which nature imitates from the marble-shops of Pisa. The whole *pension*-full is assembled, and examining stupidly the engraving which the American etcher has just brought for me, knowing me to be mad about eighteenth century music and musicians, and having noticed, as he turned over the heaps of penny prints in the square of San Polo, that the portrait is that of a singer of those days.

Singer, thing of evil, stupid and wicked slave of the voice, of that instrument which was not invented by the human intellect, but begotten of the body, and which, instead of moving the soul, merely stirs up the dregs of our nature! For what is the voice but the Beast calling, awakening that other Beast sleeping in the depths of mankind, the Beast which all great art has ever sought to chain up, as the archangel chains up, in old pictures, the demon with his woman's face? How could the creature attached to this voice, its owner and its victim, the singer, the great, the real singer who once ruled over every heart, be otherwise than wicked and contemptible? But let me try and get on with my story.

I can see all my fellow-boarders, leaning on the table, contemplating the print, this effeminate beau, his hair curled into *ailes de pigeon*,[4] his sword passed through his embroidered pocket, seated under a triumphal arch somewhere among the clouds, surrounded by puffy Cupids and crowned with laurels by a bouncing goddess of fame. I hear again all the insipid exclamations, the insipid questions about this singer: – "When did he live? Was he very famous? Are you sure, Magnus, that this is really a portrait," &c. &c. And I hear my own voice, as if in the far distance, giving them all sorts of information, biographical and critical, out of a battered little volume called *The Theatre of Musical Glory; or, Opinions upon the most Famous Chapel-masters and Virtuosi of this Century*, by Father Prosdocimo Sabatelli, Barnalite, Professor of Eloquence at the College of Modena, and Member of the Arcadian Academy, under the pastoral name of Evander Lilybæan, Venice, 1785, with the approbation of the Superiors. I tell them all how this singer, this Balthasar Cesari, was nicknamed Zaffirino because of a sapphire engraved with cabalistic signs presented to him one evening by a masked stranger, in whom wise folk recognised that great cultivator of the human voice, the devil; how much more wonderful had been this Zaffirino's vocal gifts than those of any singer of ancient or modern times; how his brief life had been but a series of triumphs, petted by the greatest kings, sung by the most famous poets, and finally, adds Father Prosdocimo, "courted (if the grave Muse of history may incline her ear to the gossip of gallantry) by the most charming nymphs, even of the very highest quality."

My friends glance once more at the engraving; more insipid remarks are made; I am requested – especially by the American young ladies – to play or sing one of this Zaffirino's favourite songs – "For of course you know them, dear Maestro Magnus, you who have such a passion for all old music. Do be good, and sit down to the piano." I refuse, rudely enough, rolling the print in my fingers. How fearfully this cursed heat, these cursed moonlight nights, must have unstrung me! This Venice would certainly kill me in the long-run! Why, the sight of this idiotic engraving, the mere name of that coxcomb of a singer, have made my heart beat and my limbs turn to water like a love-sick hobbledehoy.

After my gruff refusal, the company begins to disperse; they prepare to go out, some to have a row on the lagoon, others to saunter before the *cafés* at St. Mark's; family discussions arise, gruntings of fathers, murmurs of mothers, peals of laughing from young girls and young men. And the moon, pouring in by the wide-open windows, turns this old palace ballroom, nowadays an inn dining-room, into a lagoon, scintillating, undulating like the other lagoon, the real one, which stretches out yonder furrowed by invisible gondolas betrayed by the red prow-lights. At last the whole lot of them are on the move. I shall be able to get some quiet in my room, and to work a little at my opera of *Ogier the Dane*. But no! Conversation revives, and, of all things, about that singer, that Zaffirino, whose absurd portrait I am crunching in my fingers.

The principal speaker is Count Alvise, an old Venetian with dyed whiskers, a great check tie fastened with two pins and a chain; a threadbare patrician who is dying to secure for his lanky son that pretty American girl, whose mother is intoxicated by all his mooning anecdotes about the past glories of Venice in general, and of his illustrious family in particular. Why, in Heaven's name, must he pitch upon Zaffirino for his mooning, this old duffer of a patrician?

"Zaffirino, – ah yes, to be sure! Balthasar Cesari, called Zaffirino," snuffles the voice of Count Alvise, who always repeats the last word of every sentence at least three times. "Yes, Zaffirino, to be sure! A famous singer of the days of my forefathers; yes, of my forefathers, dear lady!" Then a lot of rubbish about the former greatness of Venice, the glories of old music, the former Conservatoires, all mixed up with anecdotes of Rossini and Donizetti,[5] whom he pretends to have known intimately. Finally, a story, of course containing plenty about his illustrious family: – "My great grand-aunt, the Procuratessa[6] Vendramin, from whom we have inherited our estate of Mistrà, on the Brenta" – a hopelessly muddled story, apparently, fully of digressions, but of which that singer Zaffirino is the hero. The narrative, little by little, becomes more intelligible, or perhaps it is I who am giving it more attention.

"It seems," says the Count, "that there was one of his songs in particular which was called the 'Husbands' Air' – *L'Aria dei Mariti* – because they didn't enjoy it quite as much as their better-halves . . . My grand-aunt, Pisana Renier, married to the Procuratore Vendramin, was a patrician of the old school of the style that was getting rare a hundred years ago. Her virtue and her pride rendered her unapproachable. Zaffirino, on his part, was in the habit of boasting that no woman had ever been able to resist his singing, which, it appears, had its foundation in fact – the ideal changes, my dear lady, the ideal changes a good deal from one century to another! – and that his first song could make any woman turn pale and lower her eyes, the second make her madly in love, while the third song could kill her off on the spot, kill her for love, there under his very eyes, if he only felt inclined. My grand-aunt Vendramin laughed when this story was told her, refused to go to hear this insolent dog, and added that it might be quite possible by the aid of spells and infernal pacts to kill a *gentildonna*,[7] but as to making her fall in love with a lackey – never! This answer was naturally reported to Zaffirino, who piqued himself upon always getting the better of any one who was wanting in deference to his voice. Like the ancient Romans, *parcere subjectis et debellare superbos*.[8] You American ladies, who are so learned, will appreciate this little quotation from the divine Virgil. While seeming to avoid the Procuratessa Vendramin, Zaffirino took the opportunity, one evening at a large assembly, to sing in her presence. He sang and sang and sang until the poor grand-aunt Pisana fell ill for love. The most skilful physicians were kept unable to explain the mysterious malady which was visibly killing the poor young lady; and the Procuratore Vendramin applied in vain to the most venerated Madonnas, and vainly promised an altar of silver, with massive gold candlesticks, to Saints Cosmas and Damian, patrons of the art of healing. At last the brother-in-law of the Procuratessa, Monsignor Almorò Vendramin, Patriarch of Aquileia, a prelate famous for the sanctity of his life, obtained in a vision of Saint Justina, for whom he entertained a particular devotion, the information that the only thing which could benefit the strange illness of his sister-in-law was the voice of Zaffirino.

Take notice that my poor grand-aunt had never condescended to such a revelation.

"The Procuratore was enchanted at this happy solution; and his lordship the Patriarch went to seek Zaffirino in person, and carried him in his own coach to the Villa of Mistrà where the Procuratessa was residing. On being told what was about to happen, my poor grand-aunt went into fits of rage, which were succeeded immediately by equally violent fits of joy. However, she never forgot what was due to her great position. Although sick almost unto death, she had herself arrayed with the greatest pomp, caused her face to be painted, and put on all her diamonds: it would seem as if she were anxious to affirm her full dignity before this singer. Accordingly she received Zaffirino reclining on a sofa which had been placed in the great ballroom of the Villa of Mistrà, and beneath the princely canopy; for the Vendramins, who had intermarried with the house of Mantua, possessed imperial fiefs[9] and were princes of the Holy Roman Empire. Zaffirino saluted her with the most profound respect, but not a word passed between them. Only, the singer inquired from the Procuratore whether the illustrious lady had received the Sacraments of the Church. Being told that the Procuratessa had herself asked to be given extreme unction[10] from the hands of her brother-in-law, he declared his readiness to obey the orders of His Excellency, and sat down at once to the harpsichord.

"Never had he sung so divinely. At the end of the first song the Procuratessa Vendramin had already revived most extraordinarily; by the end of the second she appeared entirely cured and beaming with beauty and happiness; but at the third air – the *Aria dei Mariti*, no doubt – she began to change frightfully; she gave a dreadful cry, and fell into the convulsions of death. In a quarter of an hour she was dead! Zaffirino did not wait to see her die. Having finished his song, he withdrew instantly, took post-horses, and travelled day and night as far as Munich. People remarked that he had presented himself at Mistrà dressed in mourning, although he had mentioned no death among his relatives; also that he had prepared everything for his departure, as if fearing the wrath of so powerful a family. Then there was also the extraordinary question he had asked before beginning to sing, about the Procuratessa having confessed and received extreme unction . . . No, thanks, my dear lady, no cigarettes for me. But if it does not distress you or your charming daughter, may I humbly beg permission to smoke a cigar?"

And Count Alvise, enchanted with his talent for narrative, and sure of having secured for his son the heart and the dollars of his fair audience, proceeds to light a candle, and at the candle one of those long black Italian cigars which require preliminary disinfection before smoking.

. . . If this state of things goes on I shall just have to ask the doctor for a bottle; this ridiculous beating of my heart and disgusting cold perspiration have increased steadily during Count Alvise's narrative. To keep myself in countenance among the various idiotic commentaries on this cock-and-bull story of a vocal coxcomb and a vapouring great lady, I begin to unroll the engraving, and to examine stupidly the portrait of Zaffirino, once so renowned, now so forgotten. A ridiculous ass, this singer, under his triumphal arch, with his stuffed Cupids and the great fat winged kitchenmaid crowning him with laurels. How flat and vapid and vulgar it is, to be sure, all this odious eighteenth century!

But he, personally, is not so utterly vapid as I had thought. That effeminate, fat face of his is almost beautiful, with an odd smile, brazen and cruel. I have seen faces like this, if not in real life, at least in my boyish romantic dreams, when I read Swinburne and Baudelaire,[11] the faces of wicked, vindictive women. Oh yes! he is decidedly a beautiful creature, this Zaffirino, and his voice must have had the same sort of beauty and the same expression of wickedness. . . .

"Come on, Magnus," sound the voices of my fellow-boarders, "be a good fellow and sing us one of the old chap's songs; or at least something or other of that day, and we'll make believe it was the air with which he killed that poor lady."

"Oh yes! the *Aria dei Mariti*, the 'Husbands' Air,'" mumbles old Alvise, between the puffs at his impossible black cigar. "My poor grand-aunt, Pisana Vendramin; he went and killed her with those songs of his, with that *Aria dei Mariti*."

I feel senseless rage overcoming me. Is it that horrible palpitation (by the way, there is a Norwegian doctor, my fellow-countryman at Venice just now) which is sending the blood to my brain and making me mad? The people round the piano, the furniture, everything together seems to get mixed and to turn into moving blobs of colour. I set to singing; the only thing which remains distinct before my eyes being the portrait of Zaffirino, on the edge of that boarding-house piano; the sensual, effeminate face, with its wicked, cynical smile, keeps appearing and disappearing as the print wavers about the draught that makes the candles smoke and gutter. And I set to singing madly, singing I don't know what. Yes; I begin to identify it: 'tis the *Biondina in Gondoleta*, the only song of the eighteenth century which is still remembered by the Venetian people. I sing it, mimicking every old-school grace; shakes, cadences, languishingly swelled and diminished notes, and adding all manner of buffooneries, until the audience, recovering from its surprise, begins to shake with laughing; until I begin to laugh myself, madly, frantically, between the phrases of the melody, my voice finally smothered in this dull, brutal laughter. . . . And then, to crown it all, I shake my fist at this long-dead singer, looking at me with his wicked woman's face, with his mocking, fatuous smile.

"Ah! you would like to be revenged on me also!" I exclaim. "You would like me to write you nice roulades[12] and flourishes, another nice *Aria dei Mariti*, my fine Zaffirino!"

*

234

That night I dreamed a very strange dream. Even in the big half-furnished room the heat and closeness were stifling. The air seemed laden with the scent of all manner of white flowers, faint and heavy in their intolerable sweetness: tuberoses, gardenias, and jasmines drooping I know not where in neglected vases. The moonlight had transformed the marble floor around me into a shallow, shining pool. On account of the heat I had exchanged my bed for a big old-fashioned sofa of light wood, painted with little nosegays and sprigs, like an old silk; and I lay there, not attempting to sleep, and letting my thoughts go vaguely to my opera of *Ogier the Dane*, of which I had long finished writing the words, and for whose music I had hoped to find some inspiration in this strange Venice, floating, as it were, in the stagnant lagoon of the past. But Venice had merely put all my ideas into hopeless confusion; it was as if there arose out of its shallow waters a miasma of long-dead melodies, which sickened but intoxicated my soul. I lay on my sofa watching that pool of whitish light, which rose higher and higher, little trickles of light meeting it here and there, wherever the moon's rays struck upon some polished surface; while huge shadows waved to and fro in the draught of the open balcony.

I went over and over that old Norse story: how the Paladin, Ogier, one of the knights of Charlemagne,[13] was decoyed during his homeward wanderings from the Holy Land by the arts of an enchantress, the same who had once held in bondage the great Emperor Caesar and given him King Oberon[14] for a son; how Ogier had tarried in that island only one day and one night, and yet, when he came home to his kingdom, he found all changed, his friends dead, his family dethroned, and not a man who knew his face; until at last, driven hither and thither like a beggar, a poor minstrel had taken compassion of his sufferings and given him all he could give – a song, the song of the prowess of a hero dead for hundreds of years, the Paladin Ogier the Dane.

The story of Ogier ran into a dream, as vivid as my waking thoughts had been vague. I was looking no longer at the pool of moonlight spreading round my couch, with its trickles of light and looming, waving shadows, but the frescoed walls of a great saloon. It was not, as I recognised in a second, the dining-room of that Venetian palace now turned into a boarding-house. It was a far larger room, a real ballroom, almost circular in its octagon shape, with eight huge white doors surrounded by stucco mouldings, and, high on the vault of the ceiling, eight little galleries of recesses like boxes at a theatre, intended no doubt for musicians and spectators. The place was imperfectly lighted by only one of the eight chandeliers, which revolved slowly, like huge spiders, each on its long cord. But the light struck upon the gilt stuccoes opposite me, and on a large expanse of fresco, the sacrifice of Iphigenia, with Agamemnon and Achilles[15] in Roman helmets, lappets,[16] and knee-breeches. It discovered also one of the oil panels let into the mouldings of the roof, a goddess in lemon and lilac draperies, foreshortened over a great green peacock. Round the room, where the light reached, I could make out big yellow satin sofas and heavy gilded consoles,[17] in the shadow of a corner was what looked like a piano, and farther in the shade one of those big canopies which decorate the anterooms of Roman palaces. I looked about me, wondering where I was: a heavy, sweet smell, reminding me of the flavour of a peach, filled the place.

Little by little I began to perceive sounds; little, sharp, metallic, detached notes, like those of a mandoline; and there was united to them a voice, very low and sweet, almost a whisper, which grew and grew and grew, until the whole place was filled with that exquisite vibrating note, of a strange, exotic, unique quality. The note went on, swelling and swelling. Suddenly there was a horrible piercing shriek, and the thud of a body on the floor, and all manner of smothered exclamations. There, close by the canopy, a light suddenly appeared; and I could see, among the dark figures moving to and fro in the room, a woman lying on the ground, surrounded by other women. Her blond hair, tangled, full of diamond-sparkles which cut through the half-darkness, was hanging dishevelled; the laces of her bodice had been cut, and her white breast shone among the sheen of jewelled brocade; her face was bent forwards, and a thin white arm trailed, like a broken limb, across the knees of one of the women who were endeavouring to lift her. There was a sudden splash of water against the floor, more confused exclamations, a hoarse, broken moan, and a gurgling, dreadful sound . . . I awoke with a start and rushed to the window.

Outside, in the blue haze of the moon, the church and belfry of St. George loomed blue and hazy, with the black hull and rigging, the red lights, of a large steamer moored before them. From the lagoon rose a damp sea-breeze. What was it all? Ah! I began to understand: that story of old Count Alvise's, the death of his grand-aunt, Pisana Vendramin. Yes, it was about that I had been dreaming.

I returned to my room; I struck a light, and sat down to my writing-table. Sleep had become impossible. I tried to work at my opera. Once or twice I thought I had got hold of what I had looked for so long. . . . But as soon as I tried to lay hold of my theme, there arose in my mind the distant echo of that voice, of that long note swelled slowly by insensible degrees, that long note whose tone was so strong and so subtle.

There are in the life of an artist moments when, still unable to seize his own inspiration, or even clearly to discern it, he becomes aware of the approach of that long-invoked idea. A mingled joy and terror warn him that before another day, another hour have passed, the inspiration shall have crossed the threshold of his soul and flooded it with its rapture. All day I had felt the need of isolation and quiet, and at nightfall I went for a row on the most solitary part of the lagoon. All things seemed to tell that I was going to meet my inspiration, and I awaited its coming as a lover awaits his beloved.

I had stopped my gondola for a moment, and as I gently swayed to and fro on the water, all paved with moonbeams, it seemed to me that I was on the confines of an imaginary world. It lay close at hand, enveloped in luminous, pale blue mist, through which the moon had cut a wide and glistening path; out to sea, the little islands, like moored black boats, only accentuated the solitude of this region of moonbeams and wavelets; while the hum of the insects in orchards hard by merely added to the impression of untroubled silence. On some such seas, I thought, must the Paladin Ogier, have sailed when about to discover that during that sleep at the enchantress's knees centuries had elapsed and the heroic world had set, and the kingdom of prose had come.

While my gondola rocked stationary on that sea of moonbeams, I pondered over that twilight of the heroic world. In the soft rattle of the water on the hull I seemed to hear the rattle of all that armour, of all those swords swinging rusty on the walls, neglected by the degenerate sons of the great champions of old. I had long been in search of a theme which I called the theme of the "Prowess of Ogier;" it was to appear from time to time in the course of my opera, to develop at last into that song of the Minstrel, which reveals to the hero that he is one of a long-dead world. And at this moment I seemed to feel the presence of that theme. Yet an instant, and my mind would be overwhelmed by that savage music, heroic, funereal.

Suddenly there came across the lagoon, cleaving, chequering, and fretting the silence with a lace-work of sound even as the moon was fretting and cleaving the water, a ripple of music, a voice breaking itself in a shower of little scales and cadences and trills.

I sank back upon my cushions. The vision of heroic days had vanished, and before my closed eyes there seemed to dance multitudes of little stars of light, chasing and interlacing like those sudden vocalisations.

"To shore! Quick!" I cried to the gondolier.

But the sounds had ceased; and there came from the orchards, with their mulberry-trees glistening in the moonlight, and their black swaying cypress-plumes, nothing save the confused hum, the monotonous chirp, of the crickets.

I looked around me: on one side empty dunes, orchards, and meadows, without house or steeple; on the other, the blue and misty sea, empty to where distant islets were profiled black on the horizon.

A faintness overcame me, and I felt myself dissolve. For all of a sudden a second ripple of voice swept over the lagoon, a shower of little notes, which seemed to form a little mocking laugh.

Then again all was still. This silence lasted so long that I fell once more to meditating on my opera. I lay in wait once more for the half-caught theme. But no. It was not that theme for which I was waiting and watching with bated breath. I realised my delusion when, on rounding the point of the Giudecca, the murmur of a voice arose from the midst of the waters, a thread of sound slender as a moonbeam, scarce audible, but exquisite, which expanded slowly, insensibly, taking volume and body, taking flesh almost and fire, an ineffable quality, full, passionate, but veiled, as it were, in a subtle, downy wrapper. The note grew stronger and stronger, and warmer and more passionate, until it burst through that strange and charming veil, and emerged beaming to break itself in the luminous facets of a wonderful shake, long, superb, triumphant.

There was a dead silence.

"Row to St. Mark's!" I exclaimed. "Quick!"

The gondola glided through the long, glittering track of moonbeams, and rent the great band of yellow, reflected light, mirroring the cupolas of St. Mark's, the lace-like pinnacles of the palace, and the slender pink belfry, which rose from the lit-up water to the pale and bluish evening sky.

In the larger of the two squares the military band was blaring through the last spirals of a *crescendo* of Rossini. The crowd was dispersing in this great open-air ballroom, and the sounds arose which invariably follow upon out-of-door music. A clatter of spoons and glasses, a rustle and grating of frocks and of chairs, and the click of scabbards on the pavement. I pushed my way among the fashionable youths contemplating the ladies while sucking the knob of their sticks; through the serried ranks of respectable families, marching arm in arm with their white frocked young ladies close in front. I took a seat before Florian's, among the customers stretching themselves before departing, and the waiters hurrying to and fro, clattering their empty cups and trays. Two imitation Neopolitans were slipping their guitar and violin under their arm, ready to leave the place.

"Stop!" I cried to them; "don't go yet. Sing me something – sing *La Camesella* or *Funiculi, funiculà*[18] – no matter what, provided you make a row;" and as they screamed and scraped their utmost, I added, "But can't you sing louder, d——n you! – sing louder, do you understand?"

I felt the need of noise, of yells and false notes, of something vulgar and hideous to drive away that ghost-voice which was haunting me.

Again and again I told myself that it had been some silly prank of a romantic amateur, hidden in the gardens of the shore or gliding unperceived on the lagoon; and that the sorcery of moonlight and sea-mist had transfigured for my excited brain mere humdrum roulades out of exercises of Bordogni or Crescentini.[19]

But all the same I continued to be haunted by that voice. My work was interrupted ever and anon by the attempt to catch its imaginary echo; and the heroic harmonies of my Scandinavian legend were strangely interwoven with voluptuous phrases and florid cadences in which I seemed to hear again that same accursed voice.

To be haunted by singing-exercises! It seemed too ridiculous for a man who professionally despised the art of singing. And still, I preferred to believe in that childish amateur, amusing himself with warbling to the moon.

One day, while making these reflections the hundredth time over, my eyes chanced to light upon the portrait of Zaffirino, which my friend had pinned against the wall. I pulled it down and tore it into half a dozen shreds. Then, already ashamed of my folly, I watched the torn pieces float down from the window, wafted hither and thither by the sea-breeze. One scrap got caught in a yellow blind below me; the others fell into the canal, and were speedily lost to sight in the dark water. I was overcome with shame. My heart beat like bursting. What a miserable, unnerved worm I had become in this cursed Venice, with its languishing moonlights, its atmosphere as of some stuffy boudoir, long unused, full of old stuffs and pot-pourri!

That night, however, things seemed to be going better. I was able to settle down to my opera, and even to work at it. In the intervals my thoughts returned, not without a certain pleasure, to those scattered fragments of the torn engraving fluttering down to the water. I was disturbed at my piano by the hoarse voices and the scraping of violins which rose from one of those music-boats that station at night under the hotels of the Grand Canal. The moon had set. Under my balcony the water stretched black into the distance, its darkness cut by the still darker outlines of the flotilla of gondolas in attendance on the music-boat, where the faces of the singers, and the guitars and violins, gleamed reddish under the unsteady light of the Chinese-lanterns.

"*Jammo, jammo; jammo, jammo jà,*" sang the loud, hoarse voices; then a tremendous scrape and twang, and the yelled-out burden, "*Funiculi, funiculà; funiculi, funiculà; jammo, jammo, jammo, jammo, jammo jà.*"

Then came a few cries of "*Bis, Bis!*"[20] from a neighbouring hotel, a brief clapping of hands, the sound of a handful of coppers rattling into the boat, and the oar-stroke of some gondolier making ready to turn away.

"Sing the *Camesella*," ordered some voice with a foreign accent.

"No, no! *Santa Lucia.*"

"I want the *Camesella.*"

"No! *Santa Lucia.* Hi! sing *Santa Lucia* – d'you hear?"

The musicians, under their green and yellow and red lamps, held a whispered consultation on the manner of conciliating these contradictory demands. Then, after a minute's hesitation, the violins began the prelude of that once famous air, which had remained popular in Venice – the words written, some hundred years ago, by the patrician Gritti, the music by an unknown composer – *La Biondina in Gondoleta.*

That cursed eighteenth century! It seemed a malignant fatality that made these brutes choose just this piece to interrupt me.

At last the long prelude came to an end; and above the cracked guitars and squeaking fiddles there arose, not the expected nasal chorus, but a single voice singing below its breath.

My arteries throbbed. How well I knew that voice! It was singing, as I have said, below its breath, yet none the less it sufficed to fill all that reach of the canal with its strange quality of tone, exquisite, far-fetched.

239

They were long-drawn-out notes, of intense but peculiar sweetness, a man's voice which had much of a woman's, but more even of a chorister's, but a chorister's voice without its limpidity and innocence; its youthfulness was veiled, muffled, as it were, in a sort of downy vagueness, as if a passion of tears withheld.

There was a burst of applause, and the old palaces re-echoed with the clapping. "Bravo, bravo! Thank you, thank you! Sing again – please, sing again. Who can it be?"

And then a bumping of hulls, a splashing of oars, and the oaths of gondoliers trying to push each other away, as the red prow-lamps of the gondolas pressed round the gaily lit singing-boat.

But no one stirred on board. It was to none of them that this applause was due. And while every one pressed on, and clapped and vociferated, one little red prow-lamp dropped away from the fleet; for a moment a single gondola stood forth black upon the black water, and then was lost in the night.

For several days the mysterious singer was the universal topic. The people of the music-boat swore that no one besides themselves had been on board, and that they knew as little as ourselves about the owner of that voice. The gondoliers, despite their descent from the spies of the old Republic,[21] were equally unable to furnish any clue. No musical celebrity was known or suspected to be at Venice; and every one agreed that such a singer must be a European celebrity. The strangest thing in this strange business was, that even among those learned in music there was no agreement on the subject of this voice: it was called by all sorts of names and described by all manner of incongruous adjectives; people went so far as to dispute whether the voice belonged to a man or a woman: every one had some new definition.

In all these musical discussions I, alone, brought forward no opinion. I felt a repugnance, an impossibility almost, of speaking about that voice; and the more or less commonplace conjectures of my friend had the invariable effect of sending me out of my room.

Meanwhile my work was becoming daily more difficult, and I soon passed from utter impotence to a state of inexplicable agitation. Every morning I arose with fine resolutions and grand projects of work; only to go to bed that night without having accomplished anything. I spent hours leaning on my balcony, or wandering through the network of lanes with their ribbon of blue sky, endeavouring vainly to expel the thought of that voice, or endeavouring in reality to reproduce it in my memory; for the more I tried to banish it from my thoughts, the more I grew to thirst for that extraordinary tone, for those mysteriously downy, veiled notes; and no sooner did I make an effort to work at my opera than my head was full of scraps of forgotten eighteenth century airs, of frivolous or languishing little phrases; and I fell to wondering with a bitter-sweet longing how those songs would have sounded if sung by that voice.

At length it became necessary to see a doctor, from whom, however, I carefully hid away all the stranger symptoms of my malady. The air of the lagoons, the great heat, he answered cheerfully, had pulled me down a little; a tonic and a month in the country, with plenty of riding and no work, would make me myself again. That old idler, Count Alvise, who had insisted on accompanying me to the physician's immediately suggested that I should go and stay with his son, who was boring himself to death superintending the maize harvest on the mainland: he could promise me excellent air, plenty of horses, and all the peaceful surroundings, and the delightful occupations of a rural life – "Be sensible, my dear Magnus, and just go quietly to Mistrà."

Mistrà – the name sent a shiver all down me. I was about to decline the invitation, when a thought suddenly loomed vaguely in my mind.

"Yes, dear Count," I answered; "I accept your invitation with gratitude and pleasure. I will start to-morrow for Mistrà."

The next day found me at Padua, on my way to the Villa of Mistrà. It seemed as if I had left an intolerable burden behind me. I was, for the first time since how long, quite light of heart. The tortuous, rough-paved streets, with their empty, gloomy porticoes; the ill-plastered palaces, with closed, discoloured shutters; the little rambling square, with meagre trees and stubborn grass; the Venetian garden-houses reflecting their crumbling graces in the muddy canal; the gardens without gates and the gates without gardens, the avenues leading nowhere; and the population of blind and legless beggars, of whining sacristans,[22] which issued as by magic from between the flagstones and dust-heaps and weeds under the fierce August sun, all this dreariness merely amused and pleased me. My good spirits were heightened by a musical mass which I had the good fortune to hear at St. Anthony's.

Never in all my days had I heard anything comparable, although Italy affords many strange things in the way of sacred music. Into the deep nasal chanting of the priests there had suddenly burst a chorus of children, singing absolutely independent of all time and tune; grunting of priests answered by squealing of boys, slow Gregorian modulation interrupted by jaunty barrel-organ pipings, an insane, insanely merry jumble of bellowing and barking, mewing and cackling and braying, such as would have enlivened a witches' meeting, or rather some mediaeval Feast of Fools. And, to make the grotesqueness of such music still more fantastic and Hoffmannlike,[23] there was, besides, the magnificence of the piles of sculptured marbles and gilded bronzes, the tradition of the musical splendour for which St. Anthony's had been famous in days gone by. I had read in old travellers, Lalande and Burney,[24] that the Republic of St. Mark had squandered immense sums not merely on the monuments and decoration, but on the musical establishment of its great cathedral of Terra Firma. In the midst of this ineffable concert of impossible voices and instruments, I tried to imagine the voice of Guadagni, the soprano for whom Gluck had written *Che farò senza Euridice*,[25] and the fiddle of Tartini, that Tartini with whom the devil had once come and made music.[26] And the delight in anything so absolutely, barbarously, grotesquely, fantastically incongruous as such a performance in such a place was height-ened by a sense of profanation: such were the successors of those wonderful musicians of that hated eighteenth century!

The whole thing had delighted me so much, so very much more than the most faultless performance could have done, that I determined to enjoy it once more; and towards vesper-time, after a cheerful dinner with two bag-men at the inn of the Golden Star, and a pipe over the rough sketch of a possible cantata upon the music which the devil made for Tartini, I turned my steps once more towards St. Anthony's.

The bells were ringing for sunset, and a muffled sound of organs seemed to issue from the huge, solitary church; I pushed my way under the heavy leathern curtain, expecting to be greeted by the grotesque performance of that morning.

I proved mistaken. Vespers must long have been over. A smell of stale incense, a crypt-like damp filled my mouth; it was already night in that vast cathedral. Out of the darkness glimmered the votive-lamps of the chapels, throwing wavering lights upon the red polished marble, the gilded railing, and chandeliers, and plaqueing with yellow the muscles of some sculptured figure. In a corner a burning taper put a halo about the head of a priest, burnishing his shining bald skull, his white surplice, and the open book before him. "Amen" he chanted; the book was closed with a snap, the light moved up the apse, some dark figures of women rose from their knees and passed quickly towards the door; a man saying his prayers before a chapel also got up, making a great clatter in dropping his stick.

The church was empty, and I expected every minute to be turned out by the sacristan making his evening round to close the doors. I was leaning against a pillar, looking into the greyness of the great arches, when the organ suddenly burst out into a series of chords, rolling through the echoes of the church: it seemed to be the conclusion of some service. And above the organ rose the notes of a voice; high, soft, enveloped in a kind of downiness, like a cloud of incense, and which ran through the mazes of a long cadence. The voice dropped into silence; with two thundering chords the organ closed in. All was silent. For a moment I stood leaning against one of the pillars of the nave: my hair was clammy, my knees sank beneath me, an enervating heat spread through my body; I tried to breathe more largely, to suck in the sounds with the incense-laden air. I was supremely happy, and yet as if I were dying; then suddenly a chill ran through me, and with it a vague panic. I turned away and hurried out into the open.

The evening sky lay pure and blue along the jagged line of roofs; the bats and swallows were wheeling about; and from the belfries all around, half-drowned by the deep bell of St. Anthony's, jangled the peel of the *Ave Maria*.

"You really don't seem well," young Count Alvise had said the previous evening, as he welcomed me, in the light of a lantern held up by a peasant, in

the weedy back-garden of the Villa of Mistrà. Everything had seemed to me
like a dream: the jingle of the horse's bells driving in the dark from Padua, as
the lantern swept the acacia-hedges with their wide yellow light; the grating
of the wheels on the gravel; the supper-table, illumined by a single petrol-
eum lamp for fear of attracting mosquitoes, where a broken old lackey, in an
old stable jacket, handed round the dishes among the fumes of onion;
Alvise's fat mother gabbling dialect in a shrill, benevolent voice behind the
bullfights on her fan; the unshaven village priest, perpetually fidgeting with
his glass and foot, and sticking one shoulder up above the other. And now, in
the afternoon, I felt as if I had been in this long, rambling, tumble-down
Villa of Mistrà – a villa three-quarters of which was given up to the storage of
grain and garden tools, or to the exercise of rats, mice, scorpions, and centi-
pedes – all my life; as if I had always sat there, in Count Alvise's study,
among the pile of undusted books on agriculture, the sheaves of accounts, the
samples of grain and silkworm seed, the ink-stains and the cigar-ends; as if I
had never heard of anything save the cereal basis of Italian agriculture, the
diseases of maize, the peronospora[27] of the vine, the breeds of bullocks, the
iniquities of farm labourers; with the blue cones of the Euganean hills closing
in the green shimmer of plain outside the window.

After an early dinner, again with the screaming gabble of the fat old
Countess, the fidgeting and shoulder-raising of the unshaven priest, the
smell of fried oil and stewed onions, Count Alvise made me get into the cart
beside him, and whirled me along among clouds of dust, between the endless
glister of poplars, acacias, and maples, to one of his farms.

In the burning sun some twenty or thirty girls, in coloured skirts, laced
bodices, and big straw-hats, were threshing the maize on the big red brick
threshing-floor, while others were winnowing the grain in great sieves.
Young Alvise III. (the old one was Alvise II.: every one is Alvise, that is to
say, Lewis, in that family; the name is on the house, the carts, the barrows,
the very pails) picked up the maize, touched it, tasted it, said something to
the girls that made them laugh, and something to the head farmer that made
him look very glum; and then led me into a huge stable, where some twenty
or thirty white bullocks were stamping, switching their tails, hitting their
horns against the mangers in the dark. Alvise III. patted each, called him by
his name, gave him some salt or a turnip and explained which was the
Mantuan breed, which the Apulian, which the Romagnolo, and so on. Then
he bade me jump into the trap, and off we went again through the dust,
among the hedges and ditches, till we came to some more brick farm buildings with pinkish roofs smoking against the blue sky. Here there were more
young women threshing and winnowing the maize, which made a great
golden Danaë cloud,[28] more bullocks stamping and lowing in the cool darkness; more joking, fault-finding, explaining; and thus through five farms,
until I seemed to see the rhythmical rising and falling of the flails against the
hot sky, the shower of golden grains, the yellow dust from the winnowing-

sieves on to the bricks, the switching of innumerable tails and plunging of innumerable horns, the glistening of huge white flanks and foreheads, whenever I closed my eyes.

"A good day's work!" cried Count Alvise, stretching out his long legs with the tight trousers riding up over the Wellington boots.[29] "Mamma, give us some aniseed-syrup after dinner; it is an excellent restorative and precaution against the fevers of this country."

"Oh! you've got fever in this part of the world, have you? Why, your father said the air was so good!"

"Nothing, nothing," soothed the old Countess. "The only thing to be dreaded are mosquitoes; take care to fasten your shutters before lighting the candle."

"Well," rejoined young Alvise, with an effort of conscience, "of course there *are* fevers. But they needn't hurt you. Only, don't go out into the garden at night, if you don't want to catch them. Papa told me that you have fancies for moonlight rambles. It won't do in this climate, my dear fellow; it won't do. If you must stalk about at night, being a genius, take a turn inside the house; you can get quite exercise enough."

After dinner the aniseed-syrup was produced, together with brandy and cigars, and they all sat in the long, narrow, half-furnished room on the first floor; the old Countess knitting a garment of uncertain shape and destination, the priest reading out the newspaper; Count Alvise puffing at his long, crooked cigar, and pulling the ears of a long, lean dog with a suspicion of mange and a stiff eye. From the dark garden outside rose the hum and whirr of countless insects, and the smell of the grapes which hung black against the starlit, blue sky, on the trellis. I went to the balcony. The garden lay dark beneath; against the twinkling horizon stood out the tall poplars. There was the sharp cry of an owl; the barking of a dog; a sudden whiff of warm, enervating perfume, a perfume that made me think of the taste of certain peaches, and suggested white, thick, wax-like petals. I seemed to have smelt that flower once before: it made me feel languid, almost faint.

"I am very tired," I said to Count Alvise. "See how feeble we city folk become!"

But, despite my fatigue, I found it quite impossible to sleep. The night seemed perfectly stifling. I had felt nothing like it at Venice. Despite the injunctions of the Countess I opened the solid wooden shutters, hermetically closed against mosquitoes, and looked out.

The moon had risen; and beneath it lay the big lawns, the rounded tree-tops, bathed in a blue, luminous mist, every leaf glistening and trembling in what seemed a heaving sea of light. Beneath the window was the long trellis, with the white shining piece of pavement under it. It was so bright that I could distinguish the green of the vine-leaves, the dull red of the catalpa-flowers. There was in the air a vague scent of cut grass, of ripe American grapes, of that white flower (it must be white) which made me think of the taste of peaches all melting into the delicious freshness of falling dew. From the village church came the stroke of one: Heaven knows how long I had been vainly attempting to sleep. A shiver ran through me, and my head suddenly filled as with the fumes of some subtle wine; I remembered all those weedy embankments, those canals full of stagnant water, the yellow faces of the peasants; the word malaria returned to my mind. No matter! I remained leaning on the window, with a thirsty longing to plunge myself into this blue moon-mist, this dew and perfume and silence, which seemed to vibrate and quiver like the stars that strewed the depths of heaven . . . What music, even Wagner's, or of that great singer of starry nights, the divine Schumann,[30] what music could ever compare with this great silence, with this great concert of voiceless things that sing within one's soul?

As I made this reflection, a note, high, vibrating, and sweet, rent the silence, which immediately closed around it. I leaned out of the window, my heart beating as though it must burst. After a brief space the silence was cloven once more by that note, as the darkness is cloven by a falling star of a firefly rising slowly like a rocket. But this time it was plain that the voice did not come, as I had imagined, from the garden, but from the house itself, from some corner of this rambling old villa of Mistrà.

Mistrà – Mistrà! The name rang in my ears, and I began at length to grasp its significance, which seems to have escaped me till then. "Yes," I said to myself, "it is quite natural." And with this odd impression of naturalness was mixed a feverish, impatient pleasure. It was as if I had come to Mistrà on purpose, and that I was about to meet the object of my long and weary hopes.

Grasping the lamp with its singed green shade, I gently opened the door and made my way through a series of long passages and of big, empty rooms, in which my steps re-echoed as in a church, and my light disturbed whole swarms of bats. I wandered at random, farther and farther from the inhabited part of the buildings.

This silence made me feel sick; I gasped as under a sudden disappointment.

All of a sudden there came a sound – chords, metallic, sharp, rather like the tone of a mandoline – close to my ear. Yes, quite close: I was separated from the sounds only by a partition. I fumbled for a door; the unsteady light of my lamp was insufficient for my eyes, which were swimming like those of a drunkard. At last I found a latch, and, after a moment's hesitation, I lifted it and gently pushed open the door. At first I could not understand what manner of place I was in. It was dark all round me, but a brilliant light blinded me, a light coming from below and striking the opposite wall. It was as if I had entered a dark box in a half-lighted theatre. I was, in fact, in something of the kind, a sort of dark hole with a high balustrade, half-hidden by an up-drawn curtain. I remembered those little galleries or recesses for the use of musicians or lookers-on which exist under the ceiling of the ballrooms in certain old Italian palaces. Yes; it must have been one like that. Opposite me was a vaulted ceiling covered with gilt mouldings, which framed great time-blackened canvases; and lower down, in the light thrown up from below, stretched a wall covered with faded frescoes. Where had I seen that goddess in lilac and lemon draperies foreshortened over a big, green peacock? For she was familiar to me, and the stucco Tritons also who twisted their tails round her gilded frame. And that fresco, with warriors in Roman cuirasses and green and blue lappets, and knee-breeches – where could I have seen them before? I asked myself these questions without experiencing any surprise. Moreover, I was very calm, as one is calm sometimes in extraordinary dreams – could I be dreaming?

I advanced gently and leaned over the balustrade. My eyes were met at first by the darkness above me, where, like gigantic spiders, the big chandeliers rotated slowly, hanging from the ceiling. Only one of them was lit, and its Murano-glass pendants, its carnations and roses, shone opalescent in the light of the guttering wax. This chandelier lighted up the opposite wall and that piece of ceiling with the goddess and the green peacock; it illumined but far less well, a corner of the huge room, where, in the shadow of a kind of canopy, a little group of people were crowding round a yellow satin sofa, of the same kind as those that lined the walls. On the sofa, half-screened from me by the surrounding persons, a woman was stretched out: the silver of her embroidered dress and the rays of her diamonds gleamed and shot forth as she moved uneasily. And immediately under the chandelier, in the full light, a man stooped over a harpsichord, his head bent slightly, as if collecting his thoughts before singing.

He struck a few chords and sang. Yes, sure enough, it was the voice, the voice that had so long been persecuting me! I recognised at once that delicate, voluptuous quality, strange, exquisite, sweet beyond words, but lacking all youth and clearness. That passion veiled in tears which had troubled my brain that night on the lagoon, and again on the Grand Canal singing the *Biondina*, and yet again, only two days since, in the deserted cathedral of Padua. But I recognised now what seemed to have been hidden from me till then, that this voice was what I cared most for in all the wide world.

The voice wound and unwound itself in long, languishing phrases, in rich, voluptuous *rifiorituras*,[31] all fretted with tiny scales and exquisite, crisp shakes; it stopped ever and anon, swaying as if panting in languid delight. And I felt my body melt even as wax in the sunshine, and it seemed to me that I too was turning fluid and vaporous, in order to mingle with these sounds as the moonbeams mingle with the dew.

Suddenly, from the dimly lighted corner by the canopy, came a little piteous wail; then another followed, and was lost in the singer's voice. During a long phrase on the harpsichord, sharp and tinkling, the singer turned his head towards the dais, and there came a plaintive little sob. But he, instead of stopping, struck a sharp chord; and with a thread of voice so hushed as to be scarcely audible, slid softly into a long *cadenza*.[32] At the same moment he threw his head backwards, and the light fell full upon the handsome, effeminate face, with its ashy pallor and big, black brows, of the singer Zaffirino. At the sight of that face, sensual and sullen, of that smile which was cruel and mocking like a bad woman's, I understood – I knew not why, by what process – that his singing *must* be cut short, that the accursed phrase *must* never be finished. I understood that I was before an assassin, that he was killing this woman and killing me also, with his wicked voice.

I rushed down the narrow stair which led down from the box, pursued, as it were, by that exquisite voice, swelling, swelling by insensible degrees. I flung myself on the door which must be that of the big saloon. I could see its light between the panels. I bruised my hands in trying to wrench the latch. The door was fastened tight, and while I was struggling with that locked door I heard the voice swelling, swelling, rending asunder that downy veil which wrapped it, leaping forth clear, resplendent, like the sharp and glittering blade of a knife that seemed to enter deep into my breast. Then, once more, a wail, a death-groan, and that dreadful noise, that hideous gurgle of breath strangled by a rush of blood. And then a long shake, acute, brilliant, triumphant.

The door gave way beneath my weight, one half crashed in. I entered. I was blinded by a flood of blue moonlight. It poured in through four great windows, peaceful and diaphanous, a pale blue mist of moonlight, and turned the huge room into a kind of submarine cave, paved with moonbeams, full of shimmers, of pools of moonlight. It was as bright as at midday, but the brightness was cold, blue, vaporous, supernatural. The room was completely empty, like a great hay-loft. Only, there hung from the ceiling the ropes which had once supported a chandelier; and in a corner, among stacks of wood and heaps of Indian-corn, whence spread a sickly smell of damp and mildew, there stood a long, thin harpsichord, with spindle-legs, and its cover cracked from end to end.

I felt, all of a sudden, very calm. The one thing that mattered was the phrase that kept moving in my head, the phrase of that unfinished cadence which I had heard but an instant before. I opened the harpsichord, and my fingers came down boldly upon its keys. A jingle-jangle of broken strings, laughable and dreadful, was the only answer.

Then an extraordinary fear overtook me. I clambered out of one of the windows; I rushed up the garden and wandered through the fields, among the canals and the embankments, until the moon had set and the dawn began to shiver, followed, pursued for ever by that jangle of broken strings.

People expressed much satisfaction at my recovery. It seems that one dies of those fevers.

Recovery? But have I recovered? I walk, and eat and drink and talk; I can even sleep. I live the life of other living creatures. But I am wasted by a strange and deadly disease. I can never lay hold of my own inspiration. My head is filled with music which is certainly by me, since I have never heard it before, but which still is not my own, which I despise and abhor: little, tripping flourishes and languishing phrases, and long-drawn, echoing cadences.

O wicked, wicked voice, violin of flesh and blood made by the Evil One's hand, may I not even execrate thee in peace; but is it necessary that, at the moment when I curse, the longing to hear thee again should parch my soul like hell-thirst? And since I have satiated thy lust for revenge, since thou hast withered my life and withered my genius, is it not time for pity? May I not hear one note, only one note of thine, O singer, O wicked and contemptible wretch?

Notes

Text: *Hauntings: Fantastic Stories*, Heinemann, London, 1890.

1 Richard Wagner (1813–83), German Romantic composer, considered avant garde in his own time.
2 Wolfgang Amadeus Mozart (1756–91); George Frederick Handel (1685–1759); Christoph Willibald von Gluck (1714–87).
3 Greek tragic dramatists, ?496–406 BC and ?480–406 BC respectively.
4 An elaborate hairstyle, with the hair swept up at the sides (literally 'pigeon's wings').
5 Gioachino Rossini (1792–1868), Gaetano Donizetti (1797–1848), Italian composers.
6 Wife of a Procuratore (government official).
7 Gentlewoman.
8 'Show pity to the conquered and crush the haughty', Virgil, *Aeneid* VI.853.
9 Lands granted by the Emperor in return for service.
10 Sacrament performed before death.
11 Algernon Charles Swinburne (1837–1909), English poet; Charles Baudelaire (1821–67), French poet. Both are noted for the decadence of their writings.
12 Elaborate runs in vocal music.
13 King of the Francs and Holy Roman Emperor, ?742–814 AD.
14 King of the fairies (medieval folklore).
15 The Greek king Agamemnon, helped by the warrior Achilles, attempted to sacrifice his daughter Iphigenia to the goddess Artemis, who saved her and made her a priestess.
16 Leather flaps.
17 Ornamental tables, designed to stand against a wall.
18 Popular Venetian songs.
19 Unidentified.
20 'Encore!'
21 The city of Venice, initially an independent republic, was incorportated into Italy in 1866.
22 Persons in charge of the contents of churches.
23 As the compositions of Ernst Theodor Amadeus Hoffmann (1776–1822), German writer and composer with a reputation for eccentricity.
24 Possibly René du Bellay, Baron de la Lande, *Memoires* (1569); Dr Charles

Burney (1726–1814), *The Present State of Music in France and Italy; or, the Journal of a Tour through those Countries* (1771).

25 From the opera *Orpheus and Euridice* (1756).

26 Guiseppe Tartini (1692–1770), Italian violinist, dreamed of a visit from the devil, and wrote his celebrated sonata, *The Devil's Trill*, as a result.

27 Parasitic fungus which attacks the grape-vine.

28 Danaë, mother of Perseus by Zeus, came to earth in a shower of gold.

29 Military leather boots covering the front of the knee but cut off at the back, named after Arthur Wellesley, 1st Duke of Wellington (1769–1852).

30 Robert Schumann (1810–56), German Romantic composer.

31 Virtuoso vocal practices.

32 Improvised virtuoso solo passage near the end of a piece of vocal music.

A DREAM OF WILD BEES

Olive Schreiner

Olive Schreiner, later Cronwright (1855–1920), novelist, short-story writer, writer on colonialism and feminism, was born in South Africa, the ninth child of an English mother and a repressive German Calvinist father. She educated herself and became a governess in 1874, writing in her spare time (her first, autobiographical novel, *Undine*, was not published until 1929). She slowly saved enough to travel to England in 1881 with the manuscript of her most famous work, *The Story of an African Farm* (1883). While in London she became a celebrity, and a member of a lively intellectual circle including Eleanor Marx and Havelock Ellis. She returned to South Africa in 1889, and published her two collections of allegorical short stories, *Dreams* in 1891 and *Dream Life and Real Life* in 1893. She married a politician and farmer, Samuel Cron Cronwright, in 1894, but the couple became estranged after their only child, a daughter, died soon after her birth in 1895. She became increasingly involved with politics (her allegorical, anti-war novel, *Trooper Peter Halket of Mashonaland* (1897) opposes the Boer War) and suffrage organisations. Her important feminist work, *Women and Labour*, appeared in 1911, and her writings on the politics and women's issues of her homeland in *Thoughts on South Africa* (1923).

Further reading

Berkman *et al.* (1983); Berkman (1989); Blain *et. al.* (1990); Bradford (1995); Chrisman (1990); First and Scott (1980); Harris (1993); Monsman (1992); Rive (1988–); Shattock (1993); Showalter (1977); Sutherland (1988).

A Dream of Wild Bees

A mother sat alone at an open window. Through it came the voices of the children as they played under the acacia-trees, and the breath of the hot afternoon air. In and out of the room flew the bees, the wild bees, with their legs yellow with pollen, going to and from the acacia-trees, droning all the while. She sat on a low chair before the table and darned. She took her work from the great basket that stood before her on the table: some lay on her knee and half covered the book that rested there. She watched the needle go in and out; and the dreary hum of the bees and the noise of the children's voices became a confused murmur in her ears, as she worked slowly and more slowly. Then the bees, the long-legged wasp-like fellows who make no honey, flew closer and closer to her head, droning. Then she grew more and more drowsy, and she laid her hand, with the stocking over it, on the edge of the table, and leaned her head upon it. And the voices of the children outside grew more and more dreamy, came now far, now near; then she did not hear them, but she felt under her heart where the ninth child[1] lay. Bent forward and sleeping there, with the bees flying about her head, she had a weird brain-picture; she thought the bees lengthened and lengthened themselves out and became human creatures and moved round and round her. Then one came to her softly, saying, 'Let me lay my hand upon thy side where the child sleeps. If I shall touch him he shall be as I.'

She asked, 'Who are you?'

And he said, 'I am Health. Whom I touch will have always the red blood dancing in his veins; he will not know weariness nor pain; life will be a long laugh to him.'

'No,' said another, 'let me touch, for I am Wealth. If I touch him material care shall not feed on him. He shall live on the blood and sinews of his fellow-men, if he will; and what his eye lusts for, his hand will have. He shall not know "I want."' And the child lay still like lead.

And another said, 'Let me touch him: I am Fame. The man I touch, I lead to a high hill where all men may see him. When he dies he is not forgotten, his name rings down the centuries, each echoes it on to his fellows. Think – not to be forgotten through the ages!'

And the mother lay breathing steadily, but in the brain-picture they pressed closer to her.

'Let me touch the child,' said one, 'for I am Love. If I touch him he shall not walk through life alone. In the greatest dark, when he puts out his hand he shall find another hand by it. When the world is against him, another shall say, "*You and I*."' And the child trembled.

But another pressed close and said, 'Let me touch; for I am Talent. I can do all things – that have been done before. I touch the soldier, the statesman, the thinker, and the politicians who succeed; and the writer who is never before his time, and never behind it. If I touch the child he shall not weep for failure.'

About the mother's head the bees were flying, touching her with their long tapering limbs; and, in her brain-picture, out of the shadow of the room came one with sallow face, deep-lined, the cheeks drawn into hollows, and a mouth smiling quiveringly. He stretched out his hand. And the mother drew back, and cried, 'Who are you?' He answered nothing; and she looked up between his eyelids. And she said, 'What can you give the child – health?' And he said, 'The man I touch, there wakes up in his blood a burning fever, that shall lick his blood as fire. The fever that I will give him shall be cured when his life is cured.'

'You give wealth?'

He shook his head. 'The man whom I touch, when he bends to pick up gold, he sees suddenly a light over his head in the sky; while he looks up to see it, the gold slips from between his fingers, or sometimes another passing takes it from them.'

'Fame?'

He answered, 'Likely not. For the man I touch there is a path traced out in the sand by a finger which no man sees. That he must follow. Sometimes it leads almost to the top, and then turn down suddenly into the valley. He must follow it, though none else sees the tracing.'

'Love?'

He said, 'He shall hunger for it – but he shall not find it. When he stretches out his arms to it, and would lay his heart against a thing he loves, then, far off along the horizon he shall see a light play. He must go towards it. The thing he loves will not journey with him; he must travel alone. When he presses somewhat to his burning heart, crying, "Mine, mine, my own!" he shall hear a voice – "Renounce! renounce! this is not thine!"'

'He shall succeed?'

He said, 'He shall fail. When he runs with others they shall reach the goal before him. For strange voices shall call to him and strange lights shall beckon him, and he must wait and listen. And this shall be the strangest: far off across the burning sands where, to other men, there is only the desert's waste, he shall see a blue sea! On that sea the sun shines always, and the water is blue as burning amethyst, and the foam is white on the shore. A great land rises from it, and he shall see upon the mountain-tops burning gold.'

The mother said, 'He shall reach it?'

And he smiled curiously.

She said, 'It is real?'

And he said, 'What *is* real?'

And she looked up between his half-closed eyelids, and said, 'Touch.'

And he leaned forward and laid his hand upon the sleeper, and whispered to it, smiling; and this only she heard – *'This shall be thy reward – that the ideal shall be real to thee.'*

And the child trembled; but the mother slept on heavily and her brain-picture vanished. But deep within her the antenatal thing that lay here had a dream. In those eyes that had never seen the day, in that half-shaped brain was a sensation of light! Light – that it never had seen. Light – that perhaps it never should see. Light – that existed somewhere!

And already it had its reward: the Ideal was real to it.

Notes

Text: *Dreams*, Unwin, London, 1890.
1 OS was her own mother's ninth child.

A CROSS LINE

George Egerton

'George Egerton' (Mary Chavelita Dunne), later Clairmonte, later Bright (1859–1945), short-story writer, playwright and novelist, was born in Australia of Irish parentage. She worked in Dublin and New York before eloping to Norway with Henry Higginson, a married man. While in Scandinavia she read Ibsen, Strindberg and Nietzsche, and was befriended by the novelist Knut Hamsun, whose work she later translated. After Higginson's death she returned to England and married George Egerton Clairmonte. Much influenced by Scandinavian literature, she published several volumes of short stories, of which *Keynotes* (1893) and *Discords* (1894) are the best known. Her semi-autobiographical novel, *The Wheel of God* (1898), apparently contributed to the fact that she was divorced in 1901. Remarried for a third time, she turned to playwriting in the early 1900s but never achieved the critical or popular success of her early work. Her early stories were attacked as 'erotomania' and 'crude vulgar indecency' in *The Contemporary Review* for April 1895. *A Cross Line* is one of the most admired of her short stories, and shows her innovative present-tense narrative style as well as her interest in female sexuality and independence.

Further reading

Cunningham (1978); Egerton (1983); Shattock (1993); Stubbs (1979); Stetz (1984); Sutherland (1988); White (1958).

A Cross Line

The rather flat notes of a man's voice float out into the clear air, singing the refrain of a popular music-hall ditty. There is something incongruous between the melody and the surroundings. It seems profane, indelicate, to bring this slangy, vulgar tune, and with it the mental picture of footlight flare and fantastic dance into the lovely freshness of this perfect spring day.

A woman sitting on a felled tree turns her head to meet its coming, and an expression flits across her face in which disgust and humorous appreciation are subtly blended. Her mind is nothing if not picturesque; her busy brain, with all its capabilities choked by a thousand vagrant fancies, is always producing pictures and finding associations between the most unlikely objects. She has been reading a little sketch written in the daintiest language of a fountain scene in Tanagra,[1] and her vivid imagination has made it real to her. The slim, graceful maids grouped around it filling their exquisitely-formed earthen jars, the dainty poise of their classic heads, and the flowing folds of their draperies have been actually present with her; and now? – why, it is like the entrance of a half-tipsy vagabond player bedizened in tawdry finery – the picture is blurred. She rests her head against the trunk of a pine tree behind her, and awaits the singer. She is sitting on an incline in the midst of a wilderness of trees; some have blown down, some have been cut down, and the lopped branches lie about; moss and bracken and trailing bramble, fir-cones, wild rose bushes, and speckled red 'fairy hats' fight for life in wild confusion. A disused quarry to the left is an ideal haunt of pike, and to the right a little river rushes along in haste to join a greater sister that is fighting a troubled way to the sea. A row of stepping-stones crosses it, and if you were to stand on one you would see shoals of restless stone loach 'Beardies'[2] darting from side to side. The tails of several ducks can be seen above the water, and the paddle of their balancing feet, and the gurgling suction of their bills as they search for larvae can be heard distinctly between the hum of insect, twitter of bird, and rustle of stream and leaf. The singer has changed his lay to a whistle, and presently he comes down the path a cool, neat, grey-clad figure, with a fishing creel slung across his back, and a trout rod held on his shoulder. The air ceases abruptly, and his cold grey eyes scan the seated figure with its gipsy ease of attitude, a scarlet shawl that has fallen from her shoulders forming an accentuative background to the slim roundness of her waist.

Persistent study, coupled with a varied experience of the female animal, has given the owner of the grey eyes some facility in classing her, although it has not supplied him with any definite data as to what any one of the species may do in a given circumstance. To put it in his own words, in answer to a friend who chaffed him on his untiring pursuit of women as an interesting problem.

'If a fellow has had much experience of his fellow-man he may divide him into types, and, given a certain number of men and a certain number of circumstances, he is pretty safe on hitting on the line of action each type will strike; 'taint so with woman. You may always look out for the unexpected, she generally upsets a fellow's calculations, and you are never safe in laying odds on her. Tell you what, old chappie, we may talk about superior intellect; but, if a woman wasn't handicapped by her affection, or need of it, the cleverest chap in Christendom would be just a bit of putty in her hands. I find them more fascinating as problems than anything going. Never let an opportunity slip to get new data – never!'

He did not now. He met the frank, unembarrassed gaze of eyes that would have looked with just the same bright inquiry at the advent of a hare, or a toad, or any other object that might cross her path, and raised his hat with respectful courtesy, saying, in the drawling tone habitual with him –

'I hope I am not trespassing?'

'I can't say; you may be, so may I, but no one has ever told me so!'

A pause. His quick glance has noted the thick wedding ring on her slim brown hand, and the flash of a diamond in its keeper.[3] A lady decidedly. Fast? perhaps. Original? undoubtedly. Worth knowing? rather.

'I am looking for a trout stream, but the directions I got were rather vague; might I – '

'It's straight ahead, but you won't catch anything now, at least not here, sun's too glaring and water too low, a mile up you may, in an hour's time.'

'Oh, thanks awfully for the tip. You fish then?'

'Yes, sometimes.'

'Trout run big here?' (what odd eyes the woman has, kind of magnetic.)

'No, seldom over a pound, but they are very game.'

'Rare good sport isn't it, whipping a stream? There is so much besides the mere catching of fish. The river and the trees and the quiet sets a fellow thinking – kind of sermon – makes a chap feel good, don't it?'

She smiles assentingly. And yet what the devil is she amused at he queries mentally. An inspiration. He acts upon it, and says eagerly:

'I wonder – I don't half like to ask – but fishing puts people on a common footing, don't it? You knowing the stream, you know, would you tell me what are the best flies to use?'

'I tie my own, but – '

'Do you? how clever of you! wish I could,' and sitting down on the other end of the tree, he takes out his fly book, 'but I interrupted you, you were going to say?'

'Only,' stretching out her hand (of a perfect shape but decidedly brown)

260

for the book, 'that you might give the local fly-tyer a trial, he'll tell you.'

'Later on, end of next month, or perhaps later, you might try the oak-fly, the natural fly you know; a horn is the best thing to hold them in, they get out of anything else – and put two on at a time.'

'By Jove, I must try that dodge!'

He watches her as she handles his book and examines the contents critically, turning aside some with a glance, fingering others almost tenderly, holding them daintily and noting the cock of wings and the hint of tinsel, with her head on one side; a trick of hers he thinks.

'Which do you like most, wet or dry fly?' (she is looking at some dry flies.)

'Oh,' with that rare smile, 'at the time I swear by whichever happens to catch most fish. Perhaps, really, dry fly. I fancy most of these flies are better for Scotland or England.[4] Up to this March-brown has been the most killing thing. But you might try an "orange-grouse," that's always good here; with perhaps a "hare's ear" for a change – and put on a "coachman" for the evenings. My husband (he steals a side look at her) brought home some beauties yesterday evening.'

'Lucky fellow!'

She returns the book. There is a tone in his voice as he says this that jars on her, sensitive as she is to every inflection of a voice, with an intuition that is almost second sight. She gathers up her shawl. She has a cream-coloured woollen gown on, and her skin looks duskily foreign by contrast. She is on her feet before he can regain his, and says, with a cool little bend of her head: 'Good afternoon, I wish you a full basket!'

Before he can raise his cap she is down the slope, gliding with easy steps that have a strange grace, and then springing lightly from stone to stone across the stream. He feels small, snubbed someway, and he sits down on the spot where she sat and, lighting his pipe, says 'check!'

She is walking slowly up the garden path. A man in his shirt sleeves is stooping amongst the tender young peas. A bundle of stakes lies next him, and he whistles softly and all out of tune as he twines the little tendrils round each new support. She looks at his broad shoulders and narrow flanks; his back is too long for great strength, she thinks. He hears her step, and smiles up at her from under the shadow of his broad-leafed hat.

'How do you feel now, old woman?'

'Beastly. I've got that horrid qualmish feeling again. I can't get rid of it.'

He has spread his coat on the side of the path and pats it for her to sit down.

'What is it' (anxiously)? 'if you were a mare I'd know what to do for you. Have a nip of whisky?'

He strides off without waiting for her reply and comes back with it and a biscuit, kneels down and holds the glass to her lips.

261

'Poor little woman, buck up! You'll see that'll fix you. Then you go by-and-by and have a shy at the fish.'

She is about to say something when a fresh qualm attacks her and she does not.

He goes back to his tying.

'By Jove!' he says suddenly, 'I forgot. Got something to show you!'

After a few minutes he returns carrying a basket covered with a piece of sacking. A dishevelled-looking hen, with spread wings trailing and her breast bare from sitting on her eggs, screeches after him. He puts it carefully down and uncovers it, disclosing seven little balls of yellow fluff splashed with olive green. They look up sideways with bright round eyes, and their little spoon bills look disproportionately large.

'Aren't they beauties (enthusiastically)? This one is just out,' taking up an egg, 'mustn't let it get chilled.' There is a chip out of it and a piece of hanging skin. 'Isn't it funny?' he asks, showing her how it is curled in the shell, with its paddles flattened and its bill breaking through the chip, and the slimy feathers sticking to its violet skin.

She suppresses an exclamation of disgust, and looks at his fresh-tinted skin instead. He is covering basket, hen, and all –

'How you love young things!' she says.

'Some. I had a filly once, she turned out a lovely mare! I cried when I had to sell her, I wouldn't have let any one in God's world mount her.'

'Yes, you would!'

'Who?' with a quick look of resentment.

'Me!'

'I wouldn't!'

'What! you wouldn't?'

'I wouldn't!'

'I think you would if I wanted to!' with a flash out of the tail of her eye.

'No, I wouldn't!'

'Then you would care more for her than for me. I would give you your choice (passionately), her or me!'

'What nonsense!'

'May be (concentrated), but it's lucky she isn't here to make deadly sense of it.' A bumble-bee buzzes close to her ear, and she is roused to a sense of facts, and laughs to think how nearly they have quarrelled over a mare that was sold before she knew him.

Some evenings later, she is stretched motionless in a chair, and yet she conveys an impression of restlessness; a sensitively nervous person would feel it. She is gazing at her husband, her brows are drawn together, and make three little lines. He is reading, reading quietly, without moving his eyes quickly from side to side of the page as she does when she reads, and he pulls away at a big pipe with steady enjoyment. Her eyes turn from him to the window, and follow the course of two clouds, then they close for a few seconds, then open to watch him again. He looks up and smiles.

'Finished your book?'

There is a singular soft monotony in his voice; the organ with which she replies is capable of more varied expression.

'Yes, it is a book makes one think. It would be a greater book if he were not an Englishman. He's afraid of shocking the big middle-class. You wouldn't care about it.'

'Finished your smoke?'

'No, it went out, too much fag to light up again! No (protestingly), never you mind, old boy, why do you?'

He has drawn his long length out of his chair, and kneeling down beside her, guards a lighted match from the incoming evening air. She draws in the smoke contentedly, and her eyes smile back with a general vague tenderness.

'Thank you, dear old man!'

'Going out again?' negative head shake.

'Back aching?' affirmative nod, accompanied by a steadily aimed puff of smoke, that she has been carefully inhaling, into his eyes.

'Scamp! Have your booties off?'

'Oh, don't you bother, Lizzie will do it!'

He has seized a foot from under the rocker, and, sitting on his heels, holds it on his knee, whilst he unlaces the boot; then he loosens the stocking under her toes, and strokes her foot gently.

'Now, the other!' Then he drops both boots outside the door, and fetching a little pair of slippers, past their first smartness, from the bedroom puts one on. He examines the left foot; it is a little swollen round the ankle and he presses his broad fingers gently round it as one sees a man do to a horse with windgalls.[5] Then he pulls the rocker nearer to his chair and rests the slipper-less foot on his thigh. He relights his pipe, takes up his book, and rubs softly from ankle to toes as he reads.

She smokes and watches him, diverting herself by imagining him in the hats of different periods. His is a delicate-skinned face with regular features; the eyes are fine, in colour and shape with the luminous clearness of a child's; his pointed beard is soft and curly. She looks at his hand, – a broad strong hand with capable fingers, – the hand of a craftsman, a contradiction to the face with its distinguished delicacy. She holds her own up with a cigarette poised between the first and second fingers, idly pleased with its beauty of form and delicate nervous slightness. One speculation chases the other in her quick brain; odd questions as to race arise; she dives into theories as to the why and wherefore of their distinctive nature, and holds a mental debate in which she takes both sides of the question impartially. He has finished his pipe, laid down his book, and is gazing dreamily, with his eyes darkened by their long lashes, and a look of tender melancholy in their clear depths, into space.

'What are you thinking of?' There is a look of expectation in her quivering nervous little face.

He turns to her, chafing her ankle again.

'I was wondering if lob-worms would do for – '

He stops. A strange look of disappointment flits across her face and is lost in an hysterical peal of laughter.

'You are the best emotional check I ever knew,' she gasps.

He stares at her in utter bewilderment, and then a slow smile creeps to his eyes and curves the thin lips under his moustache, a smile at her.

'You seem amused, Gipsy!'

She springs out of her chair and seizes book and pipe; he follows the latter anxiously with his eyes until he sees it laid safely on the table. Then she perches herself, resting her knees against one of his legs, whilst she hooks her feet back under the other –

'Now I am all up, don't I look small?'

He smiles his slow smile. 'Yes, I believe you are made of gutta percha.'[6]

She is stroking out all the lines in his face with the tip of her finger; then she runs it through his hair. He twists his head half impatiently, she desists.

'I divide all the people in the world,' she says, 'into those who like their hair played with, and those who don't. Having my hair brushed gives me more pleasure than anything else; it's delicious. I'd *purr* if I knew how, I notice (meditatively) I am never in sympathy with those who don't like it; I am with those who do. I always get on with them.'

'You are a queer little devil!'

'Am I? I shouldn't have thought you would have found out I was the latter at all. I wish I were a man! I believe if I were a man, I'd be a disgrace to my family.'

'Why?'

'I'd go on a jolly old spree!'

He laughs: 'Poor little woman, is it so dull?'

There is a gleam of devilry in her eyes, and she whispers solemnly –

'Begin with a D,' and she traces imaginary letters across his forehead, and ending with a flick over his ear, says, 'and that is the tail of the y!'

After a short silence she queries –

'Are you fond of me?' She is rubbing her chin up and down his face.

'Of course I am, don't you know it?'

'Yes, perhaps I do,' impatiently; 'but I want to be told it. A woman doesn't care a fig for a love as deep as the death-sea and as silent, she wants something that tells her it in little waves all the time. It isn't the love, you know, it's the being loved; it isn't really the man, it's his loving!'

By Jove, you're a rum un!'

'I wish I wasn't then. I wish I was as commonplace as ——— . You don't tell me anything about myself (a fierce little kiss), you might even if it were lies. Other men who cared for me told me things about my eyes, my hands, anything. I don't believe you notice.'

'Yes I *do*, little one, only I think it.'

'Yes, but I don't care a bit for your thinking; if I can't see what's in your head what good is it to me?'

'I wish I could understand you, dear!'

'I wish to God you could. Perhaps if you were badder and I were gooder we'd meet halfway. *You* are an awfully good old chap; it's just men like you send women like me to the devil!'

'But you are good (kissing her), a real good chum! You understand a fellow's weak points. You don't blow him up if he gets on a bit. Why (enthusiastically), being married to you is like chumming with a chap! Why (admiringly), do you remember before we were married, when I let that card fall out of my pocket? Why, I couldn't have told another girl about her. She wouldn't have believed that I *was* straight. She'd have thrown me over. And you sent her a quid because she was sick. You are a great little woman!'

'Don't see it! (she is biting his ear). Perhaps I was a man last time, and some hereditary memories are cropping up in this incarnation!'

He looks so utterly at sea that she has to laugh again, and, kneeling up, shuts his eyes with kisses, and bites his chin and shakes it like a terrier in her strong little teeth.

'You imp! was there ever such a woman!'

Catching her wrists, he parts his knees and drops her on to the rug. Then, perhaps the subtle magnetism that is in her affects him, for he stoops and snatches her up and carries her up and down, and then over to the window and lets the fading light with its glimmer of moonshine play on her odd face with its tantalising changes. Her eyes dilate and his colour deepens as he crushes her soft little body to him and carries her off to her room.

Summer is waning and the harvest is ripe for ingathering, and the voice of the reaping machine is loud in the land. She is stretched on her back on the short heather-mixed moss at the side of a bog stream. Rod and creel are flung aside, and the wanton breeze, with the breath of coolness it has gathered in its passage over the murky dykes of black bog water, is playing with the tail fly, tossing it to and fro with a half threat to fasten it to a prickly spine of golden gorse. Bunches of bog-wool nod their fluffy heads, and through the myriad indefinite sounds comes the regular scrape of a strickle[7] on the scythe of a reaper in a neighbouring meadow. Overhead a flotilla of clouds is steering from the south in a north-easterly direction. Her eyes follow them. Old time galleons, she thinks, with their wealth of snowy sail spread, riding breast to breast up a wide blue fjord after victory. The sails of the last are rose flushed, with a silver edge. Somehow she thinks of Cleopatra sailing down to meet Antony, and a great longing fills her soul to sail off somewhere too – away from the daily need of dinner-getting and the recurring Monday with its washing; life with its tame duties and virtuous monotony. She fancies herself in Arabia on the back of a swift steed. Flashing eyes set in dark faces surround her, and she can see the clouds of sand swirl, and feel the swing under her of his rushing stride. Her thoughts shape themselves into a wild song, a song to her steed of flowing mane and satin skin; an uncouth rhythmical jingle with a feverish beat; a song to the untamed spirit that dwells in her. Then she fancies she is on the stage of an ancient theatre out in the open air, with hundreds of faces upturned towards her. She is gauze-clad in a cobweb garment of wondrous tissue. Her arms are clasped by jewelled snakes, and one with quivering diamond fangs coils round her hips. Her hair floats loosely, and her feet are sandal-clad, and the delicate breath of vines and the salt freshness of an incoming sea seems to fill her nostrils. She bounds forward and dances, bends her lissom waist, and curves her slender arms, and gives to the soul of each man what he craves, be it good or evil. And she can feel now, lying here in the shade of Irish hills with her head resting on her scarlet shawl and her eyes closed, the grand intoxicating power of swaying all these human souls to wonder and applause. She can see herself with parted lips and panting, rounded breasts, and a dancing devil in each glowing eye, sway voluptuously to the wild music that rises, now slow, now fast, now deliriously wild, seductive, intoxicating, with a human note of passion in its strain. She can feel the answering shiver of feeling that quivers up to her from the dense audience, spellbound by the motion of her glancing feet, and she flies swifter and swifter, and lighter and lighter, till the very serpents seem alive with jewelled scintillations. One quivering, gleaming, daring bound, and she stands with outstretched arms and passion-filled eyes, poised on one slender foot, asking a supreme note to finish her dream of motion. And the men rise to a man and answer her, and cheer, cheer till the echoes shout from the surrounding hills and tumble wildly down the crags. The clouds have sailed away, leaving long feathery streaks in their wake. Her eyes have an inseeing look, and she is tremulous with excitement. She can hear yet that last grand shout, and the strain of that old-time music that she has never heard in this life of hers, save as an inner accompaniment to the memory of hidden things, born with her, not of this time.

And her thoughts go to other women she has known, women good and bad, school friends, casual acquaintances, women workers – joyless machines for grinding daily corn, unwilling maids grown old in the endeavour to get settled, patient wives who bear little ones to indifferent husbands until they wear out – a long array. She busies herself with questioning. Have they, too, this thirst for excitement, for change, this restless craving for sun and love and motion? Stray words, half confidences, glimpses through soul-chinks of suppressed fires, actual outbreaks, domestic catastrophes, how the ghosts dance in the cells of her memory! And she laughs, laughs softly to herself because the denseness of man, his chivalrous conservative devotion to the female idea he has created blinds him perhaps happily, to the problems of her complex nature. Ay, she mutters musingly, the wisest of them can only say we are enigmas. Each one of them sets about solving the riddle of the *ewig weibliche*[8] – and well it is that the workings of our hearts are closed to them, that we are cunning enough or *great* enough to seem to be what they would have us, rather than be what we are. But few of them have had the insight to find out the key to our seeming contradictions. The why a refined, physically fragile woman will mate with a brute, a mere male animal with primitive passions – and love him – the why strength and beauty appeal more often than the more subtly fine qualities of mind or heart – the why women (and not the innocent ones) will condone sins that men find hard to forgive in their fellows. They have all overlooked the eternal wildness, the untamed primitive savage temperament that lurks in the mildest, best woman. Deep in through ages of convention this primeval trait burns, an untameable quantity that may be concealed but is never eradicated by culture – the keynote of woman's witchcraft and woman's strength. But it is there, sure enough, and each woman is conscious of it in her truth-telling hours of quiet self-scrutiny – and each woman in God's wide world will deny it, and each woman will help another to conceal it – for the woman who tells the truth and is not a liar about these things is untrue to her sex and abhorrent to man, for he has fashioned a model on imaginary lines, and he has said, 'so I would have you,' and every woman is an unconscious liar, for so man loves her. And when a Strindberg or a Nietzche[9] arises and peers into the recesses of her nature and dissects her ruthlessly, the men shriek out louder than the women, because the truth is at all times unpalatable, and the gods they have set up are dear to them. . . .'

'Dreaming, or speering[10] into futurity? You have the look of a seer. I believe you are half a witch!'

And he drops his grey-clad figure on the turf. He has dropped his drawl long ago, in midsummer.

'Is not every woman that? Let us hope I'm, for my friends, a white one.'

'A-ah! Have you many friends?'

'That is a query! If you mean many correspondents, many persons who send me Christmas cards, or remember my birthday, or figure in my address-book? No.'

'Well, grant I don't mean that!'

'Well, perhaps, yes. Scattered over the world, if my death were belled out, many women would give me a tear, and some a prayer. And many men would turn back a page in their memory and give me a kind thought, perhaps regret, and go back to their work with a feeling of having lost something – that they never possessed. I am a creature of moments. Women have told me that I came into their lives just when they needed me. Men had no need to tell me, I felt it. People have needed me more than I them. I have given freely whatever they craved from me in the way of understanding or love. I have touched sore places they showed me and healed them, but they never got at me. I have been for myself and helped myself, and borne the burden of my own mistakes. Some have chafed at my self-sufficiency and have called me fickle – not understanding that they gave me nothing, and that when I had served them, their moment was ended and I was to pass on. I read people easily, I am written in black letter to most – '

'To your husband!'

'He (quickly) – we will not speak of him; it is not loyal.'

'Do not I understand you a little?'

'You do not misunderstand me.'

'That is something.'

It is much!'

'Is it? (searching her face). It is not one grain of sand in the desert that stretches between you and me, and you are as impenetrable as a sphinx at the end of it. This (passionately) is my moment, and what have you given me?'

'Perhaps less than other men I have known; but you want less. You are a little like me, you can stand alone. And yet (her voice is shaking), have I given you nothing?'

He laughs, and she winces – and they sit silent, and they both feel as if the earth between them is laid with infinitesimal electric threads vibrating with a common pain. Her eyes are filled with tears that burn but don't fall, and she can see his somehow through her closed lids, see their cool greyness troubled by sudden fire, and she rolls her handkerchief into a most cambric ball between her cold palms.

'You have given me something – something to carry away with me – an infernal want. You ought to be satisfied. I am infernally miserable.'

'You (nearer) have the most tantalising mouth in the world when your lips tremble like that. I . . . What! can you cry? You?'

'Yes, even I can cry!'

'You dear woman! (pause) And I can't help you!'

'You can't help me. No man can. Don't think it is because you are you I cry, but because you probe a little nearer into the real me that I feel so.'

'Was it necessary to say that? (reproachfully). Do you think I don't know it? I can't for the life of me think how you, with that free gipsy nature of yours, could bind yourself to a monotonous country life, with no excitement, no change. I wish I could offer you my yacht. Do you like the sea?;

'I love it, it answers one's moods.'

'Well, let us play pretending, as the children say. Grant that I could, I would hang your cabin with your own colours; fill it with books, all those I have heard you say you care for; make it a nest as rare as the bird it would shelter. You would reign supreme; when your highness would deign to hon-our her servant I would come and humour your every whim. If you were glad you would clap your hands and order music, and we would dance on the white deck, and we would skim through the sunshine of Southern seas on a spice-scented breeze. You make me poetical. And if you were angry you could vent your feelings on me, and I would give in and bow my head to your mood. And we would drop anchor and stroll through strange cities, go far inland and glean folklore out of the beaten track of everyday tourists. And at night when the harbour slept we would sail out through the moonlight over silver seas. You are smiling, you look so different when you smile; do you like my picture?'

'Some of it!'

'What not?'

'You!'

'Thank you.'

'You asked me. Can't you understand where the spell lies? It is the freedom, the freshness, the vague danger, the unknown that has a witchery for me, ay, for every woman!'

'Are you incapable of affection, then?'

'Of course not, I share' (bitterly) 'that crowning disability of my sex. But not willingly, I chafe under it. My God, if it were not for that, we women would master the world. I tell you men would be no match for us. At heart we care nothing for laws, nothing for systems. All your elaborately reasoned codes for controlling morals or man do not weigh a jot with us against an impulse, an instinct. We learn those things from you, you tamed, amenable animals; they are not natural to us. It is a wise disposition of providence that this untameableness of ours is corrected by our affections. We forge our own chains in a moment of softness, and then' (bitterly) 'we may as well wear them with a good grace. Perhaps many of our seeming contradictions are only the outward evidences of inward chafing. Bah! the qualities that go to make a Napoleon — superstition, want of honour, disregard of opinion and the eternal I — are oftener to be found in a woman than a man. Lucky for the world perhaps that all these attributes weigh as nothing in the balance with the need to love if she be a good woman, to be loved if he is of a coarser fibre.'

'I never met any one like you, you are a strange woman!'

'No, I am merely a truthful one. Women talk to me — why, I can't say — but always they come, strip their hearts and souls naked, and let me see the hidden folds of their natures. The greatest tragedies I have ever read are child's play to those I have seen acted in the inner life of outwardly commonplace women. A woman must beware of speaking the truth to a man; he loves her the less for it. It is the elusive spirit in her that he divines but cannot seize, that fascinates and keeps him.'

There is a long silence, the sun is waning and the scythes are silent, and overhead the crows are circling, a croaking irregular army, homeward bound from a long day's pillage.

She has made no sign, yet so subtly is the air charged with her that he feels but a few moments remain to him. He goes over and kneels beside her and fixes his eyes on her odd dark face. They both tremble, yet neither speaks. His breath is coming quickly, and the bistre[11] stains about her eyes seem to have deepened, perhaps by contrast as she has paled.

'Look at me!'

She turns her head right round and gazes straight into his face. A few drops of sweat glisten on his forehead.

'You witch woman! what am I to do with myself? Is my moment ended?'

'I think so.'

'Lord, what a mouth!'

'Don't, oh don't!'

'No, I won't. But do you mean it? Am I, who understand your very mood, your restless spirit, to vanish out of your life? You can't mean it. Listen; are you listening to me? I can't see your face; take down your hands. Go back over every chance meeting you and I have had together since I met you first by the river, and judge them fairly. To-day is Monday; Wednesday afternoon I shall pass your gate, and if – if my moment is ended, and you mean to send me away, to let me go with this weary aching . . .'

'A-ah!' she stretches out one brown hand appealingly, but he does not touch it.

'Hang something white on the lilac bush!'

She gathers up creel and rod, and he takes her shawl, and, wrapping it round her, holds her a moment in it, and looks searchingly into her eyes, then stands back and raises his hat, and she glides away through the reedy grass.

Wednesday morning she lies watching the clouds sail by. A late rose spray nods into the open window, and the petals fall every time. A big bee buzzes in and fills the room with his bass note, and then dances out again. She can hear his footstep on the gravel. Presently he looks in over the half window.

'Get up and come out, 'twill do you good. Have a brisk walk!'

She shakes her head languidly, and he throws a great soft dewy rose with sure aim on her breast.

'Shall I go in and lift you out and put you, "nighty" and all, into your tub?'

'No (impatiently). I'll get up just now.'

The head disappears, and she rises wearily and gets through her dressing slowly, stopped every moment by a feeling of faintness. He finds her presently rocking slowly to and fro with closed eyes, and drops a leaf with three plums in it on to her lap.

'I have been watching four for the last week, but a bird, greedy beggar, got one this morning early – try them. Don't you mind, old girl, I'll pour out my own tea!'

She bites into one and tries to finish it, but cannot.

'You are a good old man!' she says, and the tears come unbidden to her eyes, and trickle down her cheeks, dropping on to the plums, streaking their delicate bloom. He looks uneasily at her, but doesn't know what to do, and when he has finished his breakfast he stoops over her chair and strokes her hair, saying, as he leaves a kiss on the top of her head –

'Come out into the air, little woman; do you a world of good!' And presently she hears the sharp thrust of his spade above the bee's hum, leaf rustle, and the myriad late summer sounds that thrill through the air. It irritates her almost to screaming point. There is a practical non-sympathy about it, she can distinguish the regular one, two, three, the thrust, interval, then pat, pat, on the upturned sod. To-day she wants some one, and her thoughts wander to the grey-eyed man who never misunderstands her, and she wonders what he would say to her. Oh, she wants some one so badly to soothe her. And she yearns for the little mother who is twenty years under the daisies. The little mother who is a faint memory strengthened by a daguerreotype[12] in which she sits with silk-mittened hands primly crossed on the lap of her moiré[13] gown, a diamond brooch fastening the black velvet ribbon crossed so stiffly over her lace collar, the shining tender eyes looking steadily out, and her hair in the fashion of fifty-six. How that spade dominates over every sound! And what a sickening pain she has; an odd pain, she never felt it before. Supposing she were to die, she tries to fancy how she would look. They would be sure to plaster her curls down. He might be digging her grave – no, it is the patch where the early peas grew; the peas that were eaten with the twelve weeks' ducklings; she remembers them, little fluffy golden balls with waxen bills, and such dainty paddles. Remembers holding an egg to her ear and listening to it cheep inside before even there was a chip in the shell. Strange how things come to life. What! she sits bolt upright and holds tightly to the chair, and a questioning, awesome look comes over her face. Then the quick blood creeps up through her olive skin right up to her temples, and she buries her face in her hands and sits so a long time.

The maid comes in and watches her curiously, and moves softly about. The look in her eyes is the look of a faithful dog, and she loves her with the same rare fidelity. She hesitates, then goes in to the bedroom and stands thoughtfully, with her hands clasped over her breast.

She is a tall, thin, flat-waisted woman, with misty blue eyes and a receding chin. Her hair is pretty.

She turns as her mistress comes in, with an expectant look on her face. She has taken up a night-gown, but holds it idly.

'Lizzie, had you ever a child?'

The girl's long left hand is ringless, yet she asks it with a quiet insistence as if she knew what the answer would be, and the odd eyes read her face with an almost cruel steadiness. The girl flushes painfully and then whitens, her very eyes seem to pale, and her under lip twitches as she jerks out huskily –

'Yes!'

'What happened it?'

'It died, Ma'm.'

'Poor thing! Poor old Liz!'

She pats the girl's hand softly, and the latter stands dumbly and looks down at both hands, as if fearful to break the wonder of a caress. She whispers hesitatingly –

'Have you, have you any little things left?'

And she laughs such a soft, cooing little laugh, like the churring of a ring-dove, and nods shyly back in reply to the tall maid's questioning look. The latter goes out, and comes back with a flat, red-painted deal box and unlocks it. It does not hold very much, and the tiny garments are not of costly material, but the two women pore over them as a gem collector over a rare stone. She has a glimpse of thick crested paper as the girl unties a packet of letters, and looks away until she says tenderly –

'Look, Ma'm!'

A little bit of hair inside a paper heart. It is almost white, so silky, and so fine, that it is more like a thread of bog wool than a baby's hair. And the mistress, who is a wife, puts her arms round the tall maid, who has never had more than a moral claim to the name, and kisses her in her quick way.

The afternoon is drawing on; she is kneeling before an open trunk with flushed cheeks and sparkling eyes. A heap of unused, dainty lace trimmed ribbon-decked cambric garments is scattered around her. She holds the soft scented web to her cheek and smiles musingly. Then she rouses herself and sets to work, sorting out the finest, with the narrowest lace and tiniest ribbon, and puckers her swarthy brows, and measures lengths along her middle finger. Then she gets slowly up, as if careful of herself as a precious thing, and half afraid.

'Lizzie!'

'Yes, Ma'm!'

'Wasn't it lucky they were too fine for every day? They will be so pretty. Look at this one with the tiny valenciennes[14] edging. Why, one nightgown will make a dozen little shirts – such elfin-shirts as they are too – and Lizzie!'

'Yes, Ma'am!'

'Just hang it out on the lilac bush; mind, the lilac bush!'

'Yes, Ma'am.'

'Or Lizzie, wait – I'll do it myself!'

Notes

Text: *Keynotes*, E. Matthews and J. Lane, London, 1893.
 1 Town in ancient Boetia, Greece.
 2 Freshwater fish of the family *Cobitidae*.
 3 Ring worn to keep the wedding ring in place.
 4 The story is set in Ireland.
 5 Swellings on a horse's fetlock.
 6 White rubber extract from the sap of tropical trees, used for making dolls.
 7 Abrasive bar for sharpening a scythe.
 8 Eternal female.

9 August Strindberg (1849–1914), Swedish dramatist and novelist; Friedrich Wilhelm Nietzsche (1844–1900), German philosopher, poet and critic.
10 Questioning, inquiring.
11 Brownish-yellow.
12 Early form of photograph.
13 Watered silk.
13 Cotton or linen lace.

URMI: THE STORY OF A QUEEN

Cornelia Sorabji

Cornelia Sorabji (1866–1954), barrister, short-story writer, novelist, auto-biographer, and writer on India, was born in Nasik, in west India. She was the first woman to study law at Oxford University (1881), and became both the first British woman barrister and the first Indian barrister. She returned home in 1894 to work mainly for Indian women and children as legal adviser to the courts of various states. Her stories about India, aimed at British readers, appeared initially in periodicals and were later collected in several volumes including the popular *Life and Love Behind the Purdah* (1901). She also wrote several non-fictional works about India, including *Social Relations: India and England* (1908), as well as two autobiographical memoirs, *India Calling* (1934) and *India Recalled* (1936). Her concern about the position of women in India is reflected in *Urmi: The Story of a Queen*.

Further reading

Blain *et al.* (1990)

Urmi: The Story of a Queen

Five p.m. and Saturday. Without, a cold wet mist, a grey sky, dirty streets; within, the curtains drawn, the cosiest of lounges, the softest of cushions, the fire crackling merrily, the kettle hissing gently – how nice it was to be warm, and sleepy! . . . Presto! They don't think long about things here. A moment ago that lovely red ball nestled confidingly between the peaks of those moss-covered mountains; now it has dropped, disappeared, gone to rest, leaving only its glorious curtains for us to look upon. Or, is this the entrance to the palace of some deity – into whose presence-chamber the sun has just been ushered? The strong mountains are on guard, and the stars in motion have played the royal anthem.

All here is in darkness, save for that reflection from the west. . . . Softly – our way is through that wooded forest, under those great strong trees that embrace each other in their solitariness. Past the quiet lake, inside the gates. Another palace – large gardens, cool deep verandahs, marble halls, tall statues, Quick! Tarry not – through the courtyard. What is that? Only the sacred *tulsi*[1] in its accustomed place. Grave men in red uniforms watch the buildings. Pass them by; they question not. At last! A low dark room – there, in that corner, on the bed. Hush! A moan – she is in pain – step gently. Poor thing! small and sad, and beautiful! What eyes! What hair! What jewels! What lovely, clinging, saffron silk! Who hurt her? Her small hands are clenched – she beats her forehead – she calls on "Krishna."[2] Now she rises – listen! She speaks.

"Bukku! Come near me. Are the women there? Send them away. I want you – only you. Listen, Bukku; there is not much time. What means this sickness? Is it death? Feel my hands; they burn. My head – it's like a hot stone, lying out in an April sun. I will not live the night. What say you?"

"Hush! Light of my eyes! My child – my flower, my tender lotus-bud! That will not be, that *must* not be! Your father is measuring the ground on a long pilgrimage to Benares.[3] You will recover. Have you your amulet? Take hold of it; and see, here's a new charm. My grandmother learnt it of a faqir, and taught it me. It cured the good Akbar once, when he lay dying. The little Gulam went up to the hills this morning, and brought me the healing herb from a far-distant spot. See, too, my bracelets – they are with the priests – they will appease the gods. They were good gold. Nay! my beautiful, you will live many years. My treasure! My precious stone, the worst is past."

"No! Bukku! you are kind, you love me. You are the only true creature I

277

have beside me. All else are false, and mean me ill. They are like the hooded cobra, they sting me in the grass. Oh, Bukku! I have not loved this royal state. And they love me not here. Would that I were home again, on the cool soft banks of my own river. Remember you, Bukku, how the lotus floated on the water, and the plantain trees spread their green shade over our heads? And my father – my dear kind father – how I read with him, seated on his knee, stories of early times when the world was young; and of the beautiful Sakuntalla,[4] and the poor Nar Jehan;[5] and those verses of Kalidas,[6] when he read them to me – 'twas like the little summer brook playing with the pebbles – so pleasing to my ear. . . . It's all over now. He will miss me, my poor old father. And perhaps he, my lord whom I may not name, *perhaps* he will sigh for me, and say, 'She was young, and the gods made her beautiful, and – she is dead!' And he will be just a little grieved, and bid them play sad music, and feed poor Brahmins,[7] in my name. . . . Then he will go out, and hunt or shoot, or sit with his councillors, and forget me quite. I've loved him, Bukku. He was good to me, and strong and wise and kind; and when I talked to him of my early days and pastimes, and the things which I loved, he smiled, and said, 'It is not so with all my other wives; they know not what to talk about; they have not read your favourite books; they cannot read; they care not what occurs in other lands; they ask me for new jewels and prettier clothes; and they look modest, and sometimes beautiful; and that is all: but you.'. . . And once he praised my wisdom, and said he would I share his throne with him. See! keep you this letter; when they lift me on to the bier, and bear me to the burning ground, and put the torch to these cold limbs, go to him, put *that* in his hand. It's not long; just one line – he will know, and understand. . . .

"And now, Bukku, quick! the child! My strength is failing. Bring him to me – nearer – lift him up. How beautiful he is! His eyes, how large, how dark, how deep! I feel I am looking into a well of light, of sunshine, of clear cool water. His small round arms, how soft they are! He smiles! poor child, he wants me – and I go, whence I return not, unless perchance as some small reptile, or a tree, or a flower.

"I would it were a flower, and that I grew where *he* would touch me, and feel my petals, and say, 'I like that flower; it is as pure and fragile as my little Urmi.'. . . But, when I'm gone, take the child, carry it hence. They mean it harm. You have nursed me – nurse it; but *hide it* – hide it safely from them – from Afzul. My father will pay you, and will see to its future. Now, while it is young and helpless, you must love it and care for it. Tell it of me and of its father . . . but let *them* here think that it is dead. You know what to do; some poor baby you will purchase in the market, will have a prince's end. . . . I will tell you all, Bukku – you shall tell my father. Tell him how they hated me here. You remember, when I came, how they looked at me, and shook their heads, and said a 'God forbid!' because I read and wrote? And when the king, our lord, favoured me above them all, and sought my presence, and listened to my words, I heard them whisper. 'Bold minx!' they said, 'child of the Evil One! She knows what it does not beseem women to know, for she reads and writes as if she were some common clerk. And when she talks to *him*, she lifts her eyes and looks upon his face. How know we that in her distant home she did not break her *purdah*?[8] We hear that her father taught her many things which he learnt of the Feringhee.'[9]. . . .

"And my women who loved me, they turned against me. All but you, Bukku, whom they did not dare to touch; but they kept you from me, knowing that you loved me. I was wretched, and wrote my father word that they looked coldly on me. He said, 'Try gifts, try gold and jewels.' They took them – but it made no change; and I would I'd never left him – but for the king whom I loved – yet him I seldom saw. After the boy came, things were worse. Lying ill here one day behind this heavy curtain, I heard them talk, and Afzul was with them, and he said, 'Would that the king had hearkened to my words, and taken to wife the bride whom I had chosen. With this one I have had no commission; and she is the child of the Evil One. See how she has bewitched the king. He praises her looks, and her learning, and her ways; and, now that there is an heir, his regard for her has grown tenfold. We must *remove* her and the boy. Say the word: it shall be done!' And then, Bukku, *his* mother, whom I had tried to love as mine own, said, 'You know your work: *do it*. I give you leave: she has come between my son and me!' And Afzul – how he looked! I saw his eye gleam, and he swore an oath by his father's head. He is a terrible man. Shield my boy from him; let him not see his face. It would haunt his baby days – it would make a stain on his mind. Oh! would I were here to protect him! But what power would I have? It would but make matters worse, could I intervene. *You* will care for him, Bukku – you and my father. The king – he cannot; he must think him dead.

"You see *that* . . . Afzul . . . did . . . his work . . .

"What is this, Bukku? Is it – *death*?

"My eyes grow dim. Call on Krishna. I am falling – hold my hand. . . . The lord my king – would he were here! . . . My love! I have loved you much; love me a little."

. . . Through the open door streamed in the moonlight, and kissed the lovely figure as it lay; from the hills came the weird bark of the jackals; an owl shrieked in the mango grove. . . . What is that? the death-wail? They know, then, that all is over. Is it well with them in the agent's sanctum? in the zenana?[10] in the servants' courtyard? in the king's chamber? Is it well?

Seven p.m. – The fire is low; I am cold. Was it only a dream? Alas! would it were! It was the wail of some poor child in a London street. And it stirred the memory of other sad things in far-distant climes, across the seas. . . . Poor Urmi!

Notes

Text: *The Nineteenth Century* 33 (January 1893); reprinted in *Love and Life behind the Purdah*, Freemantle, London, 1901.

1 Species of basil, cultivated by Hindus as sacred to the deity Vishnu.
2 Hindu deity.
3 Sacred city on the Ganges.
4 Eponymous heroine of celebrated drama by Kalidasa, 5th-century Hindu dramatist and poet.
5 Another spelling of Nourjehan, wife of the 17th-century Moghul Emperor Jehangir, who built the Taj Mahal for her after her death.
6 See note 4 above.
7 Members of the highest caste, often priests.
8 Rule dictating that women remain unseen by any man apart from their husband.
9 Europeans.
10 Harem.

THE PLEASURE-PILGRIM

Ella D'Arcy

Ella D'Arcy (1851–1937), short-story writer, novelist and editor, was born in London of Irish parentage, and educated in France and Germany. Her training at the Slade School of Art was cut short owing to defective eyesight, and she turned to writing instead. Her early stories were published in *The Yellow Book*, for which she acted for a time as assistant editor, and were collected in *Monochromes* (1895) and *Modern Instances* (1898). Her friend Netta Syrett believed that 'But for her incurable idleness she should have made, if not a great, at least a very distinguished, writer of elegant and witty prose.' She wrote only one novel, *The Bishop's Dilemma* (1898). She never married, though she is reputed to have had an affair with the publisher John Lane among others. She later lived in Paris, where she translated André Maurois' fictionalised biography of Shelley, *Ariel* (1924). Her honest, pessimistic stories, which deal almost exclusively with unhappy marriages and difficult sexual relationships, are generally regarded as some of the finest of the period.

Further reading

Blain *et al.* (1990); Fitzgerald (1984); Mix (1960); Harris (1968–9); Shattock (1993); Stanford (1968); Stubbs (1979); Sutherland (1988)

The Pleasure-Pilgrim

I

Campbell was on his way to Schloss[1] Altenau, for a second quiet season with his work. He had spent three profitable months there a year ago, and he was hoping now for a repetition of that good fortune. His thoughts outran the train; and long before his arrival at the Hamelin railway station, he was enjoying his welcome by the Ritterhausens, was revelling in the ease and comfort of the old Castle, and was contrasting the pleasures of his home-coming – for he looked upon Schloss Altenau as a sort of temporary home – with his recent cheerless experiences of lodging-houses in London, hotels in Berlin, and strange indifferent faces everywhere. He thought with especial satisfaction of the Maynes, and of the good talks Mayne and he would have together, late at night, before the great fire in the hall, after the rest of the household had gone to bed. He blessed the adverse circumstances which had turned Schloss Altenau into a boarding-house, and had reduced the Freiherr Ritterhausen to eke out his shrunken revenues by the reception, as paying guests, of English and American pleasure-pilgrims.

He rubbed the blurred window-pane with the fringed end of the strap hanging from it, and, in the snow-covered landscape reeling towards him, began to recognise objects that were familiar. Hamelin could not be far off. . . . In another ten minutes the train came to a standstill.

He stepped down with a sense of relief from the overheated atmosphere of his compartment into the cold, bright February afternoon, and saw through the open station doors one of the Ritterhausen carriages awaiting him, with Gottlieb in his second-best livery on the box. Gottlieb showed every reasonable consideration for the Baron's boarders, but had various methods of marking his sense of the immense abyss separating them from the family. The use of his second-best livery was one of these methods. Nevertheless, he turned a friendly German eye up to Campbell, and in response to his cordial 'Guten Tag, Gottlieb. Wie geht's? Und die Herrschaften?'[2] expressed his pleasure at seeing the young man back again.

While Campbell stood at the top of the steps that led down to the carriage and the Platz,[3] looking after the collection of his luggage and its bestowal by Gottlieb's side, he became aware of two persons, ladies, advancing towards him from the direction of the Wartsaal.[4] It was surprising to see any one at any time in Hamelin Station. It was still more surprising when one of these ladies addressed him by name.

'You are Mr Campbell, are you not?' she said. 'We have been waiting for you to go back in the carriage together. When we found this morning that there was only half-an-hour between your train and ours, I told the Baroness it would be perfectly absurd to send to the station twice. I hope you won't mind our company?'

The first impression Campbell received was of the magnificent apparel of the lady before him; it would have been noticeable in Paris or Vienna – it was extravagant here. Next, he perceived that the face beneath the upstanding feathers and the curving hat-brim was that of so very young a girl, as to make the furs and velvets seem more incongruous still. But the sense of incongruity vanished with the intonation of her first phrase, which told him she was an American. He had no standards for American conduct. It was clear that the speaker and her companion were inmates of the Schloss.

He bowed, and murmured the pleasure he did not feel. A true Briton, he was intolerably shy; and his heart sank at the prospect of a three-mile drive with two strangers who evidently had the advantage of knowing all about him, while he was in ignorance of their very names. As he took his place opposite to them in the carriage, he unconsciously assumed a cold, blank stare, pulling nervously at his moustache, as was his habit in moments of discomposure. Had his companions been British also, the ordeal of the drive must have been a terrible one; but these young American ladies showed no sense of embarrassment whatever.

'We've just come back from Hanover,' said the girl who had already spoken to him. 'I go over once a week for a singing lesson, and my little sister comes along to take care of me.'

She turned a narrow, smiling glance from Campbell to her little sister, and then back to Campbell again. She had red hair; freckles on her nose, and the most singular eyes he had ever seen; slit-like eyes, set obliquely in her head, Chinese fashion.

'Yes, Lulie requires a great deal of taking care of,' assented the little sister sedately, though the way in which she said this seemed to imply something less simple than the words themselves. The speaker bore no resemblance to Lulie. She was smaller, thinner, paler. Her features were straight, a trifle peaked; her skin sallow; her hair of a nondescript brown. She was much less gorgeously dressed. There was even a suggestion of shabbiness in her attire, though sundry isolated details of it were handsome too. She was also much less young; or so, at any rate, Campbell began by pronouncing her. Yet presently he wavered. She had a face that defied you to fix her age. Campbell never fixed it to his own satisfaction, but veered in the course of that drive (as he was destined to do during the next few weeks) from point to point up and down the scale from eighteen to thirty-five. She wore a spotted veil, and beneath it a pince-nez, the lenses of which did something to temper the immense amount of humorous meaning which lurked in her gaze. When her pale prominent eyes met Campbell's, it seemed to the young man that they were full of eagerness to add something at his expense to the stores of information they had already garnered up. They chilled him with misgivings; there was more comfort to be found in her sister's shifting, red-brown glances.

'Hanover is a long way to go for lessons,' he observed, forcing himself to be conversational. 'I used to go there myself about once a week, when I first came to Schloss Altenau, for tobacco, or notepaper, or to get my hair cut. But later on I did without, or contented myself with what Hamelin, or even the village, could offer me.'

'Nannie and I,' said the young girl, 'meant to stay only a week at Altenau, on our way to Hanover, where we were going to pass the winter; but the Castle is just too lovely for anything.' She raised her eyelids the least little bit as she looked at him, and such a warm and friendly gaze shot out, that Campbell was suddenly thrilled. Was she pretty, after all? He glanced at Nannie; she, at least, was indubitably plain. 'It's the very first time we've ever stayed in a castle,' Lulie went on; 'and we're going to remain right along now, until we go home in the spring. Just imagine living in a house with a real moat, and a drawbridge, and a Rittersaal,[5] and suits of armour that have been actually worn in battle! And oh, that delightful iron collar and chain! You remember it, Mr Campbell? It hangs right close to the gateway on the courtyard side. And you know, in old days the Ritterhausens used it for the punishment of their serfs. There are horrible stories connected with it. Mr Mayne can tell you them. But just think of being chained up there like a dog! So wonderfully picturesque.'

'For the spectator perhaps,' said Campbell, smiling. 'I doubt if the victim appreciated the picturesque aspect of the case.'

With this Lulie disagreed. 'Oh, I think he must have been interested,' she said. 'It must have made him feel so absolutely part and parcel of the Middle Ages. I persuaded Mr Mayne to fix the collar round my neck the other day; and though it was very uncomfortable, and I had to stand on tiptoe, it seemed to me that all at once the courtyard was filled with knights in armour, and crusaders, and palmers, and things; and there were flags flying and trumpets sounding; and all the dead and gone Ritterhausens had come down from their picture-frames, and were walking about in brocaded gowns and lace ruffles.'

'It seemed to require a good deal of persuasion to get Mr Mayne to unfix the collar again,' said the little sister. 'How at last did you manage it?'

But Lulie replied irrelevantly: 'And the Ritterhausens are such perfectly lovely people, aren't they, Mr Campbell? The old Baron is a perfect dear. He has such a grand manner. When he kisses my hand I feel nothing less than a princess. And the Baroness is such a funny, busy, delicious little round ball of a thing. And she's always playing bagatelle,[6] isn't she? Or else cutting up skeins of wool for carpetmaking.' She meditated a moment. 'Some people always *are* cutting things up in order to join them together again,' she announced, in her fresh drawling young voice.

'And some people cut things up, and leave other people to do the reparation,' commented the little sister enigmatically.

And meantime the carriage had been rattling over the cobble-paved streets of the quaint mediaeval town, where the houses stand so near together that you may shake hands with your opposite neighbour; where allegorical figures, strange birds and beasts, are carved and painted over the windows and doors; and where to every distant sound you lean your ear to catch the fairy music of the Pied Piper,[7] and at every street corner you look to see his tatterdemalion form with the frolicking children at his heels.

Then the Weser bridge was crossed, beneath which the ice-floes jostled and ground themselves together, as they forced their way down the river; and the carriage was rolling smoothly along country roads, between vacant snow-decked fields.

Campbell's embarrassment began to wear off. Now that he was getting accustomed to the girls, he found neither of them awe-inspiring. The red-haired one had a simple child-like manner that was charming. Her strange little face, with its piquant irregularity of line, its warmth of colour, began to please him. What though her hair was red, the uncurled wisp which strayed across her white forehead was soft and alluring; he could see soft masses of it tucked up beneath her hat-brim as she turned her head. When she suddenly lifted her red-brown lashes, those queer eyes of hers had a velvety softness too. Decidedly, she struck him as being pretty – in a peculiar way. He felt an immense accession of interest in her. It seemed to him that he was the discoverer of her possibilities. He did not doubt that the rest of the world called her plain; or at least odd-looking. He, at first, had only seen the freckles on her nose, her oblique-set eyes. He wondered now what she thought of herself, how she appeared to Nannie. Probably as a very ordinary little girl; sisters stand too close to see each other's qualities. She was too young to have had much opportunity of hearing flattering truths from strangers; and besides, the average stranger would see nothing in her to call for flattering truths. Her charm was something subtle, out-of-the-common, in defiance of all known rules of beauty. Campbell saw superiority in himself for recognising it, for formulating it; and he was not displeased to be aware that it would always remain caviare to the multitude.[8]

The carriage had driven through the squalid village of Dürrendorf, had passed the great Ritterhausen barns and farm-buildings, on the tie-beams of which are carved Bible texts in old German; had turned in at the wide open gates of Schloss Altenau, where Gottlieb always whipped up his horses to a fast trot. Full of feeling both for the pocket and the dignity of the Ritterhausens, he would not use up his beasts in unnecessary fast driving. But it was to the credit of the family that he should reach the Castle in fine style. And so he thundered across the drawbridge, and through the great archway pierced in the north wing, and over the stones of the cobbled courtyard, to pull up before the door of the hall, with much clattering of hoofs and a final elaborate whip-flourish.

II

'I'm jolly glad to have you back,' Mayne said, that same evening, when, the rest of the boarders having retired to their rooms, he and Campbell were lingering over the hall-fire for a talk and smoke. 'I've missed you awfully, old chap, and the good times we used to have here. I've often meant to write to you, but you know how one shoves off letter-writing day after day, till at last one is too ashamed of one's indolence to write at all. But tell me – you had a pleasant drive from Hamelin? What do you think of our young ladies?'

'Those American girls? But they're charming,' said Campbell, with enthusiasm. 'The red-haired one is particularly charming.'

At this Mayne laughed so strangely that Campbell questioned him in surprise. 'Isn't she charming?'

'My dear chap,' Mayne told him, 'the red-haired one, as you call her, is the most remarkably charming young person I've ever met or read of. We've had a good many American girls here before now – you remember the good old Choate family, of course – they were here in your time, I think? – but we've never had anything like this Miss Lulie Thayer. She is something altogether unique.'

Campbell was struck with the name. 'Lulie – Lulie Thayer,' he repeated. 'How pretty it is!' And, full of his great discovery, he felt he must confide it to Mayne, at least. 'Do you know,' he went on, '*she* is really very pretty too? I didn't think so at first, but after a bit I discovered that she is positively quite pretty – in an odd sort of way.'

Mayne laughed again. 'Pretty, pretty!' he echoed in derision. 'Why *lieber Gott im Himmel*,[9] where are your eyes? Pretty! The girl is beautiful, gorgeously beautiful; every trait, every tint, is in complete, in absolute harmony with the whole. But the truth is, of course, we've all grown accustomed to the obvious, the commonplace; to violent contrasts; blue eyes, black eyebrows, yellow hair; the things that shout for recognition. You speak of Miss Thayer's hair as red. What other colour would you have, with that warm, creamy skin? And then, what a red it is! It looks as though it had been steeped in red wine.'

'Ah, what a good description,' said Campbell, appreciatively. 'That's just it – steeped in red wine.'

'Though it's not so much her beauty,' Mayne continued. 'After all, one has met beautiful women before now. It's her wonderful generosity, her complaisance. She doesn't keep her good things to herself. She doesn't condemn you to admire from a distance.

'How do you mean?' Campbell asked, surprised again.

287

'Why, she's the most egregious little flirt I've ever met. And yet, she's not exactly a flirt, either. I mean she doesn't flirt in the ordinary way. She doesn't talk much, or laugh, or apparently make the least claims on masculine atten-tion. And so all the women like her. I don't believe there's one, except my wife, who has an inkling as to her true character. The Baroness, as you know, never observes anything. *Seigneur Dieu!*[10] if she knew the things I could tell her about Miss Lulie! For I've had opportunities of studying her. You see, I'm a married man, and not in my first youth, and the looker-on generally gets the best view of the game. But you, who are young and charming and already famous — we've had your book here, by-the-by, and there's good stuff in it — you're going to have no end of pleasant experiences. I can see she means to add you to her ninety-and-nine other spoils; I saw it from the way she looked at you at dinner. She always begins with those velvety red-brown glances. She began that way with March and Prendergast and Willie Anson, and all the men we've had here since her arrival. The next thing she'll do will be to press your hand under the tablecloth.'

'Oh come, Mayne, you're joking,' cried Campbell a little brusquely. He thought such jokes in bad taste. He had a high ideal of Woman, an immense respect for her; he could not endure to hear her belittled, even in jest. 'Miss Thayer is refined and charming. No girl of her class would do such things.'

'But what is her class? Who knows anything about her? All we know is that she and her uncanny little friend — her little sister, as she calls her, though they're no more sisters than you and I are — they're not even related — all we know is, that she and Miss Dodge (that's the little sister's name) arrived here one memorable day last October from the Kronprinz Hotel at Waldeck-Pyrmont. By-the-by, it was the Choates, I believe, who told her of the Castle — hotel acquaintances — you know how travelling Americans always cotton to each other. And we've picked up a few little auto and biographical notes from her and Miss Dodge since. *Zum Beispiel*,[11] she's got a rich father somewhere away back in Michigan, who supplies her with all the money she wants. And she's been travelling about since last May: Paris, Vienna, the Rhine, Düsseldorf, and so on here. She must have had some rich experiences, by Jove, for she's done everything. Cycled in Paris; you should see her in her cycling costume, she wears it when the Baron takes her out shooting — she's an admirable shot by the way, an accomplishment learned, I suppose, from some American cow-boy — then in Berlin she did a month's hospital nursing; and now she's studying the higher branches of the Terpsichorean art.[12] You know she was in Hanover today. Did she tell you what she went for?'

'To take a singing lesson,' said Campbell, remembering the reason she had given.

'A singing lesson! Do you sing with your legs? A dancing lesson, *mein lieber*.[13] A dancing lesson from the ballet-master of the Hof Theater. She could deposit a kiss on your forehead with her foot, I don't doubt. I must ask her if she can do the *grand écart*[14] yet.' And when Campbell, in astonishment, wondered why on earth she should wish to learn such things, 'Oh, to extend her opportunities,' Mayne explained, 'and to acquire fresh sensations. She's an adventuress. Yes, an adventuress, but an end-of-the-century one. She doesn't travel for profit, but for pleasure. She has no desire to swindle her neighbour, but to amuse herself. And she's clever; she's read a good deal; she knows how to apply her reading to practical life. Thus, she's learned from Herrick not to be coy; and from Shakespeare that sweet-and-twenty is the time for kissing and being kissed.[15] She honours her masters in the observance. She was not in the least abashed when, one day, I suddenly came upon her teaching that damned idiot, young Anson, two new ways of kissing.'

Campbell's impressions of the girl were readjusting themselves completely, but for the moment he was unconscious of the change. He only knew that he was partly angry, partly incredulous, and inclined to believe that Mayne was chaffing him.

'But, Miss Dodge,' he objected, 'the little sister, she is older; old enough to look after her friend. Surely she could not allow a young girl placed in her charge to behave in such a way —'

'Oh, that little Dodge girl,' said Mayne contemptuously; 'Miss Thayer pays the whole shot, I understand, and Miss Dodge plays gooseberry, sheep-dog, jackal, what you will. She finds her reward in the other's cast-off finery. The silk blouse she was wearing to-night, I've good reason for remembering, belonged to Miss Lulie. For, during a brief season, I must tell you, my young lady had the caprice to show attentions to your humble servant. I suppose my being a married man lent me a factitious fascination. But I didn't see it. That kind of girl doesn't appeal to me. So she employed Miss Dodge to do a little active canvassing. It was really too funny; I was coming in one day after a walk in the woods; my wife was trimming bonnets, or had neuralgia, or something. Anyhow, I was alone, and Miss Dodge contrived to waylay me in the middle of the courtyard. "Don't you find it vurry dull walking all by yourself?" she asked me; and then blinking up in her strange little short-sighted way — she's really the weirdest little creature — "Why don't you make love to Lulie?" she said; "you'd find her vurry charming." It took me a minute or two to recover presence of mind enough to ask her whether Miss Thayer had commissioned her to tell me so. She looked at me with that cryptic smile of hers; "She'd like you to do so, I'm sure," she finally remarked, and pirouetted away. Though it didn't come off, owing to my bashfulness, it was then that Miss Dodge appropriated the silk "waist"; and Providence, taking pity on Miss Thayer's forced inactivity, sent along March, a young fellow reading for the army, with whom she had great doings. She fooled him to the top of his bent; sat on his knee; gave him a lock of her hair, which, having no scissors handy, she burned off with a cigarette taken from his mouth; and got him to offer her marriage. Then she turned round and laughed in his face, and took up with a Dr Weber, a cousin of the Baron's, under the other man's very eyes. You never saw anything like the unblushing coolness with which she would permit March to catch her in Weber's arms.'

'Come,' Campbell protested again, 'aren't you drawing it rather strong?'

'On the contrary, I'm drawing it mild, as you'll discover presently for yourself and then you'll thank me for forewarning you. For she makes love – desperate love, mind you – to every man she meets. And goodness knows how many she hasn't met in the course of her career, which began presumably at the age of ten, in some "Amur'can" hotel or watering-place. Look at this.' Mayne fetched an alpenstock[16] from a corner of the hall; it was decorated with a long succession of names, which, ribbon-like, were twisted round and round it, carved in the wood. 'Read them,' insisted Mayne, putting the stick in Campbell's hands. 'You'll see they're not the names of the peaks she has climbed, or the towns she has passed through; they're the names of the men she has fooled. And there's room for more; there's still a good deal of space, as you see. There's room for yours.'

Campbell glanced down the alpenstock – reading here a name, there an initial, or just a date – and jerked it impatiently from him on to a couch. He wished with all his heart that Mayne would stop, would talk of something else, would let him get away. The young girl had interested him so much; he had felt himself so drawn towards her; he had thought her so fresh, so innocent. But Mayne, on the contrary, was warming to his subject, was enchanted to have some one to listen to his stories, to discuss his theories, to share his cynical amusement.

'I don't think, mind you,' he said, 'that she is a bit interested herself in the men she flirts with. I don't think she gets any of the usual sensations from it, you know. My theory is, she does it for mere devilry, for a laugh. Or, and this is another theory, she is actuated by some idea of retribution. Perhaps some woman she was fond of – her mother even – who knows? – was badly treated at the hands of a man. Perhaps this girl has constituted herself the Nemesis[17] for her sex, and goes about seeing how many masculine hearts she can break, by way of revenge. Or can it be that she is simply the newest development of the New Woman – she who in England preaches and bores you, and in America practises and pleases? Yes, I believe she's the American edition, and so new that she hasn't yet found her way into fiction. She's the pioneer of the army coming out of the West, that's going to destroy the existing scheme of things, and rebuild it nearer to the heart's desire.'

'Oh, damn it all, Mayne,' cried Campbell, rising abruptly, 'why not say at once that she's a wanton, and have done with it? Who wants to hear your rotten theories?' And he lighted his candle without another word, and went off to bed.

III

It was four o'clock, and the Baron's boarders were drinking their afternoon coffee, drawn up in a semi-circle round the hall fire. All but Campbell, who had carried his cup away to a side-table, and, with a book open beside him, appeared to be reading assiduously. In reality he could not follow a line of what he read; he could not keep his thoughts from Miss Thayer. What Mayne had told him was germinating in his mind. Knowing his friend as he did, he could not on reflection doubt his word. In spite of much superficial cynicism, Mayne was incapable of speaking lightly of any young girl without good cause. It now seemed to Campbell that, instead of exaggerating the case, Mayne had probably understated it. He asked himself with horror, what had this girl not already known, seen, permitted? When now and again his eyes travelled over, perforce, to where she sat, her red head leaning against Miss Dodge's knee, and seeming to attract to, and concentrate upon itself all the glow of the fire, his forehead set itself in frowns, and he returned to his book with an increased sense of irritation.

'I'm just sizzling up, Nannie,' Miss Thayer presently complained, in her child-like, drawling little way; 'this fire is too hot for anything.' She rose and shook straight her loose tea-gown, a marvellous plush and lace garment created in Paris, which would have accused a duchess of wilful extravagance. She stood smiling round a moment, pulling on and off with her right hand a big diamond ring which decorated the left. At the sound of her voice Campbell had looked up, and his cold, unfriendly eyes encountered hers. He glanced rapidly past her, then back to his book. But she, undeterred, with a charming sinuous movement and a frou frou of trailing silks, crossed over towards him. She slipped into an empty chair next his.

'I'm going to do you the honour of sitting beside you, Mr Campbell,' she said sweetly.

'It's an honour I've done nothing whatever to merit,' he answered, without looking at her, and turned a page.

'The right retort,' she approved; 'but you might have said it a little more cordially.'

'I don't feel cordial.'

'But why not? What has happened? Yesterday you were so nice.'

'Ah, a good deal of water has run under the bridge since yesterday.'

'But still the river remains as full,' she told him, smiling, 'and still the sky is as blue. The thermometer has even risen six degrees.'

'What did you go into Hanover for yesterday?' Campbell suddenly asked her.

She flashed him a comprehending glance from half-shut eyes. 'I think men gossip a great deal more than women,' she observed, 'and they don't understand things either. They try to make all life suit their own pre-conceived theories. And why, after all, should I not wish to learn dancing thoroughly? There's no harm in that.'

'Only, why call it singing?' Campbell enquired.

Miss Thayer smiled. 'Truth is so uninteresting!' she said, and paused. 'Except in books. One likes it there. And I wanted to tell you, I think your books perfectly lovely. I know them, most all. I've read them away home.

They're very much thought of in America. Only last night I was saying to Nannie how glad I am to have met you, for I think we're going to be great friends, aren't we, Mr Campbell? At least, I hope so, for you can do me so much good, if you will. Your books always make me feel real good; but you yourself can help me much more.'

She looked up at him with one of her warm, narrow, red-brown glances, which yesterday would have thrilled his blood, and to-day merely stirred it to anger.

'You over-estimate my abilities,' he said coldly; 'and, on the whole, I fear you will find writers a very disappointing race. You see, they put their best into their books. So not to disillusion you too rapidly' – he rose – 'will you excuse me? I have some work to do.' And he left her sitting there alone.

But he did no work when he got to his room. Whether Lulie Thayer was actually present or not, it seemed that her influence was equally disturbing to him. His mind was full of her: of her singular eyes, her quaint intonation, her sweet, seductive praise. Twenty-four hours ago such praise would have been delightful to him: what young author is proof against appreciation of his books? Now, Campbell simply told himself that she laid the butter on too thick; that it was in some analogous manner she had flattered up March, Anson, and all the rest of the men that Mayne had spoken of. He supposed it was the first step in the process by which he was to be fooled, twisted round her finger, added to the list of victims who strewed her conquering path. He had a special fear of being fooled. For beneath a somewhat supercilious exterior, the dominant note of his character was timidity, distrust of his own merits; and he knew he was single-minded – one-idea'd almost – if he were to let himself go, to get to care very much for a woman, for such a girl as this girl, for instance, he would lose himself completely, be at her mercy absolutely. Fortunately, Mayne had let him know her character. He could feel nothing but dislike for her – disgust, even; and yet he was conscious how pleasant it would be to believe in her innocence, in her candour. For she was so adorably pretty; her flower-like beauty grew upon him; her head, drooping a little on one side when she looked up, was so like a flower bent by its own weight. The texture of her cheeks, her lips, was delicious as the petals of a flower. He found he could recall with perfect accuracy every detail of her appearance: the manner in which the red hair grew round her temples; the way in which it was loosely and gracefully fastened up behind with just a single tortoiseshell pin. He recollected the suspicion of a dimple that shadowed itself in her cheek when she spoke, and deepened into a delicious reality every time she smiled. He remembered her throat; her hands, of a beautiful whiteness, with pink palms and pointed fingers. It was impossible to write. He speculated long on the ring she wore on her engaged finger. He mentioned this ring to Mayne the next time he saw him.

'Engaged? very much so, I should say. Has got a *fiancé* in every capital of Europe probably. But the ring-man is the *fiancé en titre.*[18] He writes to her by every mail, and is tremendously in love with her. She shows me his letters. When she's had her fling, I suppose she'll go back and marry him. That's what these little American girls do, I'm told; sow their wild oats here with us, and settle down into *bonnes ménagères*[19] over yonder. Meanwhile, are you having any fun with her? Aha, she presses your hand? The "gesegnete Mahlzeit"[20] business after dinner is an excellent institution, isn't it? She'll tell you how much she loves you soon; that's the next move in the game.'

But so far she had done neither of these things, for Campbell gave her no opportunities. He was guarded in the extreme, ungenial; avoiding her even at the cost of civility. Sometimes he was downright rude. That especially occurred when he felt himself inclined to yield to her advances. For she made him all sorts of silent advances, speaking with her eyes, her sad little mouth, her beseeching attitude. And then one evening she went further still. It occurred after dinner in the little green drawing-room. The rest of the company were gathered together in the big drawing-room beyond. The small room has deep embrasures to the windows. Each embrasure holds two old faded green velvet sofas in black oaken frames, and an oaken oblong table stands between them. Campbell had flung himself down on one of these sofas in the corner nearest the window. Miss Thayer, passing through the room, saw him, and sat down opposite. She leaned her elbows on the table, the laces of her sleeves falling away from her round white arms, and clasped her hands.

'Mr Campbell, tell me, what have I done? How have I vexed you? You have hardly spoken two words to me all day. You always try to avoid me.' And when he began to utter evasive banalities, she stopped him with an imploring 'Ah, don't! I love you. You know I love you. I love you so much I can't bear you to put me off with mere phrases.'

Campbell admired the well-simulated passion in her voice, remembered Mayne's prediction, and laughed aloud.

'Oh, you may laugh,' she said, 'but I'm serious. I love you, I love you with my whole soul.' She slipped round the end of the table, and came close beside him. His first impulse was to rise; then he resigned himself to stay. But it was not so much resignation that was required, as self-mastery, coolheadedness. Her close proximity, her fragrance, those wonderful eyes raised so beseechingly to his, made his heart beat.

'Why are you so cold?' she said. 'I love you so, can't you love me a little too?'

'My dear young lady,' said Campbell, gently repelling her, 'what do you take me for? A foolish boy like your friends Anson and March? What you are saying is monstrous, preposterous. Ten days ago you'd never even seen me.'

'What has length of time to do with it?' she said. 'I loved you at first sight.'

'I wonder,' he observed judicially, and again gently removed her hand from his, 'to how many men you have not already said the same thing?'

'I've never meant it before,' she said quite earnestly, and nestled closer to him, and kissed the breast of his coat, and held her mouth up towards his. But he kept his chin resolutely high, and looked over her head.

'How many men have you not already kissed, even since you've been here?'

'But there've not been many here to kiss!' she exclaimed naïvely.

'Well, there was March; you kissed him?'

'No, I'm quite sure I didn't.'

'And young Anson; what about him? Ah, you don't answer! And then the other fellow – what's his name – Prendergast – you've kissed him?'

'But, after all, what is there in a kiss?' she cried ingenuously. 'It means nothing, absolutely nothing. Why, one has to kiss all sorts of people one doesn't care about.'

Campbell remembered how Mayne had said she had probably known strange kisses since the age of ten; and a wave of anger with her, of righteous indignation, rose within him.

'To me,' said he, 'to all right-thinking people, a young girl's kisses are something pure, something sacred, not to be offered indiscriminately to every fellow she meets. Ah, you don't know what you have lost! You have seen a fruit that has been handled, that has lost its bloom? You have seen primroses, spring flowers gathered and thrown away in the dust? And who enjoys the one, or picks up the others? And this is what you remind me of – only you have deliberately, of your own perverse will, tarnished your beauty, and thrown away all the modesty, the reticence, the delicacy, which make a young girl so infinitely dear. You revolt me, you disgust me. I want nothing from you but to be let alone. Kindly take your hands away, and let me go.'

He shook her roughly off and got up, then felt a moment's curiosity to see how she would take the repulse.

Miss Thayer never blushed: had never, he imagined, in her life done so. No faintest trace of colour now stained the warm pallor of her roseleaf skin; but her eyes filled up with tears, two drops gathered on the under lashes, grew large, trembled an instant, and then rolled unchecked down her cheeks. Those tears somehow put him in the wrong, and he felt he had behaved brutally to her, for the rest of the night.

He began to seek excuses for her: after all, she meant no harm: it was her upbringing, her *genre*:[21] it was a *genre* he loathed; but perhaps he need not have spoken so harshly. He thought he would find a more friendly word for her next morning; and he loitered about the Mahlsaal,[22] where the boarders come in to breakfast as in an hotel just when it suits them, till past eleven; but she did not come. Then, when he was almost tired of waiting, Miss Dodge put in an appearance, in a flannel wrapper, and her front hair twisted up in steel pins.

Campbell judged Miss Dodge with even more severity than he did Miss Thayer; there was nothing in this weird little creature's appearance to temper justice with mercy. It was with difficulty that he brought himself to inquire after her friend.

'Lulie is sick this morning,' she told him. 'I've come down to order her some broth. She couldn't sleep any last night, because of your unkindness to her. She's vurry, vurry unhappy about it.'

'Yes, I'm sorry for what I said. I had no right to speak so strongly, I suppose. But I spoke strongly because I feel strongly. However, there's no reason why my bad manners should make her unhappy.'

'Oh, yes, there's vurry good reason,' said Miss Dodge. 'She's vurry much in love with you.'

Campbell looked at the speaker long and earnestly to try and read her mind; but the prominent blinking eyes, the cryptic physiognomy, told him nothing.

'Look here,' he said brusquely, 'what's your object in trying to fool me like this? I know all about your friend. Mayne has told me. She has cried "Wolf" too often before to expect to be believed now.'

'But, after all,' argued Miss Dodge, blinking more than ever behind her glasses, 'the wolf did really come at last, you know; didn't he? Lulie is really in love this time. We've all made mistakes in our lives, haven't we? But that's no reason for not being right at last. And Lulie has cried herself sick.'

Campbell was a little shaken. He went and repeated the conversation to Mayne who laughed derisively.

'Capital, capital!' he cried; 'excellently contrived. It quite supports my latest theory about our young friend. She's an actress, a born comédienne. She acts always, and to every one: to you, to me, to the Ritterhausens, to the Dodge girl – even to herself when she is quite alone. And she has a great respect for her art; she'll carry out her rôle, *coûte que coûte*,[23] to the bitter end. She chooses to pose as in love with you; you don't respond; the part now requires that she should sicken and pine. Consequently, she takes to her bed, and sends her confidante to tell you so. Oh, it's colossal, it's *famos*!'[24]

IV

'If you can't really love me,' said Lulie Thayer – 'and I know I've been a bad girl and don't deserve that you should – at least, will you allow me to go on loving you?'

She walked by Campbell's side, through the solitary, uncared-for park of Schloss Altenau. It was three weeks later in the year, and the spring feeling in the air stirred the blood. All round were signs and tokens of spring; in the busy gaiety of bird and insect life; in the purple flower-tufts which thickened the boughs of the ash trees; in the young green things pushing up pointed heads from amidst last season's dead leaves and grasses. The snow-wreaths, that had for so long decorated the distant hills, were shrinking perceptibly away beneath the strong March sunshine.

There was every invitation to spend one's time out of doors, and Campbell passed long mornings in the park, or wandering through the woods and the surrounding villages. Miss Thayer often accompanied him. He never invited her to do so, but when she offered him her company, he could not, or at least did not, refuse it.

'May I love you? Say,' she entreated.

' "Wenn ich Dich liebe, was geht's Dich an?" '[25] he quoted lightly. 'Oh no, it's nothing to me, of course. Only don't expect me to believe you – that's all.'

This disbelief of his was the recurring decimal of their conversation. No matter on what subject they began, they always ended thus. And the more sceptical he showed himself, the more eager she became. She exhausted herself in endeavours to convince him.

They had reached the corner in the park where the road to the Castle turns off at right angles from the road to Dürrendorf. The ground rises gently on the park-side to within three feet of the top of the boundary wall, although on the other side there is a drop of at least twenty feet. The broad wall-top makes a convenient seat. Campbell and the girl sat down on it. At his last words she wrung her hands together in her lap.

'But how can you disbelieve me?' she cried, 'when I tell you I love you, I adore you? when I swear it to you? And can't you see for yourself? Why, every one at the Castle sees it.'

'Yes, you afford the Castle a good deal of unnecessary amusement; and that shows you don't understand what love really is. Real love is full of delicacy, of reticences, and would feel itself profaned if it became the jest of the servants' hall.'

'It's not so much my love for you, as your rejection of it, which has made me talked about.'

'Isn't it rather on account of the favours you've lavished on all my predecessors?'

She sprang to her feet, and walked up and down in agitation.

'But, after all, surely, mistakes of that sort are not to be counted against us? I did really think I was in love with Mr March. Willie Anson doesn't count. He's an American too, and he understands things. Besides, he is only a boy. And how could I know I should love you before I had met you? And how can I help loving you now I have? You're so different from other men. You're good, you're honourable, you treat women with respect. Oh, I do love you so, I do love you! Ask Nannie if I don't.'

The way in which Campbell shrugged his shoulders clearly expressed the amount of reliance he would place on any testimony from Miss Dodge. He could not forget her 'Why don't you make love to Lulie?' addressed to a married man. Such a want of principle argued an equal want of truth.

Lulie seemed on the brink of weeping.

'I wish I were dead,' she struggled to say; 'life's impossible if you won't believe me. I don't ask you any longer to love me. I know I've been a bad girl, and I don't deserve that you should; but if you won't believe that I love you, I don't want to live any longer.'

Campbell confessed to himself that she acted admirably, but that the damnable iteration of the one idea became monotonous. He sought a change of subject. 'Look there,' he said, 'close by the wall, what's that jolly little blue flower? It's the first I've seen this year.'

He showed her where, at the base of the wall, a solitary blossom rose above a creeping stem and glossy dark green leaves.

Lulie, all smiles again, picked it with childlike pleasure. 'Oh, if that's the first you've seen,' she cried, 'you can take a wish. Only you mustn't speak until some one asks you a question.'

She began to fasten it in his coat. 'It's just as blue as your eyes,' she said. 'You have such blue and boyish eyes, you know. Stop, stop, that's not a question,' and seeing that he was about to speak, she laid her finger across his mouth. 'You'll spoil the charm.'

She stepped back, folded her arms, and seemed to dedicate herself to eternal silence; then relenting suddenly:

'Do you believe me?' she entreated.

'What's become of your ring?' Campbell answered beside the mark. He had noticed its absence from her finger while she had been fixing in the flower.

'Oh, my engagement's broken.'

Campbell asked how the fiancé would like that.

'Oh, he won't mind. He knows I only got engaged because he worried so. And it was always understood between us that I was to be free if I ever met any one I liked better.'

Campbell asked her what sort of fellow this accommodating fiancé was.

'Oh, he's all right. And he's very good too. But he's not a bit clever, and don't let us talk about him. He makes me tired.'

'But you're wrong,' Campbell told her, 'to throw away a good, a sincere affection. If you really want to reform and turn over a new leaf, as you are always telling me you do, I should advise you to go home and marry him.'

'What, when I'm in love with you?' she cried reproachfully. 'Would that be right?'

'It's going to rain,' said Campbell. 'Didn't you feel a drop just then? And it's getting near lunch-time. Shall we go in?'

Their shortest way led through the little cemetery in which the departed Ritterhausens lay at peace, in the shadow of their sometime home.

'When I die the Baron has promised I shall be buried here,' said Lulie pensively; 'just here, next to his first wife. Don't you think it would be lovely to be buried in a beautiful, peaceful, baronial graveyard instead of in some horrid, crowded city cemetery?'

Mayne met them as they entered the hall. He noticed the flower in his friend's coat. 'Ah, my dear chap, been treading the – periwinkle path[26] of dalliance, I see? How many desirable young men have I not witnessed, led down the same broad way by the same seductive lady! Always the same thing; nothing changes but the flower according to the season.'

When Campbell reached his room he took the poor periwinkle out of his coat, and threw it away into the stove.

And yet, had it not been for Mayne, Miss Thayer might have triumphed after all; might have convinced Campbell of her passion, or have added another victim to her long list. But Mayne had set himself as determinedly to spoil her game, as she was bent on winning it. He had always the cynical word, the apt reminiscence ready, whenever he saw signs on Campbell's part of surrender. He was very fond of Campbell. He did not wish him to fall a prey to the wiles of this little American siren. He had watched her conduct in the past with a dozen different men; he genuinely believed she was only acting in the present.

Campbell, for his part, began to experience an ever-increasing exasperation in the girl's presence. Yet he did not avoid it; he could not well avoid it, she followed him about so persistently: but his speech would overflow with bitterness towards her. He would say the cruellest things; then remembering them when alone, be ashamed of his brutalities. But nothing he said ever altered her sweetness of temper or weakened the tenacity of her purpose. His rebuffs made her beautiful eyes run over with tears, but the harshest of them never elicited the least sign of resentment. There would have been something touching as well as comic in this dog-like humility, which accepted everything as welcome at his hands, had not been imbued with Mayne's conviction that it was all an admirable piece of acting. Or when for a moment he forgot the histrionic theory, then invariably there would come a chance word in her conversation which would fill him with cold rage. They would be talking of books, travels, sport, what not, and she would drop a reference to this man or to that. So-and-so had taken her to Bullier's, she had learned skating with this other; Duroy, the *prix de Rome*[27] man, had painted her as Hebe,[28] Franz Weber had tried to teach her German by means of Heine's[29] poems. And he got glimpses of long vistas of amourettes played in every state in America, in every country of Europe, since the very beginning, when, as a mere child, elderly men, friends of her father's, had held her on their knee and fed her on sweetmeats and kisses. It was sickening to think of; it was pitiable. So much youth and beauty tarnished; the possibility for so much good thrown away. For if one could only blot out her record, forget it, accept her for what she chose to appear, a more endearing companion no man could desire.

V

It was a wet afternoon; the rain had set in at mid-day, with a gray determination, which gave no hopes of clearing. Nevertheless, Mayne had accompanied his wife and the Baroness into Hamelin. 'To take up a servant's character, and expostulate with a recalcitrant dressmaker,' he explained to Campbell, and wondered what women would do to fill up their days were it not for the perennial crimes of dressmakers and domestic servants. He himself was going to look in at the English Club; wouldn't Campbell come too? There was a fourth seat in the carriage. But Campbell was in no social mood; he felt his temper going all to pieces; a quarter of an hour of Mrs Mayne's society would have brought on an explosion. He thought he must be alone; and yet when he had read for half an hour in his room he wondered vaguely what Lulie was doing; he had not seen her since luncheon. She always gave him her society when he could very well dispense with it, but on a wet day like this, when a little conversation would be tolerable, of course she stayed away. Then there came down the long Rittersaal the tapping of high heels, and a well-known knock at his door.

He went over and opened it. Miss Thayer, in the plush and lace tea-gown, fronted him serenely.

'Am I disturbing you?' she asked; and his mood was so capricious that, now she was standing there on his threshold, he thought he was annoyed at it. 'It's so dull,' she said persuasively: 'Nannie's got a sick headache, and I daren't go downstairs, or the Baron will annex me to play Halma.[30] He always wants to play Halma on wet days.'

'And what do you want to do?' said Campbell, leaning against the doorpost, and letting his eyes rest on the strange piquant face in its setting of red hair.

'To be with you, of course.'

'Well,' said he, coming out and closing the door, 'I'm at your service. What next?'

They strolled together through the room and listened to the falling rain. The Rittersaal occupies all the space on the first floor that the hall and four drawing-rooms do below. Wooden pillars support the ceiling, dividing the apartment lengthwise into a nave and two aisles. Down the middle are long tables, used for ceremonial banquets. Six windows look into the courtyard, and six out over the open country. The centre pane of each window is emblazoned with a Ritterhausen shield. Between the windows hang family portraits, and the sills are broad and low and cushioned in faded velvet.

'How it rains!' said Lulie, stopping before one of the south windows; 'why, you can't see anything for the rain, and there's no sound at all but the rain either. I like it. It makes me feel as though we had the whole world to ourselves.'

Then, 'Say, what would you like to do?' she asked him. 'Shall I fetch over my pistols, and we'll practise with them? You've no notion how well I can shoot. We couldn't hurt anything here, could we?'

Campbell thought they might practise there without inconvenience, and Lulie, bundling up the duchess tea-gown over one arm, danced off in very unduchess-like fashion to fetch the case. It was a charming little box of

cedar-wood and mother-o'-pearl, lined with violet velvet; and two tiny re-
volvers lay inside, hardly more than six inches long, with silver engraved handles.

'I won them in a bet,' she observed complacently, 'with the Hon. Billie
Thornton. He's an Englishman, you know, the son of Lord Thornton. I knew
him in Washington two years ago last fall. He bet I couldn't hit a three-cent
piece at twenty yards and I did. Aren't they perfectly sweet? Now, can't you
contrive a target?'

Campbell went back to his room, drew out a rough diagram, and pasted it
down on to a piece of cardboard. Then this was fixed up by means of a
penknife driven into the wood of one of the pillars, and Campbell, with his
walking-stick laid down six successive times, measured off the distance
required, and set a chalk mark across the floor. Lulie took the first shot. She
held the little weapon up at arm's length above her head, the first finger
stretched out along the barrel; then dropping her hand sharply so that the
finger pointed straight at the butt, she pulled the trigger with the third.
There was the sharp report, the tiny smoke film – and when Campbell went
up to examine results, he found she had only missed the very centre by a
quarter of an inch.

Lulie was exultant. 'I don't seem to have got out of practice any,' she
remarked. 'I'm so glad, for I used to be a very good shot. It was Hiram P.
Ladd who taught me. He's the crack shot of Montana. What! you don't know
Hiram P.? Why, I should have supposed every one must have heard of him.
He had the next ranche to my Uncle Samuel's, where I used to go summers,
and he made me do an hour's pistol practice every morning after bathing. It
was he who taught me swimming too – in the river.'

'Damnation,' said Campbell under his breath, then shot in his turn, and
shot wide. Lulie made another bull's-eye, and after that a white. She urged
Campbell to continue, which he sullenly did, and again missed.

'You see I don't come up to your Hiram P. Ladd,' he remarked savagely,
and put the pistol down, and walked over to the window. He stood with one
foot on the cushioned seat, staring out at the rain, and pulling moodily at his
moustache.

Lulie followed him, nestled up to him, lifted the hand that hung passive
by his side, put it round her waist and held it there. Campbell lost in
thought, let it remain so for a second; then remembered how she had doubtless done this very same thing with other men in this very room. All her
apparently spontaneous movements, he told himself, were but the oft-used
pieces in the game she played so skilfully.

'Let go,' he said, and flung himself down on the window-seat, looking up
at her with darkening eyes.

She sitting meekly in the other corner folded her offending hands in her
lap.

'Do you know, your eyes are not a bit nice when you're cross?' she said;
'they seem to become quite black.'

He maintained a discouraging silence.

She looked over at him meditatively.

'I never cared a bit for Hiram P., if that's what you mean,' she remarked presently.

'Do you suppose I care a button if you did?'

'Then why did you leave off shooting, and why won't you talk to me?'

He vouchsafed no reply.

Lulie spent some moments immersed in thought. Then she sighed deeply, and recommenced on a note of pensive regret.

'Ah, if I'd only met you sooner in life, I should be a very different girl.'

The freshness which her quaint, drawling enunciation lent to this time-dishonoured formula, made Campbell smile, till, remembering all its implications, his forehead set in frowns again.

Lulie continued her discourse. 'You see,' said she, 'I never had any one to teach me what was right. My mother died when I was quite a child, and my father has always let me do exactly as I pleased, so long as I didn't bother him. Then I've never had a home, but have always lived around in hotels and places: all winter in New York or Washington, and summers out at Long-branch or Saratoga.[31] It's true we own a house in Detroit, on Lafayette Avenue, that we reckon as home, but we don't ever go there. It's a bad sort of life for a girl, isn't it?' she pleaded.

'Horrible,' he said mechanically. His mind was at work. The loose threads of his angers, his irritations, his desires, were knitting themselves together, weaving themselves into something overmastering and definite.

The young girl meanwhile was moving up towards him along the seat, for the effect which his sharpest rebuke produced on her never lasted more than four minutes. She now again possessed herself of his hand, and holding it between her own, began to caress it in childlike fashion, pulling the fingers apart and closing them again, spreading it palm downwards on her lap, and laying her own little hand over it, to exemplify the differences between them. He let her be; he seemed unconscious of her proceedings.

'And then,' she continued, 'I've always known a lot of young fellows who've liked to take me round; and no one ever objected to my going with them, and so I went. And I enjoyed it, and there wasn't any harm in it, just kissing and making believe, and nonsense. But I never really cared for one of them – I can see that now, when I compare them with you; when I compare what I felt for them with what I feel for you. Oh, I do love you so much,' she murmured; 'don't you believe me?' She lifted his hand to her lips and covered it with kisses.

He pulled it roughly from her. 'I wish you'd give over such fool's play,' he told her, got up, walked to the table, came back again, stood looking at her with sombre eyes and dilating pupils.

'But I do love you,' she repeated, rising and advancing towards him.

'For God's sake, drop that damned rot,' he cried out with sudden fury. 'It wearies me, do you hear? it sickens me. Love, love – my God, what do you know about it? Why, if you really loved me, really loved any man – if you had any conception of what the passion of love is, how beautiful, how fine, how sacred – the mere idea that you could not come to your lover fresh, pure, untouched, as a young girl should – that you had been handled, fondled, and God knows what besides, by this man and the other – would fill you with such horror for yourself, with such supreme disgust – you would feel yourself so unworthy, so polluted . . . that . . . that . . . by God! you would take up that pistol there, and blow your brains out!'

Lulie seemed to find the idea quite entertaining. She picked the pistol up from where it lay in the window, examined it critically, with her pretty head drooping on one side, and then sent one of her long red-brown caressing glances up towards him.

'And suppose I were to,' she asked lightly, 'would you believe me then?'

'Oh, . . . well . . . then, perhaps! If you showed sufficient decency to kill yourself, perhaps I might,' said he, with ironical laughter. His ebullition had relieved him; his nerves were calmed again. 'But nothing short of that would ever make me.'

With her little tragic air, which seemed to him so like a smile disguised, she raised the weapon to the bosom of her gown. There came a sudden, sharp crack, a tiny smoke film. She stood an instant swaying slightly, smiling certainly, distinctly outlined against the background of rain-washed window, of gray falling rain, the top of her head cutting in two the Ritterhausen escutcheon.[32] Then all at once there was nothing at all between him and the window – he saw the coat of arms entire – but a motionless, inert heap of plush and lace, and fallen wine-red hair, lay at his feet upon the floor.

'Child, child, what have you done?' he cried with anguish, and kneeling beside her, lifted her up, and looked into her face.

When from a distance of time and place Campbell was at last able to look back with some degree of calmness on the catastrophe, the element in it which stung him most keenly was this: he could never convince himself that Lulie had really loved him after all. And the only two persons who had known them both, and the circumstances of the case, sufficiently well to have resolved his doubts one way or the other, held diametrically opposite views.

'Well, listen, then, and I'll tell you how it was,' Miss Nannie Dodge had said to him impressively, the day before he left Schloss Altenau for ever. 'Lulie was tremendously, terribly in love with you. And when she found that you wouldn't care about her, she didn't want to live any more. As to the way in which it happened, you don't need to reproach yourself for that. She'd have done it, anyhow. If not then, why later. But it's all the rest of your conduct to her that was so mean. Your cold, cruel, complacent British unresponsiveness. I guess you'll never find another woman to love you as

Lulie did. She was just the darlingest, the sweetest, the most loving girl in the world.'

Mayne, on the other hand, summed it up in this way. 'Of course, old chap, it's horrible to think of: horrible, horrible, horrible! I can't tell you how badly I feel about it. For she was a gorgeously beautiful creature. That red hair of hers! Good Lord! You won't come across such hair as that again in a lifetime. But, believe me, she was only fooling with you. Once she had you in her hunting-noose, once her buccaneering instincts satisfied, and she'd have chucked you as she did all the rest. As to her death, I've got three theories – no, two – for the first being that she compassed it in a moment of genuine emotion, we may dismiss, I think, as quite untenable. The second is, that it arose from pure misadventure. You had both been shooting, hadn't you? Well, she took up the pistol and pulled the trigger from mere mischief, to frighten you, and quite forgetting one barrel was still loaded. And the third is, it was just her histrionic sense of the fitness of things. The rôle she had played so long and so well now demanded a sensational finale in the centre of the stage. And it's the third theory I give the preference to. She was the most consummate little actress I ever met.'

Notes

Text: *The Yellow Book*, vol. v (April 1895).
 1 Castle.
 2 'Good day, Gottleib. How are you? And the Master and mistress?'
 3 Square.
 4 Waiting-room.
 5 Great hall.
 6 Board game resembling billiards.
 7 Legendary figure who charmed away the children of Hamelin when the town failed to pay him for ridding it of rats.
 8 Too refined for common tastes.
 9 Dear God in Heaven.
10 Lord God!
11 For instance.
12 Dancing.
13 My dear [friend].
14 The splits.
15 Cf. Robert Herrick, 'To the Virgins to Make Much of Time' (which begins 'Gather ye rosebuds while ye may'); *Twelfth Night* II.iii.50–1.
16 Stout stick used by mountain walkers.
17 Goddess of retribution and vengeance.
18 Official fiancé.
19 Good housewives.
20 Good appetite.
21 Type.
22 Dining-room.

23 Come what may.
24 Famous.
25 'If I love you, what business is it of yours?' (J.W. von Goethe, *Wilhelm Meister* 4:9).
26 Mayne adapts the more usual 'primrose path' (a pleasurable, but morally rep-rehensible, way of life).
27 Coveted art prize.
28 Goddess of spring and youth.
29 Heinrich Heine (1797–1856), German Romantic poet.
30 Board game.
31 Fashionable North American resorts.
32 Carved stone shield, often placed above a window.

SUGGESTION

Ada Leverson

Ada ('Mrs Ernest') Leverson, née Beddington (1862–1933), novelist, short-story writer, journalist. Unhappily married at 19, she began writing articles, sketches and parodies for *Punch* and *Black and White*. Her parodies of Oscar Wilde's writings led to a close friendship with Wilde, who nicknamed her 'the Sphinx'. She also published two stories in *The Yellow Book*. Following her husband's departure for Canada in 1905 she wrote the first of her six novels, *The Twelfth Hour* (1907). This was followed by a trilogy supposedly based on her own marriage: *Love's Shadow* (1908), *Tenterhooks* (1912), *Love at Second Sight* (1916), reprinted as *The Little Ottleys* (1962). She also wrote a weekly column, published a book on astrology, and her memoirs, *Letters to the Sphinx from Oscar Wilde with Reminiscences of the Author*, in 1930. Her novels and stories, of which 'Suggestion' is typical, are celebrated for their witty dialogue and their satiric treatment of society and of unhappy marriages.

Further reading

Blain *et al.* (1990); Burkhart (1973); Hart-Davies (1962); Mix (1960); Sitwell (1950); Speedie (1993); Shattock (1993); Wyndham (1963).

Suggestion

If Lady Winthrop had not spoken of me as 'that intolerable effeminate boy,' she might have had some chance of marrying my father. She was a middle-aged widow; prosaic, fond of domineering, and an alarmingly excellent housekeeper; the serious work of her life was paying visits; in her lighter moments she collected autographs. She was highly suitable and altogether insupportable; and this unfortunate remark about me was, as people say, the last straw. Some encouragement from father Lady Winthrop must, I think, have received; for she took to calling at odd hours, asking my sister Marjorie sudden abrupt questions, and being generally impossible. A tradition existed that her advice was of use to our father in his household, and when, last year, he married his daughter's school-friend, a beautiful girl of twenty, it surprised every one except Marjorie and myself.

The whole thing was done, in fact, by suggestion. I shall never forget that summer evening when father first realised, with regard to Laura Egerton, the possible. He was giving a little dinner of eighteen people. *Through a mistake of Marjorie's* (my idea) Lady Winthrop did not receive her invitation till the very last minute. Of course she accepted – we knew she would – but unknowing that it was a dinner party, she came without putting on evening dress.

Nothing could be more trying to the average woman than such a *contre-temps*;[1] and Lady Winthrop was not one to rise, sublimely, and laughing, above the situation. I can see her now, in a plaid blouse and a vile temper, displaying herself, mentally and physically, to the utmost disadvantage, while Marjorie apologised the whole evening, in pale blue crepe-de-chine; and Laura, in yellow, with mauve orchids, sat – an adorable contrast – on my father's other side, with a slightly conscious air that was perfectly fascinating. It is quite extraordinary what trifles have their little effect in these matters. I had sent Laura the orchids, anonymously, I could not help it if she chose to think they were from my father. I had hinted of his secret affection for her, and lent her Verlaine.[2] I said I had found it in his study, turned down at her favourite page. Laura has, like myself, the artistic temperament; she is cultured, rather romantic, and in search of the *au-dela*.[3] My father has at times – never to me – rather charming manners; also he is still handsome, with that look of having suffered that comes from enjoying oneself too much. That evening his really sham melancholy and apparently hollow gaiety were delightful for a son to witness, and appealed evidently to her heart. Yes,

307

strange as it may seem, while the world said that pretty Miss Egerton married old Carington for his money, she was really in love, or thought herself in love, with our father. Poor girl! She little knew what an irritating, ill-tempered, absent-minded person he is in private life; and at times I have pangs of remorse.

A fortnight after the wedding, father forgot he was married, and began again treating Laura with a sort of *distrait*[4] gallantry as Marjorie's friend, or else ignoring her altogether. When, from time to time, he remembers she is his wife, he scolds her about the housekeeping in a fitful, perfunctory way, for he does not know that Marjorie does it still. Laura bears the rebukes like an angel; indeed, rather than take the slightest practical trouble she would prefer to listen to the strongest language in my father's vocabulary.

But she is sensitive; and when father, speedily resuming his bachelor manners, recommended his visits to an old friend who lives in one of the little houses opposite the Oratory,[5] she seemed quite vexed. Father is horribly careless, and Laura found a letter. They had a rather serious explanation and for a little time after, Laura seemed depressed. She soon tried to rouse herself, and is at times cheerful enough with Marjorie and myself, but I fear she has had a disillusion. They never quarrel now, and I think we all three dislike father about equally, though Laura never owns it, and is gracefully attentive to him in a gentle, filial sort of way.

We are fond of going to parties – not father – and Laura is a very nice chaperone for Marjorie. They are both perfectly devoted to me. 'Cecil knows everything,' they are always saying, and they do nothing – not even choosing a hat – without my advice.

Since I left Eton I am supposed to be reading with a tutor, but as a matter of fact I have plenty of leisure; and am very glad to be of use to the girls, of whom I'm, by the way, quite proud. They are rather a sweet contrast; Marjorie has the sort of fresh rosy prettiness you see in the park and on the river. She is tall, and slim as a punt-pole, and if she were not very careful how she dresses, she would look like a drawing by Pilotelle in the *Lady's Pictorial*. She is practical and lively, she rides and drives and dances; skates, and goes to some mysterious haunt called *The Stores*,[6] and is, in her own way, quite a modern English type. Laura has that exotic beauty so much admired by Philistines; dreamy dark eyes, and a wonderful white complexion. She loves music and poetry and pictures and admiration in a lofty sort of way; she has a morbid fondness for mental gymnastics, and a dislike to physical exertion, and never takes any exercise except waving her hair. Sometimes she looks bored, and I have heard her sigh.

'Cissy,' Marjorie said, coming one day into my study, 'I want to speak to you about Laura'.

'Do you have pangs of conscience too?' I asked, lighting a cigarette.

'Dear, we took a great responsibility. Poor girl! Oh, couldn't we make Papa more –'

'Impossible,' I said; 'no one has any influence with him. He can't bear even me, though if he had a shade of decency he would dash away an unbidden tear every time I look at him with my mother's blue eyes.'

My poor mother was a great beauty, and I am supposed to be her living image.

'Laura has no object in life', said Marjorie. 'I have, all girls have, I suppose. By the way, Cissy, I am quite sure Charlie Winthrop is serious.'

'How sweet of him ! I am so glad. I got father off my hands last season.'

'Must I really marry him, Cissy? He bores me.'

'What has that to do with it? Certainly you must. You are not a beauty, and I doubt your ever having a better chance.'

Marjorie rose and looked at herself in the long pier-glass[7] that stands opposite my writing-table. I could not resist the temptation to go and stand beside her.

'I am just the style that is admired now,' said Marjorie, dispassionately.

'So am I', I said reflectively. 'But *you* will soon be out of date.'

Every one says I am strangely like my mother. Her face was of that pure and perfect oval one so seldom sees, with delicate features, rosebud mouth, and soft flaxen hair. A blondness without insipidity, for the dark-blue eyes are fringed with dark lashes, and from their languorous depths looks out a soft mockery. I have a curious ideal devotion to my mother; she died when I was quite young – only two months old – and I often spend hours thinking of her, as I gaze at myself in the mirror.

'Do come down from the clouds,' said Marjorie impatiently, for I had sunk into a reverie. 'I came to ask you to think of something to amuse Laura – to interest her.'

'We ought to make it up to her in some way. Haven't you tried any-thing?'

'Only palmistry; and Mrs. Wilkinson prophesied her all that she detests, and depressed her dreadfully.'

'What do you think she really needs most?' I asked.

Our eyes met.

'Really, Cissy, you're too disgraceful,' said Marjorie. There was a pause.

'And so I'm to accept Charlie?'

'What man do you like better?' I asked.

'I don't know what you mean,' said Marjorie, colouring.

'*I* thought Adrian Grant would have been more sympathetic to Laura than to you. I have just had a note from him, asking me to tea at his studio today.' I threw it to her. 'He says I'm to bring you both. Would that amuse Laura?'

'Oh,' cried Marjorie, enchanted, 'of course we'll go. I wonder what he thinks of me,' she added wistfully.

'He didn't say. He is going to send Laura his verses, "Heartsease and Heliotrope".' She sighed. Then she said, 'Father was complaining again today of your laziness.'

'I lazy! Why, I've been swinging the censer[8] in Laura's boudoir because she wants to encourage the religious temperament, and I've designed your dress for the Clives' fancy ball.'

'Where's the design?'

'In my head. You're not to wear white; Miss Clive must wear white.'

'I wonder you don't marry her,' said Marjorie, 'you admire her so much.'

'I never marry. Besides, I know she's pretty, but that furtive Slade-school[9] manner of hers gets on my nerves. You don't know how dreadfully I suffer from my nerves.'

She lingered a little, asking me what I advised her to choose for a birthday present for herself – an American organ, a black poodle, or an *edition de luxe* of Browning. I advised the last, as being the least noisy. Then I told her I felt sure that in spite of her admiration for Adrian, she was far too good natured to interfere with Laura's prospects. She said I was incorrigible, and left the room with a smile of resignation.

And I returned to my reading. On my last birthday – I was seventeen – my father – who has his gleams of dry humour – gave me *Robinson Crusoe*! I prefer Pierre Loti,[10] and intend to have an onyx-paved bath-room, with soft apricot-coloured light shimmering through the blue-lined green curtains in my chambers, as soon as I get Marjorie married, and Laura more – settled down.

I met Adrian Grant first at a luncheon party at the Clives'. I seemed to amuse him; he came to see me, and became at once obviously enamoured of my step-mother. He is rather an impressionable impressionist, and a delightful creature, tall and graceful and beautiful, and altogether most interesting. Every one admits he's fascinating; he is very popular and very much disliked. He is by way of being a painter; he has a little money of his own – enough for his telegrams, but not enough for his buttonholes[11] – and nothing could be more incongruous than the idea of his marrying. I have never seen Marjorie so much attracted. But she is a good loyal girl, and will accept Charlie Winthrop, who is a dear person, good-natured and ridiculously rich – just the sort of man for a brother-in-law. It will annoy my old enemy Lady Winthrop – he is her nephew, and she wants him to marry that little Miss Clive. Dorothy Clive has her failings, but she could not – to do her justice – be happy with Charlie Winthrop.

Adrian's gorgeous studio gives one the complex impression of being at once the calm retreat of a mediaeval saint and the luxurious abode of a modern Pagan. One feels that everything could be done there, everything from praying to flirting – everything except painting. The tea-party amused me. I was pretending to listen to a brown person who was talking absurd worn-out literary clichés – as that the New Humour[12] is not funny, or that Bourget[13] understood women, when I overheard this fragment of conversation.

'But don't you like Society?' Adrian was saying.

'I get rather tired of it. People are so much alike. They all say the same things,' said Laura.

'Of course they all say the same things to you,' murmured Adrian, as he affected to point out a rather curious old silver crucifix.

'That,' said Laura, ' is one of the things they say.'

About three weeks later I found myself dining alone with Adrian Grant, at one of the two restaurants in London. (The cooking is better at the other, this one is the more becoming.) I had lilies-of-the-valley in my button-hole, Adrian was wearing a red carnation. Several people glanced at us. Of course he is very well known in Society. Also I was looking rather nice, and I could not help hoping, while Adrian gazed rather absently over my head, that the shaded candles were staining to a richer rose the waking wonder of my face.

Adrian was charming of course, but he seemed worried and a little preoccupied, and drank a good deal of champagne.

Towards the end of dinner, he said – almost abruptly for him – 'Carington.'

'Cecil,' I interrupted. He smiled.

'Cissy . . . it seems an odd thing to say to you, but though you are so young, I think you know everything. I am sure you know everything. You know about me. I am in love. I am quite miserable. What on earth am I to do!' He drank more champagne. ' Tell me,' he said, 'what to do.' For a few minutes, while we listened to that interminable hackneyed *Intermezzo*, I reflected; asking myself by what strange phases I had risen to the extraordinary position of giving advice to Adrian on such a subject?

Laura was not happy with our father. From a selfish motive, Marjorie and I had practically arranged that monstrous marriage. That very day he had been disagreeable, asking me with a clumsy sarcasm to raise his allowance, so that he could afford my favourite cigarettes. If Adrian were free, Marjorie might refuse Charlie Winthrop. I don't want her to refuse him. Adrian has treated me as a friend. I like him – I like him enormously. I am quite devoted to him. And how can I rid myself of the feeling of responsibility, the sense that I owe some compensation to poor beautiful Laura?

We spoke of various matters. Just before we left the table, I said, with what seemed, but was not, irrelevance, 'Dear Adrian, Mrs. Carington –'

'Go on, Cissy.'

'She is one of those who must be appealed to, at first, by her imagination. She married our father because she thought he was lonely and misunderstood.'

'I am lonely and misunderstood,' said Adrian, his eyes flashing with delight.

'Ah, not twice! She doesn't like that now.'

I finished my coffee slowly, and then I said,

'Go to the Clives' fancy-ball as Tristan.'[14]

311

Adrian pressed my hand. . . .

At the door of the restaurant we parted, and I drove home through the cool April night, wondering, wondering. Suddenly I thought of my mother – my beautiful sainted mother, who would have loved me, I am convinced, had she lived, with an extraordinary devotion. What would she have said to all this? What would she have thought? I know not why, but a mad reaction seized me. I felt recklessly conscientious. My father! After all, he was my father. I was possessed by passionate scruples. If I went back now to Adrian – if I went back and implored him, supplicated him never to see Laura again!

I felt I could persuade him. I have sufficient personal magnetism to do that, if I make up my mind. After one glance in the looking-glass, I put up my stick and stopped the hansom.[15] I had taken a resolution. I told the man to drive to Adrian's rooms.

He turned round with a sharp jerk. In another second a brougham[16] passed us – a swift little brougham that I knew. It slackened – it stopped – we passed it – I saw my father. He was getting out at one of the little houses opposite the Brompton Oratory.

'Turn round again,' I shouted to the cabman. And he drove me straight home.

Notes

Text: *The Yellow Book*, vol. v (April 1895).

1 Setback.
2 Paul Verlaine (1844–96), French poet.
3 The beyond.
4 Absent-minded.
5 Brompton Oratory, Roman Catholic church in Knightsbridge, London.
6 Army and Navy Stores, fashionable department store in Victoria.
7 Tall narrow mirror designed to hang on a wall between two windows.
8 Container for burning incense, used in religious ceremonies.
9 Young women were admitted to the Slade School of Art (founded 1871).
10 Pseudonym of Louis Viaud (1850–1923), French naval officer and writer on the South Seas.
11 Small bunches of flowers worn in the top buttonhole of a man's jacket.
12 Ironic term deriving from the much discussed 'New Woman'.
13 Paul Bourget (1852–1935), novelist, poet, essayist.
14 Legendary Celtic hero, in love with Iseult, his uncle's wife.
15 Horse-drawn cab.
16 Horse-drawn carriage.

A CORRESPONDENCE

Netta Syrett

Netta Syrett (c.1867–1943), novelist, short-story writer, children's author and playwright, she was one of a family of five independent sisters, all of whom shared a flat in London. She taught for a time before a meeting with Aubrey Beardsley's sister Mabel led her to membership of the *Yellow Book* circle. The first of her more than thirty novels was *Nobody's Fault* (1896), followed by *The Tree of Life* (1897), *Roseanne* (1902), *Women and Circumstance* (1906) and *The Child of Promise* (1907), which is considered her best. Her last novel was *Gemini* (1940). She also wrote stories and plays for children, and edited fairy tales, including *The Garden of Delight*, illustrated by her sister Nellie (1898). She also published books on history, and wrote plays for adults. *The Sheltering Tree* (1939) contains her reminiscences of the *Yellow Book* period.

Further reading

Mix (1960).

A Correspondence

I

"I think she is perfectly lovely," Mrs. Yeo exclaimed, enthusiastically.

She made a slight indicative movement towards the far corner of the drawing-room, where the folds of a white dress and the feathery edges of a fan were just visible from her corner of the sofa.

"Ah, I thought you would be surprised."

Mrs. Lockyer spoke in the proprietary tone of one who has discovered some priceless treasure and for the first time displays it to the gaze of the multitude.

"They are altogether an ideal couple, aren't they?" she continued. "I always say *he* is quite ridiculously good-looking – *too* handsome for a mere man!"

"They met in Rome, you say?"

"Yes, quite lately; only a few weeks ago, in fact, when the Armstrongs were travelling in Italy. He'd hardly known her a week before he proposed, and it's scarcely a fortnight now since the day they met – so her mother says. This is his last evening. He's going back to-morrow to Rome; he has some work to finish there, I understand. He's a sculptor, you know. Such a romantic occupation, isn't it? – and so *suitable.* He has such classical features himself, just like Apollo, or, well, *all* those Greeky-Roman people. To me he has the air of being the *least* little bit stand-off. What do you think? I daresay that's just my fancy though, for I hear he is quite charming, but alarmingly clever. He is more than ten years older than Miss Armstrong, they say, and *I* believe there's more difference than that even – don't you think so?" But Mrs. Yeo's gaze turned in the direction of the white dress again.

"She is very lovely," she repeated, "but I don't think she seems quite happy."

The girl under discussion had risen from her seat and was standing at the corner of the mantelpiece, one hand resting on the low shelf. From where Mrs. Yeo was sitting she caught a glimpse of a very delicately tinted face; the light from a rose-shaded lamp above the girl's head fell softly on masses of rippling red-brown hair growing low on the forehead, and parted over the brows, Clytie fashion.[1] Her long trailing gown fell in white folds to her feet.

Mrs. Yeo was young and imaginative. Her friend's information about the sculptor fiancé had doubtless something to do with the fancifulness of the notion, yet, as she looked at the girl, her mind was full of vague ideas of Galatea,[2] the beautiful statue slowly awakening to this distressful life.

"Not happy?" echoed Mrs. Lockyer "Oh, why not? She *ought* to be. It's a most desirable match in every way. Mr. Margrave is well connected and rich, I believe; and" – this in a slightly lower key – "between ourselves, the Armstrongs are not *particulary* well off. She's a very *quiet* girl, I think; not that I know much of her. She's so very young, you know, only just out, in fact. This is the first dinner they've given since her engagement, and –"

There was a sound of laughter and voices outside, and the usual little stir and flutter in the room as the men came in.

"Ah, he's speaking to her. How splendid they look together," exclaimed Mrs. Yeo, who was taking more than her usual interest in the engagement. The girl looked up with a quick start as the door opened, and hastily withdrew her foot from the fender, as though she had been guilty of some impropriety. She straightened herself, and hurriedly smoothed her dress, while her hand tightened mechanically on the fan she was holding.

A close observer might have thought the movement almost a shrinking one, and in the little fleeting smile with which she greeted her lover's approach, there was perhaps as much nervousness as pleasure.

She looked very young when she raised her eyes, which were clear blue, and at first sight, singularly childlike. But their expression was puzzling; it almost seemed – and Mrs. Yeo was more interested than ever when she noticed this – as though a new nature was struggling in them tentatively, and in a half frightened way, for life and utterance. It was this uncertain air about the girl altogether, which Mrs. Yeo felt, and which appealed to her as pathetic. "She wants some one to be *very* kind to her just now," thought the tender-hearted little lady, as she watched the girl's face.

The man lingered a few moments beside her, leaning over the back of her chair, but at the first soft notes of a song, he turned towards the piano, and in the girl's attitude there was a faint suggestion of relief, though her eyes followed him rather wistfully.

The singer was a slim girl, with a somewhat striking face, and a cloud of dark wavy hair. She glanced up at Margrave with a smile of thanks, as he turned over a leaf for her, and when the song was ended he kept his place at her side. She did not move from the piano, but began to look over a pile of music as though searching for something.

There was a short silence.

"Cecily is lovelier than ever to-night," she observed, abruptly. Margrave smiled and glanced in the direction she was looking.

"Yes," he assented. "That Greek dress of hers is quite an inspiration"

The girl – her name was Gretchen Verrol – bent to pick up a stray leaf before she replied."Thank you; don't trouble," she said; then, "You are praising *me* unawares," she added.

"You designed it then?"

"And more, I made it, with these my proper hands," with a little gesture.

"I honour you equally for your inventive and creative faculties," he returned laughingly.

After a moment, with a sudden change of tone, "Cecily is very fortunate in having you with her," he said. "You read with her, I think? She is very young," and then he hesitated a little, "I have seen so little of her, and scarcely ever alone, but I fancy she needs –" he paused.

"She is beautiful enough to need nothing besides," Gretchen interrupted hastily. "Why don't you go and talk to her now? She is by herself, and I'm not her governess quite, Mr. Margrave," she added.

A young man came up to the piano at the moment, and she held out a piece of music to him. "Here is a song I know you sing, Mr. Graham! Shall! I play it for you?" she asked almost in the same breath.

Margrave looked at her a moment with an expression which was at first perplexed, and also a trifle disconcerted before he obediently went back to Cecily.

II

Five years difference in the ages of two girls is not too much to admit the possibility of intimate friendship. Not that this was the term which could, with any appropriateness, describe the relation between Cecily and Gretchen Verrol, though they were constantly together, and though Gretchen, and all that she did, occupied, or at any rate till quite recently had occupied, nearly the whole of Cecily's mental horizon.

Gretchen Verrol was a distant cousin of Mrs. Armstrong, for whom circumstances had rendered it unavoidable to do something in the way of help.

Most fortunately, both for herself and for the Armstrongs, it happened that Gretchen was clever and accomplished – "the very companion we could have chosen for our dear Cecily," as her mother frequently observed. This being the case, matters were easily arranged, and for a year previous to Cecily's engagement, Miss Verrol had lived with the Armstrongs, "reading" with Cecily, helping her with her music, and generally "forming her taste," as Mrs. Armstrong again frequently, if somewhat vaguely, remarked.

Mrs. Armstrong was a slightly vague person altogether, but kindly-natured and easy-going. Her one positive emotion being admiration for her young cousin, who soon held a very important, if not the most important, position in the household.

Whether her engagement had done anything towards lessening the exalted opinion of Gretchen which Cecily shared with her mother was a doubtful question.

"Do you like that Miss Verrol?" some one asked her once rather dubiously, and Cecily looked at her interrogator in a startled, half-awed fashion.

"She is so clever, you know," she replied, irrelevantly as it seemed, glancing furtively behind her as she spoke.

Gretchen was still an object of as much wondering reverence to Cecily a year afterwards as she had been during the first week of their acquaintance, when Miss Verrol had already summed up her impressions of the latter, once and for all.

She practically knew Cecily, as she remarked to herself, after the first day, and at the end of the first week she proceeded to recapitulate and to get her by heart. An easy task! So easy that she had to sit and look at her with an air of critical wonder.

They were reading German. That is, Gretchen was. She had been pronouncing the words with great distinctness, and Cecily, with laborious effort after imitation, had made strange and weird sounds, unlike any language that was ever imagined, far less spoken. Presently Gretchen's voice stopped, and it was then that Cecily began to move restlessly, raising apprehensive eyes to those which her companion bent quietly upon her. The silence became a little oppressive; Cecily fidgeted, dropped her eyes, and began to pull the blotting-paper to pieces with nervous fingers. Gretchen laid a hand upon it, and quietly drew it away.

"It is no good for you to read this," said Miss Verrol at last, calmly.

"No," meekly assented Cecily.

"We've tried French – you don't seem to understand anything of that."

"No," she repeated hopelessly.

"Tell me – you don't really care for music, reading, poetry, pictures, do you?"

This was practically an assertion, though put in the form of a question. Cecily felt compelled to reply.

"No," she acknowledged again, faintly.

Gretchen continued to look at her.

"It is very curious," she remarked critically, as though she had come upon a totally new species and was interested.

Cecily suddenly dropped her fair head upon her arms, and burst into tears.

Miss Verrol waited silently till the storm was passed. There was a glass opposite, and she looked across at it as the girl raised her tear-stained face.

"It doesn't matter," she said in the same critical tone. "You are pretty enough to make it of no consequence. You even look pretty when you cry. Now, *I* look hideous."

This was the first and only spoken allusion to Cecily's mental deficiencies that Gretchen ever made. The reading and music practising went on regularly as usual, and Cecily still persevered in her frantic attempts at the German accent. If there was the slightest trace of weariness in Gretchen's tone as she corrected her for the fourth or fifth time in one word, it was so faint as to be only just appreciable, and when at the end of the hour Cecily stole an apprehensive glance at her face, it was always calm and imperturbable.

"Now we will have the duet," was what she usually said as she closed the book. Indeed, her patience during the hours devoted to "mental culture" was altogether admirable, and if signs of Cecily's lack of intelligence had been otherwise wanting, they would have been supplied by the fact that, while humbly recognising the goodness and wisdom of Gretchen, and striving earnestly to be worthy of it, she would yet have found it a relief if the latter had *sometimes* lost her temper.

This absence of impatience or reproach paralysed her. Once when Gretchen had been called away in the middle of the duet, she sat vacantly staring at the keys for a moment.

All at once, with a sudden frantic movement, she half rose from her seat at the piano, a look of positive terror in her eyes.

"If only she would say something – *anything*! I can't *breathe* when she looks at me," she panted breathlessly.

When Gretchen came back she was patiently practising a bar over and over again.

"Try it once more, Cecily," Gretchen said, gazing straight before her out of the window. "It isn't right."

Mrs. Armstrong found her cousin really invaluable. She was as clever with her fingers as with her brains, and when Cecily began to go out, she not only designed, but also made most of her charming gowns for evening wear.

She always helped her to dress for dances – dressed her, in fact – for Cecily generally stood quite passive to have her hair arranged, her flowers fastened in, or the folds of her gown artistically draped.

On these occasions Gretchen never failed to praise her beauty openly and with an air of impartial criticism, and then Cecily winced and trembled a little, but said nothing.

"I have a comfortable home, but I earn my living," wrote Gretchen to a friend, when she had been with the Armstrongs about three months.

It was with real concern that a day or two after her daughter's engagement had been finally arranged Mrs. Armstrong learnt that Gretchen was thinking of leaving her.

"Cecily will be broken-hearted," she exclaimed plaintively; "and she won't be married just yet, you know. Besides, why should you go at all? I shall want you more than ever then."

But Gretchen was firm.

"As long as I could be really of use to you, with Cecily, I did not feel myself dependent," she explained. "But now it will be different. No, Cousin Mary, that is only your kindness. I should not be happy in staying on."

And Cousin Mary, though demurring, felt it selfish to stand in the way of the girl's prospects, especially as an acquaintance of hers, who was about to sail for New Zealand and wanted a governess, was overjoyed at securing such a charming person as Miss Verrol for her two girls.

"But I'm sure I don't know how to tell Cecily," she lamented again and again. "I don't know how she'll take it."

Cecily took it with a start, and an expression not easy to read.

"But she's such a strange girl," complained her mother, who was not given to analysis of character to any great extent.

III

Gretchen's departure had finally been arranged only the day before Margrave's return to Rome. He could hardly hope to finish the work he was engaged upon very speedily; it would probably be at least six months before he met Cecily again, and his complaint of having seen very little of her during his brief visit was by no means unfounded. It was difficult to tell how deeply the girl felt his absence. Perhaps her manner was even quieter and more subdued than usual, but that was the only noticeable difference in her behaviour. She very rarely mentioned his name.

There was a letter lying beside her plate on the breakfast table the morning after her lover's departure, and Gretchen, glancing across from her opposite seat, saw her quickly cover it with her hand, which she withdrew, a second after, in confusion. Her mother laughed.

"You are not going to read it now, then, Cecily?"

"No mother," she replied, flushing hotly.

An hour or two later, Gretchen opened the door of Cecily's bedroom. She was pre-occupied, and entered without knocking; indeed, she had taken the dress she had come for out of the wardrobe, and was leaving the room before she noticed that Cecily was there.

The girl sat in the corner of the window seat, trying to turn her head so as to hide that she was crying – an open letter lay on her lap.

Gretchen started. Instinctively her hand groped for the back of a chair she was passing; then she drew it away, and straightened herself.

"What is the matter, Cecily?" she asked – her voice sounded a little strained, but it was calm enough. "You have not" – she paused – "there is no bad news?"

Cecily's low sobs choked her voice. There was time for Gretchen to glance at her own face in the glass and to turn back to the light, before she replied.

"N – no," she said at last; "but –" Gretchen crossed to her side.

"Won't you tell me?" she asked. There was a little tremble in her tone now. Cecily heard it, and looked up gratefully. Gretchen seemed sorry.

"I don't like to," she murmured. "You'll say – oh, it's too silly!" Her voice broke again in a half sob.

"Never mind. Tell me"

"Only that – only – because – I shall have to answer it."

The confession broke from Cecily's lips hesitatingly, and then she laid one arm hopelessly against the window frame, and hid her wet eyes against it.

Gretchen did not speak for a minute.

"The letter, you mean?" she asked at length, quietly. "Well – there is nothing so dreadful about that, is there?"

"Oh, yes, there is — yes, there *is* — for *me!*" wailed Cecily. "You may read it." She held out the letter, looking up at Gretchen despairingly. "You'll see. He asks what I thought of some of those statues in Rome — and — and the pictures. And — I didn't think of anything. Oh, Gretchen! I know I'm very stupid — but — I had no thoughts about them, except — I wondered why they kept broken statues in such grand places. But I can't tell him that, can I? because people, clever people, think they are beautiful — without noses — or anything. And all that he says about the scenery — and you know what my spelling is like — and oh, Gretchen! Don't — don't smile like that!"

Cecily shrank back into the corner of the window seat, and covered her face with both hands. Perhaps she had never made such a long speech before — but Gretchen had seemed sorry.

There was quite a long silence. The crisp paper crackled as Miss Verrol turned the sheets; still Cecily did not look up.

"Well, do you want me to answer it for you?" The question was accompanied by a short laugh.

The girl's hands dropped from her face in a second, and her eyes sought Gretchen's inquiringly — incredulously.

"Gretchen — do you mean it? Would you? Not really?"

"Where is that silk gauze of yours?" asked Gretchen, crossing the room and stooping over a drawer.

"In that box" replied Cecily, sighing — the chance of relief was gone then.

"You see," pursued Gretchen, still turning over things in the drawer, "it's not quite the same thing as doing your exercises."

"No," agreed Cecily, despondently. Then brightening, "But Gretchen — if you would — you are so clever. You know all about those statues — and the pictures — and the palaces. You could write about them." She paused breathlessly.

"Oh, yes" replied Miss Verrol carelessly. "I dare say I could — I was considered good at composition — at school. Our relative positions would be somewhat reversed, wouldn't they? I should have to bring these excercises to you, for correction and amendment, and — naturally you are so much better up in the subject."

Another pause.

"No, I really don't think I should dare to let you see my work. There would be so many faults."

She had found the scarf now, and was busy smoothing out its creases.

"You have crushed this dreadfully," she said, reproachfully.

"Oh, you don't think it's important enough to talk about," cried Cecily desperately; "but I can *never* do it alone. Can't you help me? I shouldn't want to see the letters you wrote, you know," she assured her eagerly. "So —"

Gretchen stopped short in the midst of shaking out the filmy folds.

"Not — you mean you would not want to see the letters *I* wrote to *your* lover," she asked incredulously, fixing her eyes on the girl's face.

Cecily blushed painfully.

"No," she hesitated. "Not if you'd rather not. I know it is easier to do everything – if – people are not watching you. And you will do all the important part, about the statues, beautifully, Gretchen. The only thing I could do would be to – to send my love." Her voice faltered. "Perhaps you wouldn't mind always putting that in, at the end, after the other things, you know?"

"Yes. What am I to say?"

" Just say" – the colour flamed in her cheeks again – "I love you, Noel." She turned her head away sharply, and looked out of the window.

Gretchen still stood beside her, motionless.

"Cecily," she said at last, in a low voice, "think – do you *really* want me to do this? I won't if you –"

"Yes," she answered brokenly. "If I could do it myself, of course I – I would rather – but I *can't!* And after all, it won't matter so very much, will it, Gretchen?" She turned to her like a child, imploring to be reassured by some wise and grown up person. "I shall *mean* all the things you say."

"What about the handwriting?" asked Gretchen. Her voice sounded flat and wearied. "Has he seen yours!"

"No. I have never written to him. There has been no occasion, you see, and he doesn't know yours."

Miss Verrol went to the door. As she reached it, she paused with her hand on the lock.

"Remember, you wish it," she said, turning her head over her shoulder to look at Cecily.

The girl rose from the window seat and came towards her. Her soft hair was all disordered, her cheeks were flushed, and her pretty blue eyes were still wet.

"Yes; you are very good to me, Gretchen," she began timidly, putting out her arms. But Gretchen shrank away hastily. "Mind – you will crumple this again," she said.

IV

Thus it happened that regularly every week a letter went to Rome, beginning, at Cecily's request (her own original contribution), "My dearest Noel," and ending with "your very loving Cecily." The girl who wrote the letters sat up far into the night. Not that she was writing all the time. She read and re-read sheets of close writing on thin foreign paper. Every time she came to an endearing word her colour came and went, and she drew in her breath quickly. To be accurate, the words of love were not many. The letters were perhaps a trifle wanting in colour for a lover. They were the letters of a clever, cultivated man, a little cold by nature. Perhaps *too* highly polished. But the reader did not criticise. She changed colour when she read "my love;" she smiled triumphantly when he said how it gratified him to know that in their tastes and feelings they were so fully in sympathy. He had not been quite sure of this, he wrote – she had been so silent, so shy – and he had had to learn from her letters that he should have a wife as clever as she was beautiful. Once when she read words to this effect, Gretchen crumpled the paper fiercely in her hand, and sprang to her feet. With a smile of self-mockery, she went to the glass and deliberately studied herself. It reflected a little thin figure, with large, glittering eyes, irregular features, and a mass of rough, wavy hair. A somewhat striking apparition – picturesque, perhaps. But beautiful? A vision of Cecily's stately white loveliness swam before her eyes, and she turned away impatiently.

But the letter must be answered, and she sat down to her weekly task – a torture which she would not now forego if Cecily begged it of her on her bended knees.

She knew that Cecily already repented of her request. Every time she handed Gretchen a letter from her lover, it was with a more reluctant action, a more wistful and appealing look.

She saw, but would not heed. Cecily had decided – the act was hers – let her abide by it!

In the meantime, every week she could write, with white lips and shaking hand, "I love you, Noel." Had not Cecily herself wished it?

"Madness! Of course, I know that," she thought; "but if I like to be mad just once before I go away to live out my dull, highly respectable life, who is there to hinder me? It's an inexpensive luxury. She'll tell him, of course, when they're married – though there'll be no occasion; he'll find it out quickly enough." She smiled scornfully. "But what does that matter? I shall be thousands of miles away by that time. I shall never know how he takes it, or what he thinks." And then she sealed the letter.

Even then, though it was early morning, she sat a long time at the table, quite still, her face buried in her hands. When she looked up, it was drawn and haggard.

"And I've come to be a thing like this," she whispered, with a slow self-scorn, "about a man who has forgotten my existence. And – I am Gretchen Verrol!"

V

As time went on, drawing nearer to the expiration of the three months before her cousin's departure, Mrs. Armstrong's lamentations became more and more frequent.

"Cecily, poor child, feels it dreadfully," she repeated. "She is really getting quite thin, and I think she looks ill, though her father says it's like my fidgetiness! But I don't care; she shall take a tonic in spite of what he says. I don't like the look of her at all sometimes. She has such a – I hardly know how to explain what I mean – such a curious, frightened expression. Have you noticed it? You know, Gretchen" (confidentially), "in spite of a mother's natural feelings, and all that, I shall be glad to have her married. For my part, I don't approve of long engagements, but her father is so obstinate. The child feels unsettled, so of course she's miserable. I expect she misses Noel too, don't you? But she says so little, I hardly know *what* to think."

There was no doubt that Cecily was growing thin. Her eyes were unnaturally large and bright; they had a wistful, troubled look, and lately she had taken to starting nervously when any one spoke suddenly to her. Her mother talked of taking her away somewhere for change of air, as soon as Miss Verrol had gone.

"And I hope the voyage will do you good, too," she added, looking at Gretchen critically. "Do you know you are looking quite ill? Bless, these young people, there's always something the matter with them now. I'm sure there never used to be, in *my* young days."

The last day at the Armstrongs, after all her boxes were ready, Gretchen spent in paying farewell calls.

It was quite late in the afternoon before, the last good-bye said, and the last polite good wish for her happiness expressed, she found herself once more in front of the house she was so soon to leave. It was some moments before the door was opened in answer to her ring, and she stood on the top of the flight of steps and looked drearily up and down the street. It was a wet night – the pavements were all shining with rain, the gas lamps were reflected waveringly in the puddles on the road. Only one person was in sight – a girl in a long shiny waterproof, picking her way carefully through the mud from one pavement to the other. The rain dripped steadily, drearily from the square portico overhead.

Gretchen shivered as she looked.

The door was opened and she stepped into the dazzle of the brightly lighted hall, and began to take off her wet cloak. When the bright mist cleared, she saw that there was a portmanteau on the oak chest against the wall; a bundle of rugs lay beside it; from the drawing-room came a distant murmur of voices.

"Has any one come, then, Price?" asked Gretchen, stopping at the last button of her waterproof.

"Yes, miss; Mr. Margrave. He came unexpected, about two hours ago. I don't know why James hasn't taken up his things, I'm sure. I've told him to, times enough." Gretchen put her cloak into the maid's hands and turned to the stairs.

"Will you have some tea, miss?"

"No thank, you," she answered quietly.

Upstairs, the door of Cecily's room stood half-open. She was dressed for dinner already, and she stood before the fire, the tips of her fingers touching the mantelpiece, her forehead resting upon them.

Gretchen hesitated a moment, then went in. "This is a delightful surprise for you, Cecily, isn't it?"

"Yes," said Cecily starting. She had raised her head quickly when she heard Gretchen's step, but she did not turn round.

Gretchen stood looking at her with an indescribable expression.

"Why did he come?" she asked after a moment.

"He has been working too hard. The doctor said he was to rest a little, and take a holiday. So he made up his mind suddenly to come and see us. He wrote, but the letter hasn't come yet. We got a telegram just after you went out, about half-an-hour before he came."

Something in her voice, though she had not listened to what she said, struck Gretchen as strange.

In spite of herself. "You don't seem very glad, Cecily? You don't speak quite in the style of the orthodox engaged young lady," she said, laughing a little as she drew nearer the fire.

"I am *not* engaged," murmured Cecily.

"*What!*" Gretchen put her hand on the corner of the mantelpiece to steady herself. "What are you saying? What do you mean?"

Cecily turned a pair of frightened eyes towards her. Gretchen was going to be angry. "I – I have broken it off," she whispered in a scared way.

"Since when?"

"Since he came here this afternoon."

Gretchen broke into a shrill laugh. "What a charming reception!" she cried.

Then she recovered herself. "Tell me about it!" she exclaimed peremptorily.

Cecily glanced round the room despairingly, then at Gretchen, who had taken a low chair by the fire and was waiting with a pale face and that patient air she knew so well. There was no escape. "May I shut the door?" she said meekly crossing the room, her white dress trailing, a tall stately figure in spite of her girlishness.

She came back to her place, but did not speak.

"Well?" said Gretchen.

"I don't know what you want me to tell you."

"Why you broke it off."

There was another long pause, then Cecily began to speak low and rapidly.

"I shall never make you understand," she cried hopelessly. "I didn't mean to do it, to-day. I – I didn't even know that I had made up my mind to do it at all – till just as I was going into the drawing-room to see him. Then I seemed to see that it was all no use." Her voice sank to a whisper; she was trembling from head to foot.

"You mustn't cry. You have to go down, remember," Gretchen observed in even tones.

Cecily drew herself up. "What more shall I tell you?" she cried passionately.

Gretchen had never heard this tone from her before; it startled her. She too rose, and they stood facing one another.

"Why do you ask me?" panted Cecily. "You know – but if you like I will tell you. I don't mind now. Nothing matters now. I knew almost from the first that I could not marry him. He is so clever. And I – every moment I was afraid he would ask me something I didn't know. I didn't understand the way he talked. I didn't understand half of what he said to me. I should *never* have understood it;" she wailed, "I was always afraid when he came to talk to me, and yet when he was away –" She checked herself. All the passion had died out of her tone now. "If I hadn't known it before, his letters would have shown me. Oh, I did very wrong in asking you to write, Gretchen. I knew it, the first time he answered *your* letter, and praised what he thought I'd said."

Gretchen suddenly caught her breath. "You never –" she began.

"No, I was afraid to ask you not to go on with it when you'd been so kind, and taken so much trouble," Cecily said. "I see myself very plainly to-night. Just as though I was some one else – I see that besides – other things – I am a coward."

Gretchen was silent.

"He would not listen at first." It seemed that having begun her confession she *must* speak now, though the words came falteringly from her trembling lips. "He said he didn't understand – he said there was no reason – I was playing with him. He spoke of my letters." She paused.

"Well?" gasped Gretchen breathlessly.

"Then I thought at any rate I would not deceive him any longer – it was no good – so I told him you wrote them. . . . Gretchen! – *don't!* you – you frighten me!" she whispered hoarsely.

Gretchen had seized her by the wrist. Her eyes were burning in a face as white as death; they seemed to scorch the girl cowering down before her.

"*You little fool!*" she exclaimed, her hands dropping heavily at her sides. Each word stung like the sharp point of an icicle.

Cecily staggered back as though she had been struck.

It was out at last! This was what Gretchen had been feeling about her every minute for a whole year. The words expressed her whole attitude towards her; it was what Cecily had all the time dumbly wished, yet dreaded to hear her say. It was almost a relief – but she was dazed and confused – she did not yet understand what had forced the words, what had impelled Gretchen, at last, to give her spoken verdict. She still gazed at her bewildered, hopeless.

"What did he think of me?" inquired Gretchen mockingly. Her tone was so careless and airy that Cecily half doubted for the moment whether she could have said those words in *that voice* a second before – then she looked again at her face, and knew that her ears had not deceived her.

She stood for a second with parted lips, and then a great fear crept into her eyes, as she covered her face with both hands.

"Forgive me, Gretchen!" she murmured "You – you – know how stupid I am."

It seemed a long time before Gretchen spoke. "I shall not come down to-night," she answered calmly. "I might complicate matters perhaps. Say I have a headache, please. I shall arrange to go by the first train to-morrow. If you think you can invent any reason for this to Cousin Mary, it might be just as well. If not – it doesn't matter much."

Cecily stood motionless till the door had opened, closed again, and the room was empty.

Then with a helpless movement, she sank down on the floor before the fire, her fair hair buried in the cushions of the easy chair, to stifle her sobs.

"I can't think about Gretchen. I can't think about any one but him," she whispered to herself brokenly. "What shall I do? I didn't make myself. It isn't fair. I should have been wretched if I'd ever been his wife. He would have been ashamed of me. And yet – yet!"

Presently she rose wearily; she poured out water and bathed her eyes, and then arranged her hair carefully before the glass.

In a few minutes, except that she was terribly pale, all traces of violent grief had vanished.

Yet to herself she looked so strange that she shuddered to see her own reflection in the glass, there was something about it that was so changed.

When she turned away, it seemed as though a mask had fallen upon a trembling living face. The gong sounded, and she went quietly downstairs; it was not till the next morning that her mother knew that the engagement was at an end.

Mrs. Yeo had come up to town from her country house, on her usual spring visit, which was always devoted to shopping and incidental frivolities. She was at the theatre with her husband one evening. The house was full, and between the acts she leant forward on the red velvet cushion before her seat in the dress circle and inspected the stalls with a view to seeing how the hair was being worn this season, and whether the sleeves in the new dinner-dress she had ordered were *too* outrageous. The buzz of talk and tuneful wail of the violins fell pleasantly on her ears, as she scanned the rows of backs for a possible acquaintance.

"There's a beautiful woman. In the second box – look," her husband turned to her to say, lowering his glasses. "Do you see? In white – next to a good-looking fellow with a priggish nose."

"Why, it's Mrs. Margrave!" she exclaimed in surprise, after a moment's scrutiny. "Yes, isn't she *lovely?* And – yes, that wretched woman's there too," she added with a change of tone.

"Mrs. Margrave?" he repeated.

"Yes. You know, Jim. Cecily Armstrong. We dined at the Armstrong's once, two or three years ago, don't you remember? I thought her beautiful then. Fancy seeing her here to-night. It must be quite two years since we met her. I wonder if she would recognise me?

"She married that fellow, then? I had some idea it was all off?"

"So it was for a time. There was some mysterious fuss, don't you remember? But Mrs. Armstrong worked it. Cecily always did what she was told. I don't believe the poor child was even consulted. Look!" she broke off to exclaim indignantly. "He isn't paying her the smallest attention. He talks all the time to that horrid Miss Verrol. I *always* disliked her."

Mrs. Margrave was leaning back listlessly in her chair. Her fan lay upon her lap. She was apparently gazing straight before her, though her masses of rippling hair partly concealed her face from the Yeos.

"Who is she?"

"Why, you remember. That Miss Verrol who used to be Cecily's companion."

"I thought she went to America, or New Zealand, or somewhere?"

"So she did, but Lady Fairfield had to come home when her father died, you know, and she brought Miss Verrol with her. I believe she's living in town with them now as governess, or secretary, or something; but she's always at the Margraves', I hear." Mrs. Yeo gave vent to an untranslatable little exclamation of disgust.

"But why?" asked her husband. He alluded to the ejaculation.

"My dear Jim! Can't you *see?* Look at them!"

The lights were lowered at the moment, and the curtain rose on the last act.

When it was over, and Mrs. Yeo had collected her wraps, she turned to glance once more at the Margraves' box, but it was empty.

Down in the brightly lighted vestibule, however, when at length they reached it, she saw Cecily again.

She was standing a little out of the crush, beside one of the great doors. Her husband was wrapping a white cloak round Miss Verrol. She said something to him, with an upward glance as he did so, and they both laughed. Cecily, who stood patiently waiting at her side, shivered a little at the moment, yet Mrs. Yeo fancied she did not feel the cold. As she passed her in the doorway, their eyes met.

For a moment there was no recognition in the long wistful gaze which Cecily unconsciously fixed upon her; then, all at once, she bent her head and smiled.

The crowd swept them apart, and in a few minutes Mrs. Yeo was being whirled towards the Métropole in a hansom.

"You're very quiet," her husband remarked presently. "Didn't you enjoy the play?"

She put her hand on his, impulsively, and, as she turned to him, he saw there were tears in her eyes.

"You didn't notice her face, Jim, as we passed? I did. I shall never forget it. Poor girl! Poor child!"

Notes

Text: *The Yellow Book* vol. vii (October 1895).

1 As in the painting by Frederick, Lord Leighton of Clytie, a water nymph metamorphosed into a heliotrope because of her love for Apollo.

2 Statue brought to life by the sculptor Pygmalion.

A KNOT OF RIBBON

Laurence Alma-Tadema

Laurence Alma-Tadema (1864/7–1940), novelist, playwright, poet and short-story writer, was the daughter of the successful painter Sir Lawrence Alma-Tadema. As the story *A Knot of Ribbon* indicates, she specialised in passionate, victimised heroines, including those of her novels *Love's Martyr* (1886) and *The Wings of Icarus* (1894). She published six volumes of poetry, including *Songs of Womanhood* (1903), and wrote several plays. She never married. She was awarded a CBE for her work with Polish refugees in the First World War. *The Crucifix*, the work from which *A Knot of Ribbon* is taken, is a collection of short stories with a linking device: a crucifix is passed between the various protagonists, and acts as a silent witness to their interactions.

Further reading

Blain *et al.* (1990); Mix (1960); Sutherland (1988).

A Knot of Ribbon

It had been raining, but the rain had ceased; it lay in little pools here and there on the stones, and dripped from the cornices.

The broken clouds had sailed up to a great height, and seemed to have curdled round the moon, making her appear very far away; surrounded by a spectral halo, she shone brightly amid opal cloudlets that chased each other swiftly across the sky.

We found ourselves out of doors in a narrow street that ran down to the edge of a canal – straight down to the edge, without bar or rail, so that any one weary of life might here have slipped gently into the lap of Death. Long whipped by wind and rain, the low water beat to and fro against the slimy wall, green with sea-weed. There was no sound of life; but we saw a rat dart along the moulding of the stone just above the water's edge.

There was a door in the wall, to the right of where we stood; it was the last doorway in the street, and far from any other. We had not at first noticed that a woman sat upon the doorstep, with her elbows on her knees, and her chin upon her fists; she sat there absolutely motionless, looking at the ground before her with great dull eyes; and although she seemed otherwise in no way handsome, those eyes were singularly beautiful, large and dark and deeply-set – so liquid that it almost seemed as if they must fall from beneath their long-fringed lids.

The rain-drops gathered and fell from the lintel of the door; one after another they fell and glistened on her black hair, wet already with the rain; but she paid no heed to them, nor indeed to anything far or near. There were cats on the roof opposite, howling most dismally; then came a sudden scamper, hisses and loud yells, followed by the clatter of falling tiles. But the woman neither raised her eyes nor stirred in any way, until the approaching footfall of a man resounded on the stones.

It was just four o'clock; the bells rang out the hours from far and near. She leant forward an instant to look down the street, then drew back again. When the man was near her resting-place, she stood up suddenly, like a ghost upon the doorstep.

He was young, and handsome with a kind of brutal beauty due to a richness of life expressed by eyes and lips and teeth and hair; a beauty that would disappear when the blood of youth had slackened and coarsened.

"What in the devil's name," he cried, "are you doing here?"

The girl had risen pale and stern with smothered passion in her eyes; now, looking up at her lover, her gaze softened, and a great weakness overcame her. She spread out her hands and fell against him.

"I wanted to see you," she said.

The young man cast a rapid glance down the street, and up at the surrounding windows.

"You are wet," he said, touching her shoulders. "What folly is this? Come in."

He opened the door and led her upstairs. It was not quite dark, for the moonlight stole in at the grated windows. When they reached his room, the girl sat down heavily, and let her head sink on to the table. The young man lighted a little brass lamp, then came and stood beside her.

"What folly is this?" asked he again. His voice was harsh and masterful. "What have you got into your head? Come, take that shawl off, you are soaked; how long had you been there, you little fool?"

The girl burst into tears.

"Come, come," said he, almost as one might to a child; and he took the wet shawl, not unkindly, from her shoulders.

Stuck in the bosom of her dress was a large crucifix. The young fellow laughed, and would have seized it, had the girl allowed it; but she stayed his hand and laid the emblem on the table.

"Let that be!" she said. "I took it because – because I was alone. I had no one else. I needed God's company."

Then suddenly she seized him by both elbows and looked up at him. Her upturned face was wet with tears, the hair upon her brow all humid with the rain.

"Six days!" she said in choking voice, staying him as with impatient gesture he tried to move away, and pressing his elbows with her cold fingers – "Don't you understand? I waited – you had promised – to-night I could not bear it – I came to see."

"Do you doubt me?" asked the man.

"Yes," she replied, "I doubt you."

He looked at her searchingly an instant, then, with a shrug of the shoulders, set himself free.

He walked once or twice up and down the room, and she followed him with her eyes. Both were silent. She looked at him with that all-embracing gaze known only to a woman's eyes when they fall on the man she loves.

Her heart was full of doubt of him; yet, every time he drew near, a foolish haze of love rose between her and her hatred. She had not seen him for six days.

At last he came quite close to her and – against her will – she threw back her head and smiled a tremulous smile laden with tears. Her lover stooped and kissed her, caressing her cheek with his hand.

"You must he good," he said; "none of this, or you will spoil everything between us. What I loved best in you all along was your calm, your certainty.

Come, do you care for me or not? It depends entirely on you whether things remain as they were between us. *I* am ready. Only, no more of this nonsense."

The young woman had left off weeping, but there was no vestige of consolation on her face. She had hold of one of the buttons of his waist coat, and was twisting it round and round with trembling finger-tip, her large eyes fixed before her despairingly.

The man waited a moment as if expecting her to say something.

"Well?" asked he; and then, probably in spite of himself, he yawned.

A little shiver went through the girl; she let the button go, and pressing her hands together, looked up at him dumbly; her eyes seemed filled with speech – mute language that he once, maybe, had understood.

"Come, come," said he then, "since you have nothing to say, you had better go home. It is almost morning. – Come, – to-morrow at nine you shall see me, I promise; only don't let us begin this sort of thing again."

He almost lifted her from her chair, and wrapped her shawl about her. The girl caught his hand across her shoulder, and turning, nestled against him.

"Be kind to me!" she said, almost beneath her breath, "don't send me away without one word! Or, don't you love me any more? If that is truth, say so and let me die – only, don't play with me. I tell you, I have a horrible doubt of you in my heart; if you love another, say so – only, for the love of God, don't play with me – don't torture me!"

"Go home," replied the man, kissing her lightly on the brow; "you are mad."

But the girl went on:

"If you are going to leave me for that brown-haired girl, if already . . . say so, say so, and I swear to forgive you; perhaps I shall die, how can I tell? But I swear to forgive you."

And all the while, with her cold fingers, the only part of her that seemed beyond the calm of her control, she went to and fro along the edge of his waistcoat, there, close to where her head lay.

"You are a little fool," replied the man; "go home, it will be getting light presently."

But she that wearied him paid no heed to his words.

"Do you remember," said she, "the very first time I came here?"

He gave an almost inaudible sigh of impatience.

"It was nearly two years ago. It was a Monday. I don't know why I came, I think I was dreaming; but you had said: 'Come!' and I came.

"It rained a little, then, too; my shawl was wet, you hung it there; my kerchief,[1] too, was wet. We sat – there – and you took off my kerchief. I let you do it." The girl's voice had sunk very low; she paused awhile. "And then . . . and then . . . you wished it – how could I think, with you so near?" . . .

Her voice died away altogether; her restless fingers, which all the while had been running to and fro, to and fro, along the edge of his waistcoat, now seeking a resting-place, chanced to light upon something that lay tucked between it and his shirt, upon his breast; they pulled up a little knot of ribbon.

She fingered it an instant unconsciously, but when her eyes became aware of what they fell on she stood erect, and then, bending abruptly towards the lamp, stared at her find; without breath as it were, without a heart-throb; — there seemed a momentary cessation of life.

The little knot was of bright new ribbon, and pink in colour.

The young man grew pale, and, before he could control himself, had made a gesture as if to seize the trifle. But his mistress turned upon him. Her face was red, the veins in her neck were swollen; it was as if all the blood were driven from her stricken heart by sudden rage, veiling her eyes and deluging her brain with madness.

She fell upon him with closed fists, and thumped him once, twice, thrice upon the breast.

The young man staggered; with an oath, he seized her by both wrists; but in her rage she beat her poor head against him. And then words came; they left her throat hoarsely, almost unintelligibly, broken and distorted by fierce sobs.

"Leave off!" cried the man, "you will wake the neighbours. Leave off, I say!"

But she could not.

Seeing this, he let go her wrists, and seizing her round the body so that both her arms were imprisoned, closed her mouth with his hand.

"Mother of God!" he cried between his teeth, "I'll teach you!"

The poor wretch struggled an instant violently; then, as if stricken by the hideous disparity between her love and the shame of this embrace, she ceased suddenly, so that the man lost balance and they fell, the woman beneath the man. Then came a thud, a last stifled scream, then silence.

He lay a moment as if stunned, then raised himself.

"Get up!" he said; "I never meant to hurt you."

There were no lodgers in the room below, but he was seized with a great fear lest those on the first floor might have waked, and sat up motionless, straining his ears for the sound he feared. But all was still.

Reassured, he looked at the girl, who lay on her back with closed eyes. One hand was on the floor beside him, palm upturned; the white fingers, bent inwards, quivered slightly. He laid his own upon it, not unkindly.

"Get up," he said. "Come, little one, I never meant to hurt you."

But she recoiled from his touch with a shiver, a low moan, and rolling on to her face, lay there motionless.

"Come," said he again, "little one. . . ."

Then, in perfect silence she sat up, and pushed the hair back from her white face, and settled the kerchief about her neck.

"Wait a minute," said the man, "I will fetch you some water. Come, it's not so bad – ah! you know, you frightened me."

But the woman paid no heed to his words. With staring eyes and drooping jaw, she stood up feebly, and gathered her shawl about her; then tottered towards the door, spreading her hands before her as if wrapped in darkness.

"Where are you going?" asked he, returning with the water.

She seemed not to hear him; she opened the door slowly and went, closing it behind her.

At first he made a step forward, as if to follow her or call her back; but he merely shrugged his shoulders and stood there in the middle of the room where she had left him, jug in hand, listening to her retreating footsteps, to the fall of her loose heels upon the stairs.

As the street-door closed upon her, the bells from far and near rang out the hour; moonlight and dawn were now indistinguishably mixed.

The young man yawned; and, as he set the jug down on the table, his eyes fell on the crucifix that she had left.

He ran to the window and, leaning out, looked up the street; but there was no one to be seen. All was still. There was not even the sound of a footstep on the air, nothing but the lashing of the water as it beat to and fro against the slimy walls.

So he drew his head in again.

"Bah!" said he, "I can bring it her to-morrow."

And he closed the window.

Notes

Text: *The Crucifix*, Osgood, McIvaine and Co. London, 1895.
1 Piece of fabric worn round the neck.

AN IDYLL IN MILLINERY

Ménie Muriel Dowie

Ménie Muriel Dowie, later Norman, later Fitzgerald (1866–1945), novelist, short-story writer and travel writer, was born in Liverpool, and educated in Germany and France. Her popular *A Girl in the Karpathians* (1891) is based on a journey she made alone at the age of 20, and depicts a young woman travelling alone, dressing like a man, smoking and drinking. Her novels and stories demonstrate an interest in women's rights: they include *Gallia* (1895), which argues for the separation of love and motherhood; *The Crook of the Bough* (1898); and *Love and His Masks* (1901). Her *Yellow Book* stories were published in volume form, under the title *Some Whims of Fate*, in 1896. Her first marriage ended in divorce, and she lived for several years in India after her second marriage. She became a successful cattle breeder after her return to England towards the end of her life.

Further reading

Blain *et al.* (1990); Mix (1960); Sutherland (1988)

An Idyll in Millinery

I

The actual reason why Liphook was there does not matter: he was there, and he was there for the second time within a fortnight, and on each occasion, as it happened, he was the only man in the place – the only man-customer in the place. A pale, shaven young Jew passed sometimes about the room, in the background.

Liphook could not stand still; the earliest sign of mental excitement, this; if he paused for a moment in front of one of the two console tables and glanced into the big mirror, it was only to turn the next second and make a step or two this way or that upon the spacious-sized, vicious-patterned Axminster carpet. His eye wandered, but not without a mark of resolution in its wandering – resolution not to wander persistently in one direction. First the partings in the curtains which ran before the windows seemed to attract him, and he glanced into the gay grove of millinery that blossomed before the hungry eyes of female passers-by in the street. Sometimes he looked through the archways that led upon each hand to further salons in which little groups of women, customers and saleswomen, were collected. Sometimes his eye rested upon the seven or eight unemployed shop-ladies who stood behind the curtains, like spiders, and looked with an almost malevolent contemptuousness upon the street starers who came not in to buy, but lingered long, and seemed to con[1] the details of attractive models. More than once, a group in either of the rooms fascinated him for full a minute. One particularly, because its component parts declared themselves so quickly to his apprehension.

A young woman, with fringe carefully ordered to complete formlessness and fuzz, who now sat upon a chair and now rose to regard herself in a glass as she poised a confection of the *toque*[2] breed upon her head. With her, a friend, older, of identical type, but less serious mien, whose face pringled into vivacious comment upon each venture; comment which of course Liphook could not overhear. With them both, an elder lady, to whom the shopwoman, a person of clever *dégagé*[3] manner and primrose hair, principally addressed herself; appealingly, confirmatively, rapturously, critically – according to her ideas upon the hat in question. In and out of their neighbourhood moved a middle-aged woman of French appearance, short-necked, square-shouldered, high-busted, with a keen face of chamois leather colour and a head to which the black hair seemed to have been permanently glued – Madame Félise herself. When she threw a word into the momentous discussion the eyes of the party turned respectfully upon her; each woman hearkened. Even Liphook divined that the girl was buying her trousseau millinery; the older sister, or married friend, advising in crisp, humorous fashion, the elder lady controlling, deciding, voicing the great essential laws of order, obligation and convention; the shop-woman playing the pipes, the dulcimer, the sackbut, the tabor or the viol – Madame Félise the while commanding with invisible bâton her intangible orchestra; directing distantly, but with ineludable authority, the very players upon the stage. At this moment She turned to him and his attention necessarily left the group. How did he find this? Did he care for the immense breadth in front? Every one in Paris was doing it. Wasn't he on the whole a little bit sick of hydrangeas – every one, positively every one, had hydrangeas just now, and hydrangeas the size of cauliflowers. He made replies; he assumed a quiet interest, not too strong to be in character; he steered her away from the Parisian breadth in front, away from the hydrangeas, into a consideration of something that rose very originally at the back and had a *ruche*[4] of watercresses to lie upon the hair, and three dahlias, and four distinct colours of tulle in aniline shades,[5] one over the other, and an osprey, and a bird of Paradise, and a few paste ornaments; and a convincing degree of *chic* in its abandoned hideousness. Then he took a turn down the room towards the group aforesaid.

"It looks so *fearfully* married to have that tinsel crown, don't you know!" the elder sister or youthful matron was saying. "I mean, it suggests dull calls, doesn't it? Dull people *always* have tinsel crowns, haven't you noticed? I don't want to influence you, but as I said before, I liked you in the Paris model."

Every hat over which you conspicuously hover at Félise's, becomes, on the instant, a Paris model.

"So smart, Madam," cut in the shop-lady. "And you can't have anything newer than that rustic brim in shot straw with just the little knot of gardenias at the side. Oh I *do* think it suits you!"

Liphook turned away. After all, he didn't want to hear what these poor, silly, feeble people were saying; he wanted to look. . . .

"But Jim always likes me so much in pale blue, that I think – " began the girl.

"Why not have just a little tiny knot of forget-me-nots *with* the gardenia. Oh, I'm shaw you'd like it."

Thus flowed the oily current of the shop-lady, reaching his ear as Liphook returned down the room. He could look again in the only direction that won his eyes and his thoughts; five minutes had been killed; there was time left him yet, for She had just been seized with the idea that something with a little more brim was really her style. After all, She craved no more than to be loose at Félise's, amid the Spring models lit by a palely ardent town sun, and Harold's cheque-book looming in the comfortable shadow of his pocket.

At the back of each gilt and mirrored saloon was placed a work-table – in the manner of all hat-shops – surrounded by chairs in which, mostly with their backs to the shops, sat the girls who were making up millinery; their ages anywhere from sixteen to twenty-one. Seldom did the construction of a masterpiece appear to concern them; but they were spangling things; deftly turning loops into bows, curling feathers, binding ospreys into close sheaves; their heads all bent over their work, their neat aprons tied with tape bows at the back, their dull hair half flowing and half coiled – the inimitable manner of the London work girl – their pale faces dimly perceived as they turned and whispered not too noisily: the whole thing recalling the soft, quietly murmurous groups of pigeons in the streets gathered about the scatterings of a cab-horse's nose-bag. Sometimes shop-girls with elaborately distorted hair came up and gave them disdainful-seeming orders; but the flock of sober little pigeons murmured and pecked at its work and ruffled no plumage of tan-colour or slate. And one of them, different from the others – how Liphook's eyes, in the brief looks he allowed himself, ate up the details of her guise. Dressed in something – dark-blue, it might have been – that fitted with a difference over her plump little figure; a fine and wide lawn collar spread over breast and shoulders; a smooth head, with no tags and ends upon the pale, yellow-tinted brow; a head as sleek and as sweetly-coloured as the coat of the cupboard-mouse; a face so softly indented by its features, so fleckless, so *mat* in its flat tones, so mignon in its delicate lack of prettiness as to be irresistible. Lips, a dully greyish-pink, but tenderly curved at the pouting bow and faithfully compressed at the dusk-downy corners – terribly conscientious little lips that seemed as if never could they be kissed to lighter humour. Eyes, with pale ash-coloured fringes, neither long nor greatly curved, but so shy-shaped as ever eyes were; eyes that could only be imagined by Liphook, as he was sometimes of mind that they were that vaporous Autumn blue; and at other times that they were liquid, brook-coloured hazel.

But this was the maddest obsession that was riding him! A London work-girl in a West-end hat shop, a girl whose voice he had never heard, near whom he had never, could never, come. And Heaven forbid he should come near her; what did he want with her? Before Heaven, and all these hats and mirrors, Viscount Liphook could have sworn he wanted nothing of her. Yet he loved her completely, desperately, exclusively. What name was there for this feeling other than the name of love? Soiled with all ignoble use, this name of love; though to do him justice, Liphook was not greatly to blame in that matter. He was but little acquainted with the word; he left it out of his *affaires de cœur*,[6] and very properly, for it did not enter into them. Still his feeling for this girl, his craving for the sound of her voice, his eye fascinated by smallest movement, his yearning for the sense of her nearer presence – novel, inexplicable as this all was, might it not be love? He stood there; quiet, inexpressive of face, in jealous hope of – what next? And then She claimed his attention – in a whisper which brought her head with its mahogany hair, and her face with its ground-rice surface, close to his ear. She said:

"You don't mind five, eh? It's a model – and – don't you think it becomes me? I do think this mushroom-coloured velvet and just the three green orchids divine – and it's really very quiet!"

He assented, careful to look critically at the hat – a clever mass of evilly-imagined, ill-assorted absurdities. He had looked too long at that work-table, at that figure, at that face – he dropped into a chair – let his stick fall between his knees and cast his eyes to the mirror-empanelled ceiling; there the heads, and feet of the passers-by were seething grotesquely in a fashion that recalled the Inferno of an old engraving.

Well, it would be time to look again soon – ah! she had risen; thank goodness, not a tall woman – (She was five foot nine) – small, and indolent of outline.

"I'll take it to the French milliner now, Madam, and she'll pin a pink rose in for you to see!"

It was a shop-woman speaking to some customer, who with a hat in her hand, approached the work-table.

"If you please, Mam'zelle Mélanie," she began, in a voice meant to impress the customer, "would you pin in a rose for Madam to try? Madam thinks the pansy rather old-looking – " &c., &c., &c.

The French milliner; French, then! And what a dear innocent, young, crusty little face! what delicious surliness: the little brown bear that she was, growling and grumbling to do a favour. Well, bless that woman – and the pansy that looked old – he knew her name; enough to recognise her by, enough to address a note to her – and it should be a note! A note that would bring out a star in each grey eye – they were grey – after all. (The grey of a lingering, promising, but unbestowing twilight.) Reflecting, but unobservant, his glance left her face and focussed the pale, fair, young Jew, who was seated, in frock coat and hat, gloating over a pocket-book that had scraps of coloured silk and velvet pinned in it. He recalled his wandering senses.

"How much? Eight ten?"

"Well, I've taken a little black thing as well; it happens to be very reasonable. There, you don't mind?" Mrs. Percival always went upon the principle of appearing to be careful of other people's money; she found she got more of it that way.

"My dear! – as long as you are pleased!" It was weeks since this tone had been possible to him. He scribbled a cheque and they got away.

"I know I've been an awful time, old boy," said the mahogany-haired one, with rough good humour – the good humour of a vain woman whose vanity has been fed. "Are you coming?"

"Er – no; in fact, I'm going out of town, I shan't see you for a bit – Oh, I wasn't very badly bored, thanks."

She made no comment on his reply to her question; her coarsely pretty face hardly showed lines of relief, for it was not a mobile face; but she was pleased.

"Glad you didn't fret. I'd never dreamt you'd be so good about shopping. Yes, I'll take a cab. There is a call for 12.30, and I see it is nearly one now."

He put her into a nice-looking hansom, lifted his hat and watched her drive away. Then he turned and looked into the gaudy windows. His feelings were his own somehow, now that She had left him. He smiled; love warmed in him. Was the old pansy gone and the pink rose in its place? Had she pricked those creamy yellow fingers in the doing of it? No, she was too deft. Tired, flaccid little fingers! Was he never to think of anything or anyone again, except Mam'zelle Mélanie?

II

Now the mahogany-haired lady was not an actress: she was nothing so common as an actress; she belonged to a mysterious class, but little understood, even if clearly realised, by the public. It was not because she could not that she did not act; she had never tried to, there had been no question of capability – but she consented to appear at a famous West-end burlesque theatre, to oblige the manager who was a personal friend of long-standing. She "went on" in the ball-room scene of a hoary but ever-popular "musical comedy," because there was – not a part – but a pretty gown to be filled, and because she was surprisingly handsome, and of very fine figure, and filled that gown amazingly well. The two guineas a week that came her way at "Treasury"[7] went a certain distance in gloves and cab-fares, and the necessaries of life she had a different means of supplying. Let her position be understood: she was a very respectable person: there are degrees in respectability as in other things; there was no fear of vulgar unpleasantnesses with her and her admirers – if she had them. Mr. John Holditch, the popular manager of several theatres, had a real regard for her; in private she called him "Jock, old boy," and he called her "Mill" – because he recollected her *début*; but the public knew her as Miss Mildred Metcalf, and her lady comrades in the dressing-room as Mrs. Percival, and it was generally admitted by all concerned that she was equally satisfactory under any of these styles. Oh, it will have been noticed and need not be insisted on, that Liphook called her "my dear," and if it be not pushing the thing too far, I may add that her mother spoke of her as "our Florrie."

Liphook was a rich man whose occupation, when he was in town, was the dividing of days between the club, his rooms in Half Moon Street, his mother's house in Belgrave Square, and Mrs. Percival's abode in Manfield Gardens, Kensington. The only respect in which he differed from a thousand men of his class was, that he had visited the hat shop of Madame Félise, in the company of Mrs. Percival, and had conceived a genuine passion for a little French milliner who sewed spangles on to snippets of nothingness at a table in the back of the shop.

The note had been written, had been answered. This answer, in fine, sloping, uneducated French handwriting, upon thin, lined, pink paper of the foreign character, had given Liphook a ridiculous amount of pleasure. The club waiters, his mother's butler, his man in Half Moon Street, these unimportant people chiefly noted the uncontrollable bubbles of happiness that floated the surface of his impassive English face during the days that followed the arrival of that answer. He didn't think anything particular about it; few men so open to the attractions of women as this incident proves him, think anything particular at all, least of all, at so early a stage. He was not – for the sake of his judges it must be urged – meaning badly any more than he was definitely meaning well. He wasn't meaning at all. He cannot be blamed, either. The world is responsible for this sense of irresponsibility in men of the world – who are the world's sole making. Herein he was true to type; in so far as he did not think what the girl meant by her answer, type was supported by individual character. Liphook was not clever, and did not think much or with any success, on any subject. And if he had he wouldn't have hit the real reason; only experience would have told him that a French workgirl, from a love of pleasure and the national measure of shrewd practicality combined, never refuses the chance of a nice outing. She does not, like her English sister, drag her virtue into the question at all.

Never in his life, so it chanced, had Liphook gone forth to an interview in such a frame of mind as on the day he was to meet Mélanie outside the Argyll Baths in Great Marlboro' Street at ten minutes past seven. Apart from the intoxicating perfume that London seemed to breathe for him, and the gold motes that danced in the dull air, there was the unmistakable resistant pressure of the pavement against his feet (thus it seemed) which is seldom experienced twice in a lifetime; in the lifetime of such a man as Liphook, usually never. The Argyll Baths, Great Marlboro' Street: what a curious place for the child to have chosen, and she would be standing there, pretending to look into a shop window. Oh, of course, there were no shop windows to speak of in Great Marlboro' Street. (He had paced its whole length several times since the arrival of the pink glazed note). What would she say? What would she look like? Her eyes, drooped or raised frankly to his, for instance? That she would not greet him with bold, meaning smile and common phrase he knew – he felt. Dreaming and speculating, but wearing the calm leisured air of a gentleman walking from one point to another, he approached and – yes! there she was! A scoop-shaped hat rose above the cream-yellow brow; a big dotted veil was loosely – was wonderfully – bound about it; a little black cape covered the demure lawn collar; quite French *bottines*[8] peeped below the dark-blue skirt. But – she was not alone, a man was with her. A man whom, even at some distance, he could discern to be unwelcome and unexpected, the pale fair young Jew in dapper frock-coat and extravagantly curved over-shiny hat. Loathsome-looking reptile he was, too, so thought Liphook as he turned abruptly with savage scrape of his veering foot upon the pavement, up Argyll Street. Perhaps she was getting rid of him; it was only nine minutes past seven, anyhow; perhaps he would be gone in a moment. Odious beast! In love with her, no doubt; how came it he had the wit to recognise her indescribable charm? (Liphook never paused to wonder how himself had recognised it, though this was, in the circumstances, even more remarkable). Anyway, judging by that look he remembered, she would not be unequal to rebuffing unwelcome attention.

Liphook walked as far as Hengler's circus and read the bills; the place was in occupation, it being early in March. He studied the bill from top to bottom, then he turned slowly and retraced his steps to the corner. Joy! she was there and alone. His pace quickened, his heart rose; his face, a handsome face, was strung to lines of pride, of passionate anticipation.

He had greeted her; he had heard her voice; so soft – dear Heaven! so soft – in reply; they had turned and were walking towards Soho, and he knew no word of what had passed.

"We will have a cab; you will give me the pleasure of dining with me. I have arranged it. Allow me." Perhaps these were the first coherent words that he said. Then they drove along and he said inevitable, valueless things in quick order, conscious of the lovely interludes when her smooth tones, now wood-sweet, now with a harp-like thrilling *timbre* in them, again with the viol – or was it the lute-note? – a sharp dulcidity that made answer in him as certainly as the tuning-fork compels its octave from the rosewood board. The folds of the blue gown fell beside him; the French pointed feet, miraculously short-toed, rested on the atrocious straw mat of the wretched hansom his blindness had brought him; the scoop-hat knocked the wicked reeking lamp in the centre of the cab; the dotted veil, tied as only a French hand can tie a veil, made more delectable the creams and twine-shades of the monotonous-coloured kitten face. They drove, they arrived somewhere, they dined, and then of all things, they went into a church, which being open and permitting organ music to exude from its smut-blackened walls, seemed less like London than any place they might have sought.

And it happened to be a Catholic Church, and he – yes, he actually followed the pretty ways of her, near the grease-smeared pecten shell with its holy water, that stuck from a pillar: some Church oyster not uprooted from its ancient bed. And they sat on *prie-dieus*,[9] in the dim incense-savoured gloom; little unaspiring lights seemed to be burning in dim places beyond; and sometimes there were voices, and sometimes these ceased again and music filled the dream-swept world in which Liphook was wrapped and veiled away. And they talked – at least she talked, low murmurous recital about herself and her life, and every detail sunk and expanded wondrously in the hot-bed of Liphook's abnormally affected mind. The evening passed to night, and people stepped about, and doors closed with a hollow warning sound that hinted at the end of lovely things, and they went out and he left her at a door which was the back entrance to Madame Félise's establishment; but he had rolled back a grey lisle-thread glove, and gathered an inexpressibly precious memory from the touch of that small hand that posed roses instead of pansies all the day.

And of course he was to see her again. He had heard all about her. How a year since she had been fetched from Paris at the instance of Goldenmuth. Goldenmuth was the fair young Jewish man in the frock-coat and supremely curved hat. He was a "relative" of Madame Félise, and travelled for her, in a certain sense, in Paris. He had seen Mélanie in an obscure corner of the *Petit St. Thomas* when paying an airy visit to a lady in charge of some department there. An idea had occurred to him; in three days he arrived and made a proposition. He had conceived the plan of transplanting this ideally French work-flower to the London shop, and his plan had been a success. Her simple, shrewd, much defined little character clung to Mélanie in London, as in Paris; she had clever fingers, but beyond all, her appearance which Goldenmuth had the art to appreciate, soft but marked and unassailable by influence, told infinitely at that unobtrusive but conspicuous work-table.

Half mouse, half dove; never to be vulgarised, never to be destroyed.

Mélanie had a family, worthy *épicier*[10] of Nantes, her father; her mother, his invaluable book-keeper. Her sister Hortense, cashier at the Restaurant des Trois Epées; her sister Albertine, in the millinery like herself. Every detail delighted Liphook, every word of her rapid incorrect London English sank into his mind; in the extraordinarily narrow circumscribed life that Liphook had lived – that all the Liphooks of the world usually do live – a little, naïvely-simple description of some quite different life is apt to sound surprisingly interesting, and if it comes from the lips of your Mélanie, why . . ..

But previous to the glazed pink note, if Liphook had crystallised any floating ideas he might have had as to the nature of the intimacy he expected, they would have tallied in no particular with the reality. In his first letter had been certain warmly-worded sentences; at their first interview when he had interred two kisses below the lisle-thread glove, he had incoherently murmured something lover-like. It had been too dark to see Mélanie's face at the moment; but when since, more than once, he had attempted similar avowals she had put her head on one side, raised her face, crinkled up the corners of the grey eyes, and twisted quite alarmingly the lilac-pink lips. So there wasn't much said about love or any such thing. After all, he could see her three or four times a week; on Sunday they often spent the whole day together; he could listen to her prattle; he was a silent fellow himself, having never learnt to talk and having nothing to talk about; he could, in hansoms and quiet places, tuck her hand within his arm and beam affectionately into her face, and they grew always closer and closer to each other; as *camarades*,[11] still only as *camarades*. She never spoke of Goldenmuth except incidentally, and then very briefly; and Liphook, who had since seen the man with her in the street on two occasions, felt very unanxious to introduce the subject; after all he knew more than he wanted to about it, he said to himself. It was obvious enough. He had bought her two hats at Félise's; he had begged to do as much, and she had advised him which he should purchase, and on evenings together she had looked ravishing beneath them. He knew many secrets of the hat trade; he knew and delightedly laughed over half a hundred fictions Mélanie exploded; he was in a fair way to become a man-milliner; even Goldenmuth could not have talked more trippingly of the concomitants of capotes.[12]

One Sunday, when the sunniest of days had tempted them down the river, he came suddenly into the private room where they were to lunch and found her coquetting with her veil in front of a big ugly mirror; a mad sort of impulse took him, he gripped her arms to her side, nipped her easily off the floor, bent his head round the prickly fence of hat-brim and kissed her several times; she laughed with the low, fluent gurgle of water pushing through a narrow passage. She said nothing, she only laughed.

Somehow, it disorganised Liphook.

"Do you love me? Do you love me?" he asked rapidly, even roughly, in the only voice he could command, and he shook her a little.

She put her head on one side and made the same sweet crinkled-up kind of *moue moquante*,[13] then she spread her palms out and shook them and laughed and ran away round the table. "Est-ce que je sais, moi?"[14] she cried in French. Liphook didn't speak. Oh, he understood her all right, but he was getting himself a little in hand first. A man like Liphook has none of the art of life; he can't do figure-skating among his emotions like your nervous, artistic-minded, intellectually trained man. After that one outburst and the puzzlement that succeeded it, he was silent, until he remarked upon the waiter's slowness in bringing up luncheon. But he had one thing quite clear in his thick English head, through which the blood was still whizzing and singing. He wanted to kiss her again badly; he was going to kiss her again at the first opportunity.

But, of course, when he wasn't with her his mind varied in its reflections. For instance, he had come home one night from dining at Aldershot – a farewell dinner to his Colonel it was – and he had actually caught himself saying: "I must get out of it," meaning his affair with Mélanie. That was pretty early on, when it had still seemed, particularly after being in the society of worldly-wise friends who rarely, if ever, did anything foolish, much less emotional, that he was making an ass of himself, or was likely to if he didn't "get out of it." Now the thing had assumed a different aspect. He could not give her up; under no circumstances could he contemplate giving her up; well then, why give her up? She was only a little thing in a hat shop, she would do very much better – yes, but, somehow he had a certain feeling about her, he couldn't – well, in point of fact, her loved her; hang it, he respected her; he'd sooner be kicked out of his Club than say one word to her that he'd mind a fellow saying to his sister.

Thus the Liphook of March, '95, argued with the Liphook of the past two and thirty years!

III

Liphook's position was awkward – all the other Liphooks in the world have said it was beastly awkward, supposing they could have been made to understand it. To many another kind of man this little love story might not have been inappropriate; occurring in the case of Liphook it was nothing less than melancholy. Not that he felt melancholy about it, no indeed; just sometimes, when he happened to think how it was all going to end, he had rather a bad moment, but thanks to his nature and training he did not think often.

Meantime, he had sent a diamond heart to Mrs. Percival; there was more sentiment about a heart than a horse-shoe; women looked at that kind of thing, and she would feel that he wasn't cooling off; so it had been a heart. That secured him several more weeks of freedom at any rate, and he wouldn't have the trouble of putting notes in the fire. For on receiving the diamond heart Mrs. Percival behaved like a python after swallowing an antelope; she was torpid in satiety, and no sign came from her.

But one morning Liphook got home to Half Moon Street after his Turkish bath, and heard that a gentleman was waiting to see him.

"At least, hardly a gentleman, my lord; I didn't put him in the library," explained the intuitive Sims.

Some one from his tailor's with so-called "new" patterns, no doubt; well –

He walked straight into the room, never thinking, and he saw Goldenmuth. The man had an offensive orchid in his buttonhole. To say that Liphook was surprised is nothing; he was astounded, and too angry to call up any expression whatever to his face; he was rigid with rage. What in hell had Sims let the fellow in for? However, this was the last of Sims; Sims would go.

The oily little brute, with his odious hat in his hand, was speaking; was saying something about being fortunate in finding his lordship, &c.

"Be good enough to tell me your business with me," said Liphook, with undisguised savagery. Though he had asked him to speak, he thought that when her name was mentioned he would have to choke him. His rival – by gad, this little Jew beggar was Liphook's rival. Goldenmuth hitched his sallow neck, as leathery as a turtle's, in his high, burnished collar, and took his pocket-book from his breast pocket – which meant that he was nervous, and forgot that he was not calling up a "wholesale buyer," to whom he would presently show a pattern. He pressed the book in both hands, and swayed forward on his toes – swayed into hurried speech.

"Being interested in a young lady whom your lordship has honoured with your attention lately, I called to 'ave a little talk." The man had an indescribable accent, a detestable fluency, a smile which nearly warranted you in poisoning him, a manner — ! There was silence. Liphook waited; the snap with which he bit off four tough orange-coloured hairs from his moustache, sounded to him like the stroke of a hammer in the street. Then an idea struck him. He put a question:

"What has it got to do with you?"

"I am interested — "

"So am I. But I fail to see why you should mix yourself up with my affairs."

"Madame Félise feels — "

"What's she got to do with it?" Liphook tossed out his remarks with the nakedest brutality.

"The lady is in her employment and — "

"Look here; say what you've got to say, or go," burst from Liphook, with the rough bark of passion. He had his hands behind his back; he was holding one with the other in the fear that they might get away from him, as it were. His face was still immobile, but the crooks of two veins between the temples and the eye corners stood up upon the skin; his impassive blue eyes harboured sullen hatred. He saw the whole thing. That old woman had sent her dirty messenger to corner, to "ask his intentions," to get him to give himself away, to make some promise. It was a kind of blackmail they had in view. The very idea of such creatures about Mélanie would have made him sick at another time; now he felt only disgust, and the rising obstinacy about committing himself at the unsavory instance of Goldenmuth. After all, they couldn't take Mélanie from him; she was free, she could go into another shop; he could marry . . . Stop — madness!

"Mademoiselle Mélanie is admitted to be most attractive — others have observed it — "

"You mean you have," sneered Liphook; in the most ungentlemanly manner, it must be allowed.

"I must bring to the notice of your lordship," said the Jew, with the deference of a man who knows he is getting his point, "that so young as Mademoiselle is, and so innocent, she is not fitted to understand business questions; and her parents being at a distance it falls to Madame Félise and myself to see that — excuse me, my lord, but we know what London is! — that her youth is not misled."

"Who's misleading her youth?" Liphook burst out; and his schoolboy language detracted nothing from the energy with which he spoke. "You can take my word here and now that she is in every respect as innocent as I found her, And now," with a sudden reining in of his voice, "we have had enough of this talk. If you are the lady's guardians you may reassure yourselves: I am no more to her than a friend: I have not sought to be any more." Liphook moved in conclusion of the interview.

"Your lordship is very obliging; but I must point out that a young and

351

ardent girl is likely, in the warmth of her affection to be precipitate – that we would protect her from herself."

"About this I have nothing to say, and will hear nothing" exclaimed Liphook, hurriedly.

Goldenmuth used the national gesture; he bent his right elbow, turned his right hand palm upwards and shook it softly to and fro.

"Perhaps even I have noticed it. I am not insensible!"

Liphook had never heard a famous passage[15] – he neither read nor looked at Shakespeare, so this remark merely incensed him. "But," went on the Jew, "since she came to England – for I brought her – I have made myself her protector – "

"You're a liar!" said Liphook, who was a very literal person.

"Oh, my lord! – I mean in the sense of being kind to her and looking after her, with Madame Félise's entire approval; so when I noticed the marked attention of a gentleman like your lordship – "

"You're jealous," put in Liphook, again quite inexcusably. But it would be impossible to over-estimate his contempt for this man. Belonging to the uneducated section of the upper class he was a man of the toughest prejudices on some points. One of these was that all Jews were mean, scurvy devils at bottom and that no kind of consideration need be shown them. Avoid them as you would a serpent; when you meet them, crush them as you would a serpent. He'd never put it into words; but that is actually what poor Liphook thought, or at any rate it was the dim idea on which he acted.

"You lordship is making a mistake," said Goldenmuth with a flush. "I am not here in my own interest; I am here to act on behalf of the young lady." Had the heavens fallen? In *her* interest? Then Mélanie? Never! As if a Thing like this could speak the truth!

"Who sent you?" Liphook always went to the point.

"Madame Félise and I talked it over and agreed that I should make it convenient to call. We have both a great regard for Mademoiselle; we feel a responsibility – a responsibility to her parents."

What was all this about? Liphook was too bewildered to interrupt even.

"Naturally, we should like to see Mademoiselle in a position, an assured position for which she is every way suited."

So it was as he thought. They wanted to rush a proposal. *Must* he chaffer with them at all?

"I can tell you that if I had anything to propose I should write it to the lady herself," he said.

"We are not anxious to come between you. I may say I have enquired – my interest in Mademoiselle has led me to enquire – and Madame Félise and I think it would be in every way a suitable connection for her. Your lordship must feel that we regard her as no common girl; she deserves to be *lancée*[16] in the right manner; a settlement – and establishment – some indication that the connection will be fairly permanent, or if not, that suitable – "

"Is *that* what you are driving at, you dog, you?" cried Liphook, illuminated at length and boiling with passion. "So you want to sell her to me and take your blasted commission? Get out of my house!" He grew suddenly quiet; it was an ominous change. "Get out, this instant, before – "

Goldenmuth was gone, the street door banged.

"God! God!" breathed Liphook with his hand to his wet brow, "what a hellish business!"

It was nine o'clock when Liphook came in that night. He did not know where he had been, he believed he had had something in the nature of dinner, but he could not have said exactly where he had had it.

Sims handed him a note.

He recognised a friend's hand and read the four lines it contained.

"When did Captain Throgmorton come, then?"

"Came in about three to 'alf past, my lord; he asked me if your lordship had any engagement to-night, and said he would wait at the club till quarter past eight and that he should dine at the Blue Posts after that."

"I see; well," he reflected a moment, "Sims, pack my hunting things, have everything at St. Pancras in time for the ten o'clock express, and," he reflected again, "Sims, I want you to take a note – no, never mind. That'll do."

"V'ry good, my lord."

Yes, he'd go. Jack Throgmorton was the most companionable man in the world – he was so silent. Liphook and he had been at Sandhurst together, they had joined the same regiment. Liphook had sent in his papers rather than stand the fag of India; Throgmorton had "taken his twelve hundred" rather than stand the fag of anywhere. He was a big heavy fellow with a marked difficulty in breathing, also there was fifteen stone of him. His round eyes, like "bulls'-eyes," the village children's best-loved goodies, stuck out of a face rased to an even red resentment. He had the hounds somewhere in Bedfordshire. His friends liked him enormously, so did his enemies. To say that he was stupid does not touch the fringe of a description of him. He had never had a thought of his own, nor an idea; all the same, in any Club quarrel, or in regard to a point of procedure, his was an opinion other men would willingly stand by. At this moment in his life, a blind instinct taught Liphook to seek such society; no one could be said to sum up more completely – perhaps because so unconsciously – the outlook of Liphooks world, which of late he had positively begun to forget. The thing was bred into Throgmorton by sheer, persistent sticking to the strain, and it came out of him again mechanically, automatically, distilled through his dim brain a triple essence. The kind of man clever people have found it quite useless to run down, for it has been proved again and again that if he can only be propped up in the right place at the right moment, you'll never find his equal *in* that place. Altogether, a handsome share in "the secret of England's

353

greatness" belongs to him. The two men met on the platform beside a pile of kit-bags and suit cases, all with Viscount Liphook's name upon them in careful uniformity. Sims might have had the administration of an empire's affairs upon his mind, whereas he was merely chaperoning more boots and shirts than any one man has a right to possess.

"You didn't come last night," said Captain Throgmorton, as though he had only just realised the fact. He prefaced the remark by his favourite ejaculation which was "Harr-rr" – he prefaced every remark with "Harr-rr" – on a cold day it was not uninspiriting if accompanied by a sharp stroke of the palms; in April it was felt to be somewhat out of season. But Captain Throgmorton merely used it as a means of getting his breath and his voice under way. "Pity," he went on, without noticing Liphook's silence; "good bone." This summed up the dinner with its famous marrow-bones, at the Blue Posts.

They got in. Each opened a *Morning Post*. Over the top of this fascinating sheet they flung friendly brevities from time to time.

"Shan't have more than a couple more days to rattle 'em about," Captain Throgmorton remarked, after half an hour's silence, and a glance at the flying hedges.

Liphook began to come back into his world. After all it was comfortable world. Yet had an angel for a time transfigured it, ah dear! how soft that angel's wings, if he might be folded within them . . . old world, dear, bad old world, you might roll by.

They were coming home from hunting next day. Each man bent ungainly in the saddle; their cords were splashed; the going had been heavy, and once it had been hot as well, but only for a while. Then they had hung about a lot, and though they found three times, they hadn't killed. Liphook was weary. When Throgmorton stuck his crop under his thigh, hung his reins on it, and lit a cigar, Liphook was looking up at the sky, where dolorous clouds of solid purple splotched a background of orange, flame-colour and rose. Throgmorton's peppermint eye rolled slowly round when it left his cigar-tip; he knew that when a man – that is, a man of Liphook's sort – is found staring at a thing like the sunset there is a screw loose somewhere.

"Wha' is it, Harold?" he said, on one side of his cigar.

Liphook made frank answer.

"What's she done then?"

"Oh, Lord, it isn't *her*."

"'Nother?" said Jack, without any show of surprise, and got his answer again.

"What sort?" This was very difficult, but Liphook shut his eyes and flew it. "How old?"

"Twenty," said Liphook, and felt a rapture rising.

"Jack, man," he exclaimed, under the influence of the flame and rose, no doubt, "what if I were to marry?"

Throgmorton was not, as has been indicated, a person of fine fibre. "Do, and be done with 'em," said he. And after all, as far as it went, it was sound enough advice.

"I mean marry her," Liphook explained, and the explanation cost him a considerable expenditure of pluck.

An emotional man would have fallen off his horse – if the horse would have let him. Jack's horse never would have let him. Jack said nothing for a moment; his eye merely seemed to swell; then he put another question:

"Earl know about it?"

"By George, I should say not!"

"Harr-rr."

That meant that the point would be solved in the curiously composed brain of Captain Throgmorton, and by common consent not another word was said on the matter.

IV

Two days had gone by. Liphook's comfortable sense of having acted wisely in coming out of town to think the thing over still supported him, ridiculous though it seems. For of course he was no more able to think anything over than a Hottentot. Thinking is not a natural process at all; savage men never knew of it, and many people think it quite as dangerous as it is unnatural. It has become fashionable to learn thinking, and some forms of education undertake to teach it; but Liphook had never gone through those forms of education. After all, to understand Liphook, one must admit that he approximated quite as nearly to the savage as to the civilised and thinking man, if not more nearly. His appetites and his habits were mainly savage, and had he lived in savage times he would not have been touched by a kind of love for which he was never intended, and his trouble would not have existed. However, he was as he was, and he was thinking things over; that is, he was waiting and listening for the most forceful of his instincts to make itself heard, and he had crept like a dumb unreasoning animal into the burrow of his kind, making one last effort to be of them. At the end of the week his loudest instinct was setting up a roar; there could be no mistaking it. He loved her. He could not part from her; he must get back to her; he must make her his and carry her off.

"Sorry to be leaving you, Jack," he said one morning at the end of the week. They were standing looking out of the hall door together and it was raining. "But I find I must go up this morning."

Throgmorton rolled a glance at him, then armed him into the library and shut the door.

"What are you going to do?"

"Marry her."

There was a silence. They stood there, the closest feeling of friendship between them, not saying a word.

"My dear Harold," said Throgmorton at length, with much visible and more invisible effort; he put a hand heavily on Liphook's shoulder and blew hard in his mute emotion. Then he put his other hand on Liphook's other shoulder. Liphook kept his eyes down; he was richly conscious of all Jack was mutely saying; he felt the weight of every unspoken argument; the moment was a long one, but for both these slow-moving minds a very crowded moment.

"Come to the Big Horn Mountains with me," Throgmorton remarked suddenly, "– and – harr-ra write to her from there."

He was proud of his suggestion; he knew the value of a really remote point to write from. It was always one of the first things to give your mind to, the choice of a geographically well-nigh inaccessible point to write from. First you found it, then you went to it, and when you got there, by Jove, you didn't need to write at all. Liphook smiled in impartial recognition of his friend's wisdom, but shook his head.

"Thanks," he said. "I've thought it all over" – he genuinely believed he had – "and I'm going to marry her. Jack, old man, I love her like the very devil!"

In spite of the grotesqueness of the phrase, the spirit in it was worth having.

Throgmorton's hands came slowly off his friend's shoulders. He walked to the window, took out a very big handkerchief and dried his head. He seemed to look out at the dull rain battering on the gravel and digging yellow holes.

"I'll drive you to meet the 11.15," he said at last and went out of the room.

Liphook put up his arms and drew a deep breath; it had been a stiff engagement. He felt tired. But no, not tired. Roll by, O bad old world – he has chosen the angel's wing!

Not one word had passed about Goldenmuth, Madame Félise, or the astounding interview; a man like Liphook can always hold his tongue; one of his greatest virtues. Besides, why should he ever think or breathe the names of those wretches again? Jack Throgmorton, in his splendid ignorance, would have been unable to throw light upon the real motive of these simple, practical French people. Liphook to his dying day would believe they had given proof of hideous iniquity, while in reality they were actuated by a very general belief of the *bourgeoise*, that to be "established," with settlements, as the mistress of a viscount, is quite as good as becoming the wife of a grocer. They had been perhaps, wicked, but innocently wicked; for they acted according to their belief, in the girl's best interest. Unfortunately they had had an impracticable Anglais to deal with and had had to submit to insult; in their first encounter, they had been worsted by British brute stupidity.

With a constant dull seething of impulses that quite possessed him, he got through the time that had to elapse before he could hear from her in reply to his short letter. He had done with thinking. A chance meeting with his father on the sunny side of Pall Mall one morning did not even disquiet him. His every faculty, every fibre was in thrall to his great passion. The rest of life seemed minute, unimportant, fatuous, a mass of trivial futilities.

There were two things in the world, and two only. There was Mélanie, and there was love. Ah, yes, and there was time!

Why did she not answer?

A note from the bonnet-shop, re-enclosing his own, offered an explanation that entered like a frozen knife-blade into Liphook's heart. She had left. She was gone. Gone altogether, for good. Absurd! Did they suppose they could – oh, a higher price was what they wanted. He'd go; by God he'd give it. Was he not going to marry her? He hurried to the hat-shop; he dropped into the chair he had occupied when last in the shop, let his stick fall between his knees and stared before him into the mirrored walls. All the same tangled scene of passing people, customers, shop-women and brilliant millinery was reflected in them; only the bright hats islanded and steady among this ugly fluctuation. Pools of fretful life, these circular mirrors; garish, discomforting to gaze at; stirred surely by no angel unless the reflection of the mouse-maiden should ever cross their surfaces.

Fifteen minutes later he was standing gazing at the horrid clock and ornaments in ormolu that stood on the mantel-piece of the red velvet salon where he waited for Madame Félise.

She came. Her bow was admirable.

"I wrote to Mademoiselle, and my letter has been returned. The note says she has gone." Liphook's schoolboy bluntness came out most when he was angry. "Where has she gone? And why?"

"Aha! Little Mademoiselle! Yes, indeed, she has left us and how sorry we are! *Chère petite*.[17] But what could we do? We would have kept her, but her parents –" A shrug and a smile punctuated the sentence.

"What about her parents?"

"They had arranged for her an alliance – what would you have? – we had to let her go. And the rezponsibility – after all – "

"What sort of alliance?" The dog-like note was in his voice again.

"But – an alliance! I believe very good; a *charpentier* – a *charcutier*,[18] I forget – but *bien solide!*[19]"

"Do you mean you have sold her to some French – "

"Ah, my lord! how can you speak such things. Her parents are most rezpectable, she has always been most rezpectable – naturally, we had more than once felt anxious here in London –"

"I wish to marry her," said Liphook curtly, and he said it still, though he believed her to have been thrust upon a less reputable road. It was his last, his greatest triumph over his world. It fitted him nobly for the shelter of the angel's wing. He had learned the worst – and –

357

"I wish to marry her," said Liphook.

"Hélas! – but she is married!" shrieked Madame Félise in a mock agony of regret, but with surprise twinkling in her little black eyes.

"Married!" shouted Liphook. "Impossible!"

"Ask Mr. Goldenmuth, he was at the wedding." Madame laughed; the true explanation of my lord's remarkable statement had just struck her. It was a *ruse*; an English *ruse*. She laughed very much, and it sounded and looked most unpleasant.

"His lordship was – a *little* unfriendly – a little too – too reserved – not to tell us, not even to tell Mademoiselle herself that he desired to *marry* her," she said with villainous archness.

Liphook strode to the door. Yes, why, why had he not?

"I will find her; I know where her relatives live. If it is a lie – I'll make you sorry – "

"*Fi donc*,[20] what a word! the ceremony at the *Mairie*[21] was on Thursday last."

They were going downstairs and had to pass through the showrooms – quite near – ah, quite near – the table where the little grey and brown pigeons sat clustered, where the one ring-dove had sat too.

"It is sometimes the fate of a lover who thinks too long," Madame was saying, with an air of much philosophy. "But see now, if my lord would care to send a little souvenir" – Madame reached hastily to a model on a stand – "*comme cadeau de noce*[22] here is something quite *exquis!*"[23] She kissed the tips of her brown fingers – inimitably, it must be allowed. "So simple, so young, so innocent – I could pose a little *nœud*[24] of *myositis*. Coming from my lord, it would be so delicate!"

Liphook was in a shop. There were people about. He was a lover, he was a fool, he was a gentleman.

"Er – thank you – not to-day," he said; the air of the world he had repudiated came back to him. And a man like Liphook doesn't let you see when he is hit. That is the beauty of him. He knew it was true, but he would go to Paris; yes, though he knew it was true. He would not, could not see her. But he would go.

He stood a moment in the sun outside the shop, its windows like gardens behind him; its shop-ladies like evil-eyed reptiles in these gardens. The carpets, the mirrors on the wall, the tables at the back – and it was here he had first seen the tip and heard the flutter of an angel's wing!

"Lord Liphook," said a voice, "what an age . . . "

He turned and lifted his hat.

His world had claimed him.

Notes

Text: *The Yellow Book*, vol. x (July 1896).
 1 Learn by heart.
 2 Small round brimless hat.
 3 Relaxed.
 4 Ruff.
 5 Coloured with aniline (synthetic) dyes.
 6 Affairs of the heart.
 7 Pay-day.
 8 Small boots.
 9 Pieces of furniture made for prayer, with low surfaces for kneeling and arm-rests.
10 Grocer.
11 Comrades.
12 Close-fitting cap-like hats.
13 Mocking pout.
14 'Do I know, myself?'
15 *Merchant of Venice*, III. i. 48–58.
16 Launched.
17 Dear little thing.
18 A carpenter – a seller of cold meats.
19 Very dependable.
20 Fie, for shame.
21 The mayor's house.
22 As a wedding present.
23 Exquisite.
24 Nest.

THE SWEET O'THE YEAR

Ella Hepworth Dixon

Ella Hepworth Dixon (1857–1932), novelist, short-story writer, editor and journalist, was the daughter of William Hepworth Dixon, respected journalist and editor of the *Athenaeum*. She was educated in London and Heidelberg, and later in Paris, where she studied painting. Part of the circle of contributors to *The Yellow Book*, in which she published several short stories (later collected as *One Doubtful Hour* (1904)), she also contributed articles to *Woman's World*, and later edited *The English-Woman* (1895–1900). Her one novel, *The Story of a Modern Woman* (1894), describes the sacrifice of her own happiness which is made by an independent career woman in order not to betray another woman. She never married, and became increasingly interested in feminist issues later in life. Her autobiography, *As I Knew Them* (1930), discusses her literary acquaintances from the 1890s.

Further reading

Blain *et al.* (1990); Mix (1960); Sutherland (1988)

The Sweet o'the Year

Indoors, in the austere northern light of the studio, one hardly realised that the trees on the boulevard were all a-flutter in their pale green garments, that outside, all over Paris, the fairytale of spring was being told. The only vernal sound which the painter could hear as he worked, was the monotonous cooing of a pair of ring-doves, whose cage hung at the end of the passage, at an open door which gave on a strip of sun-flooded court. Intermittently, he could hear, too, the shuffling of a pair of feet – feet which pottered about in the aimless way of the old and tired. The familiar sound brought up a vision of Virginie, the woman who swept out the studio, kept the models from the door, and made him an excellent *tisane*[1] when he was out of sorts. Yes, Virginie certainly had her uses, although she was old, and shrivelled and unsightly. The young man hummed a love-song of Chaminade's[2] as he stepped away from his picture, screwing up his eyes the better to judge of the values. Poor, bent old Virginie, with the failing memory, the parchment skin, and the formless lips! He was sorry for women – even for old women. Being a Frenchmen, he had an innately tender regard for the sex.

"The world is made for men," he said to himself, "*tiens*,[3] I am glad I was born a man."

And all the while Virginie, busy among her pots and pans at the end of the passage, was thinking about her master. She was proud of his talent, of his success, above all, of his youth and good looks. She rejoiced that, although M. Georges was barely thirty, he was already *hors concours*[4] at the Salon, that he could afford so big a studio. The young men made more money nowadays . . . Why, it was a finer atelier than *he* used to have – the greatest painter of his day in France, the famous Jean Vaillant.

The stove had not yet been lighted, and, in spite of the sunshine outside, it was chilly in the kitchen, where Virginie was scouring the pans. At seventy, after a lifetime of anxiety and of toil; of rising at the dawn, of scrubbing, cleaning, cooking, washing: at seventy, one has no longer much warmth in one's veins. And then the blond, spring sunshine only made her feel dizzy; she had a cough which troubled her, and queer pains in her bones. . . . "Maybe," she nodded to herself, "that it is not for long that I am here. Poor M. Georges."

An imperious ring at the outer bell made her hurry to the door. Her face fell as she encountered a fantastic hat loaded with lilac, a fresh spring toilet,[5] a pair of handsome eyes, and a triumphant smile. She began to grumble.

363

"M. Georges was at home, yes. But he was busy. He was hard at work on a picture. The back-ground of a portrait which must be finished this week. Could not Mademoiselle call again?"

"Ah, but he will see me," declared the Lilac Hat, pushing by and leaving a pungent odour of chypre[6] behind her as she passed, with her rustling silk linings and her overpowering air of femininity. Virginie shuffled after her to the studio door.

"Mlle. Rose," she announced.

The young man threw down his palette and brushes, and turned, his face alight.

As Virginie went back alone down the narrow passage, there was a curious silence in the atelier, broken, at last, by the murmur of soft, happy voices.

"Tas de saletés,"[7] grumbled Virginie, "she'll not let him do any more work to-day." A strange spasm of jealousy seized her. The little incident – though she had often witnessed it before – seemed somehow to accentuate to-day her own senility, her failing powers, her rapid detachment from life. It reminded her, too, of things that had occurred half a century ago. . . . . Well, she would like to show M. Georges that she, too . . . . At any rate, she had the letters still; she would give them to him this afternoon – when Mlle. Rose had gone, before he went out. After all, who should have them except M. Georges? He, at least, would keep them if anything happened to her. . . . . Suddenly the old woman felt a lump at her throat, a curious, choking sensation. She stepped to the window, and pushed it open.

Outside, a light easterly wind was shaking an almond-tree in full blossom, making a fluttering pink cloud against the dear April sky. The ring-doves in their wicker cage were cooing in an amorous ecstasy. . . .

Presently, with her heavy step, she turned into the cupboard which served her for a bed-room. In one corner stood a locked box, dusty with disuse, at which she fumbled nervously with a rusty key. Then, with palsied, trembling fingers, she drew out an ancient packet of letters, tied with a ribbon which had perhaps once been rose-coloured.

By and bye, when the light had lessened, Virginie knocked timidly at the studio-door. Mlle. Rose had been gone some time now, yet there still hung about the room a faint odour of chypre.

"Mais entrez donc, ma vieille!"[8] called out the young painter, kindly, glancing over his shoulder as he stood at his easel. "What is it that you want?"

"Nothing, M. Georges. It is something that I thought you might like to have. You collect such things – letters, autographs. And you, too, are an artist. One day – who knows – you may be as great as him?"

He came forward, surprised, and took the bundle of letters from her shaking fingers – dingy, folded sheets of paper, which had once been fastened by wafers,[9] and which bore the dates of April and May, 1846. Running his eye across some of the yellow pages, covered with faded ink, he glanced at the signatures. "Why, they are priceless!" he cried. "Love-letters from Jean Vaillant? Where, in Heaven's name, did you get them, Virginie?"

"But they are mine! Yes, yes, M. Jean wrote them to me. Ah, but I did not always sweep studios and open doors. . . . . I was pretty once, M. Georges. I was a model. He chose me for his *Baigneuse*.[10] It is in the Luxembourg now; they say it will be in the Louvre. . . . . M. Jean was very fond of me. . . . . *Dame!*[11] that is all nearly fifty years ago, now," she muttered, stooping, with the patient humility of the poor, to pick up some of the yellow sheets which had fallen to the ground.

He knelt down, too, and helped to collect the letters.

"But read them, M. Georges!" A rosy flush of belated feminine pride had crept over her shrunken cheeks. He began to read aloud the letter he held in his hand. It was an intimate revelation of the heart of him whom the younger generation spoke of always as the Master.

"*I want to tell you again how your eyes haunt me, and how I delight in your beauty. . . .*"

She stood there timidly, as he read aloud, with her seamed face, and her little, faded eyes fixed on her master. A white cap was tied beneath her shrivelled chin; a loose camisole covered her shrunken chest, a meagre petticoat revealed her bony ankles.

"*Your beauty, which is so strangely complex, for it has not only a child's sweetness, but a woman's seduction. Ah, you are indeed an exquisite creature. . . .*"

He raised his eyes and looked at the familiar figure of Virginie. . . . . All at once the bent, unsightly form seemed invested with the sweetness, the purity, the dignity of the young girl; round her head, with its sparse white hair, there rested, for an instant, the aureole[12] of the woman who is beloved.

"*Whether you wish it or no, you will be for ever my inspiration, my dream, my reward. I was like a man asleep, and you, Virginie, have awoken me.*"

A feeble smile of satisfied vanity flickered over the old woman's face. She nodded her head as he went on reading, her knotted hands twisted nervously together. Time, with his corroding finger, had seared and branded her out of all semblance of a woman. She represented nothing but the long, the inexorable degradation of life.

"*Nothing will ever make me forget the unearthly beauty of your face, nor the hours we have passed together. . . .*"

Gently the young man laid the letter down. His eyes had filled with tears; he could no longer see the words. And then, reverently, he folded it with the rest, and, opening the drawer of an antique cabinet, he locked his new-found treasures up.

"Sapristi! Mais ce n'est pas amusant – la vie,"[13] he muttered, watching the bent figure of the old woman as she passed, presently, mumbling and nodding, out of the studio, to be swallowed up in the vague shadows of the passage. Suddenly it felt cold and dismal in the great room.

"Non, ce n'est pas gaie, la vie,"[14] he repeated; "at least, not when we live too long. Well, let us make haste to amuse ourselves while we are young."

Rapidly he cleaned up his palette, and put on another coat. Rose had promised to wait for him for dinner, he remembered, and there had even been talk of a ball in the Quartier.

Virginie was patching an old skirt as he passed out by the little kitchen. It had turned much colder, and she had drawn up a chair near the stove.

Gently, deferentially, he took her withered hand and kissed it.

"Hommage à la maîtresse de Jean Vaillant,"[15] he murmured gaily. "Has she any commission for her humble servant?"

The old woman's eyes lit up. Outside, there was already something of the cold serenity of evening in the still, primrose-coloured sky. The ring-doves were silent now, huddled together in their wicker cage, their beaks tucked beneath their wings.

"If monsieur," she said humbly, "would give himself the trouble to bring me a small bottle of some cordial? *Dame!* In the spring one feels chilly, M. Georges. . . . . Yes, the old feel chilly in the spring."

Notes

Text: *The Yellow Book*, vol. ix (April 1896).
1 Herbal tea.
2 Cécile Chaminade (1857–1944) French pianist and composer.
3 Look here.
4 Above the competition.
5 Costume.
6 Sandalwood perfume.
7 Heap of filth.
8 "Come on in, old woman!"
9 Small adhesive discs used for sealing letters before the advent of envelopes.
10 Bather.
11 Well!
12 Halo.
13 "Good God! Life is not amusing."
14 "No, life is not happy."
15 "Homage to the mistress of Jean Vaillant."

ANOTHER FREAK

Mary Angela Dickens

Mary Angela Dickens (1862–1948), novelist and short-story writer, was the eldest grandchild of Charles Dickens. She started publishing fiction in his periodical *All the Year Round*, which was edited by her father, Charles Dickens Jnr. Her novels and stories – collected in *Some Women's Ways* (1896) – deal mainly with lost love, unhappy marriages and overwhelming passion. Of her longer fiction, *Cross Currents* (1891) was the most successful, but she also published *A Mere Cypher* (1893), *A Valiant Ignorance* (1894), *Prisoners of Silence* (1895), *Against the Tide* (1897), *On the Edge of a Precipice* (1899) and *Unveiled* (1906). She became a Roman Catholic towards the end of her life, and her later works, *The Debtor* (1912) and *Sanctuary* (1916), confront religious issues.

Further reading

Blain *et al.* (1990); Sutherland (1988).

Another Freak

I

It was a very attractive room – a drawing room, perfectly harmonious as to colour and decoration, eminently up-to-date as to fittings; but the only expression in the eyes of its solitary occupant was one of vague dissatisfaction.

Mrs. Smith-Clouston stood by the fern-filled fire-place, and looked protestingly about her. She was intimately acquainted with the room. Also, she had been waiting now for nearly half-an-hour. She was a little, faded, bored-looking women; perfectly "turned out," as she would have said to herself, from the crown of her bonnet to the soles of her shoes.

Looking idly for something wherewith to amuse herself, her attention was caught by a newspaper lying on a quaint Chippendale escritoire.[1] She sauntered across; and then she stopped, and a spark of interest came into her pale eyes. On the ledge of the escritoire, arranged there by the servant, were two letters, which had arrived by the last post. One was addressed to "Miss Heseltine, 115, Bruton Street, W.," in a strong, upright, man's hand; the other, in sprawling, illiterate characters, to "Miss Heseltine, 115, Bruton Street, Hyde Park, London." The latter Mrs. Smith-Clouston merely glanced at with the slightest possible shrug of her shoulders. It was the former upon which her eyes were fastened with lively curiosity.

"I wonder whether she means it?" she said to herself. "It looks like it. It looks – "

"Mary says you've been waiting ages, Alice! How you must have been reviling me!"

It was a strong, full voice that uttered these words as the door opened; musical, in spite of a certain hardness about its careless tones; and it harmonized curiously with the appearance of the woman to whom it belonged.

She was a woman in whom the evanescent charm of girlhood, with its inexperiences, ignorances, and assumptions, had passed into a maturity which was just entering upon its most perfect stage. She was tall, well-proportioned, graceful with the unconscious ease of absolute self-possession, in spite of certain little brusqueries of manner. Her features were excellent: but no one on first meeting Bride Heseltine ever thought of her as handsome. Exactly what constituted her charm her friends would have been puzzled to say. They might have declared that she was brilliant, eccentric, kind-hearted, a good talker, a good listener, or what not, each according to his or her individual fancy; and none of their statements would have accurately represented the fact.

She sat down at the tea-table now, and drew off her gloves with deft, vigorous movements. She was dressed with the same perfection of fashionable details as was her visitor; but an unconscious emanation of originality blended her very clothes into a characteristic whole, and beside her Mrs. Smith-Clouston looked like a doll dressed from a fashion-plate. The protesting annoyance of expression with which the latter had turned to receive her hostess died feebly out, and Mrs. Smith-Clouston subsided into an easy-chair, saying with mild reproach;

"I know no one in London but you, Bride, who would have the face to waste half-an-hour of another woman's time in the busiest week of June; and I know no one but you for whom I would have waited."

Miss Heseltine laughed slightly. Society woman as she was, she did not appear to have a vast amount of respect for Society's "business."

"I expected to be in an hour ago," she said carelessly. "Well, now, tell me about the Cholmondeley's dinner last night. Was it amusing? And had they those new flower things? I want to use them next week, and I shan't if they have appeared already."

"Who have you got?" inquired Mrs. Smith-Clouston, ignoring the Cholmondeleys.

Miss Heseltine leant back in her chair, and clasped her hands behind her head with a fine, unconstrained gesture.

"Yourselves," she said, "and the Berkeleys, and Arthur Gordon. The others haven't answered yet. Any letters waiting for me, I wonder?"

She rose, and walked across the room.

Mrs. Smith-Clouston did not speak, but her eyes brightened a little as they followed the vigorous figure.

Miss Heseltine reached the escritoire, and stopped short, standing for perhaps a second looking down at the letters awaiting her. Then she turned away without touching them.

"Answers?" said Mrs. Smith-Clouston.

"No."

"Don't let me prevent your reading them, dear."

"They are not pressing – thanks."

The words were carelessly, almost brusquely uttered; and, as she spoke them, Miss Heseltine came back to her chair. She seemed to have passed into a reflective mood, and as Mrs. Smith-Clouston watched her, that lady's face became quite animated and shrewd with ardent curiosity. It was she who broke the silence.

"If you keep your visitors waiting for half-an-hour, Bride," she said, with a little laugh, but with eyes that were observant of Miss Heseltine, "they will inevitably look about the room for entertainment. Looking at that newspaper over there, my eye was caught by your letters, and I'm curious about your country correspondent. Another freak?"[2]

Miss Heseltine roused herself.

"I really don't know," she said deliberately. "I never considered the question. She is a girl at Abbotsmead – I had a house there last summer, you know. We are by way of being friends."

"Friends!" ejaculated Mrs. Smith-Clouston, with an indescribable intonation. "Really, Bride!"

"Friends," repeated Miss Heseltine, with an absolute disregard of the effect her words produced. "She interests me. She is a girl with a story."

"The usual story?" inquired Mrs. Smith-Clouston nonchalantly.

Miss Heseltine flashed one quick look at her, and nodded.

"Yes," she said, "the usual story, so far! I have a fancy for altering the end."

"Ah," returned Mrs Smith-Clouston; "that's very like you, Bride." She paused, and then added, "The other letter is from Stephen Gore, isn't it?"

"Yes."

Miss Heseltine changed her position, and, stretching out one hand, began to play with her teaspoon. It was a restless, more truly, perhaps, a sensitive movement; and it harmonized oddly with the general power and decision of the womanly personality. Apparently Mrs. Smith-Clouston found herself emboldened by it.

"Don't Stephen Gore's letters demand a little more interest from you?" she inquired, with a mixture of assertion and tentativeness, "Or, perhaps – perhaps you are paying that one the supreme compliment of desiring to read it when you are alone?"

Miss Heseltine lifted her eyes and looked at the other woman. Then she turned her face slowly away. She did not speak a word.

Mrs. Smith-Clouston's little *blasé*[3] face actually flushed, with an excitement not untouched by amusement.

"Considering that you met him at my house, Bride," she said softly, "and that you and I were girls together, I think – I can't help thinking – that you might tell me – " She let her words die away into an expressive silence, and there was a pause. Then Miss Heseltine said, in an odd, uneven tone;

"Tell you what, Alice?"

"Well, whether – you really mean it."

"Does it seem such an extraordinary thing?" The grey eyes were turned for an instant full upon Mrs. Smith-Clouston, and there was a flash of irrepressible humour in them. There was humour, too, in the brusque question, but the voice was not quite steady, and Miss Heseltine's features twitched slightly.

"I think it perfect," responded Mrs. Smith-Clouston promptly. "Extraordinary? Not in the least! But is it really so, Bride, has he spoken?"

Miss Heseltine's eyes were fixed upon the little tea-table, but she was not fidgeting now.

"Not yet," she said, in a low voice.

"But – you know he means to?"

"Yes."

"And – ?"

"Yes!"

Miss Heseltine rose abruptly as she spoke, and walked away to the window. Mrs. Smith-Clouston contemplated her with the covert amusement in her face deepening. Then she too rose, crossed the room to Miss Heseltine, and put a small gloved hand affectionately on her arm. It was trembling a little, and she patted it gently.

"I'm so glad, dear," she said. "So delighted! I consider it quite the most perfect thing I've heard of for a long time! You'll let me know as soon as it comes off? I shall be on thorns."

"In case it should not come off?" said Miss Heseltine, turning with a rather tremulous and uncertain laugh, and an obvious struggle for her ordinary demeanour. "Seriously, Alice, it's rather absurd for a woman of my age to fall in love, don't you think?"

"You know very well that I don't think any such thing, Bride. It is just the one thing you wanted, don't you know. And Stephen Gore is just the kind of man to be fallen in love with, too. So clever, and so popular, and so well off! Lots of women have cared for him, to my knowledge – only he has never responded. Oh, we've known him a long time. He used to come to our house before he came into his money and changed his name. Didn't you know about that?" as a slight sound of surprise came from Miss Heseltine. "Oh yes, it was about five years ago. He was awfully poor then – just the same brilliant, attractive creature, but too poor to get a start, I suppose, for he never did anything that I know of. His name then was Baker – Stephen Baker."

"What!"

Miss Heseltine had been leaning one arm on the escritoire playing idly with the two unopened letters on the ledge; and as the last words passed Mrs. Smith-Clouston lips she had lifted herself suddenly. She was standing erect now, the letters clenched in her hand as though every nerve and muscle had suddenly contracted.

There was a moment's pause. Mrs. Smith-Clouston felt vaguely bewildered. Before she could collect herself Miss Heseltine said slowly, and in a strange, grating voice, "Say that again, Alice. I – didn't understand!"

"About Stephen Gore's name? It's quite simple. His father was a Mr Baker – it was a good family, but horribly poor, as I said. And your Stephen was Stephen Baker until about five years ago, when he came into a heap of money on condition that he took the name of Gore. That's all."

"I – see!" said Miss Heseltine. She seemed to speak with difficulty. "It's a common name, isn't it, Alice?"

"There are Bakers and Bakers, certainly," returned Mrs. Smith-Clouston.

"But he is one of the right ones, I assure you. And now I really must go, dear! Good-bye! Again and again, so glad!"

She kissed Miss Heseltine with effusion, and was rather surprised to find her embrace only mechanically returned. A few moments later the front door closed upon her, and Miss Heseltine turned and went slowly back into the drawing-room.

Her face had changed in the last few moments strangely and completely. It was quite white. She lifted her hand to her head, forgetting, apparently, the letters crushed within it. They fell at her feet, and she stood staring down at them. "It's a common name," she said, half aloud – "a common name!"

At that instant the front-door bell rang sharply, and the sound seemed to break up at once all the strange numbness that hung about her. With every line of her face quivering and working, she sprang across the room to the door, and called to the servant who was crossing the hall in a whisper which arrested the woman's attention instantly –

"If that is Mr. Gore, tell him I cannot see him now. To-morrow – at this time, to-morrow – tell him." Then she turned and went rapidly on up the stairs.

II

Miss Heseltine's drawing-room was empty when, at half-past five on the following afternoon, Mr. Stephen Gore was shown into it.

Stephen Gore had been described as a "good-looking fellow" ever since he emerged from boyhood; and now, at forty-three, he remained a "good-looking fellow" still. He was tall, well built, and well set up; and the slight touch of grey about his temples gave additional character to his face. His features were rather worn and lined, as though he had lived vigorously. His eyes were very pleasant, full of fire, full of thought; at this particular moment full of something deeper still. It was a clever face, and yet Stephen Gore had never "done anything"; he had made no conspicuous use even of his unexpected wealth, or the position it brought him, except to enjoy. There were lines about his mouth which five years before had threatened to tinge his whole expression with the cynicism of a man who feels that Fate has been hard on him; and though since then Fate had changed her tactics, the traces of her earlier dealings with him were not wholly to be effaced.

He stood upon Miss Heseltine's hearthrug, with his eyes intently fixed upon the door; but he started violently as a touch fell on the handle. Then, as the door opened and Miss Heseltine appeared, he moved quickly forward.

"Thank you for letting me come!" he said.

Miss Heseltine had come in very quietly, and she gave him her hand in silence. She was very pale, and perhaps it was her pallor which gave so strange an expression to her face. She moved, as soon as he released her hand, and sat down with her back to the window.

"Won't you sit down?" she said.

Trivial as were the words, the tone was noticeable. All the rather hard decision usually characteristic of her voice was absent; it was dignified, composed, and indescribably womanly.

It made a quite indefinite impression upon Stephen Gore. He seated himself in silence, and then said, with an instinctive softening of his own voice:

"It was stupid of me to come yesterday! It was my mistake, of course, but I understood – "

"You were quite right," she interrupted, in a low voice. "I said – yesterday."

There was a moment's pause, and then Stephen Gore leaned forward.

"Will it seem rough to you," he said, "if I say – may I come to the point at once? I think – I hope – you know the question I have come to ask you. However you answer it, I thank you for letting me ask it."

He paused to master a huskiness in his voice – the outcome of an emotion to which he would not give rein – and then continued;

"I've nothing to offer you – nothing that you respect. It was one of your first charms for me that you made me realize what an idle, good-for-nothing fellow I am! But I love you, though I'm not a young man, as – perhaps, no young man can love. Will you be my wife?"

His voice rang with a depth of feeling which no young man, as he said, could have touched. His eyes, dark with self-restraint and suspense, looked full into hers, and on the dead silence that followed there fell a singular sound – a hardly audible sob. Miss Heseltine sat quite still, her hand clutched round the arm of her chair, her pale face a little drawn.

"Do you love me?"

There had been a long pause before the words came from her: a pause during which Stephen Gore's breath had come quick and short. And as she uttered them slowly, he leaned impulsively forward.

"You know I love you!" he said, speaking with a hardly-restrained impetuosity, which seemed to sweep away all convention and lay bare their relation each to the other. "Bride, you know it! You hold all that's best in me – not that there's much, God knows. But there is something. If you love me you could make what you like of me. Good heavens, how can a man put his very heartbeats into words?"

He had started to his feet, struggling fiercely with the passion which palpitated in every bare and broken sentence. And, as he stood looking down on her, Miss Heseltine raised her eyes to his face.

"Then you will be honest with me," she said. She moved for the first time, drawing herself upright in her chair. Something in her manner, or in the depths of her grey eyes, seemed suddenly to check Stephen Gore's excitement. He stood motionless, looking down at her, as she went on in a steady, rather hoarse voice.

"Two summers ago," she said, looking, not at him, but straight before her,

"I had a house at Abbotsmead, in Somersetshire. It is a quaint little village, and I used to go about a good deal and see after the people. There was – there is – a girl named Lucy Gibson there, in whom I took an interest. She was a kind of pariah. It is a respectable village, and she is a blot on its reputation. I made friends with her – with much difficulty, for she is very shy and shrinking – and she told me her story. It is the usual story. A man – a gentleman – staying at the inn for the fishing; an ignorant, credulous, easily-flattered girl. Lucy's powers of description are limited. She told me nothing definite about the man, except" – Miss Heseltine's voice grew a little faint – "his name, and that he lived in London. And I determined when I came back to town to find him, if I could."

Miss Heseltine paused. She had gone steadily on from sentence to sentence with no break of any kind. She did not move now, or glance at the figure by her side.

"The name she gave me was Stephen Baker," she said. "I was told yesterday that, five years ago, that was your name."

There was a moment's heavy silence. Over Stephen Gore's eager face a dull flush had stolen. He turned away, and stood with his head bent down, leaning one arm on the mantelpiece.

"Be as lenient with me as you can," he said, between his set teeth.

Miss Heseltine's head was bowed for a moment, like that of a woman in extremity of physical pain. Then she lifted it again, her pale face quite quiet. She raised her hand and pushed the hair from her forehead.

"I knew it," she said.

A long, long pause. The man stood with his head bent lower yet; the woman sat quite still, a strange absorbed look on her face. At last Stephen Gore turned suddenly.

"What can I say?" he said, with a gesture of passionate appeal. "What can I say? We are not boy and girl, Bride. You are a woman. It is because you are so large-souled a woman, because your nature is so complete on all its lines, that you have all my heart. You know – the purest woman on this earth can't but know – what brutes men are. I've been as bad as most – worse, perhaps. There was not much hope of married life for me when I was a young man – not much hope of any kind. If I had told you this in a general way – it's not an uncommon confession, Heaven knows! – you would have forgiven me, wouldn't you? You could have taken it for granted?"

"I am afraid it is possible."

The words came from her in a low voice, full of self-condemnation, full of self-contempt. But the words only reached Stephen Gore's ears. He took a quick step towards her.

"Then couldn't you – can't you – "

She stopped him with a peremptory movement of her hand, turning her face towards him at last, as she rose to her feet, her eyes flashing.

"No," she said: "thank God, I can't! It is because we do take these things for granted, we women who should know better, who should be stronger, that you men continue, as you said just now, brutes."

He drew back a pace as though she had struck him, and they stood for an instant face to face – man and woman confronted on the common ground of humanity. Then she went on;

"What I have meant to say to Stephen Baker, whenever I should meet him, I say to him now. If you have any manhood in you, if you have any sense of justice and honour, if right and wrong are anything more to you than the playthings of the moment, take the one straight course that is open to you. Share the punishment as you brought about the sin. Make Lucy Gibson your wife. Ah!" – as a startled, incredulous exclamation broke from him – "that's your first impulse, of course! The thing seems to you incredible, inconceivable! More shame to us all, men and women alike, that it should be so! You said just now that I could make what I liked of you. That is what I would make of you then – an honest man, and Lucy's husband."

She turned away from him with a strange impetuous gesture, as though the feeling that shook her voice demanded some kind of physical relief. There was an interval before either spoke again. Stephen Gore stood with his clenched hand resting on the back of a chair, his face at once alert and set, as in intense realization of the necessities of the moment. It was he who broke the silence.

"What you propose is possible, of course, from one point of view. But what is gained by it?"

"Justice!"

"Justice is a delicate thing to administer when you come to details. It is a safer thing to temper it with mercy."

He turned a chair towards her, and she sank into it unconsciously with her eyes fixed on him, as he leaned one arm on the mantelpiece and went on the same reasoning tone strongly touched with appeal.

"Look at it, Bride, from both sides! Suppose I were to marry – Lucy Gibson? The wrong is not undone by that; only a conventional varnish is applied. The girl is 'righted'; but – what about the man – the man who must destroy his every prospect and hope in life in the process? Is that justice? Consider what it is you hold in your hands – what it is you are destroying – and destroying for a set of phrases merely. You dominate me as no influence has ever dominated me before. You draw out all that is best in me. I've made nothing of my life! When I was young I didn't get a chance. When things altered I didn't care! But there is still time! You give me new thoughts, higher thoughts, true thoughts of life and all that it holds. With you I might do something, even yet. But, if you throw me over, all that goes under for ever! Bride, for God's sake have pity on me! Let us cover up the past! Let me atone in any other way! But – marry me!"

She had grown whiter as he spoke, but she never moved her eyes from his face, and they looked full into his as she answered steadily;

"Nothing can cover up the past! There is no other way!"

"No other way than ruin? No other way than utter damnation?"

The words were a fierce demand, and the colour flushed suddenly into Bride Heseltine's face as she answered it.

"What other way is there for the woman?" she cried passionately. "Oh, you men! You cowards! Ruin! Damnation! that is what you bring to a woman, without pity, without remorse, just for your pleasure! Ah! if it meant for you what it means for the woman – if you lost all as she loses all – these things would cease to be!"

Before the bitter denunciation of her voice and words he faltered, silent and abashed, though unconvinced. Then he turned back to his original argument.

"It could do no good – no real good!" he urged. "It is only in name that she would be the better."

"It is you who would be the better!" said Miss Heseltine. The sudden passion had faded from her face, leaving it white and quivering with earnestness as she lifted it to him. "It is of you I'm thinking most! You have done hideously wrong! You are as degraded in my eyes as – as is my poor Lucy in the eyes of all good women! Do the one right thing possible! Own that you've done wrong, and bear your punishment."

"It would be quixotic!"[4]

"Perhaps! Most of the things worth doing in this world are extinguished under some such label. It is the abuses of life that are called expedient, practical, necessary! It is 'necessary,' we are told, that women like Lucy should be a hopeless class, apart for ever; it is 'necessary' that the crime of the men who have tempted them should be condoned! Obviously, therefore, it must be quixotic and preposterous to try to remedy such a state of things?"

He stretched out his hand and caught hers with a desperate movement.

"Bride!" he cried hoarsely, "Bride, even if it is so – even if these things are the abuse they seem to you – what good can one man do? Things will remain as they are for anything that you and I can do! Don't sacrifice me to a theory!"

She paused a moment, her scathing passion arrested by the agony of his tone. She lifted her other hand and laid it on his breast.

"One man can do his share!" she said. "There may come a moment to any human being when his hand must touch one of the great wrongs of the world, and touching it, must lighten it or press it down. The pressure, the lightening may be imperceptible. It is the impulse in ourselves that is the point. Use the force that is in you for the right!"

She stopped; and they stood, his right hand holding her left, his left hand closed over her right as it lay upon his breast. The breath of each was coming thick and fast, and each saw nothing but the other's eyes. Then she went on again, and her voice was strong and gentle.

"But it is not sacrificing you," she said; "not the best part of you! No man deteriorates from having done the right thing. The doing of this will do more for you than I could ever do. It is because I believe, with all my heart, that you have more in you than has ever shown itself, that you are capable of great things, that I beg you to lay this one sure foundation. Without it nothing good could come. Stephen, for my sake!"

Their faces were very close together, and he was holding her in a clasp that grew unconsciously tighter and tighter.

"Do you love me, Bride?" he said.

"Yes."

"And you will never marry me?"

"Never!"

Then quite suddenly there surged over his face the dull-red flush of furious anger, and he released her almost roughly.

"Then there is no more to be said!" he said thickly. "For the rest – it is absolutely out of the question!"

An instant later the door had closed behind him.

III

"Dear Miss,

"This is to say that he come back yesterday, and I'm an honest woman, dear Miss, since this morning. Nothing can't undo what's done nor give me happiness. And it's but just it shouldn't, me having been a bad girl. He hasn't no love for me, and he and me will live parted, always. It came to me as perhaps I didn't ought to have let him do it; but he said it was your wish, and, dear Miss, this is what I write to say, that he told me it was your doing. And I wish to thank you, oh, dear, dear Miss, most hearty and humble for your kindness. He told me most particular that I was to let you know as we was married.

"I am, dear Miss,

"Your ever grateful and obedient.

"Lucy"

It was late – nearly two o'clock in the morning. Miss Heseltine stood alone in her drawing-room, the cloak in which she had just come in from a dance still about her. Just a week had passed since she had stood there face to face with Stephen Gore – since Stephen Gore had disappeared suddenly from the London world in the height of the London season. Miss Heseltine had come up the stairs and into the room with a slow and weary step, to find the letter which she held now open in her hand, lying on the edge of the escritoire where those other letters had lain a week ago.

She read the letter through, and a sudden flush rushed over her face. Then she stood there, gazing down at it, the flush slowly fading. Her face was white to the lips when she lifted it at last, tired to the uttermost. There was a strange blind look in her grey eyes as she moved mechanically, turned out the lamp and went to her room.

The world – that minute section of it, that is to say, that had expected a rather interesting wedding – considered itself much aggrieved when it found that no wedding was forthcoming, and expressed itself freely on the subject: not, however, to the two people most nearly concerned. Mrs. Smith-Clouston was particularly fluent on the subject.

"My dear, don't talk of it!" she said. "Extraordinary? She was always full of freaks, and now I think she's mad! Oh yes, it must have been her fault, of course! No doubt she refused him. Well, she'll be sorry by and by. He's gone out to India with some appointment or other, and they say he'll be a big man after all."

Notes

Text: *Some Women's Ways*, Jarrold, London, 1896.
1 Writing desk.
2 Personal whim or caprice.
3 Bored, indifferent.
4 Unrealistically idealistic.

THE OTHER ANNA

Evelyn Sharp

Evelyn Sharp, later Nevinson (1869–1955), short-story writer, novelist, journalist, suffragist, began her working life as a teacher. She published six stories in *The Yellow Book* and became a member of its circle. Her feminist ideas led her to support the women's suffrage movement. Her first novel, *At the Relton Arms*, appeared in 1896, and she later published another novel, *Nicolette* (1907), and *Rebel Women* (1910), a collection of stories fictionalising her own experience as a suffragist. She was imprisoned for suffragist activities in 1911. Her autobiography, *An Unfinished Adventure,* describing these activities as well as her quest for personal independence, was published in 1933. The same year, at the age of 64, she married Henry Nevinson, who had been a friend for over 30 years.

Further reading

Blain *et al.* (1990); Mix (1960).

The Other Anna

There were flights and flights of wide, cold, dreary stone stairs, and at the top of them three studios in a row. Pinned on the door of the furthest one was a notice to the effect that the owner had gone out to lunch and would not be back until two, and it was this that caused the discontent on the face of the girl who sat on the edge of the stairs, drumming her toes impatiently on the step below.

"And I promised to be here at half-past one," she grumbled, shivering a little as she spoke; and she got up and paced the landing quickly, and stamped her feet to keep warm. A man opened the door of the middle studio with a jerk, and looked out.

"Are you waiting for anybody? Hadn't you better go away and come again presently? Mr. Hallaford won't be back for another half-hour," he said, in short rapid sentences. There was a frown on his face, but whether it came from nervousness or annoyance she could not tell. It was evident, though, that she worried him by being there, for it was the second time he had spoken to her; and she gave her chin the slightest tilt into the air as she answered him.

"Go away? Down all those stairs? I couldn't really!" she said with an irritating smile.

"Oh well," began the man, frowning again, "if you like hanging about – "

"I don't like it a bit," she assured him, earnestly. "It is the stupidest occupation imaginable. You should just try it and see!"

But this he showed no anxiety to do, for the mere suggestion precipitated him into his studio again, and she concluded that the frown must have been nervousness after all. She returned to her seat on the stairs, but had hardly settled herself in her corner when the door opened behind her once more, and the owner of the middle studio was again jerking out his abrupt remarks at her back.

"It's no use staying out there in the cold," he said, as though she were somehow morally responsible for the inclemency of the weather. "There's a fire in here, and my model hasn't come back yet. You can come in and wait, if you like."

"All right; I don't mind if I do," she said carelessly, and followed him in. Common gratitude or even civility, she felt, would have been wasted on a man who threw his hospitality at her head; and it was only the unfriendliness of the stone stairs outside, and perhaps her desire for adventure as well, that made her accept his offer at all. But when he did not even trouble to give her a chair, and resumed his occupation of stretching a paper on a board without noticing her in the least, Anna began to feel puzzled as well as slighted. He was certainly odd, and she always liked odd people; he might be nervous into the bargain, and nervousness was a failing so far removed from her own personality that she was always inclined to tolerate it in another; but neither nerves nor eccentricity could quite explain his want of manners, and she had never had to endure discourtesy from a man before. She prepared resentfully to assert herself, but before she had time to choose her words a sudden suspicion darted into her mind. This was a studio, and the owner of it was an artist, and he had found her hanging about another man's studio. How could he be supposed to know that she was only having her portrait painted, and was not a professional model at all? The idea, when she had once grasped it, amused her immensely; and she resolved impulsively to play the part he expected from her. The adventure was promising well, she thought.

"What fun!" she said aloud, and her host glanced up at her and frowned. Of course, she wanted him to frivol with her, and he did not mean to be frivoled with. So he said nothing to encourage her, and she sat down and scanned the room critically. It was very bare, and rather dusty.

"I suppose it's because you're a man," she observed, suddenly. She was only finishing her thoughts out loud, but to him it sounded like another attempt to draw him into conversation, and he felt irritated by her persistence. He never wanted to talk much at any time, and his attitude towards the confidences of his models was one of absolute indifference. He did not care to know why they had become models, nor how their people had lost their money, nor what sort of homes they had; they were there to be drawn, that was all. But he realised vaguely that Anna was there by his invitation, and he made an effort to be civil.

"It accounts for most of my actions, yes," he said, and set down the board and began filling his pipe.

"I mean," she explained, "that if you were a woman you might make this place look awfully nice. You could have flowers, for instance, and – "

"Oh yes," he interrupted; "and photographs, and muslin, and screens."

"Well, you might," she said, calmly. "But I shouldn't. Flowers would be enough for me, and perhaps a broom and a duster. But then, I'm not a man."

"No," he said, just as calmly. "If you were, you would know that one does not take one's suggestions about these things from a woman."

Even in her assumed character she was not quite prepared for the scant courtesy of his reply, and he inferred from her silence that he had succeeded in quenching her at last. But when he glanced at her over his shoulder, he was rather disconcerted at finding her eyes fixed on his face with an astonished look in them. He was always absent-minded, and when he was not at work he was unobservant as well; and he asked himself doubtfully whether her cheeks had been quite so pink before he made his last remark. Any other man would have noticed long ago that she had not the manner or the air of the ordinary model; but Askett did not trouble to argue the point even for his own satisfaction. She was a little more ladylike than most of them, perhaps, but she resembled the rest of her class in wanting to chatter, and that in itself justified his abruptness. So there was a pause that was a little awkward, and then his model came in – an old man in a slouched hat and a worn brown coat.

"What a musty old subject to choose!" she commented, and got up instantly and walked away to the door.

"Wouldn't you care to wait until Hallaford comes back?" asked her host, a little less morosely. "I can go on working all the same, as long as you don't talk."

"I shouldn't think of it," she said, emphatically. "I am quite sure you wouldn't be able to endure another suggestion from me, and I really couldn't promise not to make one."

He could have sworn that her last words were accompanied by a lightning glance round the room, but her expression, when she turned at the door and looked at him was almost vacant in its innocence. He followed her hastily, and opened the door for her.

"You'd better wait," he said, involuntarily. "You'll catch cold or something out there."

She flashed a mocking look up in his face.

"Don't you think," she observed, demurely, "that that is one of the things about which one does not want suggestions from a man?"

Ten minutes later, she was accepting a torrent of apologies from Tom Hallaford with a queenly forgiveness that she knew by experience to be the most effective weapon at her command.

"If you weren't such an awful brick you'd never sit to me again," he avowed, humbly. "To drag you all this way, and then – ! Wasn't it beastly cold too?"

"It was cold," Anna admitted, gently. "But I didn't mind much."

And when he began afresh to abase himself, and made the confusing statement that he ought to be shot and was hanged, she felt he had suffered sufficiently, and she interrupted him by a true account of how she had spent the last half-hour.

"Well, I'm bothered!" he said. "Of course, Askett thought you were a model, a *paid* model, don't you see; and he thought it was just cheek of you to say his studio was dirty and all that. So it would have been rather, don't you know, if you'd been an ordinary model; they want jumping on sometimes. I say, Miss Angell," he added, chuckling, "what larks if Askett comes in when you've gone, and asks me for your address! Ten to one he does. What shall I say?"

"I don't fancy," said Anna, quietly, "that he will want to know."

Nevertheless, as she was hurrying past the door of the middle studio, two hours later, Askett came out hastily and called her back.

"Is all your time filled for the present?" he asked, "or could you sit to me next week, in the afternoon?"

A gleam of mischief lurked in her eyes, but he was still unsuspecting, and he mistook her hesitation for reflection.

"I could come next week," she said. "What time?"

"Two o'clock on Monday. And you can give me your name and address so that I shall know where to write to you. You'll very likely forget all about it."

"Do you really think that's possible?" smiled Anna. Askett said nothing, but looked over her head at the wall as though she were not there at all, and waited for her reply. Anna was racking her brains for a name that would be likely to belong to a model.

"Well?" he said, impatiently.

"Oh, you want my name?" said Anna, desperately. "Well, my address is care of Miss Anna Angell, 25 Beaconsfield Mansions, Belgravia. And my name is – is Poppy – Poppy Wilson. Oh dear! that's wrong – I mean – "

He was staring at her, for the first time, with something approaching ordinary human interest.

"There seems to be a difficulty about the name," he remarked. He was not surprised at all; she had probably quarrelled with her family – models always had – and so was afraid to give her real name. He put down her confusion to the fact that she had not been sitting long, and was new at the deception. "What's the matter with Wilson?" he asked, not unkindly. "It's a very nice name, isn't it?"

"Oh, Wilson's all right," she hastened to assure him. "It's the Poppy that's wrong; I mean, it's my pet name, don't you see, and it wouldn't do."

"No," he said, dryly. "Perhaps it wouldn't."

"My real name is Anna," she continued, "Anna Wilson. You understand, don't you?" Even for the sake of the disguise, she could not endure that he should think of her as Poppy.

"Real name Anna, pet name Poppy, address care of Miss Anna – hullo?" he stopped writing on his cuff and looked down at her sternly. "You seem to have the same name as the elderly lady who looks after you. How's this? I don't believe your name is Anna at all."

This was a little hard, as it was the only true statement she had made.

"My name *is* Anna," she said, indignantly. "And so is hers. It's only a coincidence that we both have the same name; in fact, it was because of that we first made friends, years ago at school. You see, we began by being at school together, and we've been together every since, more or less. And – when I left home, she let me come and live in her flat, that's all. It doesn't seem odd to me, but perhaps you don't know much about girls' Christian names? And she isn't elderly at all! She's young, and rather pretty, and – "

"Oh, all right; I don't care what she's like. Don't forget about Monday; and look here, you can come in that hat; it's rather nice. Good-bye."

"I shall wear my very oldest hat and all the clothes that don't suit me," she resolved, rebelliously, as she went downstairs.

She surprised her maid very much at dinner-time, that evening, by laughing softly to herself at intervals; and she might have been discovered, more than once, with her elbows on the mantelshelf, gazing at the reflection of herself in the mirror. But as the evening wore on she became, first fretful, then sober, then determined; and she went to bed with a carefully composed letter in her head, which was to be sent without fail on the following morning. She came down to breakfast and wrote it; kept it till lunch-time, and stamped it; re-read it at tea-time, and burnt it. She was very cross all the evening, and decided that she was run down, and wanted a change. The next morning she was convinced she had influenza, and took a large dose of ammoniated quinine, and sent a special messenger to her greatest friend. Her greatest friend was out of town, which reminded her that she wanted a change, and she telegraphed to Brighton for rooms. The reply came that they would be vacant on Monday, and she wired back that she did not want them at all. The next day was Sunday and her At Home day; and she came to the conclusion that her circle of friends was a very dull one, and that no one who was a bit nice ever called on her At Home day, and that the only interesting people were the people who never called on one at all, the people, in fact, whom one met in odd ways without any introduction; and at this point of her reflections she laughed unaccountably, and resolved to give up her At Home day. She had made two engagements with two separate friends for Monday afternoon; but when it came, she threw them both over and started for a walk across the park at half-past one. At a quarter to two she hailed a hansom in the Bayswater road, and told the cabman to drive quickly, and at his own not unreasonable request supplied him further with an address in the West of London. And at two precisely, she was toiling up the long flights of stone stairs that led to Askett's studio, wondering crossly what had induced her to embark on such an absurd enterprise, and still more what was making her persist in it now.

"It's quite reasonable to undertake to do a mad thing one day, but to go and *do* it the next is unpardonable," she grumbled to herself, as she knocked at the door of the middle studio. She remembered with relief that Tom Hallaford had gone abroad for a few weeks, which considerably lessened the chances of detection and for the rest – it was an adventure, and that was always something. So it was her usual smiling, rather impudent face that finally greeted Askett when he opened the door to her.

"So you didn't forget, after all? Made sure you would," he observed. "People who forget their own names can forget anything."

"I didn't forget my own name," said Anna, truthfully, a remark of which he naturally missed the point.

They did not talk at all for the first hour or so, and Anna began to feel distinctly bored. Being a model was not half so much fun as she had expected to find it, and it made her extremely sleepy. She had hoped for a new sensation, and the only one she felt was an overwhelming dulness. Nothing but her sense of the ridiculous prevented her from throwing up the whole game on the spot, but a single glance at his stern, uncompromising features kept her silent. "Just imagine how he would sneer!" she thought; and the mere idea made her toss her head and laugh scornfully.

"Keep still, please," he said, inexorably. "What's the joke?"

"That is precisely what I can't tell you," said Anna, laughing again. "If I did it wouldn't be a joke at all, you see."

"I'm afraid I don't, but that may be because I haven't known you long enough to have grasped your system of conversation. It's rather difficult to talk to a person who only tells you the ends of her thoughts, as it were. If I were a conjurer, or a medium, or somebody like that, it might be all right."

"It isn't half so difficult as talking to a person who doesn't talk at all," retorted his model.

"Perhaps not," said Askett, indifferently. "Will you kindly lower your chin a little, it has a tendency to – thanks. You were saying – "

"I was saying that conversation with a person who is only interested in your stupid chin isn't any fun at all," said Anna, who was beginning to feel both tired and cross. Askett glanced at her with a look of mild surprise.

"Then why be a model?" was all he said.

"That's exactly what I want to know myself. I mean," she added, hastily, "it isn't my fault. I – I wouldn't be a model if I could help it, but I can't."

"Models can never help it," said Askett, sceptically. "Troubles at home, I suppose? Your friends don't know you sit? I thought so. Never knew you'd have to come to this, and so on. Of course, yes."

"You're very unfeeling," remarked Anna, who had assented by nods the touching story of her life as related by Askett. "You should try being a model for an afternoon, and then you'd know."

"My dear young lady, one occupation at a time is always enough for a man," said Askett quietly. "Probably that is why I am interested merely in your features. Does the elderly lady, I mean the other Anna, know that you are a model?"

"Yes, she does," said Anna, fervently. "She doesn't like my doing it at all; but how can I help it? She thinks it is too hard work, and I *quite* agree with her."

"If you don't mind," said Askett, who had not been listening, "I wish you would keep to subjects that don't excite you quite so much. Whenever you are being smart, or funny, or injured, you poke your chin in the air; and it's disconcerting. Supposing you were to think of some quiet elderly topic, such as cats, or politics, or the lesser clergy?"

"Perhaps, if I were to think of nothing to say at all, you would like it better," cried Anna.

"Perhaps," said Askett, with a stony indifference.

"I may as well tell you," continued Anna, controlling her indignation with difficulty, "that whenever I am silent I have a most *horrible* expression."

"Never mind about the expression," said Askett. "That's my business, not yours. Sulk away as much as you please, as long as it keeps you quiet."

In spite of his want of interest in her and his utter lack of observation, he was considerably astonished when she sprang suddenly down from the platform, overturning the chair with a clatter, and faced him angrily. It was unlike any previous experience he had had with models and he began to realise that there was something unusual about this one, though what it was he did not precisely know, and that the moment had come for him to deal with it. So he put down his charcoal, and pulled forward a chair and a box; led her gently to the chair and sat down on the box, himself, and felt for his tobacco-pouch.

"Now, look here," he said, holding up his hand to stop her as she began to speak; "I know all about it. So, if you don't mind, I think we'll cut the first part. You've not been used to such treatment, and you didn't come here to be insulted. Very well; you didn't. But you came here to be my model, and I naturally expect you to behave like a model, and not like any other young woman who wishes to make conversation. Surely, that's reasonable isn't it?"

"It might be if – if I liked being a model, perhaps. But I don't," said Anna, rather lamely. She had found her new sensation, but it did not amuse her; she had never been lectured before, and she was not sure whether she felt angry or merely puzzled. Askett smiled slightly.

"That is hardly my fault," he replied. "I didn't suggest your vocation to you, did I?"

She was burning to tell him that he had, that he, and her own freakishness, and Fate, were entirely responsible for her vocation; but again the dread of his ridicule kept her silent, and she only baffled him once more by breaking into a peak of mirthful laughter.

"Oh, heavens!" he groaned. "How is one to deal with a thing like that? What in the name of wonder is the joke *now*?"

"It – it's the same joke as before," gasped Anna. "You really don't know what an awfully good joke it is."

"You must forgive me if I don't even want to find out," said Askett, shortly; and he got up and went to the window and looked out. The situation was not dignified, and he apostrophised the whole race of models, and wondered why they could not see that a chap wanted to work, instead of playing up to him with their hopelessly feminine ways. And then he realised that this particular one had stopped laughing, and was waiting for him to say something.

"Well?" he said gruffly.

"I'm awfully sorry," said Anna, who was secretly a little ashamed of herself. "The fact is, I'm rather a new hand at being a model, and it still makes me feel drowsy, and if I hadn't talked nonsense just now I should have gone to sleep. It isn't so very long since I had to earn my own living, and one doesn't get used to it all at once, don't you know. Shall I go on sitting, now?"

He did not answer for a second or two. For the first time he had noticed her way of speaking, and it struck him that perhaps she was less of a fraud than most models who profess to have come down in the world, and that her family might have been decent people after all. He began to feel a little remorse for having been hard on her.

"Look here," he said, still gruffly. "I'm not going to do any more to-day. and I think you won't quite do for what I wanted, so you needn't come back to-morrow. I'll pay you all the same till the end of the week, so you'll be able to take a holiday with a clear conscience. Perhaps, you won't find it so tiring when you've had a rest. And the next chap you sit for may not mind your talking."

She stood quite still while he went across the room to fetch her cloak. Somehow, she was not so pleased at her unexpected deliverance as she would have been ten minutes ago. She had an uncomfortable sensation of having behaved like a child, and added to this was a vague feeling of shame at allowing him to think she was poor and friendless, and in need of his help. So she stepped up to him and took the cloak out of his hand.

"I don't want a holiday, thank you," she said. "You are a brick, but I would sooner keep my part of the bargain if you'll let me. I wasn't really tired, I was lazy."

He shrugged his shoulders, and realised that his pity had been wasted.

"As you like," he said, shortly, and Anna climbed up to her chair again.

It was indisputable that she was an irreproachable model for the rest of the afternoon, that she abstained from all temptation to elevate her chin, and met his few attempts at conversation with subdued monosyllables; but for all that, the wish to work had completely deserted him, and he yawned at last and looked at his watch, and said it was time for tea.

"You may talk now," he said, as he put on the kettle.

"Thanks. But there isn't anything to say," said Anna.

"Does that make any difference?" he asked, with an unexpected smile that propitiated her; and she came down and offered to cut the bread and butter. He shook his head, and possessed himself of the loaf.

"Stay where you are, I'll look after this. Women always make it taste of the knife! Hullo! offended again? I'm sorry, but you know they do."

"They don't in – in the other Anna's flat. But you've never been there, of course; and I suppose you'll never go, will you?"

"Depends on the other Anna, doesn't it? Do you think she'd have me?"

"I'm quite certain she would," said his model, with such assurance that a less absorbed person would have suspected something of the truth. As it was, he only looked slightly amused and asked for a reason.

"Oh, because Anna always likes odd people who don't talk much; and she doesn't think them musty or anything like that, just because they're not usual. She'd call you interesting, and quarrel with every one who didn't agree with her, and be frightfully glad all the while because they didn't."

"Sugar?" asked Askett, who had again not been listening.

"Two lumps, please. So do you, don't you? I *knew* you would! So does Anna. I think you'd like Anna too, rather."

"Ah! What makes you think that?"

"Well, you've got some sense of humour, enough to know she wasn't really laughing at you. Most people are afraid of her, you know; and they think she doesn't feel things because she laughs; and of course she does feel them all the same. She hates people to be afraid of her; but you are never afraid of any one, are you? And you'd understand why she laughs. Oh yes, you'd like Anna."

"You are a very devoted friend," said Askett.

"I believe I do like her better than any one else I know," admitted Anna.

"Better than yourself?"

"Much better," she said, and began laughing again with no apparent reason.

"Oh dear," said Askett, "is it that joke again?"

But she was afraid of rousing his suspicions, and evaded his question. She was very anxious, just then, that his suspicions should not be roused.

When she left, he asked her again if she would not like to have a holiday till the end of the week.

"Am I such a very bad model then?" she asked.

"You are the most irritating model I have ever endured, but you can come back at two to-morrow," was his reply.

Several times that evening, she took up her pen to write and tell him that she would not come any more, and each time she laid it down again, and jerked her small chin into the air, and vowed she would go through with it.

"It is an adventure," she said, "and it is too rare to be wasted."

So for the sake of an adventure, she knocked once more at the door of Askett's studio. He opened it immediately, and held out his hand in greeting; but he was very businesslike in his manner, and set to work directly she was ready.

"I shall try your profile to-day," he said, screwing up his easel.

"You'll regret it," observed Anna.

"Possibly. Kindly turn your head a little further away; that'll do. What's wrong about your profile, please?"

"There's nothing wrong about it," she said, indignantly. "But I always show people my full face if I can; it's got more character."

"Women are so commercial," remarked Askett. "They make the most of every little advantage they think they possess."

"I must say," retorted Anna, "that for one who professes so much scorn for the whole sex, your perpetual desire to drag it into the conversation is most surprising."

"How is the other Anna?" asked Askett, rather suddenly.

"Oh, she's all right. She isn't so sure she would like you as I expected her to be."

"Indeed? Can't she contemplate my appalling silence without shuddering? Or is it because my face hasn't got any character in it?"

"Oh, no, your face is all right. And she wouldn't mind your being silent in the least, because she does all the talking herself. She'd only expect you to listen."

"What a clatter there must be when you get together," observed Askett.

"It generally has the effect of silencing us both," said Anna, gravely. "Am I sitting better to-day?"

"A little, yes. But I think I'll try the full face again; perhaps, you won't bob your head round quite so often if you are obliged to look at me."

"One would think I *wanted* to look at you," pouted Anna.

"That is certainly what you have led me to believe," said Askett, looking for another sheet of paper. "Now, don't flare up for nothing at all; I didn't mean to be rude, and I wasn't rude; and if you persist in jumping whenever I say anything you don't like, I shall relapse into silence again."

"And on the whole," said Anna, thoughtfully, "your remarks *are* a little improvement on that deadly silence."

"Now," said Askett, pressing down the drawing pins; "tell me some more about the other Anna. I like your expression when you talk about the other Anna, it's so appreciative. I believe you are a solitary instance of a woman who can endure the charms of another woman without feeling jealous."

"Perhaps it is only the charms of the other Anna," she said, carelessly. "What do you want to know about her?"

"Oh, anything, everything. What does she do, for instance?" said Askett, vaguely. His temporary interest in a woman, who was *not* there with the express purpose of distracting him, was already vanishing as he began to grow interested in his work.

"Do? Has she got to *do* anything? You surely don't suppose she is a model, or anything like that, do you? She's much too lazy to do things; she just has a good time, that's all. All her people are away or dead or at war with her; and she has some money of her own, not nearly enough of course, but still it's something. And she dresses rather well, and has a charming flat – I don't believe you are listening to a word I say, and it's too bad!"

"Indeed I am. It is my way of appearing interested. She dresses rather well, and has a charming flat. What more, please?"

"How much more do you want? That's enough for most people And why do you want to know all about Anna, when you've never seen her?"

"Oh, surely, because you wanted something to talk about. Besides you said she would like me. Isn't that enough reason for a man? Chin a little lower, please."

"I said you would like her," said Anna, slowly. "So you – do you think you would?"

"What do you think?" he asked, smiling at her sudden earnestness. She laughed.

"I think she would irritate you beyond measure! And you would hate her for being frivolous, and she would hate you for being serious."

"Decidedly, we had better not be introduced," said Askett.

The next day, the door was ajar when she arrived, and she pushed it open and walked in without knocking.

"Oh!" she exclaimed, and then paused and reddened with pleasure.

"Hullo! it's you, is it?" said Askett, coming forward. "What's up now?"

"Flowers! How beautiful! Where did they come from? I thought you never had any. Oh, doesn't it make the whole place look different?"

"They're all right, I suppose," he replied, indifferently. "Flowers always are. I'm glad you like them, they'll help you not to feel bored, perhaps. You curious child, to make all that fuss over a lot of daffodils! Does the other Anna like flowers as much as you do?"

She turned away with a little movement of dissatisfaction. Of course it was absurd, but for all that she found it impossible to control her growing jealousy for the other Anna.

After that, there were always flowers when she came for a sitting, and she came very often indeed. For Askett was at work on the illustrations for an eighteenth-century novel, and she posed several times for him as his heroine, a bewitching little figure in a quaint old cloak and large be-feathered hat. They were very good friends by the time the spring came, able to dispute without misconception, and to remain silent without embarrassment; and Askett, to judge by results, had long ago managed to grasp the system by which her conversation was made. The principal theme of it was still the other Anna; for, as the beginning of the year grew older, the difficulty of telling him the truth became increasingly greater. It would have meant, at least, some sort of an explanation, and she could not endure explaining why she did things; indeed, she rarely knew why. Besides, it would have put an end to the sittings, and the sittings amused her enormously, and she always went on doing what amused her. So she continued to impersonate the heroine of the eighteenth-century novel, and her conversation was still about the other Anna.

One day he was more silent than usual. He tried her in various positions and gave them all up in turn, made sketches on odd bits of paper and flung them aside, and ended in throwing down his pencil and saying he was no good.

"Have you got a headache?" she asked him.

"Headache? No, I'm all right," he said, in the resentful manner with which he repelled all her attempts to find out something about him. "Women always think you're ill if you feel a bit off colour," he added, as though to explain his abruptness.

"The other Anna," she observed, "always has a headache when she is off colour, as you call it. She had one this morning."

"Ah," said Askett, brightening a little, "tell me about the other Anna. Why is she off colour to-day?"

"Because she is in love," said Anna, lightly; and she crossed her feet and leaned back in her chair and looked at him.

"In love? The other Anna in love? Why, you told me she had too much sense of humour ever to fall in love. Who's the chap?" It was very ridiculous, but he could not help the sudden pang of disappointment he felt on hearing that the other Anna was in love. It disturbed his impression of her, and he had not know until that moment how strong that impression had grown.

"Oh, he doesn't know she's in love with him, and she couldn't possibly let him know, because he might have a sense of humour too; and then he'd just scoff, and she'd want to kill herself. It – it's a tragedy to fall in love if you've got a sense of humour, isn't it? Oh, of course you don't know." And she began humming a tune.

"Why don't I know? Because I am never in love, or because I have no sense of humour?"

"Oh, you've got a sense of humour right enough," she said, and went on singing softly to herself. Askett put down his pipe half-smoked.

"What is the other Anna like when she is in love?" he asked, and smiled at his wish to know.

"I only know she's very difficult to live with," replied his model, ruefully. "She's very happy or very sad all the time, and she gets impatient with me, as though I could help it. So absurd, isn't it? Poor Anna! You see, she has never been in love before, and she can't make it out. I wish, I do wish she were not in love now; it spoils everything so."

"It generally does," said Askett; and his eyes travelled slowly from the pair of pointed shoes up the pink silk cloak to the large black hat, and turned away swiftly when they rested on her face. "Have you ever been in love?" he asked, suddenly.

"Yes," she said, promptly, and fixed her eyes on him so persistently that she brought his reluctant gaze back to her, and then laughed softly in his face. "Have you?" she asked.

He smiled indulgently, and returned to the other Anna. "What a fool the fellow must be," he said, jestingly, "to give up a woman like that when she's good enough to fall in love with him."

"Oh, I don't think so," said Anna. "He doesn't know; men never do. And she can't tell him; women never can. It's such hard lines; her life is being quite spoilt because she mustn't say anything. She wouldn't mind so much if she were quite sure the man didn't like her; she'd pull herself together again, and go on. But how is she to find out?"

"Why doesn't she send you to ask him?" suggested Askett.

"Do you know," she said with a queer little smile, "you've made that same old joke again?"

But he noticed that, this time, it did not move her to one of her irresistible peals of laughter.

"After all," she added, casually, "I am not sure that it is a joke at all."

Askett got up and went to look after the kettle; tea would make a diversion, he thought, and they seemed to be in need of a diversion that afternoon. "It strikes me," he said, with his back to her, "that you let yourself worry too much about the love affairs of the other Anna."

"Perhaps I do," replied Anna with the same enigmatical smile. "But it's chiefly your fault; you always want to hear about her, and you never let me talk about anything else. It isn't very flattering to *me*, I must say!" She ended with a pout.

Askett stood up and smiled thoughtfully.

"How absurd!" he said with a half-laugh. "Go and tell your Anna that some one is in love with her, because he has heard that she is a woman with a sense of humour and a heart; and see if it doesn't cure her depression!"

"I shouldn't be surprised if it did," replied Anna.

When she made ready to go, that day, he forgot to put on her cloak for her, and stood irresolutely looking at her with the old nervous frown come back to his face; and she guessed instinctively that there was something he had to say to her.

"What is it?" she said, involuntarily.

"It's just this," he said, speaking very quickly; "I don't think I shall want you any more after next week, and – "

He stopped, although she had not said anything. She looked steadily at the pink silk cloak that hung across the chair, at the jug of wallflowers on the mantel-shelf, at the two empty cups on the upturned wooden box; and she drew in her lips with a sharp breath.

"Yes," she said, and held out her hand. "Good-bye."

"And when may I come and meet the other Anna?" he asked, smiling.

There was already a yard and half of stone passage between them; and the space was widening every minute, as she backed towards the staircase and he into the middle studio.

"I am afraid she would have too much sense of humour to receive you," she said, and laughed mockingly, and went away down the long flights of stone stairs.

"It's all right," said Askett, congratulating himself. "She doesn't care. I might have known she wouldn't. These models – ah well!" He flung the pink silk cloak on the floor, and sat down on the chair, and relighted his pipe. "I believe, if she had told me much more about the other girl, I might have fancied myself in love with her. It would be a queer thing, after holding off for all these years, to fall in love with a woman I have never seen! I wonder what it was that fetched me in that child's descriptions of her? Strange how fascinating a picture those stray bits of information have made in my mind! Probably, if I were to meet her in the ordinary way, I shouldn't discover any charm in her at all; women are so secretive. I begin to understand the reason for arranging marriages. All the same, I should like to meet her." His eyes fell on the pink cloak, as it lay in an effete and shapeless heap on the floor. "There's something very expressive in a woman's clothes, when you've known the woman," he observed, to change the current of his thoughts. But they soon wheeled round again. "I wonder how the other Anna would look in that thing? Its very odd to have kept my interest in the same woman for six, seven, eight weeks, and a woman I haven't even seen. I suppose it's true that all the constancy in a man's heart is for the women he has never seen, but still – However, it's a safe passion, and I won't risk it by making her acquaintance. No," he added, moving his chair round so that he could not see the pink silk cloak, "I will not ask for an introduction to the other Anna."

On his way home he ran against Tom Hallaford, and they walked down Piccadily together. Tom Hallaford was only just back from Rome, and it was consequently some time before the conversation became sufficiently local and personal to interest his companion, who had not been to Rome at all. But Askett got his chance after a while.

"Yes, I've been pretty busy," he said, in reply to an inquiry about his work. "By the way, you remember that model of yours I took pity on, one day in the winter, when you kept her waiting? Oh yes you do; pretty little girl rather, big hat, name Wilson, lives with a Miss Angell. My dear fellow, one would think you had never even heard her name! Well, never mind about the model; I don't want to talk about her. But I do want to know something about the girl she lives with, the other Anna, you know – Miss Angell, in fact."

"I suppose you know what you're playing at," said Tom, good-naturedly; "but I'm bothered if I do. Miss Angell doesn't live with any one as far as I know. She never introduced me to a model in her life; in fact, I only know her very slightly. Some aunt of hers commissioned me to paint her portrait; that was how she came to sit for me. Who is the model you were talking about? You must have got mixed somehow, old chap."

"Mixed?" said Askett, mechanically, standing in a vague manner on the edge of the kerbstone. "Mixed, yes, that's it, of course; certainly mixed. I suppose – in fact, I believe – well, it's that joke, you know." And to the mystification of his companion, who stood staring after him. he beckoned with an exaggerated composure to a hansom, gave the driver an address in Belgravia, and drove away without a word of farewell.

The other Anna answered her own bell, that evening, because her maid was out for a holiday. And she found Askett standing on the door mat outside.

"Oh!" was all she could find to say, though it was extremely expressive in the particular way she said it.

"It's all right," said Askett, in the most courteous and self-possessed man-ner possible. "I've only come to ask the other Anna to marry me, instead of the chap who doesn't know how to appreciate her. Do you think she will?"

There was the dawn of a laugh in her eyes as she threw the door wider.

"I believe," she replied, "that she still has a lurking fondness for the other chap. But if you'll come in I'll tell you that little joke of mine, and then – "

"No need," observed Askett, "I think I know it."

Note

Text: *The Yellow Book* vol. xiii (April 1897).

LUCY WREN

Ada Radford

Ada Radford (dates unknown), short-story writer and poet, was the sister of the writer and critic Ernest Radford, member of the Rhymer' Club, Fabian, wit, vegetarian and oarsman, who dedicated his *Translations from Heine and other Verse* (1882) to her. The Radfords were members of *The Yellow Book* circle. She contributed two stories to *The Yellow Book*, and later collaborated with her brother on a collection of poems, *Songs in the Whirlwind* (1918).

Further reading

Mix (1960).

Lucy Wren

A grey scholarly little person.

She had no degree, but her testimonials were unusual. She would be an acquisition to any staff. Refined, cultivated, literary in her tastes, and above all thoroughly conscientious and reliable.

And so although her health and her means had allowed her to do comparatively little in preparation, and although she was beginning later than some women, Lucy Wren found herself teaching in a large school, with a salary of £95 a year, and a prospect of a rise of £5 at the end of the year.

She was very fortunate; she recognised the fact, although she did not give thanks for it quite as often as her friend Katharine Grey, with whom she lived.

They sat one summer evening, exercise-books for correction piled in front of them.

"Our life," said Katharine, "is so delightfully free. Think of being a governess in a family."

Yes, Lucy Wren had been saved from that.

"Imagine being one of those girls in an idle rich family, with nothing to think about except dress and flirtations."

Her healthy-minded brisk little comrade shuddered at the thought.

Yes, she had been saved from that.

She thought little of clothes, although the soft grey dress she wore, made beautiful lines over her slight figure. And flirtations! . . . All the satisfaction there is to be gained from having no flirtations was hers, and yet somehow she wished that Katharine would give her mind to her exercise-books, instead of sitting there thanking heaven that they were not as other women.

"I don't believe you would have lived long in a life of that kind," Katharine said, looking at her broad quiet brow and long sensitive hands. "It's impossible to imagine you without work and without a purpose.

I confess there was a time when I liked a little of it; a little, you know."

Lucy Wren smiled and asked, "Of which? of dress, or of flirtation?"

"Both I think," and the blue and red pencil remained idly balanced in Katharine's fingers, and the picture of good sense grew pensive.

"I always feel that it has been knowing you that has made me look at things differently. After I knew you things seemed almost vulgar, that before I had thought only fun. In fact there are things I've never dared confess to you; they are nothing much, but I don't think you'd ever quite forgive or understand."

Lucy did not protest that she would, and so no confidence was given.

"I shan't get through these books if you will talk," was what she said, and she opened an exercise-book.

"That child's mind is a perfect chaos," she murmured as she wrote "Very poor work" across the page at the bottom.

Katharine had an unusual desire to talk; she fidgeted, and at last, finding Lucy absolutely unresponsive she left the table and her unfinished work, and sitting in the horsehair easy chair, leant back, a volume of Browning in her hand.

When at last Lucy looked up, Katharine spoke at once.

"It's a glorious love poem," she said her eyes shone, and the schoolmistress had disappeared. "Shall I read it to you?"

To listen to a glorious love poem read by Katharine, at any time required the same kind of composure as the dentist's chair, but to-night had she proposed to let loose the specimens of animal life she kept in bottles and boxes, all over the room, Lucy would have given the same involuntary shudder.

"My head aches so, I must go to bed; good night," she said firmly, and leaving her half-finished books on the table, she left the room, with what for her were rapid movements.

"Good night," said Katharine, and buried herself again in her book.

"I know you'll be very angry," said Katharine the next afternoon, as Lucy stood in her hat and cloak ready to go out, "but I never can understand your friendship with that little Mrs. Dawson. She doesn't seem to me to have a thing in her."

Lucy smiled.

"And you frighten the very little she has out of her; but I – well, I like to go and hear about things outside the school."

"But it's all gossip, isn't it?"

"Yes, it's all gossip."

"How funny of you, Lucy. What kind of man is her husband?"

"We never get more than a few words together," said Lucy. Then she added. "He looks unhappy."

It was gossip, and yet Lucy listened. Ella (Mrs. Dawson's name was Ella) always apologised. "I know these things don't interest you," she said, "but then after all you get quite enough of clever people," and so she talked and Lucy listened, and learnt many things – to-day as usual. For instance:

If Ella were Mrs. Spooner, she wouldn't like her husband to spend so much of his time with Ethel Dayley. Not that she should be jealous, of course; jealousy is a small feeling, and would show distrust in Tom; still she should distinctly dislike it. "It depends so much on the woman," she said, and looking in a kindly way at Lucy, whose tired head was resting against the back of her chair, she added: "Now I shouldn't mind Tom being friends with you. But it isn't always safe."

A vision of Ethel Dayley rose before Lucy, and she understood that she was the safer.

Then she heard that Sophie Warren was engaged to marry a man years and years younger than herself. That his people were furious. That Ella herself thought it very wrong of Sophie.

Didn't Lucy think it a wrong thing to do?

"I don't know," said Lucy.

"But imagine yourself in such a position."

"I can't," said Lucy.

With even so much encouragement Ella chatted and chattered.

"People think I'm older than Tom, but really I'm a week younger; and I've always been so glad that it wasn't the other way, for people can say such nasty things if a woman's older than her husband."

"I wish Tom would come in," she said suddenly.

Lucy wished it too. She was not as good a listener to-day as usual.

"He likes so few of my friends," Ella sighed, "and when he doesn't like them, although he doesn't mean to be rude, he hardly speaks to them. He always has something to say to you. Really Tom ought to have married a clever woman;" and Ella mentally determined to read more, in case Tom took to talking to her; but it is hard to work with such a remote end in view.

When Tom came he was very quiet, and Ella was disappointed.

"How very tired you look," he said, fixing his eyes on Lucy's face, as he gave her some tea.

"I am, very," said Lucy.

"Oh, I'm so sorry," broke in Ella, "you never told me. Why ever didn't you tell me? And here I've been chattering and chattering, and you ought to have been on the sofa, quite quiet, with your feet up. Do put them up, now. Tom won't mind, will you, Tom?"

Ella was in such a charming little fuss that Tom and Lucy exchanged a smile.

"Fancy not telling me!" said Ella.

They smiled again. "To tell Ella you are tired," the smile said, "is just putting a match to a dear little feminine bomb." Lucy pacified Ella, then she looked at Tom again, and the smile died out of her face. She understood now Ella's constant complaint that he never talked. Talk! How could he? And she? Why had she spent so much time with Ella, week after week?

Only because she was dead tired and only half alive, that was all; but Tom was, and had to be, with her always.

A leaden sky, a leaden river. Lucy stopped and looked over the bridge. In the river there was a just perceptible movement, in the sky a suppression that promised a storm, and, for who could look so far ahead, freshness after it.

Lucy thought of Katharine's cheerful companionship and the cup of cocoa awaiting her, and still she lingered.

"Low spirits are mostly indigestion," Katharine had said; Katharine, who was never original, but who threw down her commonplaces and let them ring.

Good sense, good sense.

Hadn't even Lucy nearly enough of it? Wasn't she earning her own living? Wasn't she saving a few pounds for her own enjoyable old age? Wasn't she frugal and quiet and hard-working, as any woman of the working classes? And this discontent that surged within her when she felt strong, that dragged at her spirits and clouded her brain when she was tired – it was just unreasoning womanish folly, and Katharine would say indigestion. Was it? Very well.

To-night she would not make the usual effort to throw it off. "I mustn't, I mustn't," she had always thought; "I shan't be fit for my work to-morrow." And resolutely she had turned and interested herself in some light book. To-night, in the leaden dulness, rebellion stirred.

"Good heavens! Haven't I even the right to be wretched!"

Her work constantly overtaxed her strength. Economy prevented her from getting proper rest in her holidays. But she was sensible, and rested all she could, so that although always tired and draggled, she might not be noticeably so, and lose her post.

That was the comfort common sense gave.

She looked forward. She would never get a head mistress-ship, she had neither the acquirements nor the personality; and year after year young girls came with their degrees and their inexperience, and after a time – it was years yet – but after a time, perhaps before she was forty, she would be told she was too old to teach.

Then she would fall back on her savings. If she went on limiting her pleasures at the present rate they might be £50 by that time. Her prospects looked dark as the river.

But it was the present that goaded her thoughts into the even darker future.

She hated her work and the thought of to-morrow.

She saw the rows of girls, she heard the chalk against the blackboard.

The girls, their often commonplace, heavy faces, their awkward, un-developed figures, their dress already betraying vanity and vulgarity – she saw herself grinding them.

They liked her, of course; every one liked her. She wished they would hate her. She was lonely – desperate. For friends her colleagues; their outlook, their common shop, stifled her. "What are we doing with all these girls?" she asked herself.

"We are making them upright, sensible women, who will not argue in a circle or manœuvre to get husbands," Katharine had said. Would Katharine never see that *not* doing things is not enough for a woman? She believed they were overworking these girls. "We are killing the spirit in them," she thought, "as it has been killed in me."

In the thought of her work there was no comfort.

And then, had her own nature no needs beyond being sensible? She thought of life as it had been in her imaginings, in her dreams, and as it even might be in reality. What was her part in it?

To be sensible.

There was love, and there was home, and there was reasonable rest, and there was the exaltation of spirit that art can give, and music and poetry and nature; and the voice of a hideous mockery said:

"You can be sensible."

As she heard it more and more clearly, as a voice outside, she defied it from within, where something told her that the crowning act of common sense would be a plunge, death and darkness in reality, not this horrible pretence.

And then she was walking along towards the station with Tom Dawson. Neither had spoken of the strangeness of meeting there. They were walking silently side by side. Neither spoke, but as they neared the station their steps grew slower and slower. In the light of a lamp she saw his face with sudden clearness.

"You too," she thought. "No, not you. I can bear it, but not you. Tom's moody. Tom's this and that" – came back to her in Ella's voice, with its shallow, pleasant little clang. They walked, thinking – he of her face as he had seen it before she saw him, she of him. Her heart was beating with sudden sympathy, but she was living. For him, every day, Ella's common-places – Ella's affection.

Every day to work hard at distasteful work, for an income barely sufficient for Ella's little fancies. How had it ever happened? With his face, with his mind!

On the short journey home they hardly looked at each other or spoke, but the few necessary words were spoken in the voices of loving friends.

He stopped at the garden gate of her lodgings.

"Is Miss Grey at home?"

"No, there is no light in our room."

And he followed her in, and stood close at her side while she lit the lamp. She thought she heard his heart beating.

Her common sense said "Speak – say anything – about Ella – about to-morrow, or yesterday, or the day before."

But she stood by him, motionless and trembling.

Then her common sense made a fresh effort.

"Speak" – it commanded: for the silence was drawing them closer each moment.

The commonplace words that divide were slipping further and further from her thought.

"Anything would do," she said, vaguely, to herself – "anything about the bazaar – about – the school."

But the command had become mere words in her brain. It was the evening of her revolt. Instead of speaking she lifted her eyes – and he had been waiting, knowing that she must, and that he would hold her in his arms. She had not resisted – she had leant her cheek against his, and put her arms around his neck. Not until they had moved apart for a moment, her cheeks flushed and she was frightened.

"Don't think, my darling," he said. "Don't, don't; we have such a little while together."

And he drew her closer again.

"My little one – my love – my life," he murmured to her. "And I found you in all that darkness."

"And I you. The river was so dreadful, just as things are –"

"Yes, I knew – I saw what you were feeling, and I knew – because I too –"

"Yes – yes, I know – I knew –"

There was a footstep on the gravel path.

"Katharine," said Lucy, despairingly, but without a start; and not until she heard her hand on the door she rose and stood by the mantel-piece.

"May I introduce Mr. Dawson, Katharine?"

Katharine was pleased to meet him, and she had plenty to say.

Lucy picked her hat up from the floor, and stood silent. Katharine thought, as she had often thought, it was a pity Lucy would not talk to strangers; she did not do herself justice. She had said a good deal on several subjects, before Tom Dawson rose. Public spirit in girls' schools – vegetarianism – she wished to try it, as also, it seemed, rational dress and cremation. How long was he there? Neither he nor Lucy had the slightest idea, but he knew a moment would come when he must leave.

But he must ensure seeing Lucy to-morrow.

"We shall see you to-morrow," he said to her; "it is Ella's 'At-Home' day?"

"Yes, I will come," said Lucy.

He was gone.

"Well," said Katharine, "I don't think he's very entertaining, do you? I don't think he's a great improvement on his wife. I thought you said he was interesting?"

Lucy moved.

"Don't go to bed this minute," Katharine pleaded.

Standing, her cheeks still flushed, she heard, as though in the distance, Katharine's tales.

"I know it's no use paying you compliments, but you're looking wonderfully pretty to-night, Lucy; your hair suits you loose like that."

And then, at last, she let her shut her bedroom door and be alone.

Lucy was at school again at nine o'clock the next morning.

Four hours teaching, dinner, preparation, and then Ella's "At Home."

She was counting the hours to Ella's "At Home." Seven hours more, seven hours more, six hours and three quarters, she kept saying to herself, as she explained to the elementary Euclid class the curious things about right angles.

Five minutes between each lesson.

She did not to go the teachers' room, she stayed in the empty class-rooms, and whether she shut her eyes a moment, or whether they rested on the blackboard or the maps, or the trees outside, she was absurdly, childishly happy.

No questions – no conscience – she was Lucy Wren to-day – not the safe friend of Ella's husband – not the best companion for girls – not the woman every one was the better for knowing – she was just herself. She saw a child talking in class. She ought to give her a bad mark. She did not do it, and she revelled in her little injustice.

Another lesson and another little break.

If he had not come! There by the river! What would have happened? She did not know. "Only if we had not found each other!" That was the thought that made her shudder. But they had! They had! Only five hours more to Ella's "At Home!"

It was Ella's "At Home," and Ella's husband. But what had Ella to do with either? Ella, with her mind so full of little things, so content with herself and with Tom. Did she envy Ella? Envy Ella? What a funny idea, how had it come into her head?

"Miss Wren, can I speak to you! I want to give you the fifth form next term. They are nice girls, but their tone isn't just what I should wish. It's a difficult age, their home influences are bad, frivolous. It's more advanced work than you have had, I'm afraid you'll find it hard, but I feel so sure that your influence is the best they could have."

It was the head mistress, and it was settled that next term Lucy should have the fifth form, and her salary would be raised; and there were only three hours now to get through before Ella's "At Home!"

Ella was happy. She was having quite an intimate talk with one or two dear friends before the others came.

"How shocking!" she said more than once, and when she said that, you might be sure that she was enjoying herself.

Lucy sat apart – turning over a book. Ella thought she was reading and let her alone.

Scraps of their talk reached her now and then – just now it was about some girl, a governess who had been flirting, and it seemed with somebody's husband.

"She was sent off at once."

That gave the dismayed ladies some small comfort.

"But fancy carrying on like that," one gasped.

"And trusted so, and recommended by a clergyman."

"What really happened?" asked Ella. In low tones Ella was told that some one came into the conservatory – and they were there, kissing each other.

"And recommended by a clergyman," Ella repeated.

"And dressing so quietly."

"Really one's never safe."

And tale after tale of the audacity of their sex went the round of the party.

It was a pity, even Ella thought it rather a pity, that just then Tom and a friend should come in, and the conversation should take another direction.

There was a buzz of talk, and tea-cups were handed round.

"If only she would undertake it, my friend, Miss Wren, would be an excellent person to take your girls abroad," said Ella to a lady who was making anxious inquiries for a suitable person, "but she's so much appreciated where she is. She's over there," she said in a lower voice glancing towards Lucy.

The lady looked.

"The girl your husband is standing by, a quiet reliable-looking little person?"

"Yes, that's Lucy."

"She looks the very thing. Not pretty, but not exactly a dowd. My girls wouldn't care to be sent off with a dowd."

"Sugar?" said Tom, slowly.

"No thanks," said Lucy.

He dropped a lump into her cup.

"Tom!" exclaimed Ella, whose eyes and ears were everywhere. "Lucy said no – give it me, dear, I'll take it out."

Notes

Text: *The Yellow Book*, vol. xiii (April 1897).

AMOR VINCIT OMNIA

Flora Annie Steel

Flora Annie Steel, née Webster (1847–1929), novelist, short-story writer, and educational administrator, was born in London, but moved to Forfarshire, Scotland (where her father originated) at the age of 10. She was educated privately, and 'finished' in Brussels. After her marriage, at the age of 19, to a colonial administrator, she moved to India, where she was to live for twenty years, working in educational administration and advocating education for Indian women. She founded a school for Indian girls in 1884, as well as working as a school inspector, and estimated that about 20,000 girls had benefited from her care and attention. She published a collection of tales of the Punjab, *Wide Awake Stories*, in 1884, and began writing full time after she returned to Britain in 1889. The best known of her seventeen novels, many of which are set in India, is her non-partisan account of the Indian Mutiny, *On the Face of the Waters* (1896), but she also published, among others, *Miss Stuart's Legacy* (1893), *The Potter's Thumb* (1894), *Red Rowans* (1895), *Hosts of the Lord* (1900), *Mistress of Men* (1917) (set in seventeenth-century India, the story of a girl who is abandoned and who becomes an empress) and *The Curse of Eve* (1929), which advocates birth control for women. She also collected and published folk and fairy tales, wrote a history of India and an Indian cookery book, and supported the women's suffrage movement. Her autobiography, *The Garden of Fidelity*, was published posthumously.

Further reading

Blain *et al.* (1990); Paxton (1990); Powell (1981); Sutherland (1988).

Amor Vincit Omnia

This story began and ended in a public library. An odd, forlorn little offshoot of progress, dibbled out beyond the walls of a far-away Indian city, which drowsed through the sunny to-day as it has drowsed through many a century of sunny yesterdays. True it is that in a certain mimetic and superficial manner Poorânâbad had changed with the changing years. It had evolved a municipal committee, and this in its turn had given birth to various simulacra of civilisation; but in effect the former was but the old council of elders in modern guise, and the latter but Jonah's gourd,[1] springing up in a day or night at the bidding of some minor prophet from over the seas. They came and went, these minor prophets, each with his theory, his hobby; and even when Poorânâbad knew them no more, it could remember its rulers by the libraries and band-stands, the public gardens, the schools, and the museums they had left behind them.

The library itself stood in the midst of a newly laid-out public garden, which but two summers before had been a most evil-smelling tank[2] – at least, for nine months of the year; the remaining three found it a shining lake flushed with fresh rain and carpeted with pink lotus blossom. But culture of all sorts had stepped in with drain-pipes, bricks, mortar, flowers, and books, and the result was a maze of winding walks, stubbly grass, and stunted bushes gathered round a square stuccoed building of one room encircled by an arched verandah. To east and south the deceptive walls and flat mud roofs of the native city looked like towers against the sky. To west and north stood avenues of *shìshum*[3] trees, with here and there a peep of the white bungalows wherein the minor prophets dwelt and grew gourds.

Within, under the one roof hung with two punkahs,[4] stood two tables, the one littered with English magazines and illustrated papers, the other bare, save for a few leaflets of the native press, with high-sounding names and full of still more lofty sentiments. The two bookcases, one at each end of the room, showed the same well-intentioned, but unsuccessful, impartiality; for the eastern one was nearly empty, while the western overflowed, chiefly with novels; a dozen shelves of them to one of miscellaneous literature, made up for the most part of works on the Central Asian question and missionary reports. The novels, however, had a solid appearance, since most of them had been re-bound by the district office bookbinder in the legal calf and boards which he used also for the circulars and acts by which India is governed.

411

Before this bookcase stood the only occupant of the room, a tall, weedy boy of about fifteen – a boy with remarkably thin legs, somewhat of a stoop in his narrow shoulders, and a supple brown finger travelling slowly along the ill-spelt titles of the books; ill-spelt, because the Government bookbinder could hardly be expected to grapple successfully with the title of a modern novel. The hesitations of this brown finger might have served as an index to the owner's taste, and showed a distinct leaning towards sentiment. It lingered over several suggestive titles, until it finally settled on something writ large in three volumes. After which the boy, crossing to a double desk midway between the tables, wrote in the English register in a fine bold hand any clerk might have envied –

Amor Vincit Omnia.[5] Govind Sahai, Kyasth.

So, with two volumes under his arm, and one held close to his soft, shortsighted black eyes, Govind Sahai, of the tribe of Kyasths, or scribes, made his way citywards down one of the winding paths. Thus strolling along he was typical of the great multitude of Indian boys of his age. Boys who read – great heavens! what do they not read, with their pale, intelligent faces close to the lettering? And their thoughts? – that is a mystery.

Govind Sahai's face was no exception to the rule; it was young, yet old; high-featured, yet gentle; the ascetic hollows in the temples belied by the long sweeping curves in the mouth, and both these features neutralised by the feminine oval of the cheek. He was the only son of a widow, who, thanks to his existence, led a busy and contented life in her father-in-law's otherwise childless house; for the honours of motherhood in India are great. Yet she was poor beyond belief to Western ears. Across the black water, in a Christian country, such poverty would have meant misery, but in the old simplicity of Poorânâbad the little household managed to be happy; above all, in its hopes of the future, when Govind's education should be over, and he be free to follow his hereditary trade as a writer. His father had found his ancestral level, oddly enough, in compiling sanitary statistics in an English office, until the cholera added one to the mortality returns by carrying him off as a victim; after which all the interest of life to the inhabitants of the little courtyard and slip of roof which Govind called home, centred in the clever boy, who could only follow his father's trade if he succeeded in gaining the necessary pass; for education has undermined heredity. So Govind worked hard for the scholarship which would enable him to go to college. Day after day he absorbed an amount of information which was perfectly prodigious. Month after month found him further and further adrift in the sea of knowledge. Even in play-time he gorged himself on new ideas, as might be seen by the library register. It was not only *Amor Vincit Omnia* which showed on its pages, but many another similar work –

Lost for Love,	Govind Sahai, Kyasth.
Love the Master,	,, ,,
My Sweetheart,	,, ,,
One Life, One Love,	,, ,,

And so on down one column and up another, for the boy read fast.

On this particular hot, dusty May morning he became so interested in his last book that he sat down on the parapet of the city's central sewer, and twining one thin leg round the other plunged headlong into a sentimental scene between two lovers, heedless of his unsavoury environments. The interweaving of intellectual emotion and material sensation pictured on the page seemed to this boy, just verging upon manhood, to be an inspiration, lifting the whole subject into a new world of pure passion. It appealed, as a matter of fact, though he knew it not, both to his inherited instincts and his acquired ideas, thus satisfying both.

'My darling,' said Victor, raising her sweet face to his, and pressing a kiss on those pure, pale lips, 'love such as ours is eternal. Earth has no power' – et cetera, et cetera, et cetera. The tears positively came into his eyes; he seemed to feel the touch of those lips on his, making him shiver.

'The little soft tendrils of her hair stirred with his breath as Una, shrinking to his side, whispered, 'I am not afraid when I am with you, my king. I feel so strong! so strong to maintain the Right! Strong to maintain our Love before all the world! For Love is of Heaven, is it not, dear heart?' 'Our Love is,' murmured Victor, once more raising her pure, pale – Et cetera, et cetera, et cetera.

Yes, it was very beautiful, very exalting; also very disturbing to this inheritor of a nature built on simpler, more direct lines. That ancestral past of his seemed brutally bald beside this highly decorated castle of chivalry.

'Aha! Good evening, pupil Govind,' broke in the accurate voice of Narayan Chand, headmaster of the district school. 'You have, I am glad to see, availed yourself of the advantages of the public library. With what mental pabulum[6] have you provided yourself this summer's eve?'

As he spoke, he seated himself likewise on the parapet of the sewer, and read over the boy's shoulder, 'Amor Vincit Omnia.' Then his spectacled glance travelled down the page, returning for comfort to the title; that, at least, smacked of learning. 'Ah, aha! I see. Light literature. Good for colloquial, and of paramount use in *vivâs*.[7] So far, well. For superiority of diction, nevertheless, and valuability to grammar studies, give me *Tatler*, *Spectator*,[8] and such classics.'

Govind closed his book in most unusual irritation. 'Even in English literature, master-*ji*, new things may be better than old.'

'Of that there is no possible doubt,' quoted master-*ji*, with cheerful gravity. He was a most diligent reader of the English papers, and used to sit at the library table for hours of an evening devouring the critiques on Gilbert's or Tennyson's last[9] with undiscriminating absorption in the formation and

413

style of the sentence. His quotations were in consequence more various than select. 'Of that there can be no possible probable manner of doubt,[10] as a modern poet puts it tersely,' he repeated, tilting his embroidered smoking-cap further from his forehead, and drawing the black alpaca tails of his coat round his legs; 'yet still, for all that, it is held, that – to speak colloquially – for taking the cake of scholarship, the classics – '

Govind Sahai put his feet to the ground and the first volume under his arm.

'Master-*ji*, when one labours long days at cube roots, then classics in the evening become excessive. Life is not all learning; life is love also.'

He was quoting from the book he had been reading.

'Sits the wind in that quarter,'[11] began Narayan sagely; then he looked at the boy reflectively and changed manner and language. 'That brings to memory, my son,' he said in Hindustani. 'When comes thy wedding procession? I must speak to the virtuous widow that it come in vacation time, so as not to interfere with study.'

A sullen indifference was on Govind's face.

'You need not fear, master-*ji*; I mean to have the scholarship. The wedding will make no difference.'

Narayan Chand smiled a superior smile.

'Nay, my son; it must – it should – *for a time*. So is the vacation convenient. Thou canst return to school when the festal season is over. Come, I will speak to thy relations even now.'

The widow was sifting wheat – a pleasant-faced little dump of a woman, with dimples on her bare brown arms.

'Mother,' said Govind calmly, 'is grandfather in? The master-*ji* hath come about my wedding.'

'What have men to say to such things?' she answered, with a shrill laugh; 'go tell master-*ji*, heart of mine eyes, that it is settled for the first week of vacation. Her people were here but now. *Hurri hai!*[12] but I shall laugh and cry to see thee! There shall be nothing wanting at all! Flowers and sweets and merriment. Thy granny and I have toiled and spun for it. And the bride sweeter than honey. Fie! Govind, be not shy with thy mother! Think of the bride she gives thee, and tell her thou art happy.'

She flung her arms round her tall son, kissing him and plying him with questions till he smirked sillily.

'Happy enough, mother,' he admitted, then felt *Amor Vincit Omnia* under his arm, and sighed. 'I would much rather not be married; at least, I think not. O mother, I would she had fair hair and blue eyes!'

'*Lakshmi!*[13] hear him! Wouldst marry a fright, Govind? Wait the auspicious moment; wait till I lift the veil. O the beauty! fresh from the court of Indra,[14] wheat-coloured and languishing with jewels and love.'

Govind shook his head.

'Profane not the great name of Love.' He quoted to himself, being forced to this secrecy by the fact that the only language his mother understood has no word for love – as he meant it. So he added mournfully, 'I am ready for my duty whenever you wish it, mother; that is enough.'

Nevertheless, he dreamt dreams that night as he lay curled upon his short string bed, with the second volume of *Amor Vincit Omnia* under the quilt, so as to be ready for the early summer dawn. Out under the stars in the bare, mud-walled courtyard, destitute to Western eyes of all comfort, he dreamt the dreams of his race – of a gorgeously attired bride, shy, yet alluring, looking at him for the first time.

'Thou hast a nightmare,' said his mother crossly, when just before daybreak he woke them all by sitting up in his bed and declaiming, *Amor vincit omnia* in a loud voice. ''Tis that book under thy head. Put it aside, and lie as thy forefathers lay; they dreamt not of pillows. So shalt thou sleep sound and let others sleep also.'

She went yawning back to bed, and lay awake till dawn brought work, counting over the savings she had made, and calculating how much she could spare for flowers and sweets and spiced dishes, for all the hitherto unknown luxuries which, according to custom, were to make the boy's life a dream of pleasure for a time. Only for a time, since the scholarship had to be gained.

A month afterwards a red-curtained bridal palanquin containing a mysterious bride was carried over the threshold of the little mud courtyard, and Govind Sahai, with a silver triptych on his forehead, his ears tasselled with evil-smelling marigolds, his scented tinsel coat hung with jasmine chaplets,[15] dismounted from a pink-nosed pony amidst an admiring crowd. That was an end of the spectacle as far as the outside world was concerned. Within it was only beginning for those two fond women who had spun and scraped and saved for this great occasion ever since the bridegroom was five years old. Much had to be done ere they would sit down in proud peace knowing that no possible enhancement of delight had been omitted. The boy himself went through the countless ceremonies, all tending towards an apotheosis of the senses, with a certain shy dignity; perhaps the sight of master-*ji* doing wedding guest in a copper-coloured alpaca coat gave him confidence by reminding him that even the learned stoop to folly. He was pale, partly from the turmeric baths, which are supposed to produce a complexion favourable to feminine eyes, partly because he really felt sick after the unusual sloth and sweets of the last few days. So much for his physical state. Of his mental condition this much may be presaged: that if either his inherited instincts or his acquired convictions had any reality whatever, it must have been chaos.

More chaotic than ever when, far into the night, after endless tests and trials, Nihâhli, the mysterious bride, proved beautiful as – – as – ?

Well, the fact was sure; only the comparison remained doubtful. The inherited instincts said a 'peri,'[16] the acquired convictions an angel. Both, it

415

will be observed, denizens of another world. But then there are more 'other worlds' than one.

'Master Narayan Chand hath sent to remind us that school re-opens next week,' said Govind's mother when nigh two months had passed; two months during which the path of life had been smoothed, scented, and decorated for the special use of a boy and a girl. Govind Sahai looked up from his work, which was, briefly, holding Nihâli's slim, ring bedecked fingers. The fact that he did so on pretence of teaching her to write is of secondary importance. She was undoubtedly a very pretty girl, and her delicate, refined face was at that moment full of adoring tenderness for the lad beside her. Not thirteen at the most, she was taller than English girls of that age, but far more slender, with a figure still following the straight lines of childhood. Graceful for all that, since her small head poised well over a round throat, and the want of contour was dexterously hidden by masses of jewellery, gleaming through the tinsel-shop veil. Even from wrist to elbow the thinness of the arm was concealed by the bridal bracelets of white ivory lined with red, whilst the slender ankles beneath the scarlet, gold-bordered petticoat were hung with silver-gilt jingles.

A typical bride briefly, arrayed in all attractions, save for the big nose-ring, with its dangling golden spoon hiding the lip. Govind objected to its presence, his mother to its absence – both, curiously enough, for the same reason – because it served as a check to indiscriminate kissing of the bride. The pious widow used to blush over her son's habit of saying good-bye to his wife when he had to leave her for an hour or two. It might be English fashion, warranted by all the love literature in creation; it was not decent. Neither did she approve of seeing them, as now, seated together over that ridiculous farce of pothooks.[17] Marriage was one thing, love-making was another, so she spoke sharply.

'Well,' answered the boy, utterly unabashed, 'dost think I have forgotten, *amma jan*?[18] Nay! Nihâli hath been hearing my holiday task half the morning. Hast not – O Nihâli?'

His arm, under cover of the veil, stole round the girl's waist and remained there – a flagrant breach of decorum which, fortunately for the female accomplice, remained unnoticed by mother-in-law, who was busy over a knot in a thread she was skeining from her unending pirn.[19] Yet Nihâli, despite this awful lapse, looked sweet and good enough to fill the heroine's part in any novel, and her looks did not belie her. The past two months had been a fever of delight to Govind. With the curious apathetic resignation to the limitations of custom so noticeable in clever Indian lads whose brains are full of theories, he had accepted marriage in the spirit of his forebears, only to find that Love (with a big L) such as he had read of in books was actually within his reach. To be sure, in books the object was chosen by the lover; but what did that matter in the end? So he used up all the stock-in trade of the

sentimental novelists for little Nihâli's benefit, and she listened to his rhap-
sodies on perfect marriage and twin souls, her eyes set wide with wonder,
admiration, and belief. No 'first lady' in white satin could have played her
part more prettily than this Indian child of thirteen, who from her cradle had
been taught to venerate her husband as a god, and who now, in a sort of
rapture, found herself the object of a sentimental passion absolutely novel
and bewildering. She nestled her sleek head on his shoulder, telling him that
she believed every word he said. And so she did; had he told her the world
was flat, instead of explaining to her with great pomp and precision that she
was living on an orange depressed at the poles, it would have been the same
to her. The world she lived in was of his creating. Like most Hindu girls of
the higher classes, she had a marvellous memory, and Govind had hardly
known whether to be pleased or pained at the discovery that, after hearing
him read it over a few times she knew his repetition better than he did
himself; yet, shy of her own exploit, she only replied to his laughing reference
to the holiday task by a timid squeeze of the hand still holding hers.

Mother-in-law broke the knot with a snap – a habit with the determined
little woman, who thereinafter would twirl the ends together as if nothing
had happened. One twist of the thumb, and all was as it had been.

'I know not what holiday tasks may mean,' she said scornfully. 'In my
time, work was work and play play. So must it be now. Nihâli's people have
sent to ask when she returns to them, after established custom. I have
answered, "When school begins."'

They had been so supremely, so innocently happy over their pothooks!
And now the consternation on their two young faces was quite piteous.
Mother-in-law, however, found it scandalous. Did not all decent girls cry to
go home long before the honeymoon was over? Had not she herself wept
bitterly in her time; and there was Nihâli actually snivelling at the idea of
leaving; before her husband, too! And Govind was no better.

'It is so soon,' pleaded the boy, too much taken aback for instant revolt;
besides, the situation had never come into any of the novels he had read, so
he really felt unable to cope with it.

His remark only increased the pitch of his mother's voice. Soon, was it?
Had he not had two months of billing and cooing, to gain which she and
granny had spun their fingers to the bone? Soon! Whose fault was it if time
had been wasted over alphabets and pothooks? Her shrill tones brought
granny from her labours below, and before these two eminently respectable
matrons the guilty pair could only hold each other's hands like the babes in
the wood, feeling lost and miserable.

That afternoon he went over to the public library, for the first time since
his marriage, and spent hours hunting up precedents on the subject, only to
return discomfited and hopeless. Nihâli would revolt, of course, if he bade her
follow his lead; but how could he bear to have the finger of scorn pointed at
her by those unacquainted with the theory of perfect marriage and twin

souls? That night, when the rest of the little household retired from the roof, leaving the luxury of fresh air to the younger people, he and Nihâli sat down under the stars on the still flower-strewn bed, and cried like the children they were.

So with awful swiftness the dawn came when Govind had to put on the pale-pink turban proclaiming him a first-class middle student, and set off to school with his books under his arm – books, on the whole, less disturbing than *Amor Vincit Omnia* and its congeners. Nothing further had been said about Nihâli's approaching departure. It was inevitable, of course; meanwhile, they must make the most of the time left to them. So Govind looked haggard and feverish as he took his accustomed place; nevertheless, being student by nature, the work beguiled him. By evening he was light-hearted enough to run home and race up the crumbling stairs leading to the roof, full of anecdotes and news for Nihâli. There was no one to receive them. The roof itself had resumed its normal workaday appearance, and in the very place where the little bride had sat on her lacquered bridal stool squatted his mother, piecing two broken strands of her skein together as if nothing had happened. And nothing out of the common had happened. Whose fault was it if Govind flung himself on his face and wept like a baby for what was beyond his reach?

His mother had expected so much when she planned her *coup d'etat*. But he continued to cry – which she did not expect – for something more complex than simple passion had been aroused in the boy. Of that he might have been ashamed; in this he gloried. Was it not, in short, a legitimate subject for self-glorification? So he wept himself sick in a subdued, docile sort of way. Finally, master-*ji* called one day in consternation to say that, though painstaking as ever, poor Govind could not remember the simplest problem; while as for riders,[20] he just sat and looked at them. The scholarship was thus in danger. She tried scolding the boy in good set terms, but he met her reproaches with an invulnerable superiority before which she stood aghast. What was to be done? Perhaps this spiriting away of the bride in order to avoid a scene had been an error, but was that any reason why she should be requested to return? To begin with, it would be an appalling breech of etiquette, and then there was the risk of consequences much to be deprecated between such very young people. The whole household, including master-*ji*, puzzled over the difficulty, which seemed all the more puzzling because it was so uncalled for, boys having been married at fifteen and sent to school again afterwards since time began without any fuss. But then, those boys had not read *Amor Vincit Omnia* and learned to mix sentiment with passion.

While matters were at this deadlock, Nihâli's mother arrived on the scene unexpectedly, and, *en petit comite*[21] with the women-folk, gave a new turn to affairs. The possibility suggested was in a measure disconcerting, but, on the other hand, afforded Govind's mother an opportunity of retreating with dignity, since the girl must not be allowed to fret as she had been fretting.

The result being that a week afterwards Govind Sahai did a difficult rider in a way which made Narayan Chand dream dreams of a future when folk would say, 'This eminent man received primary and secondary education at the hands of our most successful teacher of youth, Pundit Narayan Chand.' It was a dream he frequently indulged in about his pupils.

The little strip of roof was once more frequented by pigeons, and the snappings and joinings of threads relegated for the most part to the court below. Yet the boy's appetite did not return, and as winter came on he developed a teasing cough in that narrow chest of his. The fact was, that he burnt the candle of life at both ends in more ways than one. Perhaps if his soul could have been left in peace he might have passed through the ordeal safely, as many a boy manages to do in India. But it was not. Poor Govind had no rest. He strung himself up to the highest pitch in obedience to the mixed results of his birth and education. Then on this quivering instrument he proceeded to play scales. It was Tausig's exercises[22] on a zither. He had to teach himself, teach Nihâli, think of the coming baby, and go through the whole gamut of intellectual and physical emotion of which he had read. The first string gave way when his mother, laughing, crying, and blessing him all in a breath, put a boy baby into his arms on his return from school one day. He sat down stupidly on the lowest step of the mud stairs, gazing at what he held in a sort of bewildered amaze at finding himself thus, till his mother angrily snatched the child from him, saying he should be ashamed of shedding tears on a new-born baby's face. It was very like Nihâli, he thought, only years older with all those wrinkles. Then he thought helplessly how he had decided, with Nihâli's consent of course, on a thousand contraventions of old customs at this time. Yet there was she upstairs in the hands of the wise women, and the baby ready to be doctored by its grandmother. What could a boy of sixteen do against such odds? So the little proselytising pamphlet he had read was put away with a sigh; and after all Nihâli did very well under the old *régime*. He found her, when the wise women permitted him, in the seventh heaven over the baby. Was there ever such a doll, with its little sharp nose and pinched-up lips! And would he believe it? – the tiny creature was so lazy that grandmother had to tickle it so – on the mouth – before it would take any interest in the sugar and spices! By and by, when she could nurse it herself, it would be different. She lay smiling at the idea, while downstairs, as they left the house, the gossips were shaking their heads and saying calmly, 'It is an unnecessary baby, but a forerunner. Others will come. There is plenty of time.'

Even when Nihâli could not nurse the child, and they had recourse to a Maw's feeder,[23] which Govind, with many blushes, bought at the same shop which supplied him with slate pencils, those two young things feared nothing. He used to bring his books to the roof where she lay with the little quiet mouse of a thing tucked away in her veil. Then, while the sun set red over the dusty city, he worked away at all the 'ologies' – worked somewhat feverishly, since more depended now on his success. Sometimes Nihâli's smile gurgled over in laughter, and Govind, looking up, would find baby's fingers being clasped round his pen.

'Look you,' she would whisper, as if in presence of some great potentate, 'I asked my lord if he wished to be a writer too, and see how fast he holds!'

There was one thing, however, to which the baby did not hold fast, and that was life. But not till the very day before the eventful examination, which meant so much to Govind, did those two children read fear in each other's faces about that other child.

'O Govind! what shall we do? what shall we do?' wailed Nihâli, when the grandmother, seeing them wild with anxiety, told them the truth, while the great-grandmother stood by wagging her head and mumbling of others by and by. What was that to them now? How he got through the next day he never knew. He took the papers and went with them to his desk; nay, more, he did his level best with them, nerving himself to the effort chiefly by thoughts of master-*ji*'s disappointment if he failed. But his personal interest in the matter seemed gone; that was centred on a roof in the dusty city where one child sat crying over another. What were *plus* or *minus* to him save a world with or without an unnecessary infant?

All that night was passed beside Nihâli, waiting for his mother's voice to say the end had come; but the morning found the little sleeper still in the young mother's arms. Perhaps there was still hope. He hastily swallowed some breakfast, and, delayed by this hint or respite, found himself five minutes late in the examination-room. The first papers had already been given out, and to avoid possibility of fraud none save those present at the issue were allowed to compete. So Govind had to sit idle for while, knowing he had lost a definite number of chances. Nor was this the worst; the pause gave him time for thought. Hitherto, once within the familiar walls, old habits of attention and forgetfulness had possessed him. Now, with nothing to do, he remembered and yet forgot. So when the order to go up for the second paper came he rose with his brain in a whirl, a wild desire to cry, 'Let me alone, my baby is dying!' seeming to blot out everything else in the world. Perhaps had he done so he might have had a chance in the examiners' human pity; as it was, he pulled himself together, and failed hopelessly.

In the pause before the *vivâ voce* he sat looking straight before him, dully conscious that he had done badly.

'Govind has never been the same since he married,' whispered one boy, and the other giggled.

'Silence!' cried Narayan Chand fussily. 'Govind Sahai, your name is first for *vivâ*. Come up, Govind Sahai, Kyasth.' Then, as the dull yet anxious face passed him, he whispered: 'Now for value of light literature. You are best at colloquial, my pupil, so courage, and remember "Amor Vincit Omnia" and such like things.'

'Amor Vincit Omnia!' The boy's last chance fled before those words. When the ordeal was over, he turned back to his place mechanically. As he passed the master-*ji* once more, he read his fate in the disappointed face raised to his, then in the confident smile of the boy succeeding him, finally in the surprised nudging of the whole class. Something seemed to snap in his brain; he paused, and, facing the examiners, raised his hand. The rush of thought was too much for him at first; then he broke silence in a gentle, deprecating voice –

'If you will be kind enough to excuse me, sirs, I will beg leave to retire. The exigencies of the case forbid explanation, but this much is admitted – that "Amor vincit omnia."'

'That boy speaks better English than I thought for,' said one examiner to the other, when the leave had been granted. 'Give him five marks more; he's failed, of course, but it's as well to be just.'

When Govind reached home Nihâli's arms were empty. There is no need to say more. It was an unnecessary infant to all save those two.

'You have failed, failed badly, my poor pupil, owing, doubtless, to domestic bereavement,' said the master-*ji*, when he called a week or two later full of vexed sympathy. 'Such circumstances point to special privilege of entering again next year, for which we will apply. And then, Govind, there must be no killing of two birds with one stone. There must be no complicated states of mind, confusing idiom.'

But Govind Sahai, Kyasth, did not avail himself of the permission duly given, as the pundit-*ji* put it, 'in consideration of the strictly non-regulation death of his infant at a premature age.'

The old grandfather, whose small life-pension had been the prop of the household, died of autumnal fever, and during the ensuing winter the result of his failure to win the scholarship came home to Govind with depressing force, since even from that poor ten rupees a month something might have been spared to stand between those three fond women and the grindstone, that last resort of poverty. Then Nihâli's mother, coming over unexpectedly and finding her daughter at the mill, carried her off in a huff. This time Govind said nothing; the spirit had gone out of him, and for the girl's own sake he gave into custom. He worked very hard, but as the winter advanced his shoulders seemed to grow narrower and narrower, and the teasing cough became louder. Good food, care, and rest might have done something per-haps; only perhaps, for there is not much to be done when the candle of life is alight at both ends, except to put it out. That is what happened one April morning when the bougainvillea round the arched verandah of the library looked like a crimson drapery. He used to go there every morning before school-hours, for the memory of his failure in *vivâ voce* rankled keenly, and he was possessed by a curious determination to prove Master Narayan Chand wrong in attributing it to Gonvind's unwise selection of books. So, secure at those hours from interruption he used to sit and study the idiom of light literature.

'Thou art not fit to go,' said his mother tearfully one morning after the boy had been kept awake all night by cough and fever.

'Reading will not hurt me, *amma jan*,' he replied, 'and the examination is next month.'

They found him two hours afterwards seated at the desk before the ledger, his head resting on a novel he had just been entering in the register. A horrible stain of blood from the blood-vessel he had ruptured blotted the page, but through it you could still see, in his bold handwriting –

Amor Vincit Omnia. Govind Sahai, Kyasth.

Notes

Text: *In the Permanent Way*, Heinemann, London, 1898.

1 In the Old Testament, God causes a gourd (in the Jerusalem Bible, the Hebrew term is translated as 'castor-oil plant') to rise up and shelter Jonah, Hebrew prophet, but strikes it down again next day (Jonah 4: 6–7).
2 Artificial lake.
3 Large tree of genus *Dalbergia sissoo*.
4 Palm-leaf fans.
5 'Love Conquers All.'
6 Food for thought.
7 Viva voce (oral) examinations.
8 Early eighteenth-century journals, founded and written by essayists Joseph Addison (1672–1719) and Richard Steele (1672–1729).
9 Recent publications by William Schwenk Gilbert (1836–1911), comic poet and lyricist for 'Gilbert and Sullivan' comic operas; Alfred, Lord Tennyson (1809–92), Poet Laureate.
10 Lyrics by Gilbert from the opera *The Gondoliers*, Act I.
11 *Much Ado about Nothing* II. iii. 102, slightly misquoted.
12 Oh Lord!
13 Invocation to the Hindu goddess of wealth and plenty.
14 King of the Hindu gods.
15 Wreaths.
16 Beautiful supernatural being.
17 Marks made while learning to write.
18 Mother dear.
19 Shuttle spool.
20 Problems arising out of mathematical theorems.
21 In an intimate discussion.
22 *Tägliche Studien*, popular finger exercises for the piano, by Carl Tausig (1841–71), Polish pianist.
23 Baby's feeding bottle.

A STORY OF A WEDDING TOUR

Margaret Oliphant

Margaret Oliphant, née Wilson (1828–97), novelist, short-story writer, biographer, critic and historical writer, was born in Scotland. She published her first novel, the successful *Margaret Maitland* (1849), at the age of 21. She moved to London after her marriage to her cousin Francis Wilson Oliphant, a stained-glass engraver, in 1852, and produced a number of novels, the income from which helped to support not only her husband and children but also her alcoholic brother. Widowed in her early thirties, and left virtually penniless, she supported her children (and, later, her widowed brother's children) by writing, becoming one of the most prolific and skilful of Victorian writers and Queen Victoria's favourite novelist. Of her almost 100 novels, the series known as the 'Chronicles of Carlingford' is the best known, and includes *The Rector and The Doctor's Family* and *Salem Chapel* (both 1863), *The Perpetual Curate* (1864), *Miss Marjoribanks* (1866) and *Phoebe Junior* (1876). She also published several volumes of short stories (her ghost stories, collected as *Stories of the Seen and Unseen* (1885), are considered among her best), literary histories, art criticism, several biographies, travel works and two autobiographies (1868 and 1899). She also wrote over 200 articles for *Blackwoods*, and edited their Foreign Classics Series. Her history of Blackwoods, *Annals of a Publishing House* (1897), is much admired. *A Story of a Wedding Tour*, one of a series of variations on the theme of a young woman's bid for freedom, is less conventional in its treatment of marriage than her earlier fiction tends to be.

Further reading

Blain *et al.* (1990); Broughton (1987); Clarke (1981, 1986, 1989); Colby and Colby (1966); Haythornthwaite (1990); Homans (1986); Jay (1990, 1995); Schor (1993); Shattock (1993); Showalter (1977); Sutherland (1976, 1988); Terry (1983); Trela (1994); Williams (1986).

A Story of a Wedding Tour

Chapter I

They had been married exactly a week when this incident occurred.

It was not a love marriage. The man, indeed, had been universally described as being "very much in love," but the girl was not by any one supposed to be in that desirable condition. She was a very lonely little girl, without parents, almost without relations. Her guardian was a man who had been engaged in business relations with her father, and who had accepted the charge of the little orphan as his duty. But neither he nor his wife had any love to expend on her, and they did not feel that such visionary sentiments came within the line of duty. He was very honourable man, and took charge of her small – very small – property with unimpeachable care.

If anything, he wronged himself rather than Janey, charging her nothing for the transfers which he made of her farthing's worth of stock from time to time, to get a scarcely appreciable rise of interest and income for her. The whole thing was scarcely appreciable, and to a large-handed man like Mr Midhurst, dealing with hundreds of thousands, it was almost ridiculous to give a moment's attention to what a few hundreds might produce. But he did so; and if there is any angel who has to do with trade affairs, I hope it was carefully put to his account to balance some of the occasions on which he was not perhaps so particular. Nor did Mrs Midhurst shrink from her duty in all substantial and real good offices to the girl. She, who spent hundreds at the dressmaker's every year on account of her many daughters, did not disdain to get Janey's serge frocks at a cheaper shop, and to have them made by an inexpensive workwoman, so that the girl should have the very utmost she could get for her poor little money.

Was not this real goodness, real honesty, and devotion to their duty? But to love a little thing like that with no real claim upon them, and nothing that could be called specially attractive about her, who could be expected to do it? They had plenty – almost more than enough – of children of their own. These children were big boys and girls, gradually growing, in relays, into manhood and womanhood, when this child came upon their hands. There was no room for her in the full and noisy house. When she was grown up most of the Midhurst children were married, but there was one son at home, who, in the well-known contradictiousness of young people – it being a very wrong and, indeed, impossible thing – was quite capable of falling in

425

love with Janey – and one daughter, with whom it was also possible that
Janey might come into competition.

The young Midhursts were nice-looking young people enough; but Janey
was very pretty. If Providence did but fully consider all the circumstances, it
cannot but be felt that Providence would not carry out, as often is done, such
ridiculous arrangements. Janey was very pretty. Could anything more
inconvenient, more inappropriate, be conceived?

The poor little girl had, accordingly, spent most of her life at school,
where she had, let it not be doubted, made many friendships and little loves;
but these were broken up by holidays, by the returning home of the other
pupils, while she stayed for ever at school: and not at one school, but several
– for in his extreme conscientiousness her guardian desired to do her "every
justice," as he said, and prepare her fully for the life – probably that of a
governess – which lay before her. Therefore, when she had become proficient
in one part of her education she was carried on to another, with the highest
devotion to her commercial value no doubt, but a sublime indifference to her
little feelings. Thus, she had been in France for two years, and in Germany
for two years, so as to be able to state that French and German acquired in
these countries were among the list of her accomplishments. English, of
course, was the foundation of all; and Janey had spent some time at a famous
academy of music, – her guardian adding something out of his own pocket to
her scanty means, that she might be fully equipped for her profession. And
then she was brought, I will not say home: Janey fondly said home, but she
knew very well it did not mean home. And it was while Mrs Midhurst was
actually writing out the advertisement for 'The Times,' and the 'Morning
Post,' and 'The Guardian,' which was to announce to all the world that a
young lady desired an engagement as governess, that her husband burst in
with the extraordinary news that Mr Rosendale, who had chanced to travel
with Janey from Flushing, on her return, and who afterwards, by a still
greater chance, met her when asked to lunch at the Midhursts', and stared
very much at her, as they all remarked – had fallen in love with, and wanted
to marry, this humble little girl.

"Fallen in love with Janey!" Mrs Midhurst cried. "Fallen in love with you,
Janey!" said Agnes Midhurst, with a little emphasis on the pronoun. He was
not, indeed, quite good enough to have permitted himself the luxury of
falling in love with Mr Midhurst's daughter, but he was an astonishing
match for Janey. He was a man who was very well off: he could afford himself
such a caprice as that. He was not handsome. There was a strain of Jewish
blood in him. He was a thick-set little man, and did not dress or talk in
perfect taste; but – in love! These two words had made all the difference.
Nobody had ever loved her, much less been "in love" with her. Janey consented willingly enough for the magic of these two words. She felt that she
was going to be like the best of women at last – to have some one who loved
her, some one who was in love with her. He might not be "joli, joli,"[1] as they

say in France. She might not feel any very strong impulse on her own part towards him; but if he were in love with her – in love! Romeo was no more than that with Juliet. The thought went to Janey's head. She married him quite willingly for the sake of this.

I am afraid that Janey, being young, and shy, and strange, was a good deal frightened, horrified, and even revolted, by her first discoveries of what it meant to be in love. She had made tremendous discoveries in the course of a week. She had found out that Mr Rosendale, her husband, was in love with her beauty, but as indifferent to herself as any of the persons she had quitted to give herself to him. He did not care at all what she thought, how she felt, what she liked or disliked. He did not care even for her comfort, or that she should be pleased and happy, which, in the first moment even of such a union, and out of pure self-regard to make a woman more agreeable to himself, a man – even the most brutal – generally regards more or less. He was, perhaps, not aware that he did not regard it. He took it for granted that, being his wife, she would naturally be pleased with what pleased him, and his mind went no further than this.

Therefore, as far as Janey liked the things he liked, all went well enough. She had these, but no other. Her wishes were not consulted further, nor did he know that he failed in any way towards her. He had little to say to her, except expressions of admiration. When he was not telling her that she was a little beauty, or admiring her pretty hair, her pretty eyes, the softness of her skin, and the smallness of her waist, he had nothing to say. He read his paper, disappearing behind it in the morning; he went to sleep after his midday meal (for the weather was warm;) he played billiards in the evening in the hotels to which he took her on their wedding journey; or he overwhelmed her with caresses from which she shrank in disgust, almost in terror. That was all that being in love meant, she found; and to say that she was disappointed cruelly was to express in the very mildest way the dreadful downfall of all her expectations and hopes which happened to Janey before she had been seven days a wife. It is not disagreeable to be told that you are a little beauty, prettier than any one else. Janey would have been very well pleased to put up with that; but to be petted like a little lapdog and then left as a lapdog is – to be quiet and not to trouble in the intervals of petting – was to the poor little girl, unaccustomed to love and athirst for it, who had hoped to be loved, and to find a companion to whom she would be truly dear, a disenchantment and disappointment which was almost more than flesh and blood could bear.

She was in the full bitterness of these discoveries when the strange incident occurred which was of so much importance in her life. They were travelling through France in one of those long night journeys to which we are all accustomed nowadays; and Janey, pale and tired, had been contemplating for some time the figure of her husband thrown back in the corner opposite, snoring complacently with his mouth open, and looking the worst that a middle-aged man can look in the utter abandonment of self-indulgence and rude comfort, when the train began to slacken its speed, and to prepare to enter one of those large stations which look so ghastly in the desertion of the night.

Rosendale jumped up instinctively, only half awake, as the train stopped. The other people in the carriage were leaving it, having attained the end of their journey, but he pushed through them and their baggage to get out, with the impatience which some men show at any pause of the kind, and determination to stretch their legs, or get something to drink, which mark the breaks in their journey. He did not even say anything to Janey as he forced his way out, but she was so familiar with his ways by this time that she took no notice. She did take notice, however, when, her fellow-passengers and their packages having all been cleared away, she suddenly became sensible that the train was getting slowly into motion again without any sign of her husband.

She thought she caught a glimpse of him strolling about on the opposite platform before she was quite sure of what was happening. And then there was a scurry of hurrying feet, a slamming of doors, and as she rose and ran to the window bewildered, she saw him, along with some other men, running at full speed, but quite hopelessly, to catch the train. The last she saw was his face, fully revealed by the light of the lamp, convulsed with rage and astonishment, evidently with a yell of denunciation on the lips. Janey trembled at the sight. There was that in him, too, though as yet in her submissiveness she had never called it forth, a temper as unrestrained as his love-making, and as little touched by any thought save that of his own gratification. Her first sensation was fright, a terror that she was in fault and was about to be crushed to pieces in his rage: and then Janey sank back in her corner, and a flood of feeling of quite another kind took possession of her breast.

Was it possible that she was alone? Was it possible that for the first time since that terrible moment of her marriage she was more safely by herself than any locked door or even watchful guardian could keep her, quite unapproachable in the isolation of the train? Alone!

"Safe!" Janey ventured to say to herself, clasping her hands together with a mingled sensation of excitement and terror and tremulous delight which words could not tell.

She did not know what to think at first. The sound of the train plunging along through the darkness, through the unknown country, filled her mind as if some one was talking to her. And she was fluttered by the strangeness of the incident and disturbed by alarms. There was a fearful joy in thus being alone, in having a few hours, perhaps a whole long tranquil night, to herself: whatever came of it, that was always so much gained. But then she seemed to see him in the morning coming in upon her heated and angry. She had always felt that the moment would come when he would be angry, and more terrible to confront than any governess, or even principal of a ladies' college. He would come in furious, accusing her of being the cause of the accident, or doing something to set the train in motion; or else he would come in fatigued and dusty, claiming her services as if she were his valet – a thing which had, more or less, happened already, and against which Janey's pride and her sense of what was fit had risen in arms. She thought of this for a little time with trouble, and of the difficulties she would have in arriving, and where she would go to, and what she would say. It was an absurd story to tell, not to his advantage, "I lost my husband at Montbard." How could she say it? The hotel people would think she was a deceiver. Perhaps they would not take her in. And how would he know where to find her when he arrived? He would feel that he had lost her, as much as she had lost him.

Just as this idea rose in her mind, like a new thing full of strange sugges-tions, the train began to shorten speed again, and presently stopped once more. She felt it to do so with a pang of horror. No doubt he had climbed up somewhere, at the end or upon the engine, and was now to be restored to his legitimate place, to fall upon her either in fondness or in rage, delighted to get back to her, or angry with her for leaving him behind: she did not know which would be the worst. Her heart began to beat with fright and anticipa-tion. But to her great relief it was only the guard who came to the door. He wanted to know if madame was the lady whose husband had been left behind; and to offer a hundred apologies and explanations. One of those fools at Montbard had proclaimed twenty minutes' pause when there were but five. If he had but heard he would have put it right, but he was at the other end of the train. But madame must not be too much distressed; a few hours would put it all right.

"Then there is another train?" said Janey, her poor little head buzzing between excitement and relief.

"Not for some hours," said the guard. "Madame will understand that there is not more than one *rapide*² in the middle of the night; but in the morning quite early there is the train omnibus. Oh, very early, at five o'clock. Before madame is ready for her dinner monsieur will be at her side."

"Not till evening, then?" said Janey, with again a sudden acceleration of the movement of her heart.

The guard was desolated. "Not before evening. But if madame will remain quietly in the carriage when the train arrives at the station, I will find the omnibus of the hotel for her – I will see to everything! Madame, no doubt, knows which hotel to go to?"

Janey, as a matter of fact, did not know. Her husband had told her none of the details of the journey; but she said with a quick breath of excitement –

"I will go to the one that is nearest, the one at the Gare.³ There will be no need for any omnibus."

"And the baggage? Madame has her ticket?"

"I have nothing," cried Janey, "except my travelling-bag. You must explain that for me. But otherwise – otherwise, I think I can manage."

"Madame speaks French so well," the man said, with admiration. It was, indeed, a piece of good fortune that she had been made to acquire the language in the country: that she was not frightened to find herself in a foreign place, and surrounded by people speaking a strange tongue, as many a young English bride would have been. There was a moment of tremendous excitement and noise at the station while all was explained to a serious *chef de Gare*,[4] and a gesticulating band of porters and attendants, whose loud voices, as they all spoke together, would have frightened an ordinary English girl out of her wits. But Janey, in the strange excitement which had taken possession of her, and in her fortunate acquaintance with the language, stood still as a little rock amid all the confusion. "I will wait at the hotel till my husband comes," she said, taking out the travelling-bag and her wraps, and maintaining a composure worthy of all admiration. Not a tear, not an outcry. How astonishing are these English, cried the little crowd, with that swift classification which the Frenchman loves.

Janey walked into the hotel with her little belongings, not knowing whether she was indeed walking upon her feet or floating upon wings. She was quite composed. But if any one could only have seen the commotion within that youthful bosom! She locked the door of the little delightful solitary room in which she was placed. It was not delightful at all. But to Janey it was a haven of peace, as sweet, as secluded from everything alarming and terrible, as any bower. Not till evening could he by any possibility arrive – the man who had caused such a revolution in her life. She had some ten hours of divine quiet before her, of blessed solitude, of thought. She did not refuse to take the little meal that was brought to her, the breakfast of which she stood in need; and she was glad to be able to bathe her face, to take off her dusty dress, and put on the soft and fresh one, which, happily, had folded into very small space, and therefore could be put into her bag. Her head still buzzed with the strangeness of the position, yet began to settle a little. When she had made all these little arrangements she sat down to consider. Perhaps you will think there was very little to consider, nothing but how to wait till the next train brought him, which, after all, was not a very great thing to do. Appalling, perhaps, to a little inexperienced bride; but not to Janey, who had travelled alone so often, and knew the language, and all that.

But whoever had been able to look into Janey's mind would have seen that something more was there, – a very, very different thing from the question of how best to await his coming back. Oh, if he had loved her, Janey would have put up with many things! She would have schooled herself out of all her private repugnances; she would have been so grateful to him, so touched by the affection which nobody had ever bestowed upon her before! But he did not love her. He cared nothing about herself, Janey; did not even know her, or want to know her, or take into consideration her ways or her wishes. He was in love with her pretty face, her fresh little beauty, her power of pleasing him. If ever that power ceased, which it was sure to do, sooner or later, she would be to him less than nothing, the dreary little wife whom everybody has seen attached to a careless man: Janey felt that this was what was in store for her. She felt the horror of him, and his kind of loving, which had been such a miserable revelation to her. She felt the relief, the happiness, ah, the bliss, of having lost him for a moment, of being alone.

She took out her purse from her pocket, which was full of the change she had got in Paris of one of the ten-pound notes which her guardian had given her when she left his house on her wedding morning. She took out the clumsy pocket-book, an old one, in which there were still nine ten-pound notes. It was all her fortune, except a very, very small investment which brought her in some seven pounds a year. This was the remainder of another small investment which had been withdrawn in order to provide her with her simple trousseau, leaving this sum of a hundred pounds which her guardian had given her, advising her to place it at once for security in her husband's hands. Janey had not done this, she scarcely could tell why. She spread them on the table – the nine notes, the twelve napoleons of shining French money. A hundred pounds; she had still the twelve francs which made up the sum. She had spent nothing. There were even the few coppers over for the *agio*.[5] She spread them all out, and counted them from right to left, and again from left to right. Nine ten-pound notes, twelve and a-half French napoleons – or louis, as people call them nowadays – making a hundred pounds. A hundred pounds is a big sum in the eyes of a girl. It may not be much to you and me, who know that it means only ten times ten pounds, and that ten pounds goes like the wind as soon as you begin to spend it. But to Janey! Why, she could live upon a hundred pounds for – certainly for two years; for two long delightful years, with nobody to trouble her, nobody to scold, nobody to interfere. Something mounted to her head like the fumes of wine. Everything began to buzz again, to turn round, to sweep her away as on a rapidly mounting current. She put back all the money in the pocket-book – her fortune, the great sum that made her independent; and she put back her things into the bag. A sudden energy of resolution seized her. She put on her hat again, and as she looked at herself in the glass encountered the vision of a little face which was new to her. It was not that of Janey, the little governess-pupil; it was not young Mrs. Rosendale. It was full of life, and meaning, and energy, and strength. Who was it? Janey? Janey herself, the real woman, whom nobody had ever seen before.

Chapter II

It is astonishing how many things can be done in sudden excitement and passion which could not be possible under any other circumstances. Janey was by nature a shy girl and easily frightened, accustomed indeed to do many things for herself, and to move quietly without attracting observation through the midst of a crowd; but she had never taken any initiative, and since her marriage had been reduced to such a state of complete dependence on her husband's wishes and plans that she had not attempted the smallest step on her own impulse.

Now, however, she moved about with a quiet assurance and decision which astonished herself. She carried her few possessions back again to the railway station, leaving the small gold piece of ten francs to pay, and much overpay, her hour's shelter and entertainment at the hotel.

Nobody noticed her as she went through the bustle of the place and back to the crowded station, where a little leisurely local train was about starting – a slow train occupied by peasants and country folk, and which stopped at every station along the line. English people abound in that place at all hours, except at this particular moment, when the *rapide* going towards Italy had but newly left and the little country train was preparing in peace. Nobody seemed to notice Janey as she moved about with her bag on her arm. She took her ticket in her irreproachable French "acquired in the country," which attracted no attention. She got into a second-class carriage in which there were already various country people, and especially a young mother with a baby, and its nurse in a white round cap with long streaming ribbons. Janey's heart went out to these people. She wondered if the young woman was happy, if her husband loved her, if it was not very sweet to have a child – a child must love you; it would not mind whether your cheeks were rosy or pale, whether you were pretty or not, whether you had accomplishments or languages acquired in the country.

Looking at this baby, Janey almost forgot that she was going out upon the world alone, and did not know where. It is a tremendous thing to do this, to separate from all the world you are acquainted with, to plunge into the unknown. Men do it often enough, though seldom without some clue, some link of connection with the past and way of return. Janey was about to cut herself off as by the Fury's shears[6] from everything. She would never join her husband again. She would never fear her guardian again. She must drop out of sight like a stone into the sea. There was no longing love to search for her, no pardon to be offered, no one who would be heart-struck at the thought of the little girl lost and unhappy. Only anger would be excited by her running away, and a desire to punish, to shake her little fragile person to pieces, to make her suffer. She knew that if she did it at all, it must be final. But this did not overwhelm her. What troubled Janey a great deal more than the act of severance which she was about to accomplish, was the inevitable fib or fibs she must tell in order to account for her appearance in the unknown. She did not like to tell a fib, even a justifiable one. It was against all her traditions, against her nature. She felt that she could never do it anything but badly, never without exciting suspicions; and she must needs have some story, some way of accounting for herself.

This occupied her mind while the slow train crawled from station to station. It was the most friendly, idle, gossiping little train. It seemed to stop at the merest signal-box to have a talk, to drink as it were a social glass administered through that black hose, with a friend; it stopped wherever there were a few houses, it carried little parcels, it took up a leisurely passenger going next door, and the little electric bell went on tingling, and the guard cried "En voiture!"[7] and the little bugle sounded. Janey was amused by all these little sounds and sights, and the country all flooded with sunshine, and the flowers everywhere, though it was only March, and dark black weather when she had left home.

Left home! and she had no home now, anywhere, no place to take refuge in, nobody to write to, to appeal to, to tell if she was happy or unhappy. But Janey did not care! She felt a strange elation of ease and relief. All alone, but everybody smiling upon her, the young mother opposite beginning to chatter, the baby to crow to her, the nurse to smile and approve of the *bonne petite*[8] dame who took so much notice of the child. Her head was swimming, but with pleasure, and the blessed sensation of freedom – pleasure tinctured with the exhilaration of escape, and the thrill of fright which added to the excitement. Yet at that moment she was certainly in no danger. He was toiling along no doubt, fuming and perhaps swearing, on another slow train on the other side of Marseilles. Janey laughed to herself a little guiltily at the thought.

And she had escaped! It was not her doing primarily. She might have gone on all her life till she had died, but for that accident which was none of her doing. It was destiny that had done it, fate. The cage door had been opened and the bird had flown away. And how nice it would be to settle down, with this little mother, just about her own age, for a neighbour, and to help to bring the baby up! The kind, sweet faces they all had, mother and baby and *bonne*[9] all smiling upon her! When Janey looked out on the other side she saw the sea flashing in the sunshine, the red porphyry rocks reflecting themselves in the brilliant blue, and village after village perched upon a promontory or in the hollow of a bay. She had never in all her life before felt that sensation of blessedness, of being able to do what she liked, of having no one to call to her account. She did not know where she was going, but that was part of the pleasure. She did not want to know where she was going.

Then suddenly this sentiment changed, and she saw in a moment a place that smiled at her like the smiling of the mother and baby. It was one of those villages in a bay: a range of blue mountains threw forth a protecting arm into the sea to shield it: the roofs were red, the houses were white, they were all blazing in the sun. Soft olives and palms fringed the deep green of the pines that rolled back in waves of verdure over the country behind, and strayed down in groups and scattered files to the shore below. Oh, what a cheerful, delightsome place! and this was where the little group with the baby were preparing to get out. "I will go too," said Janey to herself; and her heart gave a little bound of pleasure. She was delighted to reach the place where she was going to stay – just as she had been delighted to go on in the little pottering train, not knowing where she was going; and not wishing to know.

This was how Janey settled herself on the day of her flight from the world. She scarcely knew what story it was she told to the young woman whose face had so charmed her, and whom she asked whether she would be likely to find lodgings anywhere, lodgings that would not be too expensive.

My husband is – at sea," Janey heard herself saying. She could scarcely tell what it was that put those words into her head.

"Oh, but yes," the other young woman cried with rapture. Nothing was more easy to get than a lodging in St Honorat, which was beginning to try to be a winter resort, and was eager to attract strangers. Janey had dreamed of a cottage and a garden, but she was not dissatisfied when she found herself in a sunbright room on the second floor of a tall white house facing the sea. It had a little balcony all to itself. The water rippled on the shore just over the road, the curve of the blue mountains was before her eyes.

I do not say that when she had settled down, when the thrill of movement was no longer in her brain, Janey was not without a shiver at the thought of what she had done. When the sun set, and that little chill which comes into the air of the south at the moment of its setting breathed a momentary cold about her, and when the woman of the house carefully closed the shutters and shut out the shining of the bay, and she was left alone with her candle, something sank in Janey's heart – something of the unreasonable elation, the fantastic happiness, of the day. She thought of "Mr. Rosendale" (she had never got so near her husband as to call him by any other name) arriving, of the fuss there would be about her and the inquiries.

Was it rash to have come to a place so near as this – within an hour or two of where he was? Was there a danger that some one might have seen her? that it might be found out that she had taken her ticket? But then she had taken her ticket for a place much farther along the coast. She thought she could see him arrive all flaming with anger and eagerness, and the group that would gather round him, and how he would be betrayed by his bad French, and the rage he would get into! Again she laughed guiltily; but then got very grave again trying to count up all the chances – how some porter might have noticed and might betray her, how he might yet come down upon her furiously, to wreak upon her all the fury of his discomfiture. Janey knew by instinct that though it was in no way her fault, her husband would wreak his vengeance upon her even for being left behind by the train. She became desperate as she sat and thought it all over. It would be better for her to leap from the window, to throw herself into the sea, than to fall into his hands. There would be no forgiveness for her if he once laid hands upon her. Now that she had taken this desperate step, she must stand by it to the death.

Chapter III

Ten years had passed away since the time of that wedding tour.

Ten years! It is a very long time in a life. It makes a young man middle-aged, and a middle-aged man old. It takes away the bloom of youth, and the ignorance of the most inexperienced; and yet what a little while it is! – no more than a day when you look back upon it. The train from Marseilles to Nice, which is called the *rapide*, goes every day, and most people one time or another have travelled by it.

One day last winter one of the passengers in this train established very comfortably in the best corner of a sleeping carriage in which he had passed the night luxuriously, and from which he was now looking out upon the shining sea, the red rocks, the many bays and headlands of the coast, suddenly received such a shock and sensation as seldom occurs to any one. He was a man of middle-age and not of engaging aspect. His face was red, and his eyes were dull yet fiery. He had the air of a man who had indulged himself much and all his inclinations, had loved good living and all the joys of the flesh, had denied himself nothing – and was now paying the penalties. Such men, to tell the truth, are not at all unusual apparitions on that beautiful coast or in the train *rapide*. No doubt appearances are deceitful, and it is not always a bad man who bears that aspect or who pays those penalties: but in this case few people would have doubted.

His eyes were bloodshot, he had a scowl upon his brow, his foot was supported upon a cushion. He had a servant with him to whom he rarely spoke but with an insult. Not an agreeable man – and the life he was now leading, whatever it had been, was not an agreeable life. He was staring out at the window upon the curves of the coast, sometimes putting up the collar of his fur coat over his ears, though it was a warm morning, and the sun had all the force of April. What he was thinking of it would be difficult to divine – perhaps of the good dinner that awaited him at Monte Carlo when he got there, perhaps of his good luck in being out of England when the east winds began to blow, perhaps of something quite different – some recollection of his past. The *rapide* does not stop at St Honorat, which indeed had not succeeded in making itself a winter resort. It was still a very small place. There were a few people on the platform when the train rushed through. It seemed to pass like a whirlwind, yet notwithstanding, in that moment two things happened. The gentleman in the corner of the carriage started in his seat, and flung himself half out of the window, with a sudden roar which lost itself in the tunnel into which the train plunged. There was an awful minute in that tunnel: for the servant thought his master had taken a fit, and there was no light to see what convulsions he might have fallen into, while at the same time he fought furiously against the man's efforts to loose his wrappings and place him in a recumbent position, exclaiming furiously all the time. He had not taken a fit, but when the train emerged into the light he was as near to it as possible – purple-red in his face, and shouting with rage and pain.

"Stop the train! stop the train!" he shouted. "Do you hear, you fool? stop the train! Ring the bell or whatever it is! break the – thing! Stop the train!"

"Sir, sir! if you will only be quiet, I will get your medicine in a moment!"

"Medicine, indeed!" cried the master, indignantly, and every furious name that he could think of mounted to his lips – fool, idiot, ass, swine – there was no end to his epithets. "I tell you I saw her, I saw her!" he shouted. "Stop the train! Stop the train!"

On the other hand, among the few insignificant persons, peasants and others, who had been standing on the platform at St Honorat when the *rapide* dashed past, there had been a woman and a child. The woman was not a peasant: she was very simply dressed in black, with one of the small bonnets which were a few years ago so distinctively English, and with an air which corresponded to that simple coiffure. She was young, and yet had the air of responsibility and motherhood which marks a woman who is no longer in the first chapter of life. The child, a boy of nine or ten, standing close by her side, had seized her hand just as the train appeared impatiently to call her attention to something else; but, by some strange spell of attraction or coincidence, her eyes fixed upon that window out of which the gouty travel-ler was looking. She saw him as he saw her, and fell back dragging the boy with her as if she would have sunk into the ground. It was only a moment and the *rapide* was gone, screaming and roaring into the tunnel, making too much noise with the rush and sweep of its going to permit the shout of the passenger to be heard.

Ten years, ten long years, during which life had undergone so many changes! They all seemed to fly away in a moment, and the girl who had arrived at the little station of St Honorat alone, a fugitive, elated and intoxicated with her freedom, suddenly felt herself again the little Janey who had emancipated herself so strangely, – though she had for a long time been frightened by every train that passed and every stranger who came near.

In the course of these long years all this had changed. Her baby had been born, her forlorn state had called forth great pity, great remark and criticism, in the village where she had found refuge, – great censure also, for the fact of her marriage was not believed by everybody. But she was so lonely, so modest, and so friendly, that the poor little English stranger was soon forgiven. Perhaps her simple neighbours were glad to find that a prim English-woman, supposed to stand so fierce on her virtue, was in reality so fallible – or perhaps pity put all other sentiments out of court. She told her real story to the priest when the boy was baptised, and though he tried to persuade her to return to her husband, he only half believed in that husband, since the story was not told under any seal of confession. Janey never became absolutely one of his flock. She was a prim little Protestant in her heart, standing strong against the saints, but devoutly attending church, believing with simple religiousness that to go to church was better than not to go to church, whatever the rites might be, and reading her little English service steadily through all the prayers of the Mass, which she never learned to follow. But her boy was like the other children of St Honorat, and learned his catechism and said his lessons with the rest.

There were various things which she did to get a living, and got it very innocently and sufficiently, though in the humblest way. She taught English to the children of some of the richer people in the village: she taught them music. She had so much credit in this latter branch, that she often held the organ in church on a holiday and pleased everybody. Then she worked very well with her needle, and would help on an emergency at first for pure kindness, and then, as her faculties and her powers of service became known, for pay, with diligence and readiness. She found a niche in the little place which she filled perfectly, though only accident seemed to have made it for her. She had fifty pounds of her little fortune laid by for the boy. She had a share of a cottage in a garden – not an English cottage indeed, but the upper floor of a two-storeyed French house; and she and her boy did much in the garden, cultivating prettinesses which do not commend themselves much to the villagers of St Honorat. Whether she ever regretted the step she had taken nobody ever knew. She might have been a lady with a larger house than any in St Honorat, and servants at her call. Perhaps she sometimes thought of that; perhaps she felt herself happier as she was; sometimes, I think, she felt that if she had known the boy was coming she might have possessed her soul in patience, and borne even with Mr Rosendale. But then at the time the decisive step was taken she did not know.

She hurried home in a great fright, not knowing what to do; then calmed herself with the thought that even if he had recognised her, there were many chances against his following her, or at least finding her, with no clue, and after so many years. And then a dreadful panic seized her at the thought that he might take her boy from her. He had known nothing about the boy: but if he discovered that fact it would make a great difference. He could not compel Janey to return to him, but he could take the boy. When this occurred to her she started up again, having just sat down, and put on her bonnet and called the child.

"Are you going out again, mother?" he cried.

"Yes, directly, directly: come, John, come, come!" she said, putting his cap upon his head and seizing him by the hand. She led him straight to the presbytery, and asked for the *curé*,[10] and went in to the good priest in great agitation, leaving the boy with his housekeeper.

"M. l'Abbé," she said, with what the village called her English directness, "I have just seen my husband go past in the train!"

"Not possible!" said M. l'Abbé, who only half believed there was a husband at all.

"And he saw me. He will come back, and I am afraid he will find me. I want you to do something for me."

"With pleasure," said the priest; "I will come and meet Monsieur your husband, and I will explain –"

"That is not what I want you to do. I want you to let John stay with you, to keep him here till – till – He will want to take him away from me!" she cried.

"He will want to take you both away, *chère petite dame*.[11] He has a right to do so."

"No, no! but I do not ask you what is his right. I ask you to keep John safe; to keep him here – till the danger has passed away!"

The priest tried to reason, to entreat, to persuade her that a father, not to say a husband, had his rights. But Janey would hear no reason: had she heard reason either from herself or another, she would not have been at St Honorat now. And he gave at last a reluctant consent. There was perhaps no harm in it after all. If a man came to claim his rights, he would not certainly go away again without some appeal to the authorities – which was a thing it must come to sooner or later, – if there was indeed a husband at all, and the story was true.

Janey then went back to her home. She thought she could await him there and defy him. "I will not go with you," she would say. "I may be your wife, but I am not your slave. You have left me alone for ten years. I will not go with you now!" She repeated this to herself many times, but it did not subdue the commotion in her being. She went out again when it became too much for her, locking her door with a strange sense that she might never come back again. She walked along the sea shore, repeating these words to herself, and then she walked up and down the streets, and went into the church and made the round of it, passing all the altars and wondering if the saints did pay attention to the poor women who were there, as always, telling St. Joseph or the Blessed Mary all about it. She sunk down in a dark corner, and said –

"Oh, my God! oh, my God!"

She could not tell Him about it in her agitation, with her heart beating so, but only call His attention, as the woman in the Bible touched the Redeemer's robe.[12] And then she went out and walked up and down again. I cannot tell what drew her back to the station – what fascination, what dreadful spell. Before she knew what she was doing she found herself there, walking up and down, up and down.

As if she were waiting for some one! "You have come to meet a friend?" some one said to her, with an air of suspicion. And she first nodded and then shook her head; but still continued in spite of herself to walk up and down. Then she said to herself that it was best so – that to get it over would be a great thing, now John was out of the way; he would be sure to find her sooner or later – far better to get it over! When the train came in, the slow local train, coming in from the side of Italy, she drew herself back a little to watch. There was a great commotion when it drew up at the platform. A man got out and called all the loungers about to help to lift out a gentleman who was ill, – who had had a bad attack in the train.

"Is there anywhere here we can take him to? Is there any decent hotel? Is there a room fit to put my master in?" he cried.

He was English with not much French at his command, and in great distress. Janey, forgetting herself and her terrors, and strong in the relief of the moment that he whom she feared had not come, went up to offer her help. She answered the man's questions; she called the right people to help him; she summoned the *chef de Gare* to make some provision for carrying the stricken man to the hotel.

"I will go with you," she said to the servant, who felt as if an angel speaking English had suddenly come to his help. She stood by full of pity, as they lifted that great inert mass out of the carriage. Then she gave a great cry and fell back against the wall.

It was a dreadful sight the men said afterwards, enough to overcome the tender heart of any lady, especially of one so kind as Madame Jeanne. A huge man, helpless, unconscious, with a purple countenance, staring eyes, breathing so that you could hear him a mile off. No wonder that she covered her eyes with her hands not to see him: but finally she hurried away to the hotel to prepare for him, and to call the doctor, that no time should be lost. Janey felt as if she was restored for the moment to life when there was something she could do. The questions were all postponed. She did not think of flight or concealment, or even of John at the presbytery. "He is my husband," she said, with awe in her heart.

This was how the train brought back to Janey the man whom the train had separated from her ten years before. The whole tragedy was one of the railway, the noisy carriages, the snorting locomotives. He was taken to the hotel, but he never came to himself again, and died there the next day, without being able to say what his object was, or why he had got out of the *rapide*, though unable to walk, and insisted on returning to St Honorat. It cost him his life; but then his life was not worth a day's purchase, all the doctors said, in the condition in which he was.

Friends had to be summoned, and men of business, and it was impossible but that Janey's secret should be made known. When she found herself and her son recognised, and that there could be no doubt that the boy was his father's heir, she was struck with a great horror which she never quite got over all her life. She had not blamed herself before; but now seemed to herself no less than the murderer of her husband: and could not forgive herself, nor get out of her eyes the face she had seen, nor out of her ears the dreadful sound of that labouring breath.

Notes

Text: *A Widow's Tale and Other Stories*, Blackwood, Edinburgh, 1898.
  1 Good-looking (literally 'pretty, pretty').

2 Express train.
3 Station.
4 Station-master.
5 Percentage payable for currency exchange.
6 In fact Atropos, who wields the shears which cut the thread of life, is one of the Fates, not the Furies (goddesses of vengeance).
7 All aboard!
8 Pretty little.
9 Nursemaid.
10 Priest.
11 Dear little lady.
12 See Matthew 9: 20–2; Mark 5: 25–34; Luke 8: 43–8.

REFERENCES AND FURTHER READING

Adburgham, Alison (1983) *Silver Fork Society: Fashionable Life and Literature, 1814–1840*, Constable, London.

Altick, R.D. (1957) *The English Common Reader: A Social History of the Mass Reading Public, 1800–1900*, Chicago University Press, Chicago, IL.

Alston, R.C. (1990) *A Checklist of Women Writers, 1801–1900. Fiction, Verse, Drama*, British Library, London.

Anderson, B. (1976) 'The Writings of Catherine Gore', in *Journal of Popular Culture*, 10: 404–23.

Armstrong, Isobel and Bristow, Joseph, with Sharrock, Cath (eds) (1996) *Nineteenth-Century Women Poets: An Oxford Anthology*, Clarendon Press, Oxford.

Armstrong, Nancy (1987) *Desire and Domestic Fiction: A Political History of the Novel*, Oxford University Press, Oxford.

Ashton, H. (1936) *Letty Landon*, Chivers, Bath.

Auerbach, Nina (1978) *Communities of Women: An Idea in Fiction*, Harvard University Press, Cambridge, MA and London.

Auerbach, Nina (1982) *Woman and the Demon: The Life of a Victorian Myth*, Harvard University Press, Cambridge, MA and London.

Avery, Gillian (1960) *A Selection of Victorian Stories*, Oxford University Press, Oxford.

Barbauld, Anna Laetitia (1825) *Works, with a Memoir*, edited by Lucy Aikin, Longman, Hurst, Rees, Orme, Brown & Green, London.

—— (1994) *Poems*, edited by William McCarthy and Elizabeth Kraft, University of Georgia Press, Athens, GA, and London.

Bennett, Betty T. (ed.) (1980–8) *Letters of Mary Wollstonecraft Shelley*, 3 vols, Johns Hopkins University Press, Baltimore, MD.

—— (1991) *Mary Diana Dods: A Gentleman and a Scholar*, Williamson and Morrow, New York.

—— and Robinson, Charles (eds) (1990) *The Mary Shelley Reader*, Oxford University Press, Oxford and New York.

Bennett, Bridget, (ed.) (1996) *Ripples of Dissent*, Dent, London.

Berkman, Joyce Averech (1989) *The Healing Imagination of Olive Schreiner: Beyond South African Colonialism*, University of Massachussets Press, Amherst, MA.

—— Smith, M.V. and Maclennan, D. (eds) (1983) *Olive Schreiner and After*, David Philip, Cape Town.

Blain, Virginia, Clements, Patricia and Grundy, Isobel (eds) (1990) *The Feminist Companion to Literature in English: Women Writers from the Middle Ages to the Present*, B.T. Batsford, London.

Blanchard, S.L. (1841) *Life and Literary Remains of L.E.L.*, 2 vols, Colburn, London.

Blumberg, Jane (1993) *Mary Shelley's Early Novels*, Macmillan, London.

Bradford, Helen (1995) 'Olive Schreiner's Hidden Agony: Fact, Fiction, and Teenage Abortion', *Journal of South African Studies* 21(4) (December): 623–41.

Brake, Laurel (1995) 'Endgames: The Politics of *The Yellow Book* or, Decadence, Gender and the New Journalism', in L. Brake (ed.) *The Ending of Epochs: Essays and Studies* 48, D.S. Brewer: Cambridge.

Briggs, Julia (1977) *The Night Visitors: The Rise and Fall of the Ghost Story*, Faber, London.

Broughton, Treva (1987) 'Margaret Oliphant: The Unbroken Self', *Women's Studies International Forum* 10 (1): 41–52.

Burkhart, Charles (1973) *Ada Leverson, Twayne's English Authors Series*, Twayne, New York.

Butler, Marilyn (1972) *Maria Edgeworth: A Literary Biography*, Clarendon Press, Oxford.

Chapple, J.V. and Pollard, A. (eds) (1966) *Letters of Elizabeth Gaskell*, Manchester University Press, Manchester.

Chrisman, Laura (1990) 'Allegory, Feminist Thought and the *Dreams* of Olive Schreiner', *Prose Studies* 13 (May): 126–50.

Clarke, John S. (1981) 'Mrs Oliphant's Six Unacknowledged Social Novels', *Notes and Queries*, October: 408–13.

—— (1986) *Margaret Oliphant: A Bibliography*, Victorian Fiction Research Guides II, Dept of English, University of Queensland, St Lucia, Australia.

—— (1989) 'The "Rival Novelist" – Hardy and Mrs Oliphant', *The Thomas Hardy Journal* October: 51–61.

Colby, V. and Colby, R.A. (1966) *The Equivocal Virtue: Mrs Oliphant and the Victorian Literary Market-Place*, Archon Books, Hamden, CT.

Cox, Michael (ed.) (1991) *Victorian Detective Stories: An Oxford Anthology*, Oxford University Press, Oxford.

Cox, Michael and Gilbert, R.A. (eds) (1991) *Victorian Ghost Stories: An Oxford Anthology*, Oxford University Press, Oxford.

Crook, N. (ed.) (1995–) *Works of Mary Wollstonecraft Shelley*, Pickering and Chatto, London.

Cross, N. (1985) *The Common Writer: Life in Nineteenth-Century Grub Street*, Cambridge University Press, Cambridge.

Cunningham, Gail (1978) *The New Woman and the Victorian Novel*, Macmillan, London.

Dalby, Richard, (ed.) (1992) *The Virago Book of Victorian Ghost Stories*, Virago, London.

Dowling, Linda (1986) *Language and Decadence in the Victorian Fin de Siècle*, Princeton University Press, Princeton, NJ.

Easson, Angus (1979) *Elizabeth Gaskell*, Routledge and Kegan Paul, London.

—— (1985) 'Elizabeth Gaskell and the Novel of Local Pride', *Bulletin of the John Rylands Library* 67(2) (March): 608–709.

—— (ed.) (1991) *Elizabeth Gaskell: The Critical Heritage*, Routledge, London.

Edel, Leon (1971) *Henry James: The Master, 1901–1916*, Hart-Davis, London.

Edwards, P.D. (1988) *Idyllic Realism from Mary Russell Mitford to Hardy*, Macmillan, Basingstoke.

Egerton, George (1983) *Keynotes and Discords*, with a new introduction by Martha Vicinus, Virago, London.

Eliott, Jeanne (1976) 'A Lady to the End: The Case of Isabel Vane', *Victorian Studies* 19(2): 329–44.

Faxon, F.W. (1973) *Literary Annuals and Gift Books, A Bibliography: 1823–1903*, Private Libraries Association, Pinner, Middlesex.

Etty, Robert (ed.) (1995) *New Windmill Book of Mystery Stories of the Nineteenth Century*, New Windmill Series, Heinemann, London.

Feldman, Paula R. and Scott Kilvert, Diana (eds) (1987) *Journal of Mary Wollstonecraft Shelley*, 2 vols, Clarendon Press, Oxford.

—— and Kelley, Theresa M. (eds) (1995) *Romantic Women Writers: Voices and Countervoices*, University Press of New England, Hanover, NH and London.

First, Ruth and Scott, Ann (1980) *Olive Schreiner*, Deutsch, London.

Fitzgerald, Penelope (1984) *Charlotte Mew and her Friends*, Collins, London.

Flint, Kate (1993) *The Woman Reader, 1837–1914*, Clarendon Press, Oxford.

—— (ed.) (1996) *Victorian Love Stories: An Oxford Anthology*, Oxford University Press, Oxford.

Gallagher, Catherine (1986) *The Industrial Reformation of English Fiction, 1832–1867*, University of Chicago Press, Chicago, IL and London.

Gardner, Burdett (1987) *The Lesbian Imagination: Victorian Style: A Psychological and Critical Study of 'Vernon Lee'*, Garland, New York.

Gaskell, Elizabeth (1983) *Four Short Stories*, Pandora, London.

—— (1987) *Lois the Witch and Other Stories*, Sutton.

—— (1989) *My Lady Ludlow and Other Stories*, Oxford University Press, Oxford.

—— (1992) *A Dark Night's Work and Other Stories*, Oxford University Press, Oxford.

—— (1995a) *A Moorland Cottage and Other Stories*, Oxford University Press, Oxford.

—— (1995b) *Curious, if True: Strange Tales by Mrs Gaskell*, Virago, London.

—— (1977) *The Letters of Mrs Gaskell*, (ed.) J.A.V. Chapple and A. Pollard, Mandolin, Manchester.

Gilbert, Sandra and Gubar, Susan (1979) *The Madwoman in the Attic: The Woman Writer and the Nineteenth-Century Literary Imagination*, Yale University Press, New Haven, CT.

Gunn, Peter (1964) *Vernon Lee: Violet Paget, 1856–1935*, Oxford University Press, London and New York.

Hamlin, Mike (ed.) (1993) *New Windmill Book of Nineteenth Century Short Stories*, New Windmill Series, Heinemann, London.

Hare, A.J.C. (1894) *Life and Letters of Maria Edgeworth*, Arnold, London.

Harris, Janice H. (1993) 'Feminist Representations of Wives and Work: An "almost irreconcilable" Debate', *Women's Studies* 22(3): 309–33.

Harris, Wendell V. (1968–9) 'English Short Fiction in the Nineteenth Century', *Studies in Short Fiction* 6: 1–93.

—— (1979) *British Short Fiction in the Nineteenth Century*, Wayne State University Press, Detroit, MI.

Harrison, F. (ed.) (1974) *The Yellow Book: An Anthology*, Sidgwick and Jackson, London.

Hart-Davies, Rupert, (ed.) (1962) *The Letters of Oscar Wilde*, Hart-Davis, London.

Haythornthwaite, J. (1990) 'Friendly Encounters: A Study of the Relationship Between the House of J. Blackwood and Margaret Oliphant in her Role as Literary Critic', *Publishing History* 28: 79–88.

Hickok, Kathleen (1984) *Representations of Women: Nineteenth-Century Women's Poetry*, Greenwood Press, Westport, CT.

Homans, Margaret (1986) *Bearing the Word: Language and Female Experience in Nineteenth-Century Women's Writing*, Chicago University Press, Chicago, IL and London.

Horne, R.H. (1844) *A New Spirit of the Age*, repr. Garland, New York, 1986.

Hughes, W. (1980) *The Maniac in the Cellar: The Sensation Novel of the 1860s*, Princeton University Press, Princeton, NJ.

Hunter, Shelagh (1984) *Victorian Idyllic Fiction: Pastoral Strategies*, Humanities Press, Atlantic Highlands.

Jay, Elisabeth (ed.) (1990) *The Autobiography of Margaret Oliphant*, Oxford University Press, Oxford.

Jay, Elisabeth (1995) *Mrs Oliphant: 'A Fiction to Herself'*, Clarendon Press, Oxford.

Jerdan, William (1852–3) *Autobiography*, 4 vols, Hall, Vertue, London.

Jump, Harriet Devine (ed.) (1997) *Women's Writing of the Romantic Period: An Anthology*, Edinburgh University Press, Edinburgh.

Koppleman, Susan, (ed.) (1984) *Old Maids: Short Stories by Nineteenth-Century American Women Writers*, Pandora, London.

Lansbury, Carol (1975) *Elizabeth Gaskell: The Novel of Social Crisis*, Elek, London.

Leighton, Angela and Reynolds, Margaret (1995) *Victorian Women Poets: An Anthology*. Blackwell, Oxford and Cambridge, MA.

Leighton, Angela (1992) *Victorian Women Poets: Writing Against the Heart*, Harvester Wheatsheaf, London and New York.

L'Estrange, A.G. (1870) *The Life of Mary Russell Mitford,* Bentley, London.

—— (ed.) (1882) *The Friendships of Mary Russell Mitford in Letters from her Literary Correspondents*, Hurst & Blackett, London.

Leverson, Ada (1982) *The Little Ottleys*, edited by Sally Beauman, Virago, London.

Lohafer, Susan (1983) *Coming to Terms with the Short Story*, Louisiana State University Press, Baton Rouge, LA, and London.

—— and Jo Ellyn Clarey, (eds) (1989) *Short Story Theory at a Crossroads,* Louisiana State University Press, Baton Rouge, LA and London.

Mannocchi, Phyllis F. (1983) '"Vernon Lee": A Reintroduction and Primary Bibliography', *English Literature in Translation 1880–1920* 26(4): 231–67.

—— (1986) 'Vernon Lee and Kit Anstruther-Thomson: A Study of Love and Collaboration between Romantic Friends', *Women's Studies* 12(2): 129–48.

Marshall, W.H. (1960) *Byron, Shelley, Hunt and 'The Liberal'*, University of Pennsylvania Press, Philadelphia, PA.

May, Charles E. (ed.) (1976) *Short Story Theories*, University of Ohio Press, Athens, OH.

Maxwell, William B. (1937) *Time Gathered*, Hutchinson, London.

Mellor, A.K. (1988) *Mary Shelley: Her Life, Her Fiction and her Monsters*, Routledge, London and New York.

—— (1993) *Romanticism and Gender*, Routledge, London.

Miller, Betty (ed.) (1954) *Elizabeth Barrett to Miss Mitford: Unpublished Letters*, Murray, London.

Mitchell, Sally (ed.) (1984) *Mrs Henry Wood's East Lynne*, Rutgers University Press, New Brunswick, NJ.

Mix, Katherine (1960) *A Study in Yellow: The Yellow Book and its Contributors*, University of Kansas Press, Lawrence, KS.

Moers, Ellen (1977) *Literary Women*, Doubleday, Garden City, NY.

Monsman, Gerald (1992) *Olive Schreiner's Fiction*, Rutgers University Press, New Brunswick, NJ.

Myers, Mitzi (1995) '"Completing the Union": Critical Ennui, the Politics of Narrative, and the Reformation of Irish Cultural Identity', *Prose Studies* 18(3) (December): 41–77.

Nestor, Pauline (1985) *Female Friendships and Communities*, Clarendon Press, Oxford.

Norton, Caroline (1854) *English Laws for Women in the Nineteenth Century*, printed for private circulation, London.

Paxton, Nancy (1990) 'Feminism Under the Raj: Complicity and Resistance in the Writings of Flora Annie Steel and Annie Besant', *Women's Studies International Forum* 13: 333–46.

Polsgrave, Carol (1974) 'They Made it Pay: British Short Fiction Writing 1820–1840', *Studies in Short Fiction* 11: 417–21.

Poe, Edgar Allan (1842) 'Review of Nathaniel Hawthorne, *Twice Told Tales*', *Graham's Magazine*, May; repr. in *Essays and Reviews*, (ed.) G.R. Thompson, Cambridge University Press, Cambridge, 1984, pp. 571–2.

Powell, Violet (1981) *Flora Annie Steel, Novelist of India*, Heinemann, London.

Pykett, Lyn (1992) *The 'Improper Feminine': Women's Sensation Novels and the New Woman Writing*, Routledge, London.

—— (1994) *The Sensation Novel: From The Woman in White to The Moonstone*, Northcote House, London.

—— (ed.) (1996) *Reading Fin de Siècle Fictions*, Longman, London.

Renier, Anne (1964) *Friendship's Offering*, Private Libraries Association, London.

Ritchie, Anne Thackeray (1883) *A Book of Sybils: Mrs Barbauld, Mrs Opie, Miss Edgeworth, Miss Austen*, Smith, Elder, London.

Rive, Richard (ed.) (1988–) *The Letters of Olive Schreiner*, Oxford University Press, Oxford.

Robinson, Charles (ed.) (1976) *Mary Shelley: Tales and Stories*, Johns Hopkins University Press, Baltimore, MD.

Rodgers, B. (1958) *A Georgian Chronicle: Mrs Barbauld and her Family*, Methuen, London.

Rosa, M.W. (1936) *The Silver-Fork School: Novels of Fashion Preceding Vanity Fair*, Columbia University Press, New York.

Sergeant, A. (ed.) (1897) *Women Novelists of Queen Victoria's Reign*, Hurst and Blackett, London.

Schor, Esther H. (1993) 'The Haunted Interpreter in Margaret Oliphant's Supernatural Fiction', *Women's Studies* 22(3): 371–88.

Shattock, Joanne (ed.) (1993) *The Oxford Guide to British Women Writers*, Oxford University Press, Oxford and New York.

Shaw, Valerie (1983) *The Short Story: A Critical Introduction*, Longmans, London.

Showalter, Elaine (1977) *A Literature of their Own: British Women Novelists from Brontë to Lessing*, Virago, London.

—— (1991) *Sexual Anarchy: Gender and Culture at the Fin de Siècle*, Bloomsbury, London.

—— (ed.) (1993) *Daughters of Decadence: Women Writers of the Fin-de-Siècle*, Virago, London.

Sitwell, Osbert (1950) *Noble Essences; or Courteous Revelations*, Macmillan, London.

Speedie, Julia (1993) *Wonderful Sphinx: The Biography of Ada Leverson*, Virago, London.

Spencer, Jane (1993) *Elizabeth Gaskell*, Macmillan, Basingstoke.

Stanford, Derek (1968) *Short Stories of the '90s*, Baker, London.

Stephenson, Glennis (ed.) (1994) *Nineteenth-Century Stories by Women: An Anthology*, Broadview Press, Canada.

—— (1995) *Laetitia Landon: The Woman behind L.E.L.,* Manchester University Press, Manchester and New York.

Stetz, M.D. (1984) 'George Egerton', *Turn of the Century Women* 1(1) (Summer): 2–8.

Stoneman, Patsy (1987) *Elizabeth Gaskell*, Harvester Press, Brighton.

Stubbs, Patricia (1979) *Women and Fiction: Feminism and the Novel, 1880–1920*, Methuen, London.

Sutherland, John (1976) *Victorian Novelists and Publishers*, Athlone Press, London.

—— (1995) *Victorian Fiction: Writers, Publishers, Readers*, Macmillan, Basingstoke.

—— (ed.) (1988) *The Longman Companion to Victorian Fiction*, Longman, Harlow.

Terry, R.C. (1983) *Victorian Popular Fiction*, Macmillan, London.

Trela, D. (ed.) (1994) *Margaret Oliphant: Critical Essays on a Gentle Subversive*, Susquehanna University Press, Selinsgrove, PA.

Tuchman, Gaye (1989) *Edging Women Out: Victorian Novelists, Publishers and Social Change*, Routledge, London.

Turner, Cheryl (1992) *Living by The Pen: Women Writers in the Eighteenth Century*, Routledge, London.

Uglow, Jennifer (1993) *Elizabeth Gaskell: A Habit of Stories*, Faber and Faber, London.

Williams, Merryn (1986) *Margaret Oliphant: A Critical Biography*, Macmillan, Basingstoke.

White, Terence de Vere (ed.) (1958) *A Leaf from the Yellow Book: The Correspondence of George Egerton*, Richards Press, London.

Wolff, Robert Lee (1979) *Sensational Victorian: The Life and Fiction of Mary Elizabeth Braddon*, Garland, New York.

Wood, Charles (1894) *Memorials of Mrs Henry Wood*, Bentley, London.

Wyndham, Violet (1963) *The Sphinx and her Circle: A Biographical Sketch of Ada Leverson*, Deutsch, London.